Fighters
of the
MIGHTY EIGHTH
1942·1945

William N. Hess

Thomas G. Ivie

Motorbooks International
Publishers & Wholesalers ®

First published in 1990 by Motorbooks International
Publishers & Wholesalers, P O Box 2, 729 Prospect Avenue,
Osceola, WI 54020 USA

Motorbooks International books are also available at
discounts in bulk quantity for industrial or sales-
promotional use. For details write to Special Sales Manager
at the Publisher's address

Library of Congress Cataloging-in-Publication Data
Hess, William N.
    Thomas G. Ivie.
       p.   cm.
     ISBN 0-87938-460-3
     1. United States. Army Air Forces. Air Force,
8th—History.   2. World War, 1939–1945—Aerial
operations, American.   I. Ivie,
Thomas G.   II Title.
D790.H484 1990
940.54'4973—dc20   90–30790
                                   CIP

On the front cover: Lt. William Groseclose of the 335th
Fighter Squadron, 4th Fighter Group warms up his P–51
while S/Sgt. Harry East listens to the Merlin's roar for any
symptom of mechanical failure. *USAF, via Jeff Ethell*

On the back cover: 2nd Lt. Alwin M. Jucheim and his crew
chief, S/Sgt. Robert H. McCord, of the 78th Fighter Group
stand on their P–47 at Duxford, England in 1944. Jucheim
finished the war with nine aerial and six ground victories.
USAF, via Jeff Ethell

Printed and bound in the United States of America

To the fighter pilots of the Eighth Air Force who wrote this
story in the air,
and to their dedicated ground crews who sustained their
wings.

9745641

LR

Contents

Acknowledgments

We had the help and generous assistance of many people in the preparation of this narrative history of the Eighth Air Force fighter forces. Without it this project could not have been undertaken, and to them a great debt of gratitude is owed.

A special thank you must go to a number of individuals who provided us with unit records and personal recollections. Their assistance was invaluable. They are: R. L. ("Dixie") Alexander, Col. Walter C. Beckham, James Bleidner, Vernon Boehel, Dr. George Carpenter, Lt. Col. Lewis W. Chick, Col. William Clark, Col. Gordon Compton, U. L. ("Ben") Drew, Melvin Franklin, Albert F. Giesting, Philip Gossard, Brig. Gen. James H. Howard, Jack M. Ilfrey, Col. Arthur Jeffrey, Lawrence Krantz, Bob Kuhnert, Kent Miller, J. J. McVay, William R. O'Brien, Merle Olmsted, Chet Patterson, Robert H. Powell, Jr., Pinkney L. Lackey, Maj. Gen. Dale Shafer, the late Col. Everett Stewart, Col. Jim Starnes, Col. William T. Whisner and Col. Raymond R. Withers.

Without the extensive research carried out by Dr. Frank J. Olynyk, much of the material utilized in this book would never have been available. His superlative Victory List of "USAAF Credits (European Theater) For The Destruction Of Enemy Aircraft In Air-To-Air Combat, World War 2," is highly recommended.

Many others dug through their albums and footlockers and provided numerous excellent photos for us to use in this history. Because of their efforts we have been able to provide an excellent photographic record of the life and times of the men of the Eighth Air Force fighter units. Our profound gratitude to all who contributed.

The following organizations and associations also lent their support: Air Force Museum, 4th Fighter Group Association, 55th Fighter Group Association, 20th Fighter Group Association, 339th Fighter Group Association, 352nd Fighter Group Association, 355th Fighter Group Association, 356th Fighter Group Association, 357th Fighter Group Association and 359th Fighter Group Association.

A big thanks must also go to David Bodine, John Bardwell and J. Griffin Murphey III for the many hours they spent photocopying and processing photographs for this book.

Finally, we would like to express our appreciation to our wives, Ann and Dottie, and to the Ivie children, Karen, Kathy and David, for their patience and support during the preparation of this book.

Bill Hess and Tom Ivie

Introduction

Following World War I, US Army Air Service Gen. Billy Mitchell instantly set out to prove that air power could become a dominant factor in warfare. His bombing experiments in the 1920s were successful in destroying obsolete warships which served as bombing targets in Chesapeake Bay off the Virginia coast. Unfortunately, Mitchell's exuberance for air power was to get him in trouble and his resulting court-martial forced his departure from the service.

Regardless, the US Army Air Corps of the 1930s was developed by Mitchell's disciples. Men like H. H. ("Hap") Arnold, Carl Spaatz and Frank Andrews pioneered the American air arm that carried out the nation's air offensives against the Axis forces during World War II. The introduction of the Boeing B-17 to the Air Corps bomber force in 1937 was met with great elation and the future of the striking power was ensured. The heavily armed multi-engined aircraft was labeled a virtual Flying Fortress and the name stuck. In the coming years the name would strike fear into the hearts of the Axis forces that it would oppose. Regard for the aircraft developed to the extent that when America was plunged into the global conflict on Dec. 7, 1941, there was little doubt in the minds of Army Air Corps commanders that the B-17 could carry the war to the enemy, unescorted, in broad daylight.

The loss of several B-17s to Japanese fighters early in the war in the Pacific should have foretold something, but plans were not made to compensate other than by adding a tail gun installation in the aircraft. When the newly formed Eighth Air Force was dispatched to England in 1942, its bomber forces were supplemented by two groups of P-38s from the 1st and 14th Fighter Groups, and two groups of P-39s from the 31st and 52nd Fighter Groups. The P-38s did some pioneering in overseas deployment by ferrying their aircraft, but on the strong advice of the Royal Air Force the P-39s were not deployed. Upon their arrival in England the 31st and 52nd Fighter Groups received Spitfires. Shortly thereafter these fighter forces were joined by the American Eagle Squadrons and their Spitfires, which had been operating successfully for some months with the Royal Air Force.

Such was the composition of the Eighth Air Force fighter forces when it set out on its quest. The coming weeks, months and years would present myriad problems embracing equipment, command and mission. Almost before it really existed, VIII Fighter Command was stripped of all but one of its groups to equip the North African invasion force. Its first reenforcing P-38 group was also gobbled up in the North African pipeline.

When bomber losses began to predicate that fighter escort would become necessary, the pilots of the Eagle Squadrons found themselves equipped with an aircraft they deplored—the P-47 Thunderbolt. However, replacement groups and even the Eagles began to appreciate the capability of the big fighter. As the 8th Bomber Command struck further afield, the problem of range for the fighters became critical. The quest for drop tanks was partially resolved in England after months of frustration awaiting tank development in the United States.

The merger of the North American P-51 Mustang and the British Merlin engine brought about the finest escort fighter of the war. Yet, in another frustrating move by higher command, the Eighth Air Force saw the Mustang initially assigned to the tactical Ninth Air Force. Once the P-51s became available to the Eighth Air Force, the escort was able to accompany the bombers to any point in Germany. The Mustangs were joined by long-range P-38s but their success in northwestern Europe was severely limited by mechanical troubles and a heater system that was "designed for Southern California."

Thunderbolts, Lightnings and Mustangs all joined in the campaign to defeat the Luftwaffe. When the Luftwaffe wouldn't come up to fight, the fighters of the Eighth went down to the deck to destroy its aircraft, personnel and facilities on the ground. Training fields for new Luftwaffe pilots became hazardous and the flow of young pilots to German fighter units was cut to a dribble. Casualties to veteran Luftwaffe pilots in the big air battles of 1944 cut their numbers drastically. Once air supremacy had been won by Eighth Air Force fighter forces, life became miserable throughout the Third Reich. The fighters bombed and strafed all types of military targets, lines of communication and transportation throughout the countryside. If it moved by day, they went after it.

When the German jets set out to attempt to regain Luftwaffe supremacy in the sky, the Eighth Air Force fighters rose to meet the challenge. They became adept at breaking up jet formations and downing the craft as they headed for home. The American pilots went after the jet bases and cut down the enemy before he could rise to intercept.

As the end approached, Eighth Air Force fighters ranged far and wide over northern Europe. Air supremacy was complete and there was no place in the Third Reich that was safe. This is the narrative history of the pilots, the missions and the aircraft that made total victory possible.

Chapter 1

Fledglings and Eagles

The operational birth of VIII Fighter Command took place in the spring of 1942. The initial combat units of Eighth Air Force slated for movement to the United Kingdom were placed under the jurisdiction of Brig. Gen. Frank O'D. Hunter on May 17. These units consisted of the 97th Bomb Group with B–17s, the 1st Fighter Group with P–38s, the 31st Fighter Group with P–39s and the 60th Transport Group with C–47s. The route overseas ran from Presque Isle, Maine, to Goose Bay, Labrador, then either to "Bluie West 1" on the southern coast of Greenland or "Bluie West 8" on the west coast, thence on to Reykjavik in Iceland and continuing on to Prestwick in Scotland.

It had originally been decided in April of 1942 that the 97th Bomb Group's B–17s would lead flights of up to six fighter aircraft on each leg of the flight. All the groups assembled in New England to ready themselves for the move when word came from Washington suspending all movement to Europe. The Battle of Midway was forming up in the Pacific and all units were put on alert for movement west. On June 2, the 97th Bomb Group and the 1st Fighter Group were ordered to the West Coast. After about a week and the success of US forces at Midway the units were released to return to New England, but this emergency had cost the trans-Atlantic movement a two-week delay.

On June 4, the 31st Fighter Group was ordered on to England by ship as no B–17s were available for navigation aircraft. The 31st left its P–39s and on arrival in England they were equipped with Spitfire Mark Vs. The 52nd Fighter Group was treated similarly the following month, and on their arrival in England in August 1942, they, too, were equipped with Spitfires.

On June 1 the first P–38s of the 1st Fighter Group began their trans-Atlantic trek. With B–17s doing the navigating, the route was flown without incident until July 15 when six P–38s and a B–17 were forced down on the ice cap in eastern Greenland due to weather. This did not deter further flights, however, and in August, the P–38s of the 14th Fighter Group made the trip. Although the US Army Air Force (USAAF) had been greatly concerned regarding the capability of the P–38s to make the trip, only seven failed to reach their destination, and six went down on the ice cap out of 186 dispatched during 1942.

During early August, the 31st Fighter Group was declared combat ready and its pilots joined some of the Royal Canadian Air Force squadrons for their initial sorties over enemy territory. The first claim was entered by Maj. Harrison Thyng of the 309th Squadron when he claimed damage to a Focke Wulf 190 on August 8.

Public relations photo depicting a "scramble" by pilots of the 31st Fighter Group. The 31st arrived in England less their P–39s and converted to Spitfires. USAAF

Spitfire VB belonging to the 309th Fighter Squadron, 31st Fighter Group. The "paint-outs" of the RAF roundels are quite obvious. The 31st Group saw sharp action during the Dieppe operation. USAAF

Squadrons of the 31st Fighter Group flew several missions during the Dieppe commando raid on France on Aug. 19, 1942. It was on one of these missions that Lt. Sam Junkin was credited with the first confirmed American victory for the USAAF in Europe. The Spitfires of the 309th Squadron had taken off at 0820 hours to join the aerial umbrella over the beach at Dieppe to protect the landing forces. As they positioned themselves in their defensive formations they were almost immediately attacked by approximately twenty-five FW 190s.

Lt. Sam Junkin found himself in combat with one of the enemy aircraft and was able to position himself on the tail of the Focke Wulf. Several long bursts were fired and good strikes were observed. Witnesses observed the enemy aircraft (E/A) go down and crash into the sea.

While Junkin was firing at the Focke Wulf he came under attack from another 190. His Spitfire took telling shots from E/A and Junkin was seriously wounded in the shoulder by one of the cannon shots. The American pilot was rendered unconscious for a few moments and just barely regained consciousness in time to keep from crashing into the sea. Junkin pulled the Spitfire up to about 1,000 feet, but found that the canopy had been damaged and wouldn't jettison. He finally managed to break it loose at 600–700 feet and bail out. Junkin was rescued from the sea by a motor torpedo boat which was towing two barges laden with wounded commandos returning from Dieppe.

Although the Spitfire pilots of the 31st Group claimed one E/A destroyed, three probably destroyed and two damaged, they lost seven Spitfires with most of the pilots being recovered. This time they were forced to bow to the experience of the Luftwaffe and a supe-

rior aircraft. Air Marshal Leigh Mallory cited them, saying, "Your Group played a notable part in today's battle and took their full share with the rest. They displayed great enthusiasm and fine fighting spirit."

By August, three groups of fighters were operating in England: the 1st with P–38s, and the 31st and 52nd Groups with Spitfires. They were joined soon after by the P–38s of the 14th Fighter Group. Although numerous sweeps over the Continent were performed up until October, it was not their fate to encounter any degree of enemy opposition. The training held them in good stead, however, for their deployment to North Africa came at the end of October 1942.

During September 1942 the VIII Fighter Command was assigned the newly activated 4th Fighter Group. On paper the Group was new, but in reality it was the most experienced and combat-ready fighter group in the Command. The 4th Fighter Group activated on Sept. 12, 1942, was composed of the Royal Air Force's three Eagle Squadrons, all of which were made up of American volunteer pilots. No. 71 Eagle Squadron (the original) became the 334th Fighter Squadron; No. 121 Eagle Squadron became the 335th Fighter Squadron; and No. 133 Eagle Squadron became the 336th Fighter Squadron. The formal transfer did not take place until Sept. 29, 1942, and until then all three Eagle Squadrons still operated as RAF units. It was during this interim period that the Eagles flew the mission that turned out to be the most tragic and costly in their history.

On Sept. 26, 1942, No. 133 Squadron (now the 336th FS) dispatched twelve of their new Spitfire Mk. IXs to escort B–17s attacking Morlaix, France. Up to the point of rendezvous with the Fortresses, the mission

was proceeding well, but fate played a deadly hand as they arrived over the Brest Peninsula.

Joining the bombers, the Spitfires flew south above 10/10 cloud. Unknown to them the head wind they had been given at takeoff was in reality a 100 to 135 mph tail wind at 25,000 feet. Later, in POW camp, one of the navigators from the B-17s reported that the formation at one time was over Spain!

Lt. Gene Neville had engine trouble about an hour out and was sent home escorted by Lt. Dick Beaty. After thirty minutes flying they decided to let down, and upon doing so they came under fire. At first they thought they were being mistakenly fired upon on approach of the east coast of England, but the fire continued. Neville was shot down and killed over Guingamp in France while Beaty finally reached England where he crash-landed, out of fuel.

The B-17s finally dropped their bombs—just where is anyone's guess—and the formation turned north. As fuel began to diminish the Spitfire pilots became worried. Finally, Flt. Lt. Edward Brettell, RAF, leading the squadron let down through the clouds and found the formation was directly over Brest, France. Flak opened up on them immediately and shot down most of the formation. Capt. Marion Jackson was all but out of fuel when they let down through the clouds and began looking for a spot to land. He was intercepted by a Focke Wulf 190 which attacked at too high a speed and

The squadron insignia of the Eagle Squadrons No. 71, 121 and 133 as approved by King George. These squadrons became the 334th, 335th and 336th Fighter Squadrons of the 4th Fighter Group, USAAF. USAAF

skidded right in front of Jackson as he tried to keep from overshooting. Jackson opened fire and shot him down.

Of the nine pilots who let down over Brest, two were killed and six became prisoners of war. Only Lt. Bob Smith was able to evade and come out through Spain. Flight Lt. Brettell was executed for his part in the "Great Escape" from Stalag Luft III later in the war.

When formal ceremonies took place on Sept. 29, 1942, the Royal Air Force transferred the Eagle squadrons to the USAAF. They were now in reality the 4th Fighter Group under the command of Col. Edward Anderson. The squadron commanders were Maj. Gregory Daymond, 334th FS; Maj. William J. Daley, 335th FS; and Maj. Carroll McColpin, 336th FS. For VIII Fighter Command this was a great day. It now had under its command an experienced fighter group with 73½ victories against the Luftwaffe that would benefit it in two ways. With this additional group, VIII Fighter Command could continue operations against the enemy, and at the same time utilize some of these experienced pilots to train new and inexperienced units that would be arriving in England. However, these plans had to be altered due to the requirements of Operation Torch, the invasion of North Africa.

The transition from the RAF to the USAAF for the former Eagles was not without its problems, either. Even though most of the pilots were glad to be wearing the uniform of the United States, their training and service in the RAF resulted in a jealous guarding of their ways and traditions. Any attempt by American staff officers to tamper with or change things was met with open hostility. On the other hand, receiving the rank and pay of an American officer helped balance out some of these problems.

Lt. Col. Chesley G. Peterson of No. 71 Squadron became Deputy Commanding Officer of the 4th FG. In August 1943 he was promoted to full colonel, at age twenty-three, to become Group Commander. Care

A group of former No. 71 Squadron pilots and one of their Spitfire Mark Vs. Left to right: R. D. McMinn, "Abe" O. Reagen, Stan Anderson, Chesley Peterson, Oscar Coen, Bob Boock and Jim Clark. Care

After the transfer the 4th Fighter Group remained at Debden, Essex, and about the only noticeable physical change about the base, other than the uniforms, was the American star which replaced the RAF roundel on their Spitfires.

The first "official" mission for the new group was on October 2 when it sortied twenty-three Spitfires. Strange as it may seem, the 4th continued to operate under the control of the RAF and this mission was to be led by Wing Commander Duke-Wooley. The mission was a diversion for Circus 221 (Circus was RAF vernacular for a mission comprised of a small bomber force escorted by a host of fighters) and they carried it out in fine form in the skies over Calais and Dunkirk, France. While in this area, the pilots of the 334th and 335th Squadrons encountered a large gaggle of FW 190s at 24,000 feet. Within minutes after the encounter four 190s were sent crashing to earth, and a fifth was damaged. The 334th FS emerged as high scorer in this melee, with Maj. Oscar Coen and Lt. Stanley Anderson each destroying one, and Lt. Jim Clark sharing one with Duke-Wooley. The fourth 190 was gunned down by Lt. Gene Fetrow of the 335th.

During the next several days the 4th was dispatched on a mixture of Ramrod missions (escorting RAF bombers) to France and convoy patrols. On October 14, Major Daley led eleven Spitfires on a shipping strike along the coast of Holland where they attacked and shot up three flak ships. On October 20, one of these missions cost them a pilot, Lt. Anthony Seaman, when his plane exploded in midair and crashed into the Channel.

By now the requirements for Operation Torch had whittled VIII Fighter Command's strength to just two operational groups, the 4th and the 14th. On October 25 both of these groups participated in Circus 232, escorting Bostons to Le Havre, France. When it was over the 14th FG was transferred to the Twelfth Air Force, and with their departure the 4th became the lone fighter group in the Eighth Air Force.

On November 6, the 4th Fighter Group flew its first large-scale mission as the sole fighter representative of the USAAF in England when Wing Commander Duke-Wooley led twenty-one Spitfires on a bomber escort mission to Caen aerodrome. During the next several days the Group participated in two more escort missions, but on November 18 they returned to small-scale Rhubarb (another RAF term—small nuisance missions flown by fighter planes over the occupied countries on the Continent) missions. Four Spits were sent to France and their pilots strafed numerous targets on the ground. Two of these sorties were flown by Lts. Jim Clark and Robert Boock of the 334th FS, and when Clark attacked a factory at St-Valery they received a very hot reception. The German defenders unleashed a hail of fire so intense from their light flak batteries that Clark had to undertake violent evasive maneuvers. In doing so he ran his Spitfire into a tree and damaged it. Somehow he managed to keep his staggering Spit airborne after the collision, and Boock escorted him back to base.

On November 19, the opportunity for aerial combat finally occurred near Flushing airfield. Pilots of the 335th FS were on a Rhubarb mission when they encountered four FW 190s, and Lt. Frank Smolinsky clobbered one of them. The 335th FS returned to the Continent on November 20 for another Rhubarb, this time to the Furnes, Belgium, area. While they were looking for targets in that area, Maj. Roy Evans spotted a Fiesler Fi–156 observation plane loafing along and downed it for the 335th's second victory in two days. Later on this mission Evans had to hit the silk over the Channel when he experienced mechanical difficulties with his Spitfire. After a short stay in the water, he was picked up by a rescue launch and returned to England.

Toward the end of November 1942 several changes and proposed changes in the 4th Fighter Group's Table of Organization and Equipment were announced. On November 22 there was a change of command in two of the squadrons when Major Daley of the 335th FS and Major McColpin of the 336th FS were ordered back to the United States. Maj. Donald Blakeslee was given command of the 335th and Maj. Oscar Coen was given the 336th. Several days later, 800 enlisted men who would form the Group's ground units in the United Kingdom arrived and were sent to Atcham for processing into the 4th Group.

At about the same time another announcement was made to the Group which brought forth a tremendous outcry of protest. The pilots were told that the VIII Fighter Command had made the decision to convert the 4th to the new P–47 Thunderbolt and that they would have to give up their beloved Spitfires. However, this decision could not be implemented for a

Lt. Roy Evans of the 335th FS downed an Fi 156 for his first victory. He became an ace and a major before finishing his tour. Evans returned for a second tour with the 359th FG and scored one victory before becoming a POW in February 1945. Jackman

Maj. Don Blakeslee became CO of the 335th FS in November 1942. Blakeslee went on to become CO of the 4th FG. As such he was not only one of the top leaders in Eighth AF, but one of the highest scoring aces. Jackman

A gathering of the top brass of the 4th FG and the Eighth Air Force commander. Left to right: Col. Chesley Peterson, Maj. Oscar Cohen, Maj. Don Blakeslee, Maj. Roy Evans and Maj. Gen. Ira Eaker. AF Museum

while since the P–47s had not yet arrived in England. In the meantime the 4th continued operations in their Spitfires, and during the remainder of November flew several more two-plane Rhubarbs.

On Dec. 1, 1942, VIII Fighter Command received a new fighter group. The 78th Fighter Group commanded by Col. Arman Peterson arrived in England along with their P–38 Lightnings. With their long-range P–38s, the 78th FG was expected to help the Eighth Air Force by providing escort to its bombers engaged in deep penetrations of enemy territory. With this in mind the Group was ordered to set up operations at Goxhill and begin training. Some of their aircraft and crews were sent immediately to the bomber base at Chelveston in order to train with bomber crews in escort work.

Maj. Gen. Ira Eaker, first commander of the Eighth AF (left), and Brig. Gen. Frank O'D. Hunter, first commander of VIII Fighter Command. E. Stewart

While the 78th Fighter Group was setting up operations at their new base, the 4th continued flying, and on December 6 Wing Commander Duke-Wooley led the 4th FG on a bomber escort/fighter sweep to the Lille area. They were to provide return escort to the B–17s and in doing so kept several formations of Focke Wulfs at bay until the bombers crossed the coastline at Calais. At this moment F/O Gene Fetrow of the 335th FS picked out a couple of the enemy aircraft and attacked. In short order he damaged one of them and sent the other down in flames.

On December 11, two 334th FS pilots, Lts. Duane Beeson and Stanley Anderson, were sent on a Rhubarb to Belgium where they raised hell with Wehrmacht personnel. At Knokke they caught a group of soldiers taking exercises and strafed them, hit a staff car at Ostend and gunned a group of approximately 150 German soldiers parading at Nieuwpoort, Belgium.

For the remainder of December the 4th Group flew a combination of escort missions and fighter sweeps over the Continent. The mission of December 30 enabled them to close out the year "with a bang" when pilots of the 334th FS attacked an ammunition train in Etaples, France. Their cannon shells tore into the parked train, and caused its cargo to explode violently. The final mission of 1942 by the 4th Fighter Group was convoy patrols over the Channel.

The first of the P–47s arrived in England during the last days of December, and on Christmas Eve VIII Fighter Command had its first machine to evaluate. Data on the new plane was in short supply and Col. Cass Hough's technical section began immediate testing of the Thunderbolt to try and learn its strengths and weaknesses. For two weeks Hough ran the aircraft through a series of tests which included mock combat against the FW 190. In these tests Hough determined that the FW 190 could outturn and outrun the P–47 with ease at altitudes below 15,000 feet. The only improved maneuverability demonstrated by the Thunderbolt at these low altitudes was when the air speed exceeded 250 mph. On the other hand, when operated at altitudes above 15,000 feet the P–47 showed marked superiority. In this element the Thunderbolt could easily outrun and outturn the smaller Focke Wulf. The Focke Wulf still demonstrated quicker acceleration at these altitudes, but the P–47 could easily overcome this and overtake it.

These tests certainly did not do away with the nagging doubts many pilots had about the P–47, but at least they were given some guidelines for survival in combat while flying the Thunderbolt.

In the meantime, the 4th Fighter Group was continuing to carry on in its Spitfires. During the first twelve days of 1943 their missions consisted of convoy and defensive patrols. These missions were not very popular among the pilots, and Lt. George Carpenter's comments about them are typical: "Convoy patrols were a dull, unrewarding type of work. Ships going through the English Channel were potentially vulnerable to attack, particularly by fighter-bombers. However, I never did see or get involved with any enemy aircraft on these missions. Two aircraft (a section) would fly around a convoy, perhaps as many as 50 or 60 ships proceeding in, as I recall, one or two line-astern formations. We would fly at low altitudes, usually 100–500 feet. We would stay with the convoy until relieved, usually an hour or so."

On Jan. 12, 1943, VIII Fighter Command received a new fighter group, the P-47 flying 56th. Their arrival was welcomed for two big reasons: first, they would augment the size and strength of the depleted Fighter Command, and second, the 56th Fighter Group had been trained in and *liked* the Thunderbolt.

However, before VIII Fighter Command could even start planning the time tables for putting their two new groups—the 78th and the 56th—into combat, the 78th Fighter Group's P-38s and pilots were diverted to the North African Theater. Only the Group Headquarters, a few flying personnel and some of the ground personnel remained in England. It would be quite an understatement to say that these were trying and frustrating days for General Hunter and his staff. Even so, they did try to retain somewhat of an optimistic outlook about the situation. One member of the VIII Fighter Command staff recorded their accomplishments to date as follows:

"Superficially, the whole process of the arrival of the first four fighter groups, then three more, even to include the anti-climatic addition of the 78th Fighter Group, could be crossed off as a false start for the VIII Fighter Command. It would let the record stand as having equipped and trained a large part of the 12th Fighter Command for the African invasion, maintaining for itself a depleted 4th Fighter Group and a skeleton 78th Fighter Group. But this record in training and equipment and supplies, good as it is, does not tell the

story." What that writer was saying was, in spite of training and losing the bulk of its fighter groups, VIII Fighter Command was building itself into a well-organized command structure. A staff had been brought together and it was well upon its way in preparing for the arrival of the new groups which would form the newborn VIII Fighter Command.

Meanwhile, the flying and the fighting went on. On January 13 the 4th Fighter Group was relieved of the boredom of the convoy patrols by the scheduling of some large escort missions. On the first mission of the day Lt. Col. Chesley Peterson led thirty-six Spitfires from all three squadrons on a mission to St-Omer/Ft. Rouge airfield in France. However, they were unable to locate the Boston bombers because of heavy haze at the rendezvous point. On the way back to base several enemy fighters were sighted but no air battles occurred. Later in the day Peterson led a second escort mission which was to provide protection for B-17s attacking targets in the Lille area.

The next day the 334th Squadron sent up a three-plane Rhubarb to the coastline of Belgium. Shortly after their arrival over Belgium, Lt. Hank Mills became separated from the others due to a heavy rain and returned to base alone. The other pilots, Lts. Stanley Anderson and Robert Boock, finally broke out of the weather at Gmisken, Belgium, and received a hail of flak as they did so. As they turned and were about to head home two FW 190s were encountered and a battle began. The 190s tried to attack Anderson. He evaded them by doing some violent maneuvers, and then found himself on the 190s' tails. Anderson quickly opened fire and one of the Focke Wulfs rolled over and crashed into the sea. The pilot of the second 190 quickly lost his zeal for combat and departed the scene in a hurry.

Three P-47 Thunderbolts of the 335th FS over England. The change to P-47s from Spitfires was likened as changing from "race horses to dray horses" by pilots of the 4th FG. USAAF

No sooner than this action ended, another began. Two more FW 190s came in at Anderson from one o'clock, but before they could begin firing, Boock cut them off. A burst from Boock's guns hit the German leader's 190 and sent it crashing into the sea. As the 190 was crashing, Boock nearly collided with its wingman and had to go into some sudden turns to avoid ramming the German plane. After these evasive maneuvers, Boock then found himself in overcast and separated from Anderson, so he decided to go home. He came out of the overcast in the vicinity of Ostend and immediately spotted some targets on the ground—a staff car and a truck loaded with troops. Boock dived and strafed until his ammunition was exhausted, but before he pulled up and headed back to Debden, he saw the staff car overturn and wreck in a ditch.

The dreaded day finally arrived at Debden, and on January 15 the 4th Fighter Group was ordered by VIII Fighter Command to begin its P–47 training. To accomplish this the 334th Fighter Squadron was pulled out of operational flying to become the training unit for the Group. The Thunderbolts assigned to them began arriving on January 15 and 16, and the actual training began on January 17, when twenty-four pilots representing all three squadrons reported to the 334th's area to begin the program. The remaining 334th pilots were attached to the 335th and 336th Squadrons during this time and continued to fly operational missions.

The Group participated in Circus 253 to St-Omer on January 22, escorting twelve RAF Bostons whose target was the German airfield. Just as they were crossing the French coastline they were attacked by German fighters and a wild dogfight ensued. When it was all over the Luftwaffe came out on the short end, as four of its fighters went down in flames. Lts. Boock and Anderson, and Maj. Oscar Coen of the 334th accounted for three of them and the fourth was knocked down by Lt. Joseph Matthews of the 336th Squadron. But these victories were not without cost. Lt. Chester Grim was shot down by flak in the Dunkirk area and killed.

During the remainder of the month 4th Fighter Group flew some escort missions and coastal patrols, and lost one Spitfire when Boock was forced to ditch in the Channel. He was quickly picked up by air-sea rescue and returned. The P–47 training continued, but it was not without incident as one Thunderbolt was damaged in a crash-landing and a second P–47 was nosed over during a takeoff. These troubles did not end with the beginning of a new month, either. On Feb. 1, 1943, Lt. John Mitchellweis was forced to bail out when his P–47 burst into flame during a training flight. His chute opened but somehow his parachute straps failed and Mitchellweis fell to his death.

On February 5 the 4th lost another plane and pilot. Lt. William Kelly of the 335th FS was killed when his

Always a great morale booster on Eighth AF bases were Bob Hope and Frances Langford, shown here posing in front of a P–47. E. Stewart

14

Spitfire was hit by flak during an attack on German ships off the coast of Holland.

At Goxhill, Col. Arman Peterson was trying to rebuild his depleted 78th Fighter Group when they, too, received word that the 78th was to be reequipped with the Thunderbolt. The news was as upsetting there as it had been in Debden. S/Sgt. Roy Miner of the 78th's Air Inspectors Office summed up the Group's feelings when he wrote, "Then the blow fell. The first set back of the 78th! Needed urgently in the African theater, first we lost all our pilots; then all our P–38s.

"The sky began to leak snow. The days were gray, low-toned and full of feeling. There was no mail from home. The boys were homesick and heartsick. And on top of all this, we were told that P–38s would not be sent to us, but that strange monster, called a Thunderbolt, would be our fighting weapon. The first of these strange new aircraft came to us in February 1943. Big, bulky, clumsy, the pilots and ground crew turned from them in disgust. After the trim streamlining of the twin-boomed P–38 with its two wonderful engines, these new craft were like plow horses."

Disgusted as they were, the 78th began training in earnest. VIII Fighter Command's plans were to have the 4th operational in P–47s by March 1, and followed closely by the 56th and 78th Fighter Groups. It was imperative for the 78th to complete its transition as quickly as possible.

By Feb. 28, 1943, the 334th Fighter Squadron had completed its transition from the Spitfire to the P–47.

With the completion of this training they could now go operational in the craft. During this training period the P–47 had already been mistaken for the FW 190, and VIII FC decided that recognition markings should be added. The 4th was told to paint a white band around the front of the cowl and bands around the vertical and horizontal tail surfaces. In addition, the national insignia was to be bordered by a yellow circle. To further aid the program, the 4th sent its Thunderbolts on a tour of bases on March 3.

The emphasis on the P–47 also brought about the sobriquet "Jug" due to the side view of the aircraft which was said to resemble a bottle or jug. The name stuck!

During the next several days the 334th Fighter Squadron continued its training flights in the Thunderbolts in preparation for its combat debut. Between March 4 and 9 two more Jugs were written off due to crash-landings, and a third was force-landed due to engine failure. Nevertheless, on March 10 the Squadron was declared operational and Lt. Col. Chesley Peterson led fourteen of the Thunderbolts over Europe.

The Jugs' first mission was a fighter sweep over Belgium. VIII Fighter Command placed a lot of importance on this mission because, to them, the introduction of the Thunderbolt was the real beginning of the Command. Hopefully all would go well on this mission and the pilots would start feeling more confident about the P–47. But this wasn't to be. Some of the Thunderbolts had engine problems, and others experienced terrible

A P–47C of the 56th FG. Note the enlarged wing markings and white nose and tail identification recognition bands. The fuselage insignia was outlined in yellow. USAAF

problems with their radios. Peterson experienced much interference and loud noises from his set—enough to render it useless. Fortunately the Squadron did not encounter the Luftwaffe on this mission, and they returned to vent their wrath upon the technical representatives of Republic Aircraft.

The P-47s were hastily pulled off operations after the March 10 mission so the problems of the radios and the ignition systems could be studied. Meanwhile, the other two squadrons of the 4th continued flying operations in their Spitfires. Lieutenant Colonel Peterson led two missions on March 12, the second of which cost the Group one of its pilots. It happened as the 336th Fighter Squadron was just crossing into France. They were bounced by two FW 190s near Audruieq, and during the melee Lt. Don Gentile damaged one of them, but Lt. Hazen Anderson was shot down and became a prisoner of war.

Missions were flown in Spitfires on March 13 and 14 by the 4th, but on March 16 they were ordered to turn them in. Also, at this time, pilots from the 335th and 336th Squadrons who had been attached to the 334th for P-47 training were sent back to their squadrons along with their Thunderbolts. With these trained pilots and aircraft the 335th and 336th Fighter Squadrons could now begin their transition training. The 335th was the next of the 4th's units to begin the transition, and their P-47s started arriving at Debden on March 22. During the last few days of March, the 336th continued operations from Martlesham Heath and flew convoy patrols in their "nonexistent" Spitfires. These patrols continued until the first of April when they returned to Debden and began working with the P-47.

While the 4th was continuing its transition, the other two P-47 groups were also training feverishly to become combat ready and join the fight. By early April both groups were declared ready and began the moves to their new bases. On April 5 the 56th checked in at Horsham St. Faith and the next day the 78th Fighter Group moved into facilities at Duxford.

Chapter 2

Proving the Thunderbolt

April 8, 1943, was a great day for VIII Fighter Command. On this date, aircraft representing all three Groups were sent out on a mission over the Continent. The mission was led by Lt. Col. Chesley Peterson and was composed of twenty-four P–47s (eight from the 4th FG, four from the 56th FG and twelve from the 78th FG). The mission, a fighter sweep, was uneventful, but to VIII Fighter Command it was clear that their planned fighter offensives were not too far off.

The second composite mission took place on April 13 when Peterson again led thirty-six P–47s on a fighter sweep to St-Omer, France. The 78th contingent was led by their commander Lt. Col. Arman Peterson. The mission was again uneventful in terms of aerial combat, but the 78th lost one P–47 when Lt. Col. Joseph Dickman's plane suffered engine trouble and was forced to bail out over the Channel. Dickman landed in the middle of a minefield, but was picked up by Air-Sea rescue and returned to base. He became the 78th's first man to be awarded the Purple Heart.

That afternoon Lt. Col. Chesley Peterson led the second composite mission of the day. It was also a fighter sweep over the Continent and as on the earlier mission no enemy aircraft were encountered, although

pilots of the 56th Fighter Group did see their first flak barrage. The 56th also lost an aircraft due to engine failure. This time the pilot, Captain Dyar, was lucky enough to have altitude to glide back across the Channel and crash-land in England. His luck held out as his low glide path over England was mistaken by antiaircraft crews as a low-flying Focke Wulf and they opened fire. Fortunately no hits were taken by Dyar's Thunderbolt.

The test of combat for the Thunderbolts finally came on April 15 as Lt. Col. Chesley Peterson was again leading a composite force of Thunderbolts from the 4th, 56th and 78th Fighter Groups to the Continent. When the 4th FG's 335th Fighter Squadron led by Maj. Don Blakeslee passed over Knokke, Belgium, they encountered three FW 190s. Blakeslee jumped one of them and finally shot down the German after a battle that lasted from an altitude of 29,000 feet down to 500 feet. While this was happening, the rest of the 4th Group encountered five more Focke Wulfs over the Channel. In this battle Peterson downed one of the 190s, and another was downed by Lieutenant Boock of the 334th Squadron. The 4th emerged victorious in this first encounter but only by a slim margin. Two of its pilots,

P–47D of the 63rd FS, 56th FG over England. The 56th Group had trained on Thunderbolts and were sold on them from the beginning. USAAF

The vaunted Focke Wulf 190, this one from III Group, JG 2 "Richthofen." The 190 was one of the more prominent Eighth AF opponents from the beginning. USAAF

Lts. Stanley Anderson and Richard McMinn, were shot down and killed during the battle. A third P–47 was lost on the return trip when Peterson suffered engine failure and had to bail out over the Channel.

The three aerial victories in the P–47s were welcome but the former Eagles were still not convinced that it was the plane for them. The continued malfunctions and bugs which affected the performance of their aircraft left them quite uneasy about the Thunderbolt.

During the remainder of April, the Thunderbolts of VIII Fighter Command flew five more fighter sweeps over occupied Europe. All of these missions except the mission of April 29 were uneventful. On this date all three groups were operating and the 4th and 78th Fighter Groups flew their missions without incident. However, for the 56th it was a different story.

Maj. Dave Schilling led a force of thirty-six P–47s sweeping Blankenberge, Belgium, plus Woensdrecht and The Hague in the Netherlands. Immediately after landfall was made at 30,000 feet, the 62nd Squadron was attacked by six to fifteen FW 190s and Me 109s. The attackers bored in head-on, broke under and climbed back to 28,000 to 30,000 feet to resume their onslaught. Lt. Warren Gath suffered engine damage during the pass and was forced to bail out.

Major Schilling was unable to direct the Group, for his radio was inoperable over 20,000 feet. However, the

The second half of the Luftwaffe opposition that was usually encountered was the Messerschmitt Me 109 shown here getting ready for takeoff. Kirby

Thunderbolt pilots continued to fight off the enemy attacks and while they made no claims, they did manage to disperse the German fighters. Schilling and Lt. Harrison's aircraft suffered battle damage, and Capt. John McClure was shot down by enemy fighters and was later reported to be a prisoner of war, as was Lt. Gath. The 56th had been bloodied but had succeeded in performing its mission as assigned.

During April 1943, VIII Fighter Command had been sending its P-47s on fighter sweeps over the Continent with the intention of enticing the Luftwaffe into some dogfights. However, the Germans were not interested; they were saving their fighters to attack US bombers engaged in daylight raids over Europe. In spite of the lack of action during April's fighter sweeps, VIII Fighter Command's confidence was building, as evidenced by a report that stated "Most of the sweeps produced nothing tangible, for no enemy was seen. Yet the accomplishment was a real one. The Thunderbolt was perfected and mastered. The pioneer fighter pilots learned their way over enemy territory. They gained a little confidence."

The result of this newfound confidence was that VIII Fighter Command felt that the groups were ready for bomber escort duty. The first was scheduled for May 4, 1943. Approximately 117 P-47s were sent out on this date. The 4th and 56th Fighter Groups escorted the bombers of the 91st, 303rd and 305th Bomb Groups to the primary target at Antwerp, Belgium, while the 78th Fighter Group escorted a mixed formation of B-17s and B-24s on a diversion toward Paris. The first mission was a success in that the bombing mission was completed and no bombers were lost. The 4th and 56th Groups did encounter enemy fighters, and Lt. George Carpenter of the 4th managed to damage one of them. One 4th Group P-47 was lost due to mechanical failure and its pilot, Lt. John Lutz, was killed when his chute failed to open.

The 78th Fighter Group had its first opportunity for aerial combat ten days later on May 14 when they participated in another escort mission to Antwerp. The B-17s had completed their bombing of targets in Antwerp, and the force was between Antwerp and Flushing when they encountered about twenty red-nosed FW 190s. In an air battle that took place at about 24,000 feet, the young pilots of the 78th gave a good account of themselves against an experienced foe. They were able to down three of the Focke Wulfs, but at a cost of three of their own. Credit for the 78th's first victory went to Maj. James Stone, CO of the 83rd Fighter Squadron, and the other two 190s were claimed by Capt. Robert Adamina of the 82nd Fighter Squadron and Capt. Elmer McTaggart of the 83rd. Capt. Charles London was also credited with a probable on this mission, when he tore away part of a Focke Wulf's left wing with his .50s and sent it down apparently out of control.

The 4th also met up with enemy opposition on this mission, and in running air battles between Hulst and the Channel coast downed two of the FW 190s. Credited with these victories were Maj. Don Blakeslee and

Maj. Dave Schilling was one of the 56th FG's outstanding leaders and scorers from the beginning of their combat operations. USAAF

Lt. Aubrey Stanhope, both of the 335th Fighter Squadron.

During the remainder of May the pilots of VIII Fighter Command returned to fighter sweeps over the Continent, but unlike the April sweeps they were now meeting aerial opposition. On May 15, Col. Chesley Peterson of the 4th Fighter Group claimed an FW 190, but the 78th Fighter Group lost another pilot, Lt. James Sandmeier, due to engine failure. Sixteen Thunderbolts were sent on a search mission over the Channel, but Sandmeier was never found.

The 78th Fighter Group was up again the next day, and as Col. Arman Peterson led his P-47s across the coastline of Holland, bandits were seen at eleven o'clock. The German force was at about 34,000 feet and in the vicinity of Rotterdam. Peterson called for the 84th Squadron to follow him into the attack. The encounter that ensued lasted for several minutes. When it was over, four of the German aircraft had been sent crashing to earth. The victorious 78th pilots were F/O Charles R. Brown with two, and Col. Peterson and Capt. John Irvin with one each. One of the 78th's Thunderbolts failed to return, however.

During the next few days the experienced 4th Fighter Group was engaged in several aerial skirmishes and found the going quite rough. In air battles of May 18 and 21, the 4th downed four enemy planes while losing four of their own; three of their pilots were killed in action. On May 29, the 4th was again roughed up on a Ramrod/Circus mission to Rennes, France. Fortunately no planes or pilots were lost on this show, but several of the P–47s were heavily damaged.

May 1943 was a month of increased aerial combat for the VIII Fighter Command, and its pilots were learning what it was like to battle the Luftwaffe. Although the Americans were still far from establishing control of the air, they acquitted themselves well. They had scored eleven confirmed victories during May, and were credited with several more probables. Oddly enough all the victories were scored by the two groups, the 4th and 78th, who were quite suspicious of the Thunderbolt. The 56th Fighter Group, who loved the plane, came up empty-handed.

June began with a series of uneventful fighter sweeps over France and the low countries. The missions for June 12 were also fighter sweeps but this time the Luftwaffe was up and gave battle. On the first mission of the day, Capt. Walter V. Cook downed an FW 190 and ended the 56th Fighter Group's scoring drought. During the second mission of the day the 78th FG also engaged the enemy and scored two probables, but at the cost of two of their own planes.

The 56th continued adding to their victory count when Col. Hubert Zemke shot down two, and Lt. Robert S. Johnson scored his first victory on June 13. For the next several days VIII Fighter Command continued to dispatch its Thunderbolts on sweeps over the Continent, but the Luftwaffe was not lured into battle. At the end of June 17, VIII Fighter Command had flown 1,011 sorties since June 1 and could only claim four victories for all this effort. It was becoming quite obvious to the pilots that VIII FC's plans were not working. The Luftwaffe was not interested in dogfighting against Allied fighters; the bombers were its target.

Lt. Gerald Johnson, a Kentucky quail shooter, became one of the top aces and leaders in the 56th FG. USAAF

Possibly with this thought in mind, VIII Fighter Command scheduled its fighters to escort bombers of the 1st Bomb Wing on the June 22 mission to Antwerp. All three fighter groups were dispatched but only the 4th and the 78th encountered the Luftwaffe's attack. Their rendezvous with the B–17s was to take place over Antwerp, but due to a mixup on the time the P–47s met them over Walcheren Island. The Fortresses were already under attack by a mixed force of Me 109s and FW 190s, and both the 4th and the 78th Fighter Groups rushed to their aid. During the ensuing battle, seven German planes were shot down, three by the 4th and four by the 78th. One of the enemy aircraft was downed by Capt. Charles London who described his battle as follows: "As we turned in behind the bombers I saw one B–17 straggling behind the formation. I immediately led my flight to cover this straggler. As I was pulling in over and behind the bomber I observed an FW 190 flying at about 90 degrees to me, positioning itself to attack the B–17. I fired one burst at a 90 degree deflection and closed in behind the enemy aircraft. I then started firing from about 30 degrees down to 0 degrees and closed to about 350 yards, from where I fired a second burst. As I fired I saw incendiary flashes on the wing and fuselage of the FW 190, but he took no evasive action. By this time we were down to about 5,000 feet. The 190 started a slow turn to the right and went into a 45 degree dive toward land. I then broke away and saw the enemy aircraft continue down and crash on Walcheren Island. I did not see the pilot bail out."

The 78th FG's other two victories were claimed by Col. Arman Peterson and by F/O Howard Askelson. Lt. Ernest Beatie led the 4th FG in scoring when he downed two, an Me 109 and an FW 190. The other victories by the 4th were claimed by Lts. Fonzo Smith and Jim Goodson who each downed an FW 190.

June 24 was a day of limited action for the VIII FC. Two fighter sweeps were flown over France, and Lt. Thomas Shepard of the 78th Fighter Group scored the day's only victory. This day in the annals of the 4th Fighter Group, however, was to have a special significance. Their guests of honor were Gen. Frank O'D. Hunter and the Duchess of Kent. In the name of King George, the Duchess of Kent presented the Royal Badges of the three Eagle squadrons to the 334th, 335th and 336th Fighter Squadrons. In the history of the USAF, these units are the only ones who have been so honored.

The 56th Group fought a heated air battle on June 26 when they escorted the Fortresses attacking airfields on the Continent. Shortly after making landfall they sighted the bombers under strong head-on attacks from a mixed force of Me 109s and FW 190s. From initial rendezvous to halfway across the Channel during withdrawal, the Thunderbolts were in and out of combat with the determined and experienced opposition. Lts. Gerald Johnson and Charles Harrison both downed FW 190s, but the Group lost four pilots, Captains Eby, Wetherbee and Dyar, and Lt. Baron. Lt. Ralph Johnson returned with his P–47 so badly damaged that he was

Damage photos of the P-47 that Lt. Robert S. Johnson of the 56th FG brought home after absorbing all the punishment a Focke Wulf 190 could inflict. USAAF

unable to get but one gear down. Colonel Zemke went up and took a look and advised Johnson to head the aircraft out to sea and bail out, which he proceeded to do.

The miracle of the day, however, was the return of Lt. Robert S. Johnson. Focke Wulf 190s swept through his flight and his aircraft was hit effectively by 20 mm and machine gun fire. The plane caught fire and large pieces of the wings, fuselage and cowling were shot away. Johnson was drenched in hydraulic fluid, his oxygen mask was shot away and he had been cut by the flying glass from his canopy. The Thunderbolt pilot resigned himself to defeat and attempted to open the canopy. It was stuck! Cannon fire had curled the grooves and there was no way it would open. Johnson struggled with all his might to open it, but it would not budge.

As he dropped below the bombers' formation he cut his engine in an attempt to kill the fire. Sure enough, that did the trick. He restarted the engine and it seemed to perform satisfactorily at low power settings. Johnson set course for home. However, things were far from over for the day. A Focke Wulf dropped down and caught up with him easily. The Luftwaffe pilot pulled alongside, waved to him and dropped back on the tail of the Thunderbolt to deliver the coup de grâce. Johnson made himself as small as possible and shuddered as bullets and cannon shell pounded the armor plate behind his seat. He pushed the stick forward to get under the 190. The enemy overran, but lined up again and gave him another burst.

Johnson was now headed for England. The German pilot pulled alongside again and motioned for him to land and surrender. Johnson would have none of it. Another wave of the hand and the Luftwaffe pilot went back at it again. Once more the P-47 shook under the

pounding from the 190's guns, but it kept flying. For the last time the enemy pilot pulled alongside. Apparently all his ammunition had been expended. This time he threw up his hands in resignation and peeled off for home. Shortly thereafter Johnson brought to England the most damaged fighter plane that anyone had ever seen. Jubilant, Johnson was helped from the cockpit and was able to survey firsthand the damage that his aircraft had taken. But for the rugged construction of the maligned Thunderbolt, there would never have been a twenty-seven-victory fighter ace by the name of Robert S. Johnson.

During the remainder of June the Thunderbolts escorted bombers attacking targets in France, and in doing so scored six more victories at a cost of five P-47s.

As June ended the 78th Fighter Group under the command of Col. Arman Peterson was establishing itself as the hottest of the three P-47 groups in the Command. His dynamic leadership in the air and on the ground generated a tremendous esprit de corps within the Group and earned him both admiration and respect from his men. Because of this, the events of July 1, 1943, were to have a devastating and lingering effect on the 78th Fighter Group.

The 78th participated in a fighter sweep over Holland on July 1, and in a big battle over Schouwen Island they destroyed four enemy planes, probably destroyed one more and damaged five others at the cost of one of their own men, Col. Arman Peterson. No one seems to know for sure exactly what happened to the colonel. As he was leading his flight in a steep dive, Peterson pulled out directly into the sun and wasn't seen again. Numerous search missions were flown but all were in vain. The morale, which had been so high at Duxford, plummeted to the point that even Bob Hope and his USO show couldn't bring them out of it.

There could be no doubt that Lt. Robert S. Johnson would christen one of his P–47s "Lucky"! R. S. Johnson

On July 14 the 78th got the opportunity for revenge while escorting B–17s to Amiens, France. The Group encountered numerous enemy aircraft and claimed three, but at a cost of three of their own. One of the victorious pilots, Lt. August DeGenaro, was also one of the Group's losses. He was severely wounded during the air battle, and turned away to nurse his crippled aircraft back to England. He wanted to attempt a crash-landing on the English coastline, but when he made landfall he was over the village of Newhaven. Rather than risk hitting the village, DeGenaro turned back to the Channel and bailed out. Fortunately a fishing boat was nearby and quickly hauled him out of the water. For his actions and selflessness DeGenaro was later awarded the second highest award for bravery, the Distinguished Service Cross (DSC).

These early escort missions into France were viewed with mixed emotions by the pilots and Fighter Command alike. They were proud of the advances they were making in taking the fight to the enemy, but frustrated that their range of combat was so limited. These early missions were described by an VIII FC historian as follows: "The first escort missions had a David and Goliath nature—at least in that No Man's air beyond the range of the Spits, which became the hunting ground for the stubby Thunderbolts." The three fighter groups were facing an enemy force that outnumbered them approximately three to one, and were handicapped by a relatively short range.

The orders to the fighter pilot were "stick to the bombers," and don't go below 18,000 feet. The result of these orders was that the initiative of battle was handed over to the enemy. He used hit-and-run tactics to strike at the bombers, and offered our fighters very limited combat. The feelings of many of the pilots were summed up by Capt. L. W. ("Bill") Chick who was assigned to the 4th Fighter Group during this period:

"Our missions were taking us into France a little further than we could go in the Spits and we were dreaming of the days when we could have drop tanks that would let us go all the way to Paris. We were escorting a handful of Forts or Libs a little way on to the mainland, but the theory was that we had to be at nearly 30,000 feet and believe me there weren't any Jerries up there. They were at 24,000 feet where the bombers were, but we had to sit up there and fly a nice tight formation. Pretty damned senseless and we were getting no victories, but at least the bombers knew we were up there to protect them even though we weren't. This line of action persisted in England up to the time that I left in November 1943. The only victories were going to those wild eyed rebels who would get chewed out upon landing for breaking formation."

In spite of this stick-with-the-bombers doctrine, some victories were being scored. The real problem that had to be solved was the limited range of the P–47s. It was just too easy for the Luftwaffe fighter pilots to wait until the escort had to turn back and hit the bombers.

Up to this point in the war every possible means was used to extend the range. When raids were to be directed at France, US planes took off from forward bases in the south of England. When they were to be directed toward Holland or Germany, east Anglian bases were used. The answer to the problem was, of course, drop tanks. As far back as January 1943, General Hunter asked his Air Technical Section under the command of Col. Ben Kelsey to look into this matter. The project was handed to Kelsey's deputy, Col. Cass Hough, who began to immediately acquire and test droppable tanks. The first were P–47 ferry tanks which held 200 gallons, but they were unpressurized and totally unsuitable for use above 20,000 feet. While these were being tested, the Air Service Command designed a pressurized metal tank, and it tested out successfully at altitudes up to 35,000 feet. Because of a sheet steel shortage in England, production could not commence for at least three months, so Hough's team began testing a British-designed paper tank. This design also looked quite promising, but continued problems delayed its operational use until the fall of 1943.

Because of the design and production problems of the two types of pressurized drop tanks, the decision was made to try an escort mission utilizing the 200 gallon unpressurized ferry tanks. From his test data Hough determined that these tanks could be used to supply fuel from takeoff to the enemy coast, and would add at least seventy-five miles of range to the P–47s.

On July 28, 1943, Thunderbolts of the 4th and 78th Fighter Groups were prepared for the first belly-tank mission in the European Theater of Operations. They were to provide withdrawal support for B–17s attacking targets in northwestern Germany.

The 4th Fighter Group, led by Maj. Gilbert Halsey, was scheduled for the deepest penetration into Germany. In the vicinity of Emmerich, Germany, the 4th sighted Fortresses under heavy attack by enemy fighters. In an instant, Halsey gave the signal to attack and his pilots charged into the middle of the stunned Germans. Within twenty minutes the 4th had downed nine German fighters, two of which were claimed by the 4th's thirty-nine-year-old commanding officer, Col. Edward Anderson.

On the July 28 mission the 78th Fighter Group met no opposition, but two days later it was an entirely different story. Their mission was to escort B–17s on their withdrawal from Germany. The 78th had no sooner crossed the German border near Haldern when they spotted the bombers under attack by at least 100 German fighters. In their first air battle over Germany, the 78th had perhaps their most memorable mission. The commanding officer, Maj. Eugene Roberts, downed two Me 109s and one FW 190 to become the first US pilot to score a triple victory over Europe. Capt. Charles London of the 83rd FS downed an FW 190 and an Me 109 to become VIII FC's first ace. Eleven other enemy aircraft were destroyed by pilots of the 78th Group to make a grand total of sixteen victories for the day.

Major Roberts related his memorable mission as follows: "When we sighted the bombers off to our left we made a 90 degree turn and picked them up near Winterswijk. One straggling bomber was observed flying below the main formation in a dive, trailing black smoke and being attacked by about five E/A. I peeled my flight down and to the rear of the straggler. This would be about 1,000 feet below the main formation at about 21,000 feet. All E/A sighted us and took evasive

Maj. Eugene Roberts of the 78th FG performed the first "hat trick"—getting three victories in one combat on July 30, 1943. USAAF

A formation from the 84th FS, 78th FG form up laden with 75 gallon tear drop auxiliary fuel tanks. USAAF

Capt. Charles London, shown here in his P-47 with "El Jeppe" nose art, of the 78th FG became the first Eighth Air Force ace when he downed an FW 190 and a Messerschmitt 109 on a July 30, 1943, mission. London

action to the extent that I was unable to close, although I did fire a burst with improper deflection. The E/A was in a diving attack from the rear on this straggler. I initiated my attack from the port side rear of the fighters, swinging in behind them to the right and broke sharply downward to the rear. I followed them in the climb, attempting to get a deflection shot. When he broke downward I found I was directly beneath the bombers and saw a number of ball turret gunners firing at my flight. I broke down and to the rear, and pulled up to starboard side of the bombers about 1,000 yards out and at about their level.

"Looking up, I observed six E/A flying parallel to the bombers and about 1,000 feet directly above me. They failed to see us and did not take any action, so after they passed I made a climbing turn to the left to come up to their level and behind them. At this point I missed my second element and found myself alone with my wingman. In our pull up we missed the original six E/A sighted but sighted a single E/A ahead on same level at about 1,500 yards. I dived slightly below, opened full throttle and closed to about 400 yards. I pulled up directly behind the E/A and opened fire. Several strikes were observed on E/A, his wheels dropped and he spun down trailing a large volume of dark smoke and flame.

"I continued parallel to the bombers and sighted two more E/A about 2,000 yards ahead. I used the same tactics, closing to 400 yards astern, pulled up and opened fire on port aircraft. Observed strikes and E/A billowed smoke and flame, rolled over and went down. I was closing so fast that I had to pull up to avoid hitting him. I observed my wingman, F/O Koontz, firing at the

second aircraft but did not see the results. Both of these aircraft were FW 190s.

"After this second engagement, we were about two miles ahead of the bombers still well out to their starboard side. About this time I observed one E/A queuing up on port side and ahead of the bombers. I cut across, falling in behind him. We started to close again, using the same tactics as before to get in range. The E/A, an Me 109, peeled to starboard to attack the bombers head-on, and I followed closing to 500 yards before opening fire. Two bursts were behind but the third burst caught him and he spun down, trailing smoke and flame, some 1,500 yards ahead of the bombers."

In addition to the high-altitude dogfighting, Lt. Quince Brown demonstrated what the Thunderbolt's eight fifty-caliber machine guns could do to targets on the ground. During the air battle, he lost considerable altitude and decided to head back to Duxford on the deck. In doing so he caught a German train and a gun position and strafed them thoroughly with his guns. He had flown VIII FC's first strafing mission and had shown the way for missions that would be flown during 1944 in support of the invasion.

Outstanding as this mission was for the 78th, it was dampened by the loss of Colonel McNickle, their new CO, and two other pilots. The Group now began to think of itself as jinxed because of losing two commanding officers within thirty days, a feeling that lasted for quite some time.

The 4th and 56th Fighter Groups also took part in the combat action of July 30, and scored an additional nine victories. The 4th intercepted enemy fighters in the vicinity of Emmerich and scored five victories against two losses, while the 56th claimed four enemy planes against a loss of two of their own. As on July 28, German pilots not expecting the Thunderbolts that deep in Germany were caught by surprise and suffered high losses.

In August 1943 another fighter group, the 353rd, joined VIII Fighter Command. The 353rd Fighter Group, under the command of Lt. Col. Joseph A. Morris, had trained on the P-47 in the United States and were well indoctrinated on the craft before coming to England. The pilots had to wait, restlessly, for two months after their arrival in the UK before their new P-47Ds arrived. In the meantime, Morris and five senior pilots had been dispatched out to the other three veteran P-47 units for their initial combat flights before leading the men of the 353rd into combat.

On August 12 the 4th, 56th and 78th Groups were dispatched on escort missions into Germany. As the 4th FG rendezvoused with the Forts over Holland, they made contact with six enemy fighters preparing to attack the bombers. Maj. Jim Clark of the 334th FS quickly jumped the 109s and destroyed one. As this action took place, another eight fighters attacked the B-17s and were attacked themselves. Two of these 109s were downed by Captain O'Regan and Lt. Pisanos of the 334th FS. The last victory of the day went to Lt.

Cadman Padgett of the 335th FS. These victories were scored without loss to the 4th and were a prelude to the mission of Aug. 16, 1943.

The mission of August 16 was a Ramrod to Paris, and the 4th was to escort B–17s of the 1st Bomb Division. The Fortresses were already under attack when the 4th encountered them at the rendezvous point, and Col. Don Blakeslee led his men into the fight. In a wide-ranging air battle lasting nearly an hour, the 4th destroyed eighteen enemy fighters and handed the Luftwaffe its most resounding defeat to date. Of equal importance, the bombers got through and all of them returned safely. One P–47 was lost, but its pilot, Lt. Joe Matthews, escaped and made his way back to Debden. Fifteen pilots shared the victories, but the *real* star of the show was Blakeslee. He showed real leadership in his direction of the battle. The young colonel orbited above the air battle and directed his men to the enemy formations, and in doing so won a great victory. VIII FC's other three groups were also up on August 16 but were unable to score even though contact was made with enemy fighters. For the 353rd FG, which was flying its third mission, the contact was to cost them their commanding officer, Lt. Col. Joe Morris. His P–47 disappeared soon after he had led his flight in an attack on a gaggle of Focke Wulf 190s.

Aug. 17, 1943, was a day of maximum effort for the Eighth Air Force. The missions were the first attacks on Schweinfurt and Regensburg, Germany, the famous shuttle raid in which bombers of the 4th Bomber Wing continued on to bases in North Africa. This was, by far, the most ambitious effort undertaken by the Eighth Air Force to date. Escort for the mission was to be provided by all four of the Thunderbolt groups. Due to fuel limitations the P–47s could accompany the Fortresses only as far as Eupen, Germany, which is near the Rhine River. At this point the bombers were left to fight their way to the target. The initial mission to Regensburg was airborne as scheduled, but due to ground fog the mission to Schweinfurt did not get off until nearly noon.

The escort on penetration saw only limited action as the Luftwaffe fighters waited for the P–47s to depart before attacking the bombers. Two fighters were downed by the 78th Fighter Group, and one Me 109 was downed by Maj. Loren McCollom, who had just taken over command of the 353rd Fighter Group. This marked the first victory for the new unit.

When the mission to Schweinfurt didn't get off until late, this gave the Thunderbolts time to return to England and prepare to mount a second mission for the day. The 353rd and the 56th Groups took off in midafternoon to pick up the bombers on their withdrawal. The 353rd met with no opposition, but for the 56th it was to mark the beginning of a scoring streak that would continue throughout the war.

Col. Hubert Zemke led fifty-one P–47s on the mission, rendezvousing with the bombers at 1621 hours on their way home from Germany. Upon their arrival they found the Big Friends under heavy attack from some fifty to sixty enemy aircraft. Instead of their customary head-on attacks the German fighters were flying at the same level as the bombers and about five miles ahead. The attacks then would be initiated by making sharp 180 degree turns and then diving head-on toward the bombers. The 56th chose to break up the attacks by diving from above on the enemy as they went into their dive.

Lt. Spiros ("Steve") Pisanos was one of the early-scoring pilots of the 4th FG while they flew P–47s. Jackman

Capt. Walker ("Bud") Mahurin of the 56th FG was one of the most successful pilots during the Group's early days in combat. USAAF

Amongst those making the attacks was Capt. Walker Mahurin who described the action: "We started off to the left of the bombers and up forward of them. There was a FW 190 going parallel to the bombers and trying to reach a position forward to them. I sneaked up behind it and started to fire from about 300 yards closing to 200 yards. It blew up.

"We pulled up to the right and into the bombers. We completed our orbit and found ourselves in the same position with a FW 190 ahead of us. We followed him until he started to make a turn into the front end of the bombers, when I took a deflection shot at him at about 100 yards and watched him blow up.

"We again made a right turn into the bombers and this time wound up in the same spot. We spotted a Me 109 starting a head on approach to the bombers, so we started after him going down on him. I fired but observed no strikes. I pulled up and Lt. Hall, my number two man, followed him, fired at him, and started him smoking."

The 56th Group completed the mission with a total of seventeen German fighters destroyed, one probably destroyed and nine damaged for the loss of three P-47s and pilots in their largest and most victorious air battle to date. Excerpts from radio telephone (R/T) recorded the battle in this way:

1628 hours: Some more behind—maybe friendly—looks like 190s at 9 o'clock.
Focke Wulf at left.
Here comes something from the rear.
1630 hours: I got a 110.
O.K. take them.
Good show—beautiful show.
O.K. Let's go home gang.
What's at 6 o'clock? Can't identify it?
There's a 47 all alone—pick him up.
They're making head-on attacks on the 17s.

1632 hours: Let's get those guys.
There's another bunch going into them.
Come on up.
I can't get any more out of it.
They're getting under us.
O.K. Watch out, they're coming around from behind and off to the right.
1633 hours: Come up, they're shooting at you.
Two at 3 o'clock left.
I got you covered, boy.
I'm out of ammo.
Let's go home—we've been here long enough.

The 56th Group enjoyed another good day on August 19 when they escorted the Big Friends attacking Gilze-Rijen airdrome in Holland. The Thunderbolts encountered enemy aircraft immediately after rendezvous and continued to mix it up until the bombers finally departed for home. There was some confusion when the bombers passed over the target, orbited, went back over to make the bomb run and orbited once more before departure. The Thunderbolts claimed nine victories including an Me 109 for Capt. Gerald Johnson, making him the 56th's first ace. Lieutenant Hodges was lost, but it was due to mechanical failure and not enemy action.

As August 1943 drew to a close, it became quite obvious that VIII Fighter Command's aggressiveness was beginning to turn the tide in the airwar over the Continent. During the month its pilots had knocked down German aircraft at a rate of 6:1, but more importantly it was now carrying the fight deep into Germany.

In spite of these successes there was still a lot of work to be done. The increased fighter range was still not enough. The loss of sixty unescorted bombers over Schweinfurt and Regensburg proved that. For Bomber Command to carry out daylight precision bombing, it had to have a complete escort or face total disaster.

Often seen in early air battles was the Messerschmitt 110 which often fired rockets into Eighth AF bomber formations.
USAAF

Chapter 3

Extending the Limit

Work continued in Col. Cass Hough's technical branch to achieve the long-range goal, and in late August some of the new seventy-five-gallon pressurized tanks began to arrive. Soon thereafter the 4th and 56th Fighter Groups began mounting the new shackles on their Thunderbolts in preparation for these new tanks.

Meanwhile, the length and duration of fighter missions was being debated by General Hunter and the man who would replace him, Gen. William Kepner. General Hunter was much more conservative in his ambitions than Kepner. In an interview with Dr. Bruce Hopper and Lt. C. A. Foster on July 15, 1944, Kepner related the story this way: "In fact, my predecessor General Hunter told me that he thought 175 miles was a practical limit for fighters to go. I told him if I had anything to do with it, we would certainly have to go to Berlin, that we would set that as our objective—and I think he almost fainted when I told him that. He didn't say that we wouldn't do it, because he is a fighter. He kind of grinned and said, 'Well luck to you if you can—but the British say that 175 miles is the practical limit, and they have been at this for some time. I have been somewhat inclined to follow their lead. We follow their lead in many other things.' But he did admit that it probably could go, maybe, 250 or 300 miles, but not much over 300 miles. At about that time I took over. I ran around here as Deputy Commander to General Eaker and was looking over the situation. I don't know whether anyone knew that I came over here for the purpose of taking over this Fighter Command, but I did. General Arnold sent me over here personally. Hunter's tour was about finished and I was here to take the job when Hunter should leave."

On Aug. 29, 1943, General Kepner assumed command of VIII Fighter Command. The Command's new leader was fifty years old and a veteran of thirty-one years of service. Originally an infantry officer during World War I, Kepner had transferred to the Air Service in 1920 and was a pioneer in lighter-than-air operations. He became a conventional pilot in 1931 and by the early 1940s had extensive experience in pursuit aviation.

Soon after his appointment, Kepner received two new fighter groups. The 352nd under the command of Col. Joe Mason and the 355th under Col. William Cummings pushed up the strength of VIII FC to six combat-ready Thunderbolt units. From the operational and administrative standpoints important changes could now take place. The VIII FC historian summed them up this way: "It was possible for the first time for General Kepner and his organization to offer the bombers escort in relays, by which one group of fighters would accompany the bombers for the first leg of the penetration, relieve them by a second for the succeeding lap, then another over the target, and still others for the steps of their withdrawal. The increased number of fighters, the belly tanks that extended their range, and more than anything else, a growing sense of confidence all helped to make the relays a reality."

During the early months, fighters had been responsible directly to VIII FC, but in the summer of 1943 wings came into being—first the 65th, taking over the old RAF Control Station at Saffron Waldon, not far from Debden, then the 66th and later the 67th.

The principal function of wings was control of aircraft in the air. To the complicated and elaborate pattern of relays, the wing saw that each group got to its rendezvous point and that it was warned of the presence of enemy fighter as discovered by radar.

During the first five days of September the Thunderbolts participated in bomber escort and fighter sweeps into France and faced little opposition. Five enemy fighters were destroyed, but VIII FC also lost five of its own. On September 6, 122 P-47s were dispatched to escort bombers attacking Stuttgart, Germany. Again, the Luftwaffe was reluctant to mix it up with the P-47s and only one German fighter was downed. It was destroyed by Maj. Roy Evans of the 4th FG during the return flight over France.

On September 7 the P-47s escorted bombers hitting at targets in Belgium, and during the flight the 56th Fighter Group was able to claim three more victories. The 4th FG lost Lt. Aubrey Stanhope when he was downed by flak.

On September 9, VIII FC launched a massive escort mission of 215 Thunderbolts in support of B-17s attacking targets in France. Escort to the targets was provided by the 4th, 56th, 78th and 353rd Fighter Groups, while the 352nd Fighter Group flying its first operational mission provided cover for the return and landing of the 56th and 353rd Fighter Groups.

The Luftwaffe opposition was heaviest over the targets of the 3rd Bomb Division. The B-17 gunners claimed sixteen kills, two probables and nine damaged while losing two of their own over Paris and Beaumont Sur Oise. Fighter action was somewhat inconclusive during this encounter, but for Lt. Vernon Boehle of the 334th Fighter Squadron this was a day he would not soon forget.

The 4th Fighter Group's mission was to escort B-17s attacking Paris. The Group led by Lt. Col. Don Blakeslee crossed over the French coastline at Dieppe at 24,000 feet and rendezvoused with the Forts at Elbeuf, France. The timing of their arrival was nearly perfect because a mixed force of thirty Me 109s and FW

190s had just begun head-on attacks against the B-17s from out of the sun. The 334th and 336th Fighter Squadrons waded into the German fighters, drove them off and then regrouped to resume the escort. Within a few minutes a second force of sixteen enemy aircraft approached from the southwest and above. The 334th broke to intercept this attack and the Germans turned away. Maj. Oscar Coen and Capt. James Clark both fired deflection shots at long range but claimed no hits.

While this action was taking place, Lt. Vernon Boehle spotted an FW 190 and peeled off after it. Too late! The German pilot saw him coming and ran for it. The ensuing encounter was recalled by Boehle as follows: "As I turned and began climbing to rejoin the squadron I realized my wingman was no longer there. Almost simultaneously four FW 190s spotted me and one of them attacked. I hauled my P-47 around and headed for the B-17 formation in the hope that their gunners would knock the Focke Wulf off my tail. No fire came from the Forts though, so I began three violent turns and descended to 9,000 feet. All this time the German was staying right with me and I could feel hits all over my plane. At this point I quit trying to outturn the 190 and put my Jug in a steep dive and pulled out just above the trees. A quick check of my tail showed that he was still there and still firing. Suddenly the firing stopped and he was out of ammo. The German then pulled alongside my plane, surveyed the damage, waggled his wings and flew off. My plane had received quite a number of hits, but except for some vibration everything seemed to be o.k. I climbed back to 10,000 feet and then put the plane in a very gentle dive to gain a little airspeed. As I pulled the throttle back a tremendous vibration shook the plane violently and within seconds a propeller blade broke loose. Next the engine was ripped loose from its mounts and fell away, then I felt the plane go into a flat spin. It fell in a circle like a leaf falling from a tree and I knew I'd better get out

quick. I tried to jump but was pinned against the wing by airpressure. Finally I was able to push myself off the wing and fell free, but even then my troubles weren't over because the plane was right above me. I continued to free fall until I drifted out of its path and then opened my chute. Shortly thereafter I hit the Channel, got rid of the chute and climbed into the dinghy."

Although he was about forty miles off Dieppe, Boehle didn't feel too badly about his situation. His supplies were present and he found the flare gun with three shells. A short time later a flight of Spitfires passed over and he used the flare gun to try to get their attention. The first shell was a dud and the second went off but was unnoticed. Night then fell on the disappointed pilot.

During the night Boehle found his "operational" whiskey and sipped on it to ward off the cold. The next morning he heard aircraft, waited until they were overhead and fired his last flare. No luck! He remained unnoticed. As night began to fall once more a storm hit. The dinghy was bounced around like a rubber ball until the seas finally subsided. A bit later a ship was heard and a now desperate Boehle began using his flasher continuously in the hope that it would be seen. Again no luck.

Disheartened once again, Boehle began to sip on his whiskey. About an hour later he heard a ship's engine approaching from the opposite direction: "I grabbed the flasher and began signaling, and this time the ship came toward me and within a few minutes I was pulled aboard British Torpedo Boat 249. During the ride back to England the Skipper told me that he had seen my signals the first time but ignored them because they were coming from a charted mine field

A happy Vernon Boehle shown following his rescue from the Channel. V. Boehle

Lt. Vernon Boehle in his P-47C Indianapolis. This 4th FG pilot was to learn that ditching in the English Channel could be a cold and desperate experience. V. Boehle

and he was sure it was a trap. It was only on his return trip and when he saw my signals that he decided to investigate."

No more missions were flown until September 14 when the 355th Fighter Group flew its first mission. During the missions flown from September 14 through 26, little Luftwaffe opposition was encountered. A major reason for this was that the Luftwaffe High Command was realizing that escorted bombing raids over the Third Reich were now a real and dangerous threat. As a result it began a major realignment of its fighter defense zones. It transferred a number of coastal defense units which stretched from Denmark to Bordeaux, France, to bases in Germany. Other units were brought in from the Mediterranean and Russian theaters to augment this strength. Defenses were now being planned in depth.

On Sept. 27, 1943, the Luftwaffe put its plan into effect. The target for the day was Emden, Germany, and for the first time the fighters were to escort the bombers all the way to the target area and back. The first wave of bombers was to be escorted by the 4th and 353rd Fighter Groups, and the second wave by the 78th and 56th Fighter Groups. The 352nd and 355th Fighter Groups were assigned to carry out diversionary sweeps over Holland.

The 4th and 353rd made their rendezvous with the bombers over the Frisian Islands in bad weather and headed for Emden.

The P-47s of the 353rd under the leadership of Maj. Glenn Duncan were making their first deep penetration carrying new seventy-five-gallon jettisonable tanks. Shortly after joining the bombers, Maj. Ben Rimerman spotted a formation of twelve Me 109s flying at approximately 31,000 feet, which was 1,000 feet above him. He immediately took his 350th Squadron up to that level and attacked. In the ensuing fight, four of the Messerschmitts were downed and two damaged; one each by Major Rimerman and Lt. Dwight A. Fry, while Lt. William W. Odom destroyed one and shared another with Capt. Dewey Newhart. Capt. Orville Kinkade and Lt. Harry Hunter succeeded in shooting Me 109s off the tail of a P-47 in the target area to put the 351st Squadron on the scoreboard. A bit later, Lt. William J. Maguire destroyed one Me 109 and damaged another which were trying to get through to the bombers. One pilot was forced to bail out over England on return and another made a crash-landing, but it had been a most successful day for the 353rd.

On the way out Lt. Willard Millikan of the 4th FG added one more victory when he downed an FW 190 over Norderney Island (Frisian Islands) near Wilhelmshaven.

By the time the 56th and 78th FGs were to rendezvous with the second wave of bombers the weather had worsened. Because of this, the 78th missed the bombers at their rendezvous point over the North Sea, and did not join up with them until they were over the target

The 352nd FS of the 353rd FG gets in some formation time over England. USAAF

area. The result was, the 78th was about to enter its most decisive air battle since July. Their mission summary describes the action as follows: "Six Me 109s made 6 o'clock attacks on rear box of B–17s, which blew up three of the enemy aircraft. Approximately fifty enemy aircraft, mostly Me 109s, flew in small gaggles or singles. A few were painted pale blue but most were the conventional slate gray. Several Ju 88s, Me–110s, and Me–210s were identified. All squadrons made attacks, with flights breaking off to engage enemy aircraft at altitudes from 20,000 to 26,000 feet. Fight continued out over North Sea, northwest of Norderney (Frisian Islands). Blue flight (84th FS) was bounced seven times, four of which were aggressive and aimed at Flight leader, Captain (Harold) Stump. Flight warned each time by Lt. Belliveau, wingman of the second element. This flight of four destroyed four of the enemy."

Four enemy aircraft were downed by Captain Stump and F/O Peter Pompetti, each scoring two victories. In addition to these, the 78th scored six more victories for a total of ten for the day. They didn't lose a man during the battle and returned to Duxford with the high score of the day. The 56th FG added five more victories against one loss.

It was a tremendous victory for VIII Fighter Command. They had flown their first massive belly-tank raid into Germany, a trip exceeding 400 miles of which most was over water, and had inflicted a twenty-one to one victory over the German Luftwaffe.

It had a stunning impact upon the Luftwaffe. They had simply not expected to meet American fighters that deep into Germany. When the Thunderbolts returned to Emden, Germany, on October 2 the Luftwaffe reception was very timid. As a result, encounters were quite limited, but the P–47s were still able to claim six enemy aircraft destroyed as well as three probables and one damaged. Best of all, no American fighters were lost.

The Thunderbolts found themselves heading for Frankfurt on October 4, and for the 56th Fighter Group the mission turned into a real turkey shoot.

Maj. David Schilling was leading the Group to rendezvous when it was noted that one box of approximately forty bombers was a considerable distance behind the main force. He directed the 61st and 62nd Squadrons to cover the front boxes of bombers while he led the 63rd Squadron east to cover the rear box. The Thunderbolts approached the bombers from ten o'clock and slightly low. At that moment Schilling sighted a large number of twin-engined enemy aircraft maneuvering for stern attacks from five to seven o'clock position on the bombers.

Schilling took his formation over in front of the bombers and made a diving 270 degree turn which brought the fighters at a six o'clock position to the bombers, at an altitude of 28,000 feet and approximately 1,500 to 2,000 yards behind the bombers and the enemy aircraft.

Schilling picked out an Me 110 flying at six o'clock to the bombers and closed to 600 yards before firing a short burst from dead astern. Strikes were seen from wing tip to wing tip, and the left engine streamed glycol and the right engine burst into flames. A second burst brought more hits and the enemy aircraft caught fire and fell off in a shallow diving turn with both engines burning.

Capt. Walker Mahurin was leading Postage Blue Section of the 63rd during the attack and reported: "I

Capt. Harold Stump of the 78th FG was forced to fight off continued fighter attacks during the Ramrod to Emden, Germany, on September 27, 1943. He is shown in his P–47 Bad Medicine. Bertrand

F/O Peter Pompetti, 78th FG, downed two enemy aircraft on the Ramrod to Emden. He sits on the cockpit rail of his P–47 "Axe the Axis." P. Pompetti

sighted a Me 110 and notified Lt. Vogt that I was leaving him to attack it. At the time it was flying at about 20,000 feet parallel to the bombers. I throttled back and bounced down-sun on it and opened fire at 300 yards to the rear. I observed several strikes on both engines and the fuselage. I was closing so fast that I over-ran it and passed by about twenty feet away from it. At the time the right engine was on fire. I broke up to the left and started to climb. When I looked back I could see the Me 110 flaming and going straight in.

"As I pulled back up, several 110s passed in front and slightly above me, but short bursts got no hits. When I had gained two thousand feet I saw another single Me 110 flying away from the bombers at right angles to them. I again throttled back and bounced. When I opened fire from 300 yards I saw a couple of strikes. The enemy aircraft flipped over on its back and I did the same. I fired at it upside down and saw a few strikes. The Me 110 then started to head straight down. I followed and saw more strikes on it."

Mahurin's flight members saw the 110 burst into flames and break up as it hurtled earthward. "I climbed back to about 20,000 feet when I again sighted a Me 110 in a dive heading directly away from the bombers. He looked like he was going home. I started down on him and when I got to about 300 yards I again opened fire from the rear. This time I saw many strikes about the engines and the fuselage. I closed fast and before I pulled up I went past the bandit. I pulled up and started to climb. When I looked back I saw the Me 110 with the right engine flaming and pieces falling off. As the flames extended along the fuselage I saw parachutes start to open behind it."

The four Me 110s downed by Schilling and Mahurin were part of a total of fifteen of the twin-engined fighters shot down by the 56th that day. Lt. Vance P. Ludwig also got three, and singles were credited to seven other successful Thunderbolt pilots. The Me 110s apparently had been queuing up to fire rockets into the bomber formation, but without escort for themselves the 110s were certainly no match for the American fighters. They carried out little evasive action and a number of pilots reported that they encountered no return fire from rear gunners on the craft and seemed to doubt that gunners were even aboard some of the planes.

The bombers returned to Germany on October 8 and were escorted to Bremen by 274 Thunderbolts. The Luftwaffe was again up in force and a series of air battles broke out. High scorer for the day was the 4th Fighter Group with six victories. In doing so it acquired its first two aces. The Group provided penetration support, and just as it made rendezvous with the bombers over Texel Island, northwest of the Netherlands, enemy fighters attacked. The 334th FS climbed toward the German fighters and several dogfights broke out. F/O Ralph Hofer scored the first victory when he downed an Me 109 that had just shot down a P-47. Moments later Maj. Jim Clark downed a 109 and then Lt. Duane Beeson clobbered two Messerschmitts, his fifth and

Maj. Gen. William E. Kepner and his personal P-47. Kepner took over VIII Fighter Command in August 1943 and immediately set out to increase its long-range potential. USAAF

sixth kills. Meanwhile, pilots of the 335th FS got into the action and claimed two more victories. Maj. Roy Evans downed an FW 190 for his fifth victory and the other was claimed by Lt. Donald Ross. The 56th FG added another five victories and the 353rd chipped in two more, giving the command a total of thirteen victories for the day against three losses.

The victories scored by the 56th were made during withdrawal when a bevy of ten to fifteen enemy fighters (mostly FW 190s) were sighted attacking straggling B-17s attempting to get back to England. The 61st and 62nd Squadrons bounced the attackers from the rear and managed to down a number of them. Capt. Leroy Schreiber caught one FW 190 closing to pointblank range on a B-17 whose tail gunner apparently was dead. The Focke Wulf had closed to approximately fifty yards of the Fortress when the concentrated firepower of Schreiber's fifty calibers caught him unawares. Several strikes were observed and on a second pass at the Focke Wulf flame emerged as it staggered off, apparently with a dead Luftwaffe leader at the controls, for it carried a large black "V" behind the cockpit.

Two days later on the mission to Munster, Germany, the Jug pilots gave the Luftwaffe another battering. This time the score was twenty victories against the loss of one P-47. Unfortunately the victory was tempered by the fact that the bombers suffered heavy casualties.

The Luftwaffe had modified its tactics and now seemed to concentrate its attacks on the bombers over the target area. On this mission the 56th were late for their rendezvous because of a navigational error, and by the time they arrived on the scene German fighters had decimated the B-17s of the 13th BW. Hardest hit was the 100th Bomb Group which lost twelve of its fourteen planes.

When the 56th did arrive they did their best to even the score, destroying ten fighters. Maj. David Schilling, who led the 56th Group on the mission, stated: "After crossing the Dutch Coast, we were advised that the bombers were nine minutes late. To compensate for the difference I brought the Group a bit to the southeast of our planned course, and shortly after began to pick up the flak bursts over the track flown by the B-17s. This proved to be a good marker for, due to the haze, it was difficult to sight the bombers from any distance. We flew directly over Munster, at about 30,000 feet and then picked up the bombers in the vicinity of Altenberge, 15 miles northwest of the target. As we approached them I observed about 60–75 enemy aircraft making frontal, side and rear attacks and rocket bombs were being employed.

"As we came in on the right side of the bombers, I saw 6 to 8 enemy aircraft making a frontal attack on the lead box. I figured we would be too late if we attempted to head them off so I made a sharp 180 degree turn and picked them up as they finished their pass."

Major Schilling destroyed an FW 190 in his attack, which marked his fifth confirmed victory.

A number of Messerschmitt 110s and 210s were lobbing rockets into the decimated bomber formations, and Capt. Walter V. Cook found that the Me 210 could be a tough nut to crack. Following two bursts from dead astern which sent pieces flying off the plane, Cook pulled up, rolled to the left and looked down upon the enemy craft. What he saw was the left elevator gone, the rudder with a large hole in it, a large piece off the left wing, the right engine cowling shot away and the trailing edge of the right wing broken up. As Cook pulled off, the Me 210 began to burn, went into a tight spin and went down.

Capt. Gerald Johnson added two victories to his growing score—an Me 210 and an Me 110. Lt. Robert S. Johnson got an Me 109 and an Me 210, and Lts. Robert B. Taylor, James M. Jones, Anthony Carcione, John B. Eaves and Glen D. Schlitz got singles.

The 78th and 353rd Fighter Groups each added five more victories to bring the day's total to twenty. Two of the 78th's victories were credited to Maj. Eugene Roberts who downed an Me 110 and an Me 210 in an air battle over Enschede, Netherlands. These two kills raised his total to eight, the highest in VIII FC.

The 353rd Group also took part in the withdrawal of the "Big Friends" and scored a further five victories. Lieutenant Hurst destroyed one FW 190 and shared

Maj. Walter E. Beckham of the 353rd FG, shown here with his Little Demon *and ground crew, became a top scorer through his excellent marksmanship and tactics.* USAAF

32

another with Lt. William Tanner, but the big kill of the day was scored by Capt. Walter C. Beckham who got three to become the first ace of the 353rd, and whose accomplishments that day were sufficient to win him the Distinguished Service Cross. In the vicinity of Munster he sighted several enemy aircraft attacking a straggling Fortress. He started down but sighted an Me 210 much nearer and flying toward the rear box of bombers, so he attacked. The German pilot saw Beckham and went into a vertical dive. Throttling back to keep from going into compressability, Beckham gave the 210 a burst from astern, observing strikes, pieces flying off and black smoke emitting.

As he pulled up to rejoin the P-47s in his flight, he sighted an Me 110 coming at about right angles toward him. Beckham turned into the 110 for a head-on pass but the Luftwaffe pilot pulled up and to the left. The Thunderbolt pilot pulled to the right and took a few deflection shots which didn't score. When he finally positioned himself directly at the six o'clock position, Beckham saw pieces flying off the craft and smoking heavily.

Beckham then headed for home in an effort to catch up with the bombers and their P-47 escort. As he climbed to 21,000 feet he sighted a single plane off to the right at his level. Using a little more throttle, Beckham climbed to 23,000 feet and swung right hoping to get between the enemy aircraft and the sun. When he finally began to close the gap, the craft was identified as an Me 110. At that time a second Me 110 appeared and pulled in parallel to the first and a bit behind him. As he was closer to the second craft, Beckham pulled in and tried to get as close as possible, for he knew his ammunition supply was low. On his second short burst, tracers appeared telling him that he had only fifty rounds left in each gun.

Beckham then pulled in dead astern and let fly with the rest of his ammo, observing strikes, pieces and smoke. The first Me 110 was now turning into him, and Beckham had empty guns! He employed poker tactics and bluffed. He turned into the Me 110 which broke violently downward, making Beckham "the happiest guy in the world." Beckham then headed for home, but as he pushed the throttle forward he looked back to clear his tail and sighted eight or ten single craft following, but too far out to do damage. Full throttle and 1,000 feet a minute diving speed were sufficient to get him away and on his final course.

On Oct. 14, 1943, a day which became known later as Black Thursday, the Eighth Air Force embarked on the second Schweinfurt mission. To counter the attack, the Luftwaffe fighter force again changed its tactics, and this time it met and attacked the fighter escort as it reached the coastline of the Continent. The objective was to separate the bombers from the fighter escort at this point of the mission, and then hit the unescorted bombers in the target area.

The 353rd Group had to wait on the bombers which were ten minutes late at the rendezvous due to weather, which cut the fighters' escort time to an abso-

lute minimum before their fuel ran short. Shortly after landfall, the Luftwaffe made its only offensive move on the fighters during the day. About twenty Me 109s and FW 190s dove from 32,000 feet and attacked the 352nd Fighter Squadron flying on the right side of the bomber stream. Maj. Bill Bailey took his four flights in to meet the challenge, and was successful in breaking up the fighter onslaught. Lieutenant Junttila and Lt. R. A. Newman were successful in downing 109s in the initial attack. Maj. Bill Bailey sighted a P-47 with a 109 on his tail, immediately attacked and destroyed the Luftwaffe fighter. Lt. William Streit then downed another 109 that attacked him and his wingman.

The 351st Fighter Squadron came under attack at about the same time and were able to break up the enemy formation. Capt. Orville A. Kinkade shot down one of the Messerschmitt 109s.

Following these engagements the 353rd continued to escort the bombers until they sighted B-17s under attack from about thirty FW 190s in the vicinity of Duren, Germany. Maj. Ben Rimerman took his squadron into the fray and quickly shot down one of the Focke Wulfs. Captain Newhart got another. Lt. Dwight Fry shot a 190 off Lt. Wayne Blickenstaff's tail and then chased a second German fighter down to the deck. Unfortunately, Fry lost the second combat and was shot down. Fortunately, he was able to avoid capture and returned to the Group in February of 1944.

Once more, Capt. Walter C. Beckham of the 351st Squadron was in the forefront of the scoring. About the same time that Maj. Rimerman's squadron was engaged, Beckham took his flight in to intercept twenty plus FW 190s that were attacking the bomber stream from three o'clock. The P-47s made a steep diving turn and came out almost on top of the enemy formation. Beckham opened fire and got good strikes all over his target. The FW 190 went down smoking and shedding pieces in his slipstream. Beckham quickly lined up on another and flamed it.

Lieutenant McGuire, flying as Beckham's wingman, was attacked from astern by a Focke Wulf and called to Beckham for help, but the radio transmission was not heard. However, McGuire outflew the German pilot, got on his tail and sent him down flaming.

The destruction of eleven enemy aircraft by the 353rd Fighter Group and three by the 56th were the only bright spots in the day for the Eighth Air Force. The 353rd was cited by General Kepner for "superior support afforded the bombers."

Regardless, the German plan worked. While the 353rd was occupied with German single-engined fighters, the bombers continued on and were hit over the target area by twin-engined rocket-firing interceptors. Sixty bombers were lost—600 men went down with them. American fighters succeeded in destroying thirteen enemy planes during the day, but this in no way even came close to balancing the ledger. This could not be allowed to happen again. To quote from the VIII FC records, "It made doubly evident that the fighters had to go all the way."

Chapter 4

The Lightnings Cometh

The VIII Fighter Command was reinforced on October 15 when two more fighter groups became operational. They were the 55th, commanded by Lt. Col. Frank B. James, and the 356th, commanded by Lt. Col. Harold Rau. The 55th FG was equipped with the P-38 Lightning which promised deeper penetrations into Germany. The 356th was flying the P-47. The new groups flew their first mission, a fighter sweep over the Dutch Islands. The mission also marked the return of the Lightning to the Theater. It had been more than a year since the VIII FC sent its last P-38s off to North Africa.

During the remaining two weeks of October, VIII FC flew a total of seven missions. Three were fighter sweeps over the Dutch Islands and two were medium bomber escorts. The remaining two were heavy bomber

escort missions into Germany. On the mission of October 20 to Duren, Germany, the Luftwaffe was encountered and escorting pilots claimed 6-1-7 (numerals denote six claimed destroyed, 1 probably destroyed and seven damaged) enemy planes. The VIII FC suffered no losses on this mission, but nine bombers went down.

As October 1943 came to a close, VIII FC score sheets listed seventy-three confirmed victories during the month. Fourteen of its P-47s had gone down, but it was becoming quite obvious that the Command was making its presence felt. Since it had begun using the Thunderbolt, 237 German aircraft had been downed, and equally important its escort missions into Germany had helped to reduce bomber losses.

To help meet the Combined Bomber Offensive, the Germans continued to augment their fighter forces and in November had at least 800 planes. On the other side of the Channel, Allied planners knew that if their bombing offensive of Germany was to be successful, complete air superiority must be maintained. It was hoped that the P-38, which could penetrate at least 100 miles deeper into Germany, was the answer.

The P-38's first big test was to come on November 3. The 55th FG provided cover for the 40th Bomb Wing over the target area of Wilhelmshaven, Germany. The P-38 made rendezvous and escorted their charges to the target.

Lt. Jack S. Jenkins gave the P-38s the order to go home, and they started along the line of bombers to see if all was well. At that moment the Lightnings were attacked from out of the sun by a determined unit of Messerschmitt 109 pilots. While some of the German aircraft attacked the P-38s, others headed for the bombers. Lt. Robert L. Buttke's wingman was attacked and Buttke was forced to go down in a screaming dive to rescue his partner. He finally caught the enemy aircraft still on his wingman's tail at 14,000 feet and used his dive flaps to pull up, enabling Buttke to fire a long burst into the 109. Good strikes were observed, the canopy came off and the German pilot bailed out.

The P-38 pilots were under very strict orders to stay with the bombers at all costs, so Buttke pulled back up to 25,000 feet to join the bomber stream. There he sighted two 109s headed for the Big Friends, oblivious to the oncoming Lightning. Buttke closed to 300 yards on one of the E/A but couldn't get closer due to turbo failure. However, his first burst was effective and once more a German pilot bailed out.

Buttke's two kills and one by leader Lieutenant Colonel Jenkins gave the 55th Group their initial three

Lt. Robert L. Buttke was one of the first scorers for the 55th FG which marked the return of the P-38 to the Eighth AF. USAAF

victories, and it was much more meaningful in that they suffered no losses. Had they not been restricted to the bomber stream, the Lightning pilots might have scored even more kills.

The P-47s were also up on the 3rd and they, too, made their presence felt. Pilots of the 4th, 56th, 78th and 353rd Fighter Groups accounted for another ten German planes, making it thirteen confirmed victories for the day. Two US fighters and seven bombers were lost during the raid.

The Lightnings returned to Germany on November 5. This time the three squadrons of the 55th Fighter Group were accompanied by eight pilots of the newly arrived 20th Fighter Group. On the day's mission the Lightnings were escorting B-24 Liberators to Munster, Germany.

The 20th FG pilots who were accompanying the 55th met with difficulties early. Two of their P-38s were forced to abort with mechanical trouble and then their leader, Major Blanton, had trouble with his belly tank. Through a radio misunderstanding, the balance of the 20th pilots aborted when Blanton turned back.

Although plagued by further mechanical trouble and extreme cold, the P-38s of the 55th continued on to the target but had difficulty locating the bombers at the rendezvous point. Only the 38th Squadron located them, but their arrival was most timely. Sixteen P-38s had to take on an attack of Me 109s and rocket-laden Dornier Do 217s. In the heated battle, the Lightnings claimed three of the enemy for no loss and were able to bring some of the straggling bombers home.

While this mission was in progress, the Thunderbolts were escorting two bomb divisions to Gelsenkirchen, Germany. The P-47s encountered numerous enemy fighters during the mission and destroyed thirteen while losing four of their own. Among the thirteen kills that day was number 100 for the 56th Fighter Group—the first Eighth Air Force group to reach that goal. The honor went to Lt. George F. Hall who downed one of the rocket-carrying Do 217s.

On the afternoon of November 11 formations of P-47s escorted 172 bombers back to Munster to attack

Col. Jack Jenkins, CO of the 55th FG, and his personal aircraft Texas Ranger. Jenkins led the 55th through some trying times in their efforts to "stay with the bombers at all costs." USAAF

Two 20th FG pilots bicycle by one of their P–38s. The 20th was the second Lightning unit to enter combat with the Eighth Air Force in late 1943. USAAF

Col. Hubert ("Hub") Zemke, CO of the 56th FG, proved early that he was a masterful fighter tactician and prime advocate of the P–47. USAAF

marshaling yards. Several forces of enemy aircraft made their way through heavy clouds to intercept the bomber stream. The 56th Group tangled with a number of them and downed five but lost two of their own. The 353rd Group intercepted a group of twenty to twenty-five Focke Wulf 190s and broke up their formation before they could hit the heavies. Maj. Walter Beckham downed his ninth E/A while Maj. Glenn Duncan got two.

Duncan downed one of the Focke Wulfs in the initial combat but became separated from his flight. He finally found one flight of four under the bomber stream on the way out, but almost immediately he received a call from his number four man stating that he was under attack. Duncan went right back to find him but was unable to. While involved in his quest he sighted twelve to fifteen Me 109s attacking the bombers. He climbed to 22,000 feet and made a diving attack on the 109s, scattering their formation. Upon pulling up he sighted another four 109s lined up to make a pass on the bombers. Duncan lined up on the number three aircraft, which was off to one side, gave him a squirt and sent him down to crash in Holland. As Duncan headed for the coast, he sighted a straggling Fortress under attack. Two passes at the four Focke Wulfs scored no hits but gave the bomber a chance to make its run to sea.

Saturday, November 13 proved to be unlucky for the 55th Fighter Group. When the heavies went to Bremen, the P–38s were assigned to give them target support. The force that was intercepted by the Lightnings was a mixture of everything that the Luftwaffe could put up. There were Me 109s, FW 190s, Do 217s, Me 210s and Ju 88s—all up after the bombers. The Lightning pilots did their utmost to fight off the attackers, and by adhering to their rule of staying with the bombers were able to prevent other than minimal losses. However, the P–38s lost seven of their number while downing eight enemy aircraft. Capt. Joseph Myers accomplished an almost impossible task by escorting a straggling bomber and two P–38s, each on one engine, out of enemy territory.

The mission of November 25 marked the inauguration of bombing by Thunderbolts of VIII Fighter Command. The P–47s of the 353rd and 56th Fighter Groups were loaded with 500 pound bombs. Escort was provided by the 78th and 356th Fighter Groups, and the targets were airfields in the St-Omer area of France. Col. Hubert ("Hub") Zemke of the 56th Group had decided that a good way to bring the Luftwaffe up to fight was by bombing the airfields. The plan was for the 353rd to dive-bomb Ft. Rouge while the 56th did a horizontal bombing attack at Longunesse airfield.

Lt. Col. Loren McCollom led the fighter-bombers of the 353rd to their target where they immediately encountered heavy flak from ground batteries in the area. McCollom had just begun to roll into his attack from 15,000 feet when his aircraft was hit by flak. The P–47 immediately burst into flames. Fortunately, McCollom was able to pull out and go over the side about 10,000 feet. His parachute opened and he drifted down to become a prisoner of war.

Fourteen remaining P–47s completed their dive-bombing mission, but the effect of their bombing left a lot to be desired. Most of the bombs fell short of the target and six of the Thunderbolts returned with flak damage.

The 56th Group came in over their target at 24,000 feet led by a B–24 with a bombardier. On release of the bombs by the bombardier, each of the P–47s dropped its lone 500 pound bomb. A malfunction of the release mechanism on the B–24 caused the bombs to be released late. This in turn caused the fighters to miss with most of their bombs. What might have been a successful mission went for practically nil.

November 26 was a day of superlatives for both VIII FC and VIII Bomber Command. The targets for the day were Bremen, Germany, and Paris, France. To hit the targets, Bomber Command dispatched its largest force to date: eleven combat wings, a total of 633

"Bombs away" by B–17s attacking a Luftwaffe airfield in October 1943. These B–17Fs were particularly prone to be attacked head-on due to light nose armament. At the same time the escort fighters lacked the range to go to the target with them. USAAF

bombers. Joining in the task force were 381 fighters from VIII FC, and when the day was over the fighters had set a new record for enemy aircraft destroyed in a single day.

The scoring honors went to the veteran 56th Fighter Group who destroyed twenty-three enemy aircraft in the air, probably destroyed two more and damaged seven. At rendezvous point, some fifty to sixty twin-engined Me 110s and 210s were seen assembling to make rocket attacks astern of the bombers. They were being protected by a bevy of FW 190s and Me 109s, some of which were flying at up to 30,000 feet. As the 56th flew to the attack, a number of the single-engined fighters dived down to attempt to break up the Thunderbolt formations intercepting the rocket-carrying force.

Capt. Walker Mahurin made one pass after another at the Me 110s and wound up flying from one sighting to another at full throttle. In the lengthy encounter his P-47 flew at top performance for nearly half an hour, during which he managed to down three of the enemy aircraft and probably destroyed a fourth.

All total, sixteen of the twin-engined fighters were downed. Majors Gabreski and Craig, plus Captains Cook and Ralph Johnson and F/O Valenta all scored double victories for the day. The only thing that marred the triumphant feat was the loss of Lt. Byron Morrill who was seen bailing out over Amsterdam.

The day also carried special significance to at least two other fighter groups, the 20th and the 352nd. On this day each scored their initial aerial victories of the war.

The 77th Fighter Squadron of the 20th FG was attached to the 55th Fighter Group for this mission, and they were to provide penetration escort for the bombers attacking Bremen. Their encounter took place just as

Capt. (later, Major) Jack C. Price, in his Thunderbolt Feather Merchant, *was one of the early aces of the 78th FG.* Bertrand

they had rendezvoused with the bombers. Maj. Herbert Johnson, who was leading the 77th, spotted five Dornier Do 217s preparing to attack the B-17s. He immediately signaled the other pilots in his section to follow and they dived to attack the Dorniers. At 175 yards he opened fire at one of the 217s, devastating its cockpit area and left engine. The Dornier's engine burst into flames, then the plane began to shake and quickly spun violently out of control.

After breaking up this German attack on the bombers, Johnson and his men resumed the escort with no further encounters.

For the 352nd Fighter Group, it was mission number twenty-seven and they were providing withdrawal support from Bremen. Shortly after their rendezvous with the bombers, the Luftwaffe struck at a box of B-24s. The 487th Fighter Squadron led by Maj. John Meyer peeled off from out of the sun and hit the attacking 109s. In the ensuing air battle, three of the Messerschmitts were knocked out of the sky, one each by Major Meyer and Capt. Donald Dilling, and the third shared by Lts. John Bennett and Robert Berkshire. Meyer also scored a probable and a damaged.

The bombing mission to Paris had been aborted due to heavy cloud cover over the assigned targets, but the elements did not eliminate German opposition. The B-17 formation was flying through intense flak when the first Me 109s appeared and began their attack. The 78th Fighter Group, which was providing escort, wheeled around to head off the German strike, but were too late to save one B-17 which blew up in a ball of flames. They arrived just as the 109s were pulling away, and Maj. Eugene Roberts attacked one but was unable to make a claim. The other three 109s broke into a dive, so Roberts climbed to resume the escort.

While Roberts' encounter was taking place, Maj. Jack Price saw two FW 190s parallel to the B-17s at about 18,000 feet. He immediately attacked and destroyed one of them and then re-formed his flight at eleven o'clock off the first box of bombers. Within moments he saw twenty-five to thirty more enemy aircraft (Me 109s) climbing and turned to attack once more. As he approached an element of Messerschmitts, one of them flipped over and dived. Price went after him and from 300 yards exploded the 109 with a two-second burst from his fifties.

The P-47s had broken up the German attack but were unable to escape the assault of one 109. Just as Price was regrouping his element the Me 109 sneaked in from behind. Price saw him and yelled, "Break!" but Lt. Dougherty didn't get away. He was last seen going straight down.

There were more encounters to come and the 78th downed two more fighters before the mission ended. Lt. Warren Wesson hit an FW 190 with a long burst and apparently killed the pilot, because it went into a steep dive and straight down to a fiery crash. The final victory of the day was scored by Lt. Askelman.

As the results of the day's action became known it was quite obvious that VIII Fighter Command was truly coming of age. Now that its fighters were fitted with drop tanks and were capable of carrying the fight to the enemy, it was possible to destroy them in record numbers. The total score for the day was thirty-six destroyed, three probables and nine damaged for a loss of four!

Three days later, fighters of VIII FC again headed for Bremen on another escort mission. For the Lightning pilots of the 55th FG November 29 was a black day. Seven of their P-38s went down under enemy guns against only two victories. The Group had started out with fifty-five aircraft airborne, but by the time they reached Aschendorf seventeen P-38s had aborted primarily due to mechanical trouble. At 1410 hours the unit was bounced by forty-plus Me 109s attacking from head-on and above. At the same time another force of forty-plus enemy aircraft was sighted climbing to join the fracas at 27,000 feet. The Lightning pilots immediately dropped their belly tanks, but so sudden was the onslaught that some of them may have been hit before they could get rid of the bulky objects. The initial fight lasted fifteen to twenty minutes, and four P-38s were known to have been lost at this time.

One of the pilots who met the initial onslaught was Capt. Chet Patterson: "We were met head-on by thirty-plus Me 109s. I dropped my belly tanks and turned to the right to engage the enemy. I noticed four P-38s about 2 miles behind being attacked by two E/A at about 2,000 feet below me so I started a gentle dive with moderate power. I then saw one P-38 go down through the overcast, which appeared shot down. The three remaining P-38s continued evasive action with the E/A still on their tails. One of the P-38s broke left so I started my attack on the E/A on his tail. I gave a moderate burst at 300 yards and saw several hits. I dropped flaps to stay turning and gave another short burst as I mushed by at 75 yards. I pulled up and saw white smoke coming out of the E/A as he spun through the clouds."

This was one of two bright points for the 55th that day as they were only able to down two of the enemy aircraft in the melee. Colonel James, leading the group, made several 360s attempting to round up his charges before heading for home. Maj. Milton Joel of the 38th Squadron had taken one element forward during the fight, but when it came time to head for home, he, too, was amongst the missing.

The Thunderbolt pilots, on the other hand, had a much better showing. The 56th FG led in scoring with six victories, and the less experienced 356th FG was second with five.

Things had started off badly for the 356th. When they took off to escort the returning bombers, they encountered very bad weather over the Continent—10/10 cloud cover—in some areas. The B-17s returning from Bremen, Germany, were also late for the rendezvous so the 356th had to continue flying inland until they

P-38s of the 55th FG in formation. The Lightning pilots suffered from extreme cold and the engines from supercharger *troubles on the high-altitude missions with the Eighth AF. USAAF*

saw the bombers. The 360th FS slid into its position as top cover at an altitude of 28,000 feet and within three minutes the Luftwaffe was seen maneuvering to attack the Forts.

The squadron leader spotted a 109 positioning itself on the rear bombers and called for "White Flight" to bounce it. Lt. Raymond Withers was flying as number three in the flight. When the alert was sounded, he followed Lt. Bob L'Heureux and his wingman as they made a gentle diving turn and came in directly behind the German. Withers throttled back to keep from overrunning the target while L'Heureux and his wingman made their firing pass. The first two P-47s broke away after firing at and missing the 109 and then Withers closed in to 250 yards and opened fire. After a long burst from his guns he saw heavy concentrations of strikes around the cockpit, wingroot and tail section. Within seconds the 109 began trailing dense smoke, started breaking up and then went into a vertical dive totally out of control. After scoring the squadron's first victory, Withers joined back up with his unit and headed back to England. On the return trip the weather worsened and the scattered P-47s were covering the airwaves with calls for homings. Most made it back, but the weather claimed five of the 356th's Thunderbolts.

At the end of their first month of intensive operations the men of the Lightnings were licking their wounds, but they had proved they could do a good job, regardless. The P-38 suffered some mechanical shortcomings, primarily in turbo failure at high altitude and improper operation of the intercoolers. However, the biggest problem for the Lightning pilots was the inadequate cockpit heater. They were forced to wear so many layers of clothing they could hardly move, much less have their limbs free for violent maneuvering in the heat of battle. They experimented with many kinds of clothing, but finally in 1944 some of the men got hold of some blanket-lined equipment that had been designed for the men in the tanks. These seemed to work well and were prized by the pilots who possessed them.

Second, the men of the Lightnings had been strictly ordered from the beginning that they were the only aircraft capable of going all the way with the bombers, and they were to stay with the bombers at all costs. It mattered not how great the temptation and how the Luftwaffe baited the trap; the P-38s had to stick with the bomber stream and this they did. Once they started escorting the bombers in the target areas, losses to the Big Friends began to drop immediately. While the P-38s may never have run up the long string of victories nor produced many aces, their popularity never waned with the men of the bombers.

As the men of the Lightnings lamented their fortunes at the end of November 1943, events were taking place behind the scenes that had an overwhelming effect on the offensive for 1944. The reason for excitement was the arrival of the North American P-51B Mustang in England and the promise of air superiority it projected. This plane with its Merlin engine was revolutionary in several respects. It combined the features of excellent maneuverability, high speed and when compared to the P-47 and the P-38, a miserly fuel consumption rate. General H. H. Arnold, Chief of the Army Air Forces, recognized its possibilities early and in September 1943, while on an inspection of the Eighth Air Force, issued a directive that Mustangs be sent to the Eighth as soon as possible.

Chapter 5

Seven League Boots—The Mustang

Oddly enough, when the first Mustangs reached England during the fall of 1943 they were not issued to the Eighth Air Force, but went instead to the 354th Fighter Group of the Ninth Air Force. Naturally, the Eighth Air Force cried foul and protested this decision vehemently, but to no avail. The apparent reason for this decision is that the original Mustang, the Allison-engined P-51A, had been used as a tactical aircraft by both the RAF and the USAAF, and Army Air Force planners could not be persuaded to change the P-51B's mission to escort duty. VIII FC did continue to argue its case and finally won a partial victory. The agreement reached was that the 354th FG was to fly escort missions under the control of VIII FC until further notice.

The 354th FG began receiving its Mustangs on Nov. 11, 1943, and Group Commander Col. Kenneth Martin began to prepare his men for their first combat. To assist with this training and to gain his own Mustang experience, VIII FC sent Lt. Col. Donald Blakeslee of the 4th FG to Boxted in November 1943. The transition to Mustangs was not easy for the 354th, since none of its pilots had ever flown the plane. The Group had arrived in England during October but was not able to begin

operational missions until Dec. 1, 1943. On that date Blakeslee led twenty-eight Mustangs of the 354th on a sweep over the Continent. They made landfall at Knokke, Belgium, and continued inland. The trip was uneventful until they turned and headed back to England. Over St-Omer, France, they encountered heavy and accurate flak, and a second flak barrage occurred over Calais. All planes returned safely and only Lt. James Lane suffered minor damage to his plane.

While this was going on the bulk of VIII FC was engaged in an escort mission to Solingen and Leverkusen, Germany. On this mission, four wings of B-17s from the 1st Air Division and two B-24 wings of the 2nd Air Division were to hit these targets. The first force of bombers was supported by the 78th A Group (by now some of the older P-47 groups had enough aircraft and pilots to put up two groups, each having three twelve-plane sections on any mission) and the 355th, 353rd and 352nd FGs. The second force was shepherded by the 78th B Group, as well as the 4th, 56th, 356th and 55th FGs.

The 78th A Group had no sooner made rendezvous with the bombers when they encountered more than

P-51B of the 354th FG being fitted with drop tanks. Although a Ninth Air Force unit, the 354th did yeoman escort duty with the Eighth until after D-Day in June 1944. USAAF

forty enemy fighters. In a series of air battles they knocked four enemy aircraft out of the sky. Meanwhile, the 355th also found targets aplenty and claimed another four, but at the cost of two of their own. The 353rd and 352nd Groups then combined for another four victories.

P–47 pilots escorting the second force accounted for another eight German fighters. The P–38s of the 55th didn't fare too well, as they were bounced before they could get rid of their drop tanks, and two Lightnings were quickly shot down.

Maj. Ben Rimerman led the 353rd Fighter Group on their second dive-bombing mission on December 4. Each P–47 of the 351st Fighter Squadron was loaded with a 500 pound bomb and escorted to the target—the Gilze-Rijen airfield in Belgium—by the 350th and 352nd Fighter Squadrons and the 56th Fighter Group. On this mission the flak didn't begin until the target was attacked and all sixteen aircraft were able to get a much better pattern on the airfield. Attack altitude was 16,000 to 18,000 feet, and dive angles varied from fifty-five to seventy degrees, with pullout being accomplished at between 6,000 and 10,000 feet. Even though the mission was considered successful it still didn't draw the Luftwaffe into the air.

The Mustangs of the 354th FG flew their first escort mission on December 5, but it was uneventful as no enemy aircraft were encountered.

Lt. Paul Conger was one of the more aggressive pilots of the 56th FG in its early fights. He became an ace on his first combat tour and returned to fly again in 1945. P. Conger

On December 11, 388 fighters were dispatched to escort three bomb divisions to Emden, Germany. The enemy was again up in force, and was vigorously engaged. When the shooting was over, twenty-one enemy fighters had gone down, seventeen of which were dispatched by the 56th FG.

Once more the 56th Group was "Johnnie on the spot" when twin-engined rocket carriers began to line up on the bombers. A formation of more than fifty Me 110s and Ju 88s were sighted off Langeoog Island off the German coast as they were preparing to turn in on the rear of the Big Friends. The Thunderbolts immediately turned in on the stern of the German fighters. Lt. Paul Conger led his flight in behind a formation of Me 110s and proceeded to blast away. He put a short burst into the first 110 and pulled over to line up on the leader. Conger began firing at 500 yards and closed to 150 before he let up on the trigger. There was a small explosion on the right engine and black smoke began pouring back from it. The 110 was observed to go into a spin until it finally hit the ground.

Conger then lined up on a Junkers Ju 88 flying with an Me 110, one well ahead of the other. These two aircraft took him on a chase that culminated at 10,000 feet. At 500 yards he began to fire on the Ju 88 from dead astern and closed to 100 yards. The right engine caught fire and pieces began to fly off the aircraft. As Conger went by underneath the plane he saw the Me 110 hit the water. As he pulled up, the Ju 88 went into the water. Both were victims of his sustained bursts.

Maj. Francis Gabreski got his eighth kill that day but was lucky to get home. As he took his section down to attack a formation of Me 110s there was a huge explosion above and to the left. Gabreski immediately climbed to 30,000 feet to get away from the rain of debris that was falling. Unknown to him and his pilots, the debris came from the midair collision of Lieutenants Strand and Kruer of the 61st Squadron.

Gabreski then picked out three Me 110s in string formation at 24,000 feet and dropped down on their six o'clock position. The German aircraft continued to drop earthward, and the Thunderbolt pilot could not close until they reached 18,000 feet. As he fired, good strikes were seen on the fuselage and canopy. The nose of the 110 dropped and shortly after, two men went over the side.

Following recovery, Gabreski climbed and attempted to join up with a flight of six fighters ahead of him. Much to his surprise, when he got close enough to look down on the formation all six aircraft were sporting black crosses on their wings. Gabreski exited at full throttle.

Now low on fuel, the Thunderbolt pilot headed for home. As he was leaving the Emden area, he sighted a Messerschmitt 109 approaching from three o'clock but well underneath. Gabreski hoped that he would not be seen, but alas, a determined Luftwaffe pilot came up to do battle. Gabreski did two or three turns with the 109, then broke out and headed for the bomber stream hoping he could elude the enemy aircraft. Still climbing, Gabreski saw the German nose-down, pick up speed and come climbing after him. Immediately the Thunderbolt pilot broke hard right, stalled and while in the stall was hit by 20 mm fire. The shell came up through the skin of the aircraft, nicked Gabreski's right boot, hit the right rudder pedal and exploded. At this time the P–47 lost power and went into a spin. Gabreski grabbed the canopy, opened it and made ready to exit.

With the canopy still open Gabreski looked back and saw that he was still being attacked. Rolling to the left and putting the heavy P–47 into a dive, the Jug pilot headed for cover. Finally at about 1,000 feet he found cloud cover and safety. Bobbing up once in a while, he made his way to the Dutch coast and headed out across the North Sea. He had lived to fight another day.

On Dec. 13, 1943, another P–47 group, the 359th FG based at East Wrentham and commanded by Col. Alven P. Tacon, Jr., began operations. Their first mission was a fighter sweep to the Pas de Calais area while the remainder of VIII FC was escorting bomber missions to Germany.

The mission for December 20 was to Bremen and was to be regarded as a perfect example of fighter escort. Ten combat wings of bombers were sent on the mission and were escorted by twelve fighter groups. Ten groups of P–47s provided escort to the target area Initial Point where they were relieved by the longer range Mustangs and Lightnings which escorted the bombers to the target and back. There were numerous and continuing attacks by German fighters, but these were continually broken up by the disciplined escorts. The escorting fighters shot down nineteen enemy aircraft, probably destroyed three and damaged six others. US losses were five planes and pilots. The 352nd FG led by Col. Joe Mason accounted for six of these victories. Within ten minutes of rendezvousing with the bombers, the 352nd encountered enemy fighters. Blue Flight of the 486th FS was the first to be bounced when a single Me 109 struck from out of the sun. It missed and Capt. Franklyn Greene quickly turned and downed the 109 with several well-placed bursts.

The 352nd P–47s then resumed their escort for another ten minutes but as they reached Friesoythe, they made their turn and headed for Bodney. During the return flight the 487th FS caught a gaggle of Messerschmitts attacking a B–17 straggler. Capt. Donald Dilling led the attack and quickly blasted one 109 out of the sky. Within minutes after his victory three other enemy planes went down under the guns of Capt. Winfield McIntyre, Lt. Daniel Britt and Lt. Harold Riley. After disrupting the German attack the Thunderbolts escorted the heavily damaged B–17 back to the Channel.

The 56th FG also claimed six victories during the mission, and the Mustangs of the 354th claimed three more. One of the 354th's victories was claimed by Lt. Col. Don Blakeslee who now was completely infatuated with the P–51 and was already planning his campaign to get the Mustang for the 4th FG.

Another new fighter group, the 358th, joined the fray on the day's mission. They participated in the

Maj. Francis Gabreski of the 56th FG was an aggressive scorer from his entry into combat. Before he became a POW in July 1944 he ran up a score of 28 enemy aircraft destroyed in the air and three on the ground. USAAF

bomber escort in their P–47s and encountered plenty of flak but were not able to engage enemy fighters.

The impact on VIII FC and its planners is made quite obvious by the comments in its mission summary which read in part as follows: "One fighter group of the twelve (10 Thunderbolt, 1 Mustang and 1 Lightning) employed by this command carried out its part of the mission exactly as set down in field orders, while the other eleven stayed with the bombers longer and penetrated into German territory farther than had been originally intended. Three of the groups carried out their share of the program and in addition overlapped along the bomber track to such an extent that they gave double support for the whole of the next portion of the allotted fighter support area. It is interesting to note that this additional fighter support was carried out in the face of adverse wind conditions.

"All in all, with a very few exceptions, the plan as set down in Field Order 204 was carried out in an exceptionally fine manner, and both from a defensive and offensive standpoint, the mission was decidedly a great success. The fighter groups are to be commended for doing their job well and then in most cases continuing on to do additional work not expected of them."

With this mission under their belts, VIII FC was now beginning to see the results of a year and a half's planning. They were able to provide a complete escort to the bombers, and the Mustang demonstrated its extreme long range and offensive capabilities.

The next day four groups—the 78th, 356th, 358th and 359th—were sent up to escort Ninth Air Force B-26s striking at Crossbow (German V-1 rocket sites) targets in western France. Because of unfavorable weather conditions the bombers were able to hit only two of their primary targets. The mission was uneventful for all of the fighter groups except for 78th B, which encountered twenty-five to thirty German fighters in the vicinity of Doullens, France. They arrived just as the Germans began attacking the B-26s, and quickly struck at mixed groups of Me 109s and FW 190s. Within a few minutes, three Focke Wulfs had been destroyed by Lieutenants Silsby, Hunt and Doyle of the 84th FS, and Capt. J. D. Irvin, also of the 84th, claimed a 109.

The bombers and fighters of the Eighth Air Force returned to Germany on December 22, this time hitting at transportation installations in the Osnabruck and Munster area of Germany. Four combat wings of B-17s of the 1st Division and two wings of B-24s of the 2nd Division attacked Osnabruck, while a second task force composed of four wings of B-17s of the 3rd Division and one wing of B-24s of the 2nd Division attacked Munster. Each attacking force was provided with six fighter groups for escort.

Enemy reaction to the first force hitting at Osnabruck was considerably heavier and numerous encounters took place.

Pilots of the 56th, 352nd and 353rd Fighter Groups were engaged in several battles and accounted for eleven enemy fighters of the fifteen claimed by Fighter Command. The 56th destroyed four shortly after breaking off from penetration escort, and the high scorers of the day were the 352nd FG which claimed six

enemy fighters. The encounters took place just after rendezvous with the bombers had been made and continued for about another thirty minutes. Victories were claimed by Lt. Col. John Meyer, Capt. George Preddy and Lieutenant Bennett of the 487th FS with one each, and Lieutenants Horn and Coleman of the 328th FS. The final victory of the day was an Me 110 which was shared by Maj. Everett Stewart and Lt. Bob Powell of the 328th.

Everything went according to the timetable on the second mission, and all rendezvous were made properly. Enemy resistance to this force was considerably lighter, but the fighters did engage the Luftwaffe and claimed another four enemy fighters. Three of these claims were made by the 4th FG, and the fourth was made by the 78th A FG. Lt. John Godfrey of the 4th FG claimed 1½ of these victories, but almost became a victim himself. His plane was hit during the skirmish and went into a spin at about 10,000 feet. Godfrey had quite a struggle with his stricken plane and finally brought it out of the dive just above the ground.

Attacks upon targets in Ludwigshafen, Germany, were made on December 30 by twelve combat wings of bombers. Support and escort was provided all the way by VIII FC. This mission marked one of the deepest penetrations by fighters into Germany to date. One of the groups participating was the 20th FG based at King's Cliffe. This was their first escort mission and for them it was uneventful. However, this wasn't the case for all of the groups, as enemy action and accidents made this a rough day for a number of the units. Thirteen escort fighters went down on December 30, four as a result of two midair collisions. In spite of the losses, the pilots were able to claim nine victories during the day, four going to the 78th. In the vicinity of Reims, France, the lead box of bombers that they were escorting called for help as they were being hit by attacks from at least thirty Me 109s. Immediately after the call, pilots of two flights from the 83rd FS bounced six of the 109s and three of them were downed by Lts. Martinez,

Lt. Col. John C. Meyer of the 352nd FG distinguished himself in the Group's early operations in Thunderbolts. An outstanding leader, Meyer became a leading ace in the Eighth AF. USAAF

P-47 of the 486th FS, 352nd FG being readied for a mission in the early morning fog so typical of England. USAAF

Wesson and Hagman. The fourth enemy fighter was claimed a few minutes later by Lt. Julian of the 83rd FS.

On the last day of 1943, Eighth Air Force bombers struck at a variety of targets in occupied France. One task force had two combat wings of the 3rd Division striking at targets in the Paris area, while the largest force consisting of the B–17s of the 1st and 3rd Divisions and 120 B–24s of the 2nd Division headed for targets in the Bordeaux and La Rochelle area. Accompanying the force headed for Bordeaux were the 20th, 55th and 354th FGs on what was to date the longest escort mission attempted by VIII Fighter Command. The 20th FG led by Lt. Col. Jack Jenkins met the bombers over the water west of Bordeaux, and then covered the target area for about twenty minutes. During this time frame several enemy fighters were observed in the target area and Lt. Lindol Graham of the 79th FS damaged one FW 190 before he lost it in an overcast. The long mission consumed great quantities of fuel, and several pilots barely made it back to England. One pilot, Lieutenant Garrett, had to crash-land on the Isle of Wight.

The 55th Group went all the way to the target with the bombers and saved several stragglers who had been hit by flak. Col. Frank James destroyed one FW 190, and Capt. Joseph Myers destroyed an Me 109. Myers went into a bit of a turning match with his opponent, but even twenty degrees of flap utilized by the German went for naught. Myers still pulled the nose through and clobbered him.

Fighters escorting the mission to Paris also encountered enemy opposition and claimed four destroyed and one damaged in the fights that ensued.

With the beginning of the New Year, the long-planned bomber offensive struck regularly into the heart of Germany. It could do so with the realization that the bombers would now be afforded cover all the way to the target and back. With the growth of VIII FC, which occurred in late 1943, it, along with some Ninth AF units, could provide escort and also turn its eyes to other goals.

The mission for 1944 was to reach complete air superiority over the Luftwaffe. To accomplish this General Kepner and his staff began the New Year with decisions that would take the leash off the fighter pilots, so that they could strike at the Luftwaffe wherever they found it. As the Command had grown in strength, it found that the German fighters were avoiding combat whenever possible. About the only time enemy fighters could now be engaged was while they were attempting to intercept the bombers. Under the 1944 rules the escort fighter pilot, once his escort was completed and if his fuel supply allowed, could search out and attack the Luftwaffe wherever he found it—in the air or on the ground.

In addition, the fighter pilot was further aided by some new engineering advances. The P–47s were being fitted with water-injection systems which provided short-term emergency power, and new paddle-bladed propellers which greatly enhanced their climbing abil-

ity. Along with these improvements the Thunderbolts were being modified to carry wing tanks. With two 108 gallon wing tanks the P–47 now had a range of 475 miles. This was comparable to the range of the P–51 without tanks. However, with two seventy-five-gallon wing tanks the P–51 could range 650 miles from base. Later the Mustang was provided with the 108 gallon tanks which gave it an unheard of range of 850 miles!

In January 1944 other changes occurred in the manner in which the escort missions were carried out. During 1943 the fighter groups rendezvoused with the bombers at a certain point and flew with them until relieved by another unit. Under the new policy, a group was assigned to a particular area of the bomber route to patrol until the bomber force passed through it.

The New Year's first mission was on January 4 and the targets were Kiel and Munster. The new tactics were utilized and proved to be quite successful. The VIII FC mission narrative commented on these tactics: "There was never less than one group of fighters on each combat wing of bombers from the time they entered the Dutch Coast, flew over and bombed their target, Munster, and retired to the Belgian Coast. The bomber losses were quite light when viewed from the fact that the bomber force was extremely large and the fighters were operating at the extreme of their range."

Lt. Gen. James H. Doolittle assumed command of the Eighth Air Force on January 6, 1944. He led the command up to the end of the war in Europe. USAAF

During the course of the day's mission, pilots of VIII FC destroyed eight enemy fighters and claimed another as a probable. Six of the day's victories went to the 78th Fighter Group. In addition to the aerial victories, the 78th pilots destroyed a locomotive and several other ground targets while strafing.

On Jan. 5, 1944, the Eighth Air Force dispatched four task forces of bombers attacking targets in France and Germany. With such a wide diversion the Luftwaffe was not able to give adequate target coverage to all locations and had to concentrate on one point. The air battle of the day was centered over the target area of

Kiel, Germany, where the P–38s of the 55th Fighter Group and the P–51s of the 354th Fighter Group encountered large numbers of both single- and twin-engined German fighters. On approaching the target area the 55th Group sighted six Me 210s headed for the rear of the bomber formation. As they proceeded to intercept, down came thirty-plus Messerschmitt 109s out of the sun. The P–38s rose to meet the attack and went into a double Lufbery Circle, one at 28,000 feet and one at 28,500 feet. The vicious dogfight lasted some twenty minutes. The P–38s managed to down six of the E/A, with Maj. Charles Jones and his flight taking honors for the day with three. The 55th lost four P–38s in the fight.

The big victory of the day was turned in by the Mustangs of the 354th Fighter Group led by Maj. Jim Howard. Once more the Luftwaffe put its twin-engined fighters up in mass and once more they were decimated. The P–51 pilots downed fifteen of them and Lt. Glen Eagleston scored the only kill over a single-engined fighter when he downed an FW 190. The outstanding feature of the encounter was that the 354th didn't lose a single Mustang.

The chemical works at Ludwigshafen, Germany, was the target on January 7. The Luftwaffe was up and several battles were fought during the target escort and the withdrawal stage of the mission. Seven enemy fighters were destroyed in these encounters, but at the cost of six US fighters.

Maj. James H. Howard, ex-AVG Flying Tiger and 354th FG pilot, and his Mustang, Ding Hao! *Howard won the Medal of Honor for his performance in defending the 401st BG on January 5, 1944. USAAF, via W. Louie*

46

The outstanding performance of the day was turned in by the 353rd Fighter Group. While providing withdrawal support to the B-24s from the 2nd Task Force, the formation was pulled far to the south by two bomber groups flying off course. This pulled the aircraft into the vicinity of Orleans, southwest of Paris. The P-47s knew that it was imperative that they head for home, but as they departed the bombers were attacked head-on by a dozen Me 109s and FW 190s. Disregarding their fuel shortage the P-47s headed back to do battle. They were successful in breaking up the attack. Three FW 190s were downed by Lt. Jesse Gonnam.

The mission on January 11 was in support of bombers striking deep into Germany and would become a historic mission for VIII FC. To escort the strike force, all thirteen groups available to the Command were dispatched. The day's scoring honors went to the 354th FG which downed sixteen enemy fighters. Second in scoring was the 56th FG with ten and the remaining three went to the 356th FG. The high point of the mission was the exceptional bravery and skill demonstrated by Maj. James Howard of the 354th FG.

The tactical commander's report for the mission of Jan. 11, 1944, states that "the twin targets of Halberstadt and Oschersleben were the objectives of the bombers that the 354th Fighter Group was assigned to give general target area support. Forty-nine P-51s took off from base and steered a direct course to the rendezvous point. The group climbed through an overcast at 4,000 feet and continued up to 25,000 feet. At this altitude, from the point of landfall to about 100 miles in the enemy coast, cloud mists were present and made visibility alternately bad. We rendezvoused with the rear two boxes of bombers at 1115, fifteen minutes ahead of schedule, but a message was received from Tackline informing us that the bombers were on time; so it was understood that there were boxes up ahead. From this first point of rendezvous to the target, the overcast was broken. Over the target and on the withdrawal route it was clear with heavy snow blanketing the ground which made visibility excellent.

"Enemy aircraft opposition was encountered on these lead bombers from the point of rendezvous until 1230, when we had to leave. Attacks were directed at bombers usually from below or from the sides and some were head-on. E/A did not have any definite formations, but seemed to float around individually. Many twin-engine were seen."

This report is signed by Maj. James H. Howard. It in no way ascribes to his performance on that mission, which is cited in the following manner by Col. Harold W. Bowman, Commanding Officer of the 401st Bombardment Group: "The magnificent fight which you put up in the ensuing struggle was one which had elicited the praises and admiration of every one of the Fortress fliers who witnessed your actions. Members of this Group, returning from the operation, were lavish in their descriptions of the way you shot down enemy planes and, in particular, spoke in glowing terms of the attempts you made to protect the Combat Wing, against enemy attacks."

It seems that when the first enemy opposition was encountered, Major Howard was separated from his flight. Climbing up, all alone, Howard spotted a box of bombers up ahead that was under concentrated enemy attack by thirty-plus fighters. Without hesitation the former Flying Tiger piled into the enemy and continued to do battle for over an hour. How many attacks he broke up and how many of the bombers he saved will never be known, but the bomber boys were willing to swear that he downed at least six of the enemy and damaged many more.

The reticent Howard saw it his own way: "When I regained bomber altitude after the first melee in which I became separated from my flight, I discovered I was alone and in the vicinity of the forward boxes of bombers. There was one box of B-17s in particular that seemed to be under attack by six single- and twin-engined enemy fighters. There were about twenty bombers in a very compact formation and the fighters were working individually.

"The first plane I got was a two-engined German night fighter. I went down after him, gave him several squirts and watched him crash. He stood out very clearly, silhouetted against the snow that covered the ground.

"After that a Focke Wulf came cruising along beneath me. He pulled up into the sun when he saw me. I gave him a squirt and almost ran into his canopy when he threw it off to get out. He bailed out.

"Then I circled trying to join up with the other P-51s. I saw an Me 109 just underneath and a few hundred yards ahead of me. He saw me at the same time and chopped his throttle, hoping my speed would carry me ahead of him. It's an old trick. He started scissoring underneath me but I chopped throttle and started scissoring at the same time, and then we went into a circle dogfight and it was a matter of who could maneuver best and cut the shortest circle.

"I dumped 20 degree flaps and began cutting inside him, so he quit and went into a dive with me after him. I got on his tail and got in some long distance squirts from 300 or 400 yards. I got some strikes on him but I didn't see him hit the ground.

"I pulled up again and saw an Me 109 and a P-51 running together. The P-51 saw me coming in from behind and he peeled off while the Me 109 started a slow circle. I don't remember whether I shot at him or not. Things happen so fast it's hard to remember things in sequence when you get back.

"Back up with the bombers again, I saw an Me 110. I shot at him and got strikes all over him. He flicked over on his back and I could see gas and smoke coming out—white and black smoke. It would seem that he had some sort of smoke equipment to make it appear that he was damaged worse than he was.

"I saw an Me 109 tooling up for an attack on the bombers. They often slip in sideways, the way this one was doing. We were pretty close to the bombers and I was close to him. I gave him a squirt and he headed down with black smoke pouring out.

"I saw an Me 109 over on the starboard side getting in position to attack the bombers. I dived on him from where I was and got strikes all over him with my one gun. [Howard had all four fifty calibers firing on his first attacks, but on his third attack only two were working. In his last two attacks only one of his guns was working.] He turned over on his back and skidded out. He thought that he had lost me with the skid and he pulled out into a 45 degree dive. I followed him down and kept on shooting.

"I'd been with the bombers for more than a hour altogether by then and just before I left I saw a Dornier 217 coming alongside the bombers, probably to fire rockets. I dived on him and he left, but I never did fire a shot at him.

"I seen my duty and I done it. I never saw thirty fighters all at once the way the bomber people tell it. I'd see one, give him a squirt and go up again. There were an awful lot of them around; it was just a matter of shooting at them."

Officially Howard was awarded three confirmed kills for the day, but much more importantly his superiors viewed the combat from the standpoint of the bomber men he saved. Howard was awarded the Medal of Honor for his feat that day.

The weather began clearing over the coastal areas of the Continent which prompted the Eighth Air Force to switch its attention to Crossbow targets (German long-range rocket sites) in the Pas de Calais area. On January 14 Fighter Command's responsibility was to provide an aerial umbrella for the bombers attacking these targets. The 20th FG, which was covering the westernmost area of all the fighter groups, was the first to encounter enemy action. Their first encounter came in the vicinity of Fecamp, France, when the pilots of the 79th FS bounced eight FW 190s. In the ensuing fight which took place at 14,000 feet and continued almost down to the deck, two 190s were destroyed. One of the planes was claimed by Lt. Merle Nichols and the second was shared by Col. Barton Russell and F/O Markrel Byrd. Several minutes later the Group encountered fifteen FW 190s and Me 109s and a second air battle ensued, during which Maj. Richard Ott was credited with a downed 190.

Almost simultaneously the 4th Fighter Group, which was engaged in a fighter sweep, encountered a gaggle of fifteen FW 190s near Margny, France. The 336th Squadron bounced the Germans immediately and in a ferocious dogfight that ranged from 18,000 feet down to the deck, four Focke Wulfs were downed. High scorer in this battle was Capt. Don Gentile who destroyed two but in doing so nearly became a victim

Capt. Don Gentile's P-47 Donnie Boy *in which he scored some of his Thunderbolt victories.* T. Ivie

Lt. Col. Glen T. Eagleston was one of the top scorers of the 354th FG on escort missions. The resemblance of the Mustang silhouette to that of the Me 109 caused him to be shot up so badly by a P-47 on one mission that he had to bail out over England. USAAF

himself. He described his encounter as follows: "I saw and reported a gaggle of fifteen 190s flying east—5,000 feet below. We were flying south. I took my section down—consisting of F/O Richards, Lt. Norley, Lt. Garrison. As soon as we went down the 190s split fan shaped into two groups. I picked two stragglers flying north and attacked at eight o'clock to the E/A, which were in a 50 degree dive. I closed to about 300 yards and fired a long burst at the #2 190 and observed strikes around the left side of the cockpit after which I saw smoke coming out. He rolled over (at 8,000 feet) very slowly and went into a spiral dive vertically. He crashed into open country, near woods.

"I slid over immediately in back of the #1 190 and closed to about 250 yards and started firing, closing to about 150 yards. We were in a very shallow dive from 4,000 feet. I observed strikes around the cockpit and engine. As I was trying to follow him down in his slipstream to get another shot, he hit the woods and I pulled out just missing the woods myself.

"Just as I pulled up I was jumped by two 190s and the fun really started. The #1 190 was so close to me that I heard his guns, and then he hit me. I broke and the first 190 went over me. I stayed in a port turn because the #2 man was still coming in, but he was not firing. In the meantime the #1 had pulled up sharply to position himself for another attack, but I quickly swung to starboard and fired a short burst at the #2, who I never saw again. All this action took place at treetop level. I swung port to get away from the #1 man who was firing, but giving too much deflection; as his tracer was going in front of me, I used the last of my ammo on the last burst at the #2 190. I was trying to out turn him, but he stayed inside me. I suddenly flicked and just about wiped myself out on the trees. [All this time Captain Gentile was screaming into the mike, "Help, help, I'm being clobbered," but was so occupied by self-survival he never heard his mates asking for his position—an incident that caused him considerable kidding after the mission.] Recovering I reversed my turn to starboard, and there he was, still inside me and still shooting like hell. I kept on turning and skidding—all I could do. He slid under and overshot, and I reversed again port. We met head-on, and he was still firing. For the next ten minutes we kept reversing turns from head-on attacks, trying to get on each other's tails. The last time he didn't shoot; so he must have been out of ammunition. He then left and I felt like getting out and doing the rumba. All my temperatures were in the red, so I climbed up slowly and came home."

With these two victories, Gentile reached acedom with a total of five victories. While Gentile was engaged in his adventure, Lieutenant Garrison downed one FW 190 and shared another with Lieutenant Norley.

After the group re-formed from this encounter it headed toward Soissons, France. After arriving there they spotted another gaggle of 190s, and the 334th Squadron dove to attack. In the ensuing battle four more 190s were downed, one each claimed by Lieutenants Beeson, Montgomery and Biel, and the fourth

shared by Lieutenants Whelan and Rafalovitch. The last victory of the day was scored by Lieutenant Richards of the 336th, who downed a 190 in the vicinity of Compiegne, which brought the day's total to ten. All of the 4th's planes returned safely.

The 354th FG scored one victory during the January 14 mission, but the pioneer Mustang group was losing opportunities for more due to continuing and serious gun failures. Because of the angled position of the guns in the wings, they could not fire while turning or in a violent maneuver. The pressure caused by force of the maneuvers caused the belts of ammunition to buckle and jam the guns. It was a serious problem that took Fighter Command technicians several weeks to solve. In addition, the P-51B was also suffering other teething troubles such as coolant leaks and rough engines due to faulty spark plugs.

In spite of these malfunctions, VIII FC could see that the Mustang was the plane that would give the command complete air superiority, and stuck with it. While these gremlins were being worked out of the machine, the VIII FC was also lobbying hard to get the 354th FG transferred to the Eighth Air Force. The Ninth Air Force would not give up its star Group, but was required during the month of January 1944 to trade its second Mustang group, the 357th FG, to the Eighth Air Force in exchange for the 358th FG which was equipped with Thunderbolts. The Ninth Air Force felt it was a fair deal since it received an experienced group, but the Eighth Air Force felt as if it had won the bargain when it gained possession of the prized P-51.

The missions of January 24 were to escort bombers that were striking at targets in western Germany. Because of the distances involved and the bomber track, a new system of escort was devised for this mission. A continuous escort was set up as follows: Each of the twelve P-47 groups was assigned to a definite area along the bomber track, and it was to provide support and protect that section until the entire string of bombers had passed through. As soon as the bombers had passed, they would return to base and another group would take over the responsibility for the next leg. This continued right up to the target. Here the longer range P-38s and P-51s took up the escort through the target run. As the bombers made the return trip after bombing, the P-47s again assumed the responsibility. The plan worked well until bad weather intervened. A recall was sent out to the bombers, but since it wasn't clear that all the bombers received the message, the fighters continued on their mission. The day's bombing mission, of course, didn't achieve the planned objectives, but the weather did not affect the fighter mission. Luftwaffe fighters were seen throughout the mission and several of the groups engaged in battle against them. Nineteen German fighters were downed and the 356th FG was on top with ten victories.

Another deviation from the norm was inaugurated on this particular mission: one fighter squadron within its force was to be known as the "bouncing squadron." While this designated squadron would carry out its customary role of fighter escort, it was subject to being ordered out anytime the group commander so desired to investigate and attack any enemy aircraft at any visual distance away from the bomber route.

Regarding penetration support with the 356th FG, Maj. Gerald Johnson stated: "It was the hottest dogfight I ever got into. And on top of that I never heard of another flight of four planes bouncing a whole squadron of Jerries, shooting down six of them without losing a single man, then reforming after the fight for the trip home.

"I was leading my flight. Our squadron escorted the lead box of B–17s to their target and back out. Coming out, as we neared Brussels I saw a formation of 15 FW 190s flying parallel with the bombers about 3,000 feet below and a mile south. I reported them on my radio and started after them with my flight of four.

"Since they were flying in the middle of a thin layer of clouds, I lost sight of them several times before we finally came out in an open spot northeast of Ypres at about 15,000 feet. There I saw them again, 5,000 feet below being attacked by P–38s. I immediately headed for the attack on the nearest one and saw my bullets striking along the fuselage and right wing before I overran him and pulled up to let my wingman finish him.

"I took a good healthy look around and saw the P–38s leaving for home. I also saw that each of the other three in my flight had at least one Jerry in his sights and figured the odds were still in our favor. I got onto the tail of another Jerry and gave him a three second burst. There were strikes on the fuselage forward of the cockpit and a huge puff of black smoke as the FW rolled over. As I pulled up the pilot bailed out. I called my flight to re-assemble but my transmitter was out so after circling above them and racking my wings I picked up two of them, went down to tree-top level and came home.

"I wish to commend highly the other members of my flight, Lts. Maxwell, Vitali (who got three FW 190s) and Niemi for their aggressiveness and force with which they drove home their attacks."

Lt. Col. Glenn Duncan was leading the 353rd Group on withdrawal as the bombers headed for home. Duncan "was just getting the red ass at having flown another milk run mission" when he sighted two twin-engined "bogies" down low. As he led his flight down he sighted four more Me 110s flying in formation: "They were at about 5,000 feet . . . I had pulled my hand full of throttle, turbo and prop levers all back in order to slow down but I was closing too fast. I made a sharp left turn then swung around so as to come in behind the last Me 110. Still I was closing too fast so I threw in a few good hearted skids and then at the last moment as I would have over shot, and messed up a good shot, I barrel rolled and came in position on the Hun's tail. I closed up to about 250 yards, centered the needle and ball, put the pip on the top of the cockpit then squeezed in a nice long burst. The Me 110 immediately began

P–47D Oily Boid, *the mount of Lt. Robert Booth who became one of the aces of the 359th FG.* USAAF

Thunderbolt from the 350th FS, 353rd FG outbound laden with drop tank. USAAF

losing excess parts and flamed up (they burn nicely). I must have killed the rear gunner in the first few rounds because he was not shooting. This Me 110 veered off to the left and down; then crashed."

There were still three Me 110s flying in formation as Duncan closed in on the number three aircraft: "This rear gunner was really excited and shooting like mad. They must be very poor gunners because I held my fire until I pulled up to about 250 or 300 yards then gave him a long squeeze. (I found out later that I got one slug in the right side of my engine.) He immediately burst into flames and pieces flew everywhere. Those eight fifties sure pack a wallop. This Me 110 went into a spiral and crashed into a woods causing the whole area to be enveloped in a blazing inferno. Neither the pilot nor the gunner got out . . ."

Duncan chased a third Me 110 at low altitude but ran out of ammunition before he could finish it off. Capt. Dewey Newhart pulled in and sent the 110 crashing into the woods.

What had appeared to be a routine mission resulted in costing the Germans five Me 110s plus an Me 109, which one of the flights caught over an airfield on the way home.

The new escort system pleased VIII FC's planners and so they put the plan back into action for the mission on January 29. This time the thirteen groups provided escort for the three air divisions heading for Frankfurt. The Luftwaffe was also showing its teeth of late and it, too, put up fighters in strength to meet the American aerial armada. With both sides massing their strength, a

Capt. Lindon Graham of the 20th FG was one of the more successful P-38 pilots. He scored 5½ victories before being killed strafing on March 18, 1944. He is pictured with his P-38 Susie. USAAF

showdown was inevitable and VIII FC came out the undisputed victor with forty-two victories, five probables and ten damaged against fourteen losses. The 20th FG flying P-38s was high with ten kills, followed closely by the 4th which added nine more. The 4th, providing penetration support to the 1st Task Force, gained its victories after it had broken off escort and was heading back. As they approached Maastricht, Belgium, they spotted a formation of Me 109s, and the 334th FS bounced them. Two of them, Lt. Spiros Pissanos and Capt. Hank Mills, scored double victories.

The 20th, which was providing target support for the 3rd Task Force, went into action immediately on rendezvous with the bombers that were already under attack. Capt. Lindol Graham of the 97th FS led the assault and destroyed an FW 190 that was attacking a B-17. Moments later he gunned down two more and with a total of three victories became the 20th's top scorer of the day. While this was going on, Lt. Royal Frey of the 55th FS saw two Me 110s below him and bored in and destroyed one of them. In doing so he nearly fell victim to his target's rear gunner, who scored numerous hits on Frey's P-38.

The 352nd Fighter Group had been part of the withdrawal support for the day and were successful in downing a half-dozen enemy fighters. Amongst the victors were Capt. George Preddy, who scored his third victory, and Lt. Bill Whisner, Preddy's wingman, who got his first. Preddy later became one of the top scorers in the Eighth Air Force, but on this day he nearly brought his combat career to an abrupt end due to his complete disdain for German flak.

Preddy and Whisner had become separated from their squadron in the course of their combats and were heading for home at about 1,500 feet. Whisner noted the industrial area ahead and warned Preddy over the radio, but Preddy later stated: "It was my own fault, really. I knew that this was an industrial area from the many smokestacks in the area. While I didn't have a lot of gas I could have done a lot more twisting. But I didn't do nearly enough squirming. My ship was hit by flak and started smoking badly from the tail. Also, the smoke started to fill the cockpit. I called Whisner and asked him if he was o.k. He said, 'Yes.' Well I ain't, I'm smoking I told him. I told him to keep an eye on me, as I didn't think I could make it across the Channel. Just before I left the ship I let out with some 'Maydays.'"

Preddy went over the side and descended into the waters of the English Channel. "I hit the water and went six feet under . . . but I came up again. I had undone the

Thunderbolt ace Lt. Virgil K. Meroney of the 352nd FG. Meroney met with early success in the P-47 and became an ace in January 1944. USAAF

Flight leader Capt. George Preddy, left, and wingman Lt. Bill Whisner, right, both became high-scoring aces in the 352nd FG. B. Whisner

leg straps of my chute before I landed so I was able to move around pretty freely, though a gust of wind caught the chute when I came to the surface and carried me a little way.

"I inflated my Mae West and as I came to the surface I started to inflate my dinghy, which I always wear under the seat of my pants. After the right number of cuss words, I found the right valve, pulled the pin out and then pulled another valve, which does the inflating. I crawled in, threw out my anchor and started to bail with the canvas bucket."

Three flares failed to get any recognition from passing aircraft and now Preddy was down to his last: "I got my last flare ready, kept blowing the hell out of my whistle and waving my red flag. Another ship! I pulled the pin out of my last flare—but no good. This one wouldn't work either. But the airplane saw me. The pilot flew right above me, no more than 200 feet and flipped his left wing. I felt even better when I recognized the markings of the Thunderbolt. It was from my own group. I later found that Lt. Frederick Yochim was flying that day as a spotter.

"No more than three minutes after Lt. Yochim showed up an air-sea rescue Supermarine Walrus came out of the clouds. But it kept right on course and passed me by! Lt. Yochim saw what was happening and caught the Walrus and brought it back. They managed to drop a few smoke flares and landed near me. After four attempts with the rope they finally got me out of the water. I had been in the water 40 minutes and was getting tired and the sea was getting rough.

"So rough, the Walrus couldn't take off. The crew radioed for a launch which showed up after a bit and I was transferred."

Many of the fighter pilots and bomber crewmen as well came to owe their lives to the magnificent work of the RAF air-sea rescue teams. With their antiquated Walrus amphibians and motor launches, they picked up hundreds of cold and weary fliers whose aircraft were unable to make it across the English Channel to their bases in England. Regretfully, despite their valiant efforts there were many men whose final resting place was in the depths of the frigid waters of the Channel and the North Sea.

The next day the Eighth Air Force returned to Germany, this time hitting targets in Brunswick and Hanover, and again the enemy was up in strength. Over 200 enemy fighters were waiting to meet the American strike force made up of 742 bombers and 635 fighters. Air battles broke out throughout the mission and the results surpassed the totals of January 29. The fighters claimed forty-five victories, fifteen probables and thirty-one damaged against four losses. High scorers were the pilots of the "Wolfpack" (56th FG) which on this mission scored sixteen victories.

The 56th had put up an A Group under Lt. Col. Schilling and a B Group under Lt. Col. Gabreski to take part in the withdrawal support. The A Group encountered one flight of ten Me 109s, broke them up and

downed one of them. A lone Me 210 was sighted and Lt. Carcione took care of it.

The B Group ran into heavier opposition. In the vicinity of Lingen, Germany, Gabreski sighted ten to fifteen twin-engined German fighters. He ordered the other two squadrons to proceed to the rendezvous with the bombers while he took the 61st Squadron to intercept, but things didn't work out that way. One flight of the 63rd Squadron got eager and beat the 61st to the punch. They cut in front of the 61st's P-47s and caused the Luftwaffe pilots to scatter. Gabreski and his wingman, Lieutenant Klibbe, dived down after the twin-engined fighters and finally were able to bounce one after making several chases. Gabreski pulled in on the tail of an Me 210, opened up and his armor-piercing ammunition proceeded to eat up the craft, sending pieces flying in all directions. The right engine caught fire and the plane went down trailing gray smoke.

About ten minutes later Gabreski and Klibbe encountered two Me 109s climbing toward the bomber formation. Gabreski took the aircraft on the right and Klibbe the one on the left. They both closed in to pointblank range to make sure they were pursuing Messerschmitts and not Mustangs. Gabreski closed to fifty feet firing all the way and the enemy aircraft went down spinning and smoking. Klibbe's victim also went down in flames. These two victories were numbers ten and eleven for Gabreski.

Other 56th Group top aces were mixed up in the fracas; Lt. Robert S. Johnson scored two victories to push his total to fourteen destroyed, and Capt. Walker Mahurin downed a Ju 88 to run up his score to 14½. The B Group accounted for thirteen E/A without a loss. This also marked the 200th victory for the 56th Group, another milestone in their outstanding record.

The 352nd FG also fared quite well during the withdrawal support of bombers. They encountered

One-time wingman to Maj. Francis Gabreski, Lt. Frank Klibbe was one of the eager young aces of the 56th FG. F. Klibbe

numerous E/A between Ruhlortwist and the Channel and downed nine, six of which went to the pilots of the 328th FS.

After the two biggest days in its history the VIII FC closed out the month of January 1944 with a real change of pace. While two of its groups, the 56th and the 356th, escorted seventy-four B–24s to St-Pol, France, the 4th, 78th and 355th FGs participated in a dive-bombing mission to Holland. A total of seventy-five P–47s from the three groups were armed with 500 pound bombs and were escorted to the targets by their fellow pilots. Seventy of the P–47s dropped their bombs on the targets. The 4th bombed the airfield at Gilze-Rijen and scored numerous hits on the facilities. While they were busy bombing, the escorting fighters of the 4th were mixing it up with over twenty Me 109s and downed six of them.

The 55th FG added to the day's scoring when they downed another seven German fighters while on a fighter sweep in the Eindhoven/Venlo/Arnhem area of Netherlands. Combats for the Lightnings of the 55th were rather unusual in that the P–38 pilots experienced some of the highest altitude combat encountered by the pilots of VIII Fighter Command. The 38th Squadron was providing top cover for Thunderbolts dive-bombing when they were bounced by fifteen to twenty Me 109s from 5,000 feet above. The P–38s turned into them and started climbing but the enemy aircraft zoomed back up to altitude and refused to let the Lightnings get above them. Capt. Joseph Myers led his flight to 33,000 feet but was unable to get above the enemy. As the P–38s started down to join their squadron, the enemy came down once more. Lt. Gerald Brown called Myers to cover him while he set out after a 109 that was on the tail of a P–38 flown by Capt. Chet Patterson. Brown hit the gun tit at 100 yards and got good strikes all over the right side of the canopy. As he closed in to fifty yards, still firing, the tail section of the Messerschmitt broke off and went down out of control. In the meantime, Patterson met a 109 head-on after Brown got the E/A off his tail. Patterson and the Luftwaffe pilot then did a couple of turns, and the Lightning pilot got good hits on the right wing root. As the 109 attempted to pull out of the spin that he had gone into, his right wing fell off, no doubt due to the damage previously done.

With these final thirteen victories, VIII Fighter Command closed out the month with a total of 172 victories for a loss of sixty-five. The scale of the air war had grown during January and continued to do so in February as the Germans stubbornly defended their centers of production.

Chapter 6

Down to Earth and Big Week

Feb. 8, 1944, was a most memorable date for the assigned units of VIII Fighter Command. On this date the Field Order included a directive which stated: "If bombers are not being attacked groups will detach one or two squadrons to range out searching for enemy aircraft. Upon withdrawal, if endurance permits, groups will search for and destroy enemy aircraft in the air and on the ground." In a determined effort to destroy the Luftwaffe, VIII Fighter Command also directed that pilots who destroyed enemy aircraft on the ground would have these destructs credited to them personally in the same manner that they received credit for enemy aircraft destroyed in the air. Although the pilots were to learn that strafing enemy airfields was a bit more hazardous to one's well-being than was tangling with most Luftwaffe pilots, the opportunity was still there if the fighter units or individuals so desired.

Although the weather was bad and the bombers attacking targets in Frankfurt had to bomb blindly using radar techniques, a limited amount of enemy opposition was encountered. Capt. William Julian was leading the P-47s of 78th B Group on a Type 16 Penetration Support when control reported bandits in the area. Type 16 control was an RAF type ground control whose high tower radar sets had a limited range of some 160 miles. Therefore their ability to give the American fighters vectors to intercept enemy aircraft was useful only shortly after they arrived over the Continent.

The 78th Group went searching for the bandits in the area northwest of Paris but was unable to make a successful contact. Lt. Warren Wesson and his flight sighted a Heinkel He 111 bomber making an approach to the airport at Le Bourget and attacked immediately. They caught the twin-engined craft right after touchdown and proceeded to shoot it to pieces. Flak immediately opened up and Wesson got his flight out of the area. However, a few miles to the north they discovered another aerodrome, where Wesson was successful in destroying an He 177 in a hangar.

The long-range Mustangs and Lightnings continued to do yeoman service on penetration and target area coverage of the bombers. The P-38s of the 20th Fighter Group under the leadership of Lt. Col. Montgomery were about sixteen miles north of Kaiserslautern, Germany, on the way out when one of the Lightning pilots, Lieutenant Frakes, called to report that his turbo was out. Montgomery dropped to the lower level of 12,000 feet to enable Frakes to stay in formation. At this time, a single-engined bandit was sighted and Montgomery led his flight down to bounce. As he pulled in behind the Me 109, Montgomery's windshield frosted up and he was unable to fire.

Lt. James M. Morris, element leader, slid in dead astern of the 109 and gave him a two-second burst closing to 100 yards. Large pieces fell off the craft which cocked up, and as it started down the pilot bailed out.

"Shortly after as we were flying line abreast at 50 feet I saw a train moving north across our path," reported Morris. "I asked Leader if I could shoot it up. He said O.K., so I opened fire at 500 yards observing strikes on the locomotive. Steam and fire broke out . . . Continued on out on deck and in the vicinity of Sedan saw two FW 190s carrying belly tanks which had just taken off from aerodrome below. Leader called me and said, 'Let's get 'em.' I made a sharp turn to left dropping maneuvering flaps to aid in turning. They turned toward us and Col. Montgomery and I made a head-on pass on them. I fired very short bursts at 400 yards as they went by. Immediately dropped flaps on passing and racked it in to left and came down on one 190's tail. Fired one second burst from 150 yards at 30 degrees deflection and slid in dead astern at 100 yards firing another short burst. Saw strikes on E/A as he went out of control. Last saw E/A tumbling end over end toward ground from 400 feet. Immediately saw second E/A approximately 90 degrees from course so maneuvered in behind him. Fired short burst at 50 degrees at 75 yards, as he made sharp pull up into overcast. Followed E/A into rain cloud—fired another short burst from dead astern at about 50 yards in turn past vertical. Saw E/A go out of control and followed it out of overcast to regain bearing. E/A was spinning at 400 feet.

"I tried to find flight but could not see any aircraft and as light flak was intense in this area, immediately took up safe course home. Flew for about 10 minutes in clouds at 2,800 feet to avoid AA which was firing at intervals over inhabited areas. In vicinity of Dena saw Me 109 ahead flying at 45 degrees to me. Not wishing to give him the advantage of trailing me I did a 90 degree turn into him, closing dead astern as he made sharp pull up at which time I fired a two second burst from 200 yards . . . Saw strikes near canopy and airplane went into falling leaf . . . at approximately 2,500 feet. I made a sharp turn to head out toward coast and looking back saw the E/A within 300 feet of small village still in falling leaf. Flak was coming up from airport off to one side, although light and inaccurate. Came out of overcast at 2,800 feet, skirted Lille and dodged moderate flak thrown at me."

Lt. Morris was credited with the destruction of one locomotive and four enemy aircraft destroyed in the air. His destruction of four E/A on one mission was a first for a pilot of VIII Fighter Command and a real

morale booster for the Lightning pilots throughout the Command.

The 353rd Group was providing withdrawal support when 109s were encountered. Maj. Walter Beckham latched onto one of them, got in a couple of bursts and the 109 went down in a screaming vertical dive with Beckham in his Thunderbolt hot on his tail. Beckham's speed built rapidly to compressibility, and it took all his strength to pull out of the dive. The 109 was seen to continue in his dive into the ground.

Shortly afterward Beckham and his squadron engaged a flight of twenty-plus FW 190s and shot down four of them. Beckham destroyed one of the four to notch up his eighteenth victory and become far and away the top scorer in the Eighth Air Force. Taking advantage of the new strafing edict, Beckham let down through a break in the clouds to make a pass on eight or ten airplanes parked on an aerodrome. He got in a number of hits on a twin-engined object but to his chagrin, as he passed directly over the aircraft he discovered that they were dummies. In closing on his combat report he stated, "Recommend that we confine our attacks on planes on the ground to those more definitely identifiable as the real McCoy."

The target for February 10 was Brunswick, Germany, and 466 fighters rose to escort 169 B–17s of the 3rd Bomb Division. The enemy was up in greater strength than had been seen before and engaged the US fighters in combat continually from the Dutch border to the target area and back. The enemy pilots were very

Lt. James M. Morris, flying the P–38 My Dad, *became the first Lightning ace of the Eighth AF on Feb. 11, 1944. His four* victories on February 8 marked the first time such a feat had been performed in the Eighth. *J. M. Morris*

56

aggressive in their attacks against the bombers and fighters. During the course of the mission, ten of the eleven groups dispatched by VIII FC were engaged in air battles and all ten shared in the claims of 56-1-40. The victories were distributed quite evenly, with the 354th and 356th FGs being high with ten apiece and the 78th A Group placing a close second with nine. Four Thunderbolts, four Lightnings and one Mustang were lost.

The massive size and intense ferocity of the Luftwaffe's interception is easily indicated by the confusion that was rampant from the time the P-47s flying penetration support made rendezvous with the bombers. Lt. Willard W. Millikan of the 4th Group was leading his section when they were bounced from ten o'clock by ten to twelve Thunderbolts. Although no enemy aircraft could be sighted, Millikan immediately took his section in a breakup and to the left and met all the aircraft head-on. As he looked down he sighted a P-47 chasing an enemy aircraft and firing while at the same time it was being fired upon by an FW 190 on its tail. Millikan managed to latch onto the pursuing FW 190 and shot it off the tail of the Thunderbolt.

Lt. Robert Buttke was leading an element of the 55th Fighter Group which arrived a few minutes later to provide target cover. Upon arrival at 1125 hours at 30,000 feet, the P-38s sighted P-51s and another P-38 group in the area at the same time. There were several engagements taking place, but the majority of the enemy craft appeared to be twin-engined types with flights of 109s and 190s above and to the sides of the bomber stream.

Capt. Paul Hooper, Buttke's flight leader, led the P-38s down to attack a bevy of twin-engined fighters that had a straggling B-17 under attack. Buttke immediately managed to line up on one of the Me 210s and send it down in flames. The combat was down around 4,000 to 5,000 feet when Buttke was told to break: "I did a sharp turn to the right, winding up in a sloppy spin. I looked behind and saw two Me 210s shooting at me. The range was long and they missed, so I started after them in a climbing spiral turn. The fight wound up in a tight Lufbery, at about 7,000 feet. I could outturn the 210s so I pulled my nose quite a bit ahead of the last one and started firing, relaxing a little pressure on the wheel and letting him fly through my field of fire. I observed hits on the left engine and the fuselage, and the last I saw of him he was out of control and spinning straight down.

"At this time I was alone, my flight being engaged elsewhere. I started after the other 210, but I was hit from one direction by two Me 210s and a Ju 88 and from another direction by four German twin-engined ships. The lead and second ships were Me 110s, and I didn't get a good look at the other two. The leader came onto me from 30 degrees head-on starboard, turned over on his back, shooting all the time. I took violent evasive action and he missed me. I then found myself in another Lufbery with seven German ships, a formation of three trying to get on my tail and I was trying to pick off the

fourth man in a four ship flight ahead of me. This E/A was a 110. Being in a Lufbery again I had to pull my nose way ahead of him. I gave him a burst and saw hits around the cockpit. This is the enemy aircraft that I claim to have damaged. About this time something hit my left engine and I saw a piece of cowling fly off. The engine stopped as I grabbed the mixture control, hit the feathering switch, poured the coal to the good engine and spun to the left. I never saw who hit my left engine, he must have come from underneath. I hit the deck heading for home by myself."

Buttke had shown his heels to the German twin-engined fighters, but was most fortunate in surviving the battle and getting home to fight another day.

The air war over Germany had grown in size and intensity during January and early February; however, beginning with the mission of February 10 the bombing effort decreased suddenly. This bombing lull lasted a little over a week and the reason behind it was to entice the Luftwaffe fighters to come up. VIII Fighter Command's purpose was to get the opportunity to competely explore the Luftwaffe's tactics and better prepare its fighters for what they would encounter during the coming bomber offensive.

During these cold winter missions the P-38s of the 20th and 55th FGs suffered many problems, the most frequent being engine problems. The engines and turbos were especially susceptible to the cold at high altitudes, and the Luftwaffe scored several victories over crippled P-38s. Because of this the Lightnings rarely operated at altitudes over 30,000 feet. The result was that they were at a disadvantage against the Me 109s which patroled at 35,000 feet. This problem eventually led to a tragic defeat for the 20th FG on the mission of Feb. 11, 1944.

The 20th was a portion of 606 fighters who escorted 223 bombers attacking targets in the Frankfurt area. They were to provide target cover and withdrawal support. During the entire escort they were constantly attacked by vicious and concentrated groups of enemy fighters. In the series of running battles the pilots of the 20th were able to down two enemy fighters, but at a cost of eight of their own—including the Group CO, Lt. Col. Robert Montgomery.

The other thirteen fighter groups involved in the mission fared considerably better, as they combined for twenty-eight victories against six losses. High scorer for the day was the 354th FG with fourteen victories.

The next two missions, flown on February 12 and 13, were against targets in France. The 356th FG had a field day on the thirteenth when they encountered twenty enemy fighters in the vicinity of Chartres and in a series of battles against very aggressive enemy pilots downed six German fighters and damaged four others.

The long awaited bomber offensive, which was to be known as Big Week, began on February 20 and continued for five days. On the twentieth, 1,003 bombers and 832 fighters were sent to bomb German aircraft factories in Tutow, Brunswick, Halberstadt, Gotha and other targets east of Berlin. The reason:

seventy percent of Germany's single-engined fighters, ninety percent of its twin-engined fighters and sixty percent of its bombers were produced in factories located in the target cities.

Eighth Air Force's battle plan was twofold. It had expanded VIII FC to fifteen fighter groups to meet and destroy Luftwaffe fighters in the air, while the bombers disposed of the factories and assembly lines that provided replacement aircraft. The day's mission was beginning a new phase of Operation Pointblank—the destruction of Germany's aircraft production program. These plants were some of Germany's most closely guarded facilities and were located in the heart of the country.

The B-17s, under a massive umbrella of P-47s, droned into the skies over the Continent untouched until the 56th A Group was about to break escort in the vicinity of Hanover. At that time, Lt. Justin Foster of the 61st Squadron called Lt. Col. Gabreski, leading, to report a formation of nineteen Me 110s flying at 12,000 feet at the seven o'clock position. He suggested that the squadron make a 180 degree turn to the left and the P-47s would be in a perfect position for a bounce. This was accomplished and down the Thunderbolts dove in three flights directly astern of each other. With their P-47s lined up beautifully on the two flights of Me 110s, they opened fire from 800 yards and closed rapidly. Gabreski shot the wing and tail off the first victim. He immediately lined up on the second flight of E/A and proceeded to close on another Me 110, which he blew up. Lt. Don Smith also flamed two of the 110s. Lt. Robert S. Johnson said, "I got excited and started firing at the lead plane and then the next, getting only 2 or 3 strikes on the second." But then he settled down and proceeded to blow up two Me 110s for victories fifteen and sixteen. All total the pilots of the 61st were credited with the destruction of seven, probable destruction of

two and damage to the balance of the German twin-engined fighters from III/ZG 26 Horst Wessel. No P-47s were lost in what may be termed a perfect fighter attack.

The Eighth Air Force's first Mustang Group, the 357th, which had flown its first mission on February 11, was present under the leadership of Lt. Col. Don Blakeslee, CO of the 4th Fighter Group. The twenty-eight P-51s made rendezvous with the bombers south of Brunswick at 1256 hours at 25,000 feet. In the course of fighter sweeps over the bombers' return route, the Mustangs encountered several single-engined fighters. Lt. Donald R. Ross destroyed an Me 109, but in the encounter with five or six E/A present, he, too, was hit, and forced to bail out over Leipzig, Germany. Lt. Calvert L. Williams also managed to down a 109 in the same combat. These were the all-important initial victories for the 357th Fighter Group.

The high scorers for the day were the Mustangs of the 354th Fighter Group with sixteen destroyed. Their Mustangs constantly broke up attacks by Me 109s in the Leipzig area. The intensity of the interception is best described by Capt. Jack T. Bradley who was leading

Capt. Jack T. Bradley, a 354th FG Mustang pilot, was in the thick of the fighting during Big Week. J. Bradley

Lt. Donovan Smith of the 56th FG was one of the first pilots to experience compressibility during dives in combat with the P-47. F. Klibbe

the 353rd Fighter Squadron: "The Group Leader assigned our squadron to the middle box of bombers. The first box was under attack and I called this out to the Group Leader. I assigned half of my squadron to the right of the bomber formation and I led the other eight ships giving support to the left side. About 20 minutes after rendezvous, Blue Flight attacked four Me 109s coming in at 8 o'clock, to the bomber formation. At approximately 1310 I saw a B-17 straggler from the 1st bomber box being stalked by a Me 109. I gave my flight instructions to drop belly tanks and attacked the E/A. As I closed into range, a member of Blue Flight cut me off and shot the E/A down . . . I assembled the flight and rejoined the bomber formation at 1320. I saw another Me 109 preparing to attack a second B-17 that was aborting. I opened fire on the E/A before he could fire on the Fortress. The 109 split-essed and dived down. I dived with him and fired a short burst which was not effective. I closed to 350 yards and fired a four second burst and saw strikes on the right wing and fuselage and the E/A went into a vertical dive. I started circling to pick up my wingman and watch the E/A hit the ground . . . I saw an explosion on the ground with white smoke and flame . . . My wingman and I climbed back to the bomber formation and gave support to the last two boxes around the target."

The long range and ability of the Mustangs to loiter in the target area no doubt made escapes possible for many of the bombers who heretofore would never have been able to fight their way back from the distant targets and return home to England.

The enemy forces hung on doggedly, and some Thunderbolts that covered withdrawal support saw extensive combat. The 352nd FG destroyed twelve E/A, with their 328th Squadron being committed intermittently from almost the time of rendezvous with the bombers. Lt. Col. Roy W. Osborn downed one Me 110 and shared another. Just as the second 110 crashed, Osborn and his flight were bounced by eight FW 190s: "This broke the flight up as each one of us was being attacked, and I found myself in a very tight turn with a FW 190 about 50 yards behind me," reported Osborn. "He was getting close and I could hear his guns firing at me but he evidently was not getting enough deflection to hit me. I was at about 300 feet at this time and I increased my turn to such an extent that my airplane stalled and snapped off on its back. I recovered by rolling it clear around the other way and came out in a steep turn in the other direction. I think this surprised the FW 190 pilot as much as it did me, and I never saw him again. I called the flight to pick up a course of 300

This P-38 flown by Capt. Carl E. Jackson of the 20th FG went down in Holland on Feb. 20, 1944. H. Holmes

degrees, get up in the clouds and get the hell out of there."

The effect of the escort for the 1st Task Force is exemplified by the fact that only thirteen B-17s out of a striking force of 700 were lost and only a few of these to enemy aircraft.

The 2nd Task Force of 264 B-24s attacked Gotha, Brunswick and Halberstadt. The 56th B Group helped provide penetration support to the B-24s, and just as they broke escort east of Hanover a flight of Me 109s was sighted. Capt. Leroy Schreiber took his flight down to attack, and knocked three of the 109s down before they knew what hit them. On the way home the Thunderbolts of the 62nd FS sighted a Dornier Do 217 going in to land on an aerodrome at Wunstorf, Germany. Schreiber attacked and hit him, then Lts. Fred Christensen and Stanley Morrill finished him off. Christensen sighted a Ju 88 in the air as the flight continued home, and sent it down in flames.

The 20th Fighter Group got some revenge for the losses earlier in the month when they tangled with numerous Luftwaffe fighters in the target area and downed eight of them. Their only loss was Capt. Carl Jackson, who failed to make it home after having downed two FW 190s in the earlier combats.

The following day, the Eighth Air Force dispatched 615 B-17s and 244 B-24s to attack Me 110 component plants at Brunswick, Achmer aerodrome, Diepholz aerodrome and Luftwaffe airparks in western Germany. Most enemy air opposition was weak to moderate, depending on the particular area. The only sizable force to arise was intercepted by Mustangs of the 354th FG in the vicinity of Steinhuder Lake before they made rendezvous with the bombers. In the ensuing fight, ten Luftwaffe fighters were downed for the loss of two P-51s.

The 56th B Group met some enemy forces east of the Zuiderzee on the bombers' withdrawal route. Most of these single-engined fighters were hoping to queue up on crippled bombers limping home. Eleven of these birds of prey were downed by the Thunderbolts.

As Big Week continued, on February 22 the Eighth Air Force sent out a force of 289 B-17s and 177 B-24s to bomb aircraft plants in central Germany and an airfield in Denmark. Due to cloud cover over the English coast that made assembly almost impossible, the 2nd Bomb Division in its entirety was recalled, sending 103 B-24s back to their bases. Another seventy-four B-24s bombed targets of opportunity near the Dutch-German border. Most of the Continent was covered by clouds, but 161 B-17s went on to attack targets through breaks in the overcast. The B-17s came under intense enemy fighter opposition and lost thirty-eight of their number, while the fighters claimed fifty-nine enemy aircraft destroyed for the loss of eleven.

Due to the weather the bombers were scattered and many missed their rendezvous with the proper fighter units. However, the fighters did their utmost to scout up and down the route and find the Big Friends as

quickly as possible in order to protect them from the determined attacks of the Luftwaffe.

The 361st Group met the initial attacks north of Eindhoven, Netherlands, at 1223 and were able to down two enemy aircraft out of a dozen 109s and 190s that came up to intercept. Col. Avelin Tacon was leading the 359th Fighter Group, and the first sign of enemy opposition appeared at 1303 hours when they saw a B-17 explode. Tacon immediately took his flight down to intercept the attacking FW 190 some 6,000 feet below. Opening fire from 500 yards, he observed good strikes on the E/A, then he overshot. However, his wingman, Lt. George Doersch, was right there to carry on the attack which sent the 190 spinning earthward.

At about the same time, "Wheeler Red Section" of the 370th Fighter Squadron of the 359th Group was bounced by ten Me 109s. Maj. John B. Murphy called in the break and his section scattered to the four winds. He immediately brought his flight back around in a 180 degree turn and met four Me 109s head-on. Murphy took a 20 mm hit in the wing but kept going. At this time he spotted another flight of six Me 109s below. He immediately dived down and fired at the leader of the flight. This apparently missed due to extreme range, but his fire at the leader's wingman from 400 yards didn't. Very dense smoke streamed from the engine of the 109 and it went into a dive straight down.

Lt. Col. Francis Gabreski was bringing 56th A Group into the fray and while twenty minutes from the first box of bombers and in the vicinity of Arnhem, Netherlands, a huge explosion was seen in the area around the first box of bombers. The Thunderbolts proceeded at full throttle, and on overtaking them sighted fifteen single-engined E/A recovering from their passes on the Big Friends. The enemy aircraft went into a gentle turn to the left, which put the P-47s in a position to attack from dead astern. Gabreski rocked his wings in a friendly gesture as he dove to the attack. Whether the enemy took this as a friendly gesture is unknown, but it did enable the P-47s to close to 300 yards before they began to break formation. Gabreski's target broke up and to the left, but the Thunderbolt stayed right with him, firing all the while. Suddenly the FW 190 burst into flames and went down in a vertical dive.

Lt. Donovan Smith was in on the attack and he, too, latched onto an FW 190: "I then held my fire and was just going to shoot again when I felt my plane start to kick from side to side. I guess it was the beginning of compressibility so I trimmed the ship tail heavy and started to reef it back up. At this moment the FW pilot bailed out and he went by me like a shot. I finally pulled out at about 9,000 feet. As I got a quick glance back I saw his chute fully open above me."

Smith rejoined his wingman, Lt. Klibbe, and they climbed back up to 20,000 feet: "We started another pass at four other ships at 12 o'clock below us. We closed up and identified them as P-47s with white noses and tail stripes. They had their heads up as I had three other fellows with me and they didn't even act like they were going to break; so I deliberately pulled right up between the leader and his wingman. When he saw our Red noses I guess they all but bailed out for they split up all over the sky."

Mustangs of the 354th Fighter Group were in almost constant combat from the time of rendezvous. Capt. Robert J. Brooks leading the 356th Squadron sighted a formation of sixteen bogies five minutes into escort. He identified them as Me 110s, so the P-51s dropped tanks and engaged. Brooks got a good burst into one of the 110s which dove sharply downward and out of the area. The Mustangs then pulled up to meet the attack of the high-cover 109s: "As we worked toward the rear of the bombers about four 109's came down and we engaged them. I maneuvered for position on one of the E/A who was then at about 2,000 feet. I lined up and got in a 20 degree deflection shot from high, right astern . . . I saw strikes along the right wing and the cockpit area . . . he flicked to the left as I hit him and went straight down."

Brooks then climbed back up to the level of the bomber stream and engaged two Me 110s that were after a straggling Fortress. He had trouble getting lined up due to violent evasive tactics of the enemy pilot, but Brooks dropped twenty degrees of flaps and fired a four-second burst. At this the right engine began to emit great quantities of black smoke and the aircraft rolled over on its back very slowly and spiraled down.

Climbing back to 23,000 feet Brooks spotted a lone Me 109 which he was able to line up on from astern. A long burst from his guns registered good strikes and suddenly there seemed to be an explosion along the wing roots. The 109 went into a tight spin and was seen to crash.

Brooks took his flight back up to join the bombers for the fifth time. This time three 109s were sighted.

The Messerschmitts maneuvered around astern of the Mustangs and as soon as they began to close, Brooks called a break to his P-51s: "The flight split up. I checked my tail, saw it was clear and pulled up in a tight spiral for an attack. I saw two E/A coming down on me, head-on from 20,000 feet. The lead ship was a 109 and I presume the second one was his wingman. The 109 was in my sights and I fired at almost point blank range. The 109 was not firing at me. I saw his yellow spinner and continued to fire, observing strikes on his ship. I thought that we were going to collide, but at the last moment he lifted one wing to break and so doing hit my left wing, shearing off a three foot section of the tip. I maneuvered to avoid a spin and saw the second aircraft, who was a 51 on the 109's tail position, pouring shots into the already smoking E/A. The P-51 was Lt. Welden, my wingman. The entire flight joined up and we started home."

Brooks had damaged two, probably destroyed one, destroyed one and shared a second with Lt. Robert Welden. All total the 354th FG was credited with twelve destroyed, one probable and seven damaged for the afternoon's work. Their lone loss was their beloved Chinese-American Lt. Wah Kong whose Mustang was seen to explode during an attack on an Me 410.

Maj. Jack Oberhansly was leading the 78th A Group on withdrawal and they broke up numerous enemy attacks on the bombers heading for home. In intense fights that went down to the deck, the Thunderbolts were able to down six of the enemy while losing one of their own. The 353rd Group's Thunderbolts were also providing withdrawal support when Lt. Col. Glenn Duncan spotted an aerodrome northeast of Bonn, Germany, with forty aircraft parked on it. He led two flights of the 351st FS down to strafe while the

Crew chief checks out Little Demon, *the mount of Maj. Walter Beckham, before takeoff time.* USAAF

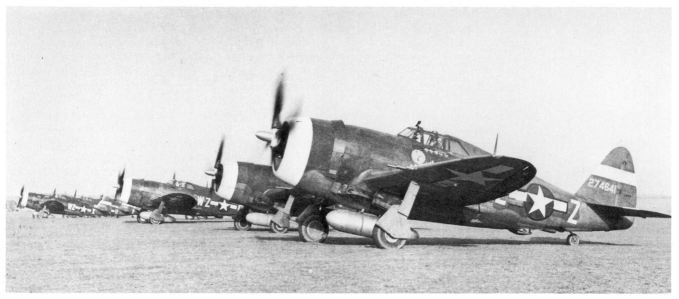

The Jugs of the 84th FS, 78th FG lined up for taxi before an escort mission. All aircraft are carrying 108 gallon paper tanks. USAAF

balance of the force continued their escort. Maj. Walter Beckham's section gave top cover while Duncan's section strafed. When they had made their passes, Beckham positioned his section and went down.

Beckham called that he was lined up on a row of FW 190s and proceeded on his run. Lt. Gordon Compton, leading "Roughman Yellow Flight," related: "As I closed I saw three FW 190s parked close together. I strafed and saw hits on all three, and saw one burst into

flames. I pulled up off the target, turning about 90 degrees to the left and heard Major Beckham say that he had been hit, was on fire and for everyone to get out. I was about 500 feet high at this time and saw tracers coming from every direction, also flak was bursting uncomfortably close, so I hit the deck." What the German fighters had been unable to do, the ground fire had accomplished. Beckham managed to bail out, but was captured shortly thereafter and remained a prisoner of war for the duration. At the time, Beckham was the leading ace of VIII FC with eighteen victories.

Compton took his flight out on the deck, but as he approached Diest-Schaffen aerodrome in Belgium he spotted a Ju 88 that had apparently just taken off. Compton pulled in astern, hung on and continued to blaze away until the twin-engined craft struck the ground in a violent explosion. Tragedy was to strike the 351st again, however, for as the flight broke landfall over Noord Beveland Island, Netherlands, both Lt. Hurlburt and Lt. Wood were hit by flak and turned inland.

Weather prevented the Eighth Air Force from continuing Big Week operations on February 23 and was not much better the following day, when the heavies were sent to bomb targets at Rostock, Gotha and Schweinfurt, Germany. Due to winds aloft and the lead bombardier suffering from anoxia due to a faulty oxygen mask, 2nd Bomb Division B-24s were scattered and some bombed the wrong target. The Luftwaffe also reversed its tactics and attacked the Liberators in force almost as soon as they crossed their landfall into the Continent. For this reason the B-24s suffered heavy losses to determined Luftwaffe attacks before the escort could get to them. However, the enemy was reluctant to mix it up with the escort when they did

Col. Glenn Duncan of the 353rd FG was a dynamic fighter tactician and pioneer in Eighth AF strafing tactics. USAAF

arrive. Only one large enemy force was sighted in the target area, and opposition on the way out was limited.

Col. Glenn Duncan led the 353rd B Group on penetration and saw no enemy fighters until they were called up to the lead boxes nearing the target area. Duncan stated: "I saw about 10–12 FW 190s coming in on the Libs at 10 o'clock so went down. The FWs were just going up on the B–24s bellies but were sorta discouraged when we came in on them.

"I came in behind a dirty looking FW and was just getting lined up when another P–47 pokes his nose in and blew up the Hun. I pulled up over the debris and got on another FW. This time I shot at a little greater range before anyone could steal him. I opened up at 450–500 yards and immediately got plenty of strikes . . . The FW rolled over, sluffed off and went down sorta twisting lazily . . . He fell into a river.

"By this time there was another FW in front of me but he didn't fly straight and level. In the following dogfight I was finally able to obtain a shooting position but the fellow had hollered for help and another FW was coming in on me at 10 o'clock. I saw him coming and turned into him but he had the advantage of the first deflection shot. He must have counted the right number of rings cause soon after he shot I flew into one of the 20 mm's. It hit my right wing mid-way out and tore a mansized hole taking the aileron bar out. Due to the loss of good aileron control I could not hope to do any more turns with the Huns so I went down on the deck and out."

Even in his crippled condition, Duncan was able to strafe and damage a Ju 88 and a large boat on the way out. Fortunately, he managed to get home but with no fuel to spare. In addition to Duncan's FW 190, the Thunderbolts of the 353rd got four more of the FW 190s.

Other target opposition came when the P–38s of the 55th FG were bounced by a force of thirty-plus single-engined fighters from 33,000 feet out of the sun. The P–38 pilots managed to break up the German attack but destroyed only a single Me 109 while losing two of their own.

The B–17s of the 1st Bomb Division attacked the ball bearing plants at Schweinfurt and targets north and west of Berlin. The latter targets were cloud covered, so they bombed Rostock through 10/10 cloud utilizing PFF (radar bombing) methods. The 236 B–17s attacking Schweinfurt met with good results.

Opposition during the escort of the B–17s was sporadic and not pressed as intently as on the prior day's raid. The majority of enemy opposition was encountered on the penetration phase of operations. Maj. James Stewart was leading the 61st Squadron of 56th A Group and reported attacks by single-engined fighters in twos and threes predominating. As P–47s broke off to do combat, most of the German aircraft split-essed and headed for the deck. Stewart and his wingman did latch onto a pair of Me 109s, and Stewart blew up one of them by hitting his still-attached belly tank. As Stewart broke off the combat he immediately saw that his wingman

Two of many who fell to the guns of Eighth fighters during Big Week: Me 109 shown taking hits and an Me 410 shown going down smoking. USAAF

was about to come under attack from a second FW 190. The German pilot spotted Stewart, broke off his attack and took evasive action. As Stewart lined up on the 190 it suddenly nosed over, did a half roll and hit the deck. Stewart, who was low on fuel, gathered up his wingman and headed home.

Col. H. R. Spicer, CO of the 357th FG, led his Mustangs on target area support and upon making rendezvous found things a bit snafued. The B–17s were flying directly above the B–24s, and then it seemed that both bomber streams went off in the wrong direction. However, the B–24s in due time wound up on the right course and turned in on the Initial Point of the bomb run: "At this time the bulk of the squadron had aborted (engine trouble and out of oxygen) leaving myself and wingman (bless his heart) to cover some 40 to 50 bombers. Two 109s were scared off and one 190 hit the deck as we drove up on him. The bomb run was completed with excellent results, a right turn was made and the next five miles continued without incident. At this time a Ju 88 was sighted about 2,000 feet below (23,000) and two miles to the left. As Goldie said he was o.k. I pulled off and gave chase. He went down fast, losing altitude in a steep spiral. At 3,000 feet I turned tight inside of him and he obligingly straightened out, allowing me to do the same, so I closed in straight down the alley and opened fire at about 600 yards in an attempt to discourage the rear gunner. Steady fire was held until he burst into flames. I overran him rapidly (cause seeming to be excessive airspeed as I was indicating 550 mph at the time) so I yanked it out to the side to watch the fun. The whole airplane was coming unbuttoned. My wingman, good old Beal, had slowed down a bit and later stated he saw two men jump and their chutes open. The ship continued straight ahead, diving at an angle of about 40 degrees until contact with Mother Earth was made, which caused the usual splendid spectacle of smoke and flame.

"Looking up suddenly, lo and behold if there wasn't a Me 110 dashing across the horizon. He showed a little sense and tried to turn, so I was forced to resort to deflection shooting opening up and spraying him up and down, round and across (I believe I was a little excited at this point). Fortunately, the left engine blew up and burst into flames. As I overran him the pilot dumped the canopy and started to get out. I lost sight at this point and again pulled out to the side. No chute was seen, but the aircraft descended impolitely into the center of the town of Enfurt, causing rather understandably confusion as it blew up and burned merrily.

Col. Henry R. Spicer, CO of the 357th FG, and his ground crew. Spicer was a colorful and capable leader. Unfortunately, he went down early in March 1944. M. Olmsted

"Again as I looked up (this is getting monotonous) a FW 190 whistled up and just as I began to turn with him my engine quit, embarrassing me no end. Believing I had been hit by the 110 gunner, and being at a loss as to the next step I opened fire (90 degrees deflection) at zero lead and pulled it around clear through him until he passed out of sight below, this intended to frighten him off more than anything else. Here the engine caught again, laboring and pounding badly."

From that point Spicer and his wingman managed to make it home. The 357th P-51s accounted for two more of the enemy that day in addition to the two by Spicer.

February 25 marked the last day of Big Week. A total of 559 B-17s and 196 B-24s were dispatched to attack Messerschmitt aircraft production centers at Regensburg, Augsburg and Furth, Germany, in addition to an attack on the Norma ball bearing plant at Stuttgart. There was only limited enemy aircraft opposition, and very few twin-engined fighters were sighted. Most of the single-engined fighters that were encountered were not aggressive, and the majority of the twenty-six that were downed during the day were caught preying on stragglers who were limping home with flak damage. The 354th Group led the scoring for the day with seven, followed by the Mustangs of the 357th Group who accounted for five.

During Big Week, the Luftwaffe chose to concentrate its attacks in defense of extremely vital targets. A frequent tactic was to mass a large attack during the penetration or withdrawal stage of the mission. To quote an VIII FC historian: "The route across Holland, north of Amsterdam, the Zuiderzee, Zwolle, Lingen, Dummer and Steinhuder lakes to Brunswick and Hannover, became a cowpath. The area between Dummer and Steinhuder Lake was a favorite rendezvous point for the German Fighter Force; for other targets, the area south of Cologne."

Most of the furious battles took place in the vicinities mentioned. In these battles VIII Fighter Command scored 287 victories during the month of February against a loss of eighty-five fighters, for a ratio of better than three to one. In January it had been two to one, and by the marked increase in the ratio in February it was obvious that the offensive was obtaining the desired results.

In late February, the battle for the new Mustangs continued. Now there were two Mustang groups in the Theater, the 354th and the 357th, and VIII FC planned to convert other groups to the Mustang. The 355th FG was next on the schedule. Because of this the 4th FG's new CO, Col. Don Blakeslee, was furious. He argued that the 4th should be first since the Eagle Squadrons had flown Merlin-powered Spitfires and were more familiar with the liquid-cooled engine. He finally convinced General Kepner with the argument, "Give me the Mustangs, General, and I give my word I'll have them on operations within 24 hours."

During the next several days new P-51Bs began arriving at Debden and Blakeslee began giving his pilots "the short course" in flying the Mustang. By February 27 enough Mustangs had arrived and enough pilots "converted" to be operational. True to his word, Blakeslee launched his first Mustang mission on February 28. The Luftwaffe over France that day was conspicuous by its absence, and the first mission nearly ended without incident. However, as the P–51s passed over the northeastern section of Paris, a section peeled off to strafe an airfield near Soissons. As they made a pass over the field, a Ju 88 was caught preparing to take off and was cut to pieces by four of the Mustang pilots.

The next day the 4th FG headed on its first Mustang mission to Germany. After making rendezvous near Minden and traveling to the target and back without seeing an enemy aircraft, some of the pilots decided to strafe some targets. During this attempt some of the P–51s experienced serious mechanical problems, so the pilots headed home.

On March 2 the 4th FG again headed for Germany to escort the bombers on their return from Frankfurt. In the vicinity of St. Goar, six enemy fighters turned and made a head-on attack on the formation. In the attack, Lt. Vasseure ("Georgia") Wynn destroyed one of the Me 109s and in a second attack two minutes later by ten FW 190s, Lt. Glen Herter destroyed a 190 and Lt. John Godfrey damaged another. Other 4th Group pilots dove toward the ground in search of other targets and claimed several vehicles, a barrage balloon and damaged numerous buildings at Deelen airfield. Except for the loss of Lt. George Villinger, the mission was a real success.

The 355th FG also met sporadic action in covering the B–24s of the 2nd Air Division away from the target. Maj. Raymond Meyer sighted three Me 109s in trail behind the last box of bombers and about 500 feet below. The 109s were seemingly oblivious to the presence of the P–47s and all fell victim to the attacking Thunderbolts. Lt. Walter V. Gresham was leading Green Flight of the 358th FS when two other E/A were sighted at about 18,000 feet. Gresham was ordered to attack and took his flight down in a diving bounce out of the sun. As the Thunderbolts approached, the two Focke Wulfs broke, one to the right and one to the left. Gresham sent his number three and number four aircraft after the second 190 while he took the leader who was in a left turn: "I gave him a short burst at 400–500 yards, and closed up to 300 and opened fire. Hits were seen in and around the cockpit and on both wings. I saw

Mustang of the 363rd FS, 357th FG being fueled. The range of the P–51 made it an immediate success for bomber escort. USAAF

an explosion on the right wing root and about this time half of his left wing disintegrated and broke off immediately. The E/A snapped and did a half cartwheel and then went into a violent spin. The contact took place between 15,000 and 12,000 feet and at the time of the attack I was indicating 500 mph and not closing too fast. I closed to about 100 yards."

Also escorting the bombers that day were the Thunderbolts of the Ninth Air Force's 365th Fighter Group. In the vicinity of Bastogne, Belgium, fourteen Focke Wulf 190s were intercepted as they came through the bomber formation. A big dogfight immediately developed and four of the 190s were destroyed and two probably destroyed. The victors were Maj. Rockford V. Gray with two, Capt. Edward F. Boles and Lt. Arlo C. Henry with one apiece. Probables were scored by Gray and Capt. David Harmon.

Taking into consideration the location and time of this combat, it is highly probable that one of the victors in that fight was responsible for the downing of Oberstleutnant Egon Mayer, Kommodore of JG 2. Mayer had been credited with the destruction of 102 Allied aircraft, including twenty-five four-engined bombers. It was Mayer who pioneered the head-on pass tactics that were used so successfully against the B–17s in late 1943.

Chapter 7

Big B

For weeks the airmen of the Eighth Air Force had been speculating and whispering about Berlin. When will we strike Big B? During February, at least six missions to Berlin had been scheduled and then scrubbed, and the nervousness and tension increased. An Eighth Air Force historian noted that the Germans were feeling the pressure, too: "The Germans must have known and felt it coming, too, for on a number of raids forces were assembled to intercept the bombers and then seemingly called off or at least failed to press their attacks, when it was found that the target was not Berlin."

The word to go was given on March 3, but the mission was again recalled due to terrible weather conditions. Leading the escort force was the 4th FG in their new Mustangs and they, too, were hindered by the weather which scattered their formation. They made rendezvous with some formations of bombers at 1120 hours and stayed with them until they reached Terschelling Island, Netherlands, at 1240 hours on the return trip. During their one hour and ten minute escort the Luftwaffe made its presence known. Near Wittenberge, Germany, the 336th FS found itself in an enormous encounter with more than sixty German fighters. The Luftwaffe was everywhere and the 336th pilots chose targets while at the same time evading German

gunfire. Capt. Don Gentile gave an idea of the intensity of the battle in his combat report: "A group of Me 110s, Do 217s and Ju 88s passed underneath us coming head-on. I rolled over starboard and started down but was bounced by 10 FW 190s, which Lt. Millikan, doing an outstanding job, engaged and drove away from me. I dove on down and got on the tail of a twin-engined plane, but my canopy was so badly frosted over that I couldn't see anything. I was scared of hitting him so pulled up and turned my defroster on and when the canopy started to clear there was a 110 right beside me and firing at me. I broke away and was again bounced by 3 FW 190s. I turned into them, met them head-on and they just kept going. I then bounced the Do 217 in a port turn, fired a short burst above and astern, and my gunsight went out. I pulled up, gave another short burst and saw strikes. Just then two 190s flashed past, one on each side so I pulled away.

"I asked Lt. Millikan if he was with me and he said, 'Hell, I'm fighting ten FWs,' so I figured he needed help. I tried to gather the odd Mustang I saw floating around telling him to join up. Then I saw a gaggle beneath me going around in a pretty good formation. I half-rolled and went down, but suddenly found myself in the midst of 12–14 190s, with no Mustangs around. I did a port,

Lt. Willard W. Millikan's P–47 Missouri Mauler *in which he scored his first three victories.* 4th FG Assn.

steep climb turn full bore. On the way up a FW 190 was in front of me. I pulled around and put him under my nose and fired a burst. I then repeated the process, saw some pieces come off and the pilot bail out."

This was the first of two victories he was to score in the melee. In addition to Gentile's kills, Lieutenants Carlson, Garrison and Millikan each downed an Me 110. Garrison also flamed a Focke Wulf 190 in this encounter, and Lt. Philip ("Pappy") Dunn damaged an Me 210. The Mustang had seen them through the fight and the 336th had scored significantly against one loss, Lt. Glenn Herter. Unfortunately, fate was to play its hand on the way home and cost the 336th two of its outstanding pilots. Lt. Vermont Garrison who had scored 7.33 aerial victories was downed by flak near Boulogne, France, and became a POW. The second loss was Lt. Philip Dunn who got lost on the way home. He decided to try and make it to Spain but ran out of fuel and he, too, became a POW. Dunn did, however, manage to shoot up a Heinkel He 111 on his attempted route to Spain.

Although half of their P-38s had been forced to abort the mission, the 55th Fighter Group led by Lt. Col. Jack Jenkins in *Texas Ranger IV* continued to plod through heavy weather to the target area. Unaware that the bombers had turned back, they searched for fifteen minutes on a sweep that took them to the outskirts of Berlin, but the Luftwaffe was not up to challenge. They did sight a small flight of Me 110s on the southwestern edge of Berlin as they headed home, but once the Lightning pilots dropped their tanks the enemy aircraft scooted into the protection of the clouds.

Another attempt to bomb Berlin was made on March 4, but again the weather severely hampered the

Lt. Willard Millikan in the cockpit of his P-51. 4th FG Assn.

mission. One combat wing did make it and bombed the southwestern section of the city, but with unobserved results.

As the bombers passed over Berlin they and their escort, twenty-eight Mustangs of the 4th FG, were bounced by more than twenty enemy fighters. Eight of the German fighters struck at the bombers while the remaining twelve attacked the 4th. Their attack was somewhat timid, though, and one of the 109s was claimed as a probable. Lt. Hugh A. Ward then went into a dive after another 109. Ward was followed into the dive by another 109 which Lt. Nicholas Megura then

Lightning of the 383rd FS, 364th FG above cloud build-up. The 364th entered combat in March 1944. USAAF

went after. As the four planes plummeted downward from 31,000 feet, Ward's Mustang came apart in midair and parts of it hit Megura's P-51. Ward was able to jump, and Megura chased the 109 down to 3,000 feet where its pilot bailed out. On the way home the 4th claimed two more E/A while strafing aerodromes.

The biggest tragedy of the day was the loss suffered by the Ninth Air Force's new Mustang unit, the 363rd Fighter Group. The day had begun when Major Culbertson led thirty-three P-51s off for the mission. Once more the weather was bad and the general consensus of the pilots was that most of the eleven Mustangs that did not return that day undoubtedly fell victim to the weather. Lt. Robert Spencer nearly became the twelfth victim when he spun out while doing an instrument climb-out, and recovered at an altitude of only 200 feet. Whatever the cause, this was the worst loss that a Mustang unit assigned to bomber escort for the Eighth Air Force would ever suffer.

The mission for March 5 shifted to airfields in France. Again bad weather was a factor and the bombers had to strike at their secondary targets. For the fighters, the mission was a little more successful. The target escort was again provided by the Mustang groups, and they found several targets for their guns. Pilots of the 357th found three FW 200 bombers taking off from their airfield near Cholet and destroyed all three. Shortly thereafter they mixed it up with enemy fighters and claimed another four victories. Unfortunately, they lost their Group CO, Colonel Spicer, to flak on the return trip. Also lost in the air battle was F/O Charles ("Chuck") Yeager who later became an ace and world renowned test pilot. Yeager managed to evade after falling to the guns of an FW 190, and made his way to Spain and eventually back to England. The 190 that downed him was attacked and probably destroyed by Capt. William ("Obie") O'Brien.

The 4th FG also enjoyed a good day at the expense of the Luftwaffe. They had escorted the bombers to the Linoges area and encountered German fighters near Bordeaux. In a short but tenacious air battle four German fighters were claimed, two each by Lt. Steve Pissanos and Lt. "Deacon" Hively. A few minutes later the Mustangs caught eight FW 200s in the circuit above Bergerac aerodrome and destroyed two in the air and then strafed several others on the ground. West of Parthenay, France, another FW 200 was shot out of the air. When the mission was over they claimed 7-0-8 victories against one loss, Lt. Steve Pisanos, who managed to survive a crash-landing and later made it back to England.

A mixed force of 730 B-17s and B-24s again headed for Berlin on March 6, 1944. Accompanying them was an escort of 803 fighters from the VIII and IX Fighter Commands. Everyone expected this to be a rough mission and it certainly was. The weather over the target was bad, and the Luftwaffe struck with unexpected numbers and fury. The weather and cloud cover prevented the bombers from bombing any of the primary targets, and results were not very impressive.

With the weather as its ally, the German fighter force tore into the bombers with a vengeance. Their attack was described in an Eighth Air Force summary: "The enemy's method of attack against the 3rd Bomb Division was skillfully executed. From both the offensive standpoint of the enemy fighters and from the escort standpoint of our fighters, the bombers presented a column of combat wing pairs, covering from head to tail a distance of perhaps as much as 60 miles. The enemy controller, apparently having detected a gap in fighter escort in the center of the column, dispatched out of his concentration two formations of fighters to harass the front and the rear of the column and to occupy the attention of the escort fighters at those two positions. Then he slammed his remaining 100 plus fighters against the momentarily unprotected center of the column. Working against time and with unusual aggressiveness, these fighters reaped a harvest of perhaps as many as 20 bombers during a period of less than 30 minutes."

The bomber crews suffered terribly during the day and at least sixty-nine of the big planes went down.

The 1st Air Task Force of B-17s was not intercepted during the escort by the 359th and 358th Fighter Groups, but when the 56th A Group under the leadership of Col. Hubert Zemke passed Dummer Lake, the cry went out. "Suddenly the 61st Fighter Squadron said they were being engaged," reported Zemke. "Their position was 15 to 20 miles to the north and with the last or rear combat wing of the five. As their cry was for help in that they'd encountered 75 to 100 E/A, we immediately turned to the northwest and proceeded toward them."

The balance of the Thunderbolts were not able to find the 61st during the initial fight but they had, indeed, been encountered. Lt. Robert S. Johnson had just taken over the lead of the 61st, as Maj. James Stewart was experiencing radio trouble. Johnson related: "I was on the left side of the bombers and going 180 degrees to them when I noticed a large box of planes coming into us at the same level at 2 o'clock to us and 7 o'clock to the bombers. There were about 40 to 50 to a box and I saw 2 boxes at our level and one box at 27,000 or 28,000 feet. I called in to watch them, that they were FW 190s. There were only eight of us. We pulled up head-on and went through them. I then identified both FW 190s and Me 109s.

"I rolled over on their tails and warned everyone to watch his own tail as the top box was coming down on us. I was gaining on a few of the last ones when they went through the bombers. I was then with my wingman as the others were already engaged. We went between two boxes of bombers and I jumped 4 FW 190s at 18,000 feet. I came in from 5 o'clock, they broke up in pairs, and I hit one of the FW 190s. He bailed out. I pulled up into 2 or 3 FW 190s or 109s coming down on us from 5 o'clock out of the sun. They broke off. I then spotted two FW 190s firing at some 4 or 5 parachutes and made an attack from 2 o'clock and above them. I chased them several seconds . . . I then saw a Fort by itself being attacked by 6 FW 190s and Me 109s. I went into them with my wingman and drove them to the deck. Altogether, I remember breaking into six attacks on myself and my wingman. Then as we climbed back up to 16,000 feet, we covered four other P-47s climbing.

"The enemy employed new tactics, hitting the bombers as a mass in a formation similar to the ones the bombers use. Today the enemy, I'd say at least 100 of them in boxes of 40 to 50, flew through the bombers head-on and then went to the stragglers and to the deck. It damn well worked. If our whole group had been there we could have stopped them. But a squadron on one side of the bombers and possibly 3 to 5 miles from the rest of the group, cannot stop this new attack."

Major Stewart shot down two of the enemy fighters as the 61st broke up the German formation. Zemke and the rest of the 56th P-47s still found plenty of action upon their arrival in the combat area and scored another five kills. Zemke got two.

When the Mustangs of the 4th Fighter Group joined in the escort as the bombers approached their targets in the Berlin area, further formations of Luftwaffe fighters were queuing up for the kill. Lt. Nicholas Megura sighted twenty-plus single-engined fighters 6,000 feet below his altitude that were sweeping the area for more than 20 twin-engined rocket-laden aircraft. The Mustangs went after the enemy, Megura picking out a flight of three Me 110s that immediately split without firing their rockets at the bombers. He was forced to break off his attack when he thought that he was being bounced from above, but this proved to be another Mustang. He then latched onto another trio of Me 110s that had just fired their rockets at the bombers. Megura proceeded to rake the entire trio, which was flying wingtip to wingtip. As the number one E/A broke into the P-51, strikes were observed all over the cockpit and both engines as he passed below. Megura then positioned himself on the tail of the number two 110 and fired until an explosion was noted in the cockpit area. The twin-engined craft went down in a dive, streaming black smoke.

An attack on a third Me 110 wound up on the deck. Although Megura had only one gun working he closed and proceeded to blaze away, getting hits on the port engine and cockpit. The Messerschmitt finally crashed into the ground near an enemy aerodrome. Megura found himself on the tail of an FW 190 still on the deck, but when he hit the gun tit nothing happened. Still hugging the deck he proceeded home.

The P-51 pilots of the 4th Group downed twelve twin-engined fighters in the melee and got another three single-engined types for good measure but lost four of their own.

The 355th Fighter Group fought with a number of FW 190s and Me 109s while giving withdrawal support for the Fortresses of the 1st Air Task Force. Many of them were after the stragglers but became the hunted as the fighter escort made attacks from overhead. Capt. Walter Koraleski attacked Uffz. Sens of JG 2 who was after a B-17 and scored with a good deflection shot.

The Me 109 went down to its destruction but Sens was able to bail out.

As Koraleski broke off, his wingman, Lt. Fortier, called out two Me 109s off to the left just above the treetops. Koraleski was on one immediately and a telling burst sent the E/A cartwheeling into the ground. The second 109 took violent evasive action, but Koraleski finally managed to get some strikes on him. At that time F/O Barger pulled up and got further hits on the E/A as did Fortier. With only one or two guns firing, Koraleski put the final bursts into the elusive enemy craft and it crashed into the ground.

Thunderbolts of the 353rd Fighter Group under the leadership of Lt. Col. Glenn Duncan were escorting the B-17s of the 2nd Air Task Force on their penetration and engaged some ten to twelve FW 190s in the vicinity of Steinhuder Lake. The P-47s were a bit late to head off the attack but did manage to engage just after the first pass. Duncan was able to nail two of the FW 190s, and a third was shared by Capt. Byers and Lt. Terzian.

Lt. Col. George Bickell and his Mustangs of the 354th Fighter Group ran into much heavier opposition in the target area. The P-51s were weaving in formation over the bombers when a mixed force of twin-engined rocket-bearing aircraft and single-engined fighters commenced their attack. Bickell dived down on one of the twin-engined craft, made a pass and blacked out as he zoomed up. As he recovered he sighted a single Me 109 stooging around. Closing on him, Bickell blew the right wing off the craft. The pilot bailed out.

Lt. Dalglish of the 355th Fighter Squadron chased two Me 109s up to 30,000 feet that were in an apparent attempt to outclimb the Mustangs. When this didn't work, they dived straight for the deck. Dalglish went after them, picked out one 109 and kept firing at it from 800 to 100 yards in a twisting dive all the way. At 7,000 feet the enemy aircraft's wings collapsed over the canopy and tore off.

Lt. Lowell Brueland attacked a formation of six Ju 88s flying a head-on pass at the B-17. Brueland imme-

Lt. Nicholas Megura of the 4th FG shot down two Me 110s and damaged another on the Big B show. AF Museum

diately got on the tail of one of the Junkers and blew it up. He then collaborated with Lt. Harris in downing a second Ju 88. As Brueland climbed back up to the bomber stream he sighted a lone Me 109 which he lit up like a Christmas tree before the pilot bailed out.

Maj. Gerald Johnson led the 56th Fighter B Group on their penetration escort of the 3rd Air Task Force made up of B-17s and B-24s. A small force of enemy aircraft was encountered in the vicinity of Dummer Lake, and two Focke Wulf 190s were destroyed by Capt. Walker Mahurin and Lt. Fred Christensen. The Thunderbolts strafed Vechta aerodrome on the way home, destroying one aircraft on the ground.

The Mustangs of the 357th Fighter Group led by Maj. Thomas Hayes escorted the 3rd Air Task Force in the target area and ran into all kinds of opposition and accounted for twenty of the enemy to become the high scorers of the day. The P-51s rendezvoused with the bombers at 26,000 feet over Berlin, where several flights proceeded to escort each box of B-17s over the targets and then provided cover for the B-24s as they arrived. During this time the remaining Mustangs drove a large number of enemy aircraft down below the bomber stream where they were engaged. On the way home the squadrons split up in order to assist bombers that were crippled and that continued to be attacked. The high scorer for the day was Capt. Davis T. Perron: "I was approaching a box of bombers at 24,000 feet from five o'clock when I saw two FW 190s attacking a crippled B-17 at 18,000. They broke from the B-17 and I picked up the lead enemy plane and dived for his tail. I caught him at around 15,000 feet and began to fire three long bursts from 600 yards. I kept closing to 300 yards and continued firing. I saw strikes on his left wing. His

wing tank blew up and he caught fire and went into an inverted spin. I saw no parachute.

"Immediately after the second FW 190 pulled in front of me at 12,000 feet. I fired two very long bursts which hit him on the left wing and fuselage. He burst into flames and pieces of the fuselage blew off. He gave two lurches to the left and then went straight down. I did not see him crash, nor did I see a parachute.

"I was climbing up from the two encounters and saw an Me 210 pulling up under the bombers slightly to my left. I swung over behind and a little below him. I began firing from 300 yards and closed to about 50 feet. His right engine caught fire. I then began to shoot at his left engine, which started smoking and burst into flames. Pieces came off his fuselage. I swung high and to the left of the enemy plane to clear the smoke and debris. When last seen he was spinning in. I did not notice any parachutes."

The Lightnings of the 364th Group and Thunderbolts of the 356th Fighter Group provided cover for the 3rd Tactical Air Force's withdrawal. Capt. John Lowell of the 364th Group found one of the B-24s under intense attack from a bevy of Me 109s and through his repeated passes was able to down two of the 109s. The 356th Group also encountered a number of the enemy and managed to down five while bringing home the Big Friends.

The savagery of the ongoing air battle is clearly indicated by the fact that the bomber crews claimed the destruction of ninety-seven German fighters and the escort claimed eighty-two, for a total of 179! Postwar figures obtained from official German sources confirm the loss of sixty-six German fighters, the majority of which fell to the escorting fighters. The fighter pilots of the Luftwaffe claimed 108 bombers and twenty fighters, while American losses were actually sixty-nine bombers and eleven fighters.

One of the net results of the March 6 mission was that it highlighted the "ace race" that was brewing. At this point the bulk of VIII FC's aces served with the 56th

Col. Hub Zemke, CO of the 56th FG "Wolfpack" flanked by his top-scoring fighter ace contenders, Capt. Robert S. Johnson, left, and Capt. Bud Mahurin, right. USAAF

The 4th FG fighter top gun contenders, Capt. Duane Beeson, right, and Capt. Don Gentile, left. USAAF

FG "Wolfpack." Two of the 56th pilots, Capt. Walker Mahurin and Lt. Robert S. Johnson, were tied at seventeen for the lead and were closely followed by at least five other "Wolfpack" pilots. The second highest scoring ace, Col. Glenn Duncan of the 353rd Fighter Group with fifteen, was also a Thunderbolt pilot. Right behind him with fourteen was Capt. Duane Beeson of the 4th Fighter Group, now flying the Mustang.

The rivalry between the 4th and 56th Fighter Groups for scoring honors had been ongoing, but now the aircraft were becoming part of the rivalry. The 4th, which had long hated the P–47, now had an aircraft in which they really felt comfortable, and Col. Don Blakeslee was exhorting his men to recapture the VIII FC scoring honors.

The press also began picking on the ace race and heavily covered the pilots involved. The VIII Fighter Command kept the ball rolling by deciding to give the same credit for planes destroyed on the ground by strafing as for those destroyed in aerial combat. They felt this would encourage pilots to go down and perform the dangerous strafing missions against German airfields. This decision, which would give a pilot the title of ace when he destroyed five or more planes on the ground, was a controversial one. In retrospect, the results are mixed. The strafing cost the VIII FC some of its most gifted pilots. Final postwar victories credited to these pilots do not include the ground credits, due to the fact that other numbered Air Forces did not give credit for planes destroyed on the ground. Therefore a number of men who became aces by facing the withering ground fire have had this accolade denied them today.

Both sides licked their wounds the following day, but the bombers returned to Berlin in force on March 8. A total of 411 B–17s and 209 B–24s were sent out to bomb the VKF ball bearing plant at Erkner, which they accomplished with good results. A force of 876 fighters took part in the mission and once more encountered stiff opposition. Their claims for the day totaled seventy-nine in the air and seven on the ground. They lost seventeen fighters. The biggest difference in the enemy opposition was the lack of twin-engined fighters, which had suffered losses that all but decimated these units during Big Week and on March 6.

The 56th Fighter Group had a terrific day with the A Group, escorting the 1st Air Task Force (ATF), claiming sixteen E/A destroyed. The B Group escorted the 2nd Air Task Force, chalking up fourteen victories. Maj. James Stewart was leading Red Flight of the 61st Squadron in A Group when three bunches of twenty-plus single-engined aircraft were sighted in the Dummer Lake area. The 109s and 190s were positioning themselves for head-on passes, but when the Thunderbolts attacked they split-essed and headed for the deck. Stewart managed to down an FW 190 before regrouping his P–47s for the flight home. While outbound he sighted an Me 110 nosing around ten parachutes that had exited from one of the bombers. Diving down, he latched onto the tail of the 110 and sent it crashing into the trees.

The 4th Fighter Group was assigned target support for 1st ATF, and they, too, met with heated opposition from primarily single-engined fighters, fifteen of which they downed. Lt. Nicholas Megura of the 334th Squadron ran into some of the first opposition while climbing through 33,000 feet. At this time the Mustangs were attacked by five Me 109s coming down head-on. As they passed through, Megura did a 180 and gave chase. The E/A continued to dive, but Megura finally caught it at 8,000 feet and sent it down in flames.

He then found himself with an FW 190 at his six o'clock position but managed to lose it in a couple of turns. Breaking clear he went after another 190 peppering a crippled Fortress. The 190 burst into flames as the fifty calibers struck home, and its pilot bailed out.

Megura then followed an Me 109 into the landing pattern at a nearby airfield. Joining in the pattern, he lined up on a German fighter on final approach. Just as he set to fire, however, he sighted two 109s coming in from three o'clock that had no doubt identified the intruder. Megura broke into them, hit the deck and sped out at full throttle.

By this time Megura was on the east side of Berlin so he headed southward, spotted a train and shot up the locomotive. Then he headed west and was sighted by another half-dozen enemy fighters but managed to lose

The pilot who became the partner in the scoring game with Capt. Don Gentile—Lt. Johnny Godfrey. AF Museum

71

them on the deck. Still heading for home, Megura climbed to 14,000 feet. There he spotted a lone Ju 88 at 10,000 feet. He gave chase and the two wound up just off the rooftops, with the Mustang blazing away with one gun. This ran out of ammunition so Megura pulled up alongside the Ju 88, which had its starboard engine out. He then climbed and continued homeward, satisfied after a full day's action.

Capt. Don Gentile, one of the up-and-coming aces of the 4th Group, teamed up with Lt. Johnny Godfrey over Berlin to put on a great act and form a team that led to continued successes for both of them. As Gentile reported: "I was flying Red 1 when the combat started; at that time Lt. Godfrey and I were alone and we went down to break up a head-on attack on the lead box of Forts by a large gaggle of Me 109s. There were about fifty 109s in the area flying in two's and four's. I picked out two and we did six or seven turns with them. Lt. Godfrey got one. He had a hard time turning without flaps, but when I used them I closed in to 75 yards and clobbered him. He rolled over and went down streaming white smoke. He was spiraling out of control and almost obscured by smoke. We attacked another 109 head-on. Using combat flaps I got line astern on him,

The famed Polish fighter ace of the 56th FG, Capt. Mike Gladych, is shown here with his crew chief. P. Conger

closed to 100 yards, got good strikes and saw the pilot bail out. I then noticed two 109s flying almost abreast and close together. I told Lt. Godfrey to take the one on the right and I took the one on the left. I opened fire at 250 yards and closed in until I almost rammed him. I got good strikes. The plane went down spinning and smoking badly and the pilot bailed out. Lt. Godfrey's E/A exploded.

"Then Lt. Godfrey was attacked from 4 o'clock. We turned into him and got him between us. I fired first and got strikes but overshot, so I told Lt. Godfrey to take over. He got strikes but ran out of ammunition. I told him to cover me while I finished him off. His belly tank caught fire and he went down to 1,000 feet and bailed out.

"During this combat many 109s were in the area and we were able to pick the best bounces. It was the way that Lt. Godfrey stayed with me in every maneuver that made our success possible. We then picked up a Fort 40 or 50 miles west of Berlin and brought him back to England. They thanked us over the R/T and we came home."

Gentile claimed three Me 109s destroyed and shared one destroyed with Godfrey. Godfrey claimed two 109s of his own in addition to the share.

The 56th B Group led by Lt. Col. Gabreski picked up the enemy fighters in the Dummer Lake area as their A Group had done. They were also successful in breaking up many of the Luftwaffe formations, but the most unusual story of the day was the encounter of Capt. Mike Gladych, the famed Polish ace who flew with Zemke's "Wolfpack." He gave chase to three FW 190s and in order to catch them turned on his water injection, giving him war emergency power. Unfortunately, they spotted him and began to climb. Gladych leveled off in order to gain speed and came under attack from two of the 190s. He went back down on the deck in a turning match, while the third 190 stayed above the fight. One of the 190s changed the turn which enabled Gladych to get on his tail, and a burst from very close range sent him crashing into the trees.

Gladych recalled: "At this time I felt the shock and saw two holes, probably from a 20 mm shell, in my right wing. The remaining two 190s were firing at me flying very close to each other. I made two more circles but finally straightened out and flew west as low as I could go. The E/A kept firing and I saw the hits on the ground very close to me. Then I noticed I had no water left and they began to close in on me. They were so close I could see the pilots in the cockpits. They flew on my sides but didn't fire anymore. When I looked in front of me I saw an airfield and the town close to it. I had no choice and flew right across the field. There were 3 or 4 FW 190s lined up and I saw the mechanics standing on the wings apparently refueling the planes. I fired a long burst and saw strikes on the planes and the men falling down. The AA opened fire but missed me, all shells exploding behind me. The accurate and intense fire must have scared my escort as they broke off."

The leader of the flight that had spared Gladych was Capt. Georg Peter Eder, who became known as "Lucky 13" in view of the fact that more than one Allied pilot was spared by him, and he was identified by his aircraft number. Eder was credited with seventy-eight victories at the end of the war, including at least forty four-engined bombers.

The 364th Group did yeoman duty in bringing the bombers home, downing nine enemy aircraft which were after the stragglers. The 355th Group didn't encounter many E/A in the air, although Major Dix did manage to blast a 190 that had just downed a P-38. Five Ju 88s were destroyed on an aerodrome near Hesepe on the way out.

During the next mission to Berlin on March 9, the cloud cover was so thick that the bombardiers had to bomb by radar. The Luftwaffe did not appear, not wanting to risk its valuable fighters in this type of weather. For the next several days the bad weather continued over Germany, so the Eighth Air Force struck at targets in France.

The missions to Germany resumed on March 15 with Brunswick as the target. On this mission the fighter escort was to try a new tactic. It was felt that the escort had flown too close to the bombers before intercepting enemy fighters on previous missions. So on this mission the fighters spaced themselves at greater distances from their Big Friends. The new tactic apparently worked well, as the escort blasted 38-3-13 enemy fighters from the sky. Twenty-four of the victories went to the "Wolfpack," and Lt. Robert S. Johnson scored three victories to raise his total to twenty-one. He became VIII FC's new top ace.

Lt. Quince L. Brown and his flight from the 78th B Group were on their way home and just west of Munster, Germany, when they sighted a big dogfight above them. Realizing that the German fighters would break for the deck, the Thunderbolts positioned themselves above the only opening in the clouds at 8,000 feet. Brown reported: "As we got right under the dogfight, I saw a Me 109 come spinning down on fire. I also saw two P-47s chasing a Me 109 going straight down. I saw two Me 109s about one o'clock to us and down about 500 feet. As we got about 600–800 yards from them they broke left and the fight was on. The two Me 109s tried everything they could to get away. I easily outturned them from 9,000 to 2,000 feet. Finally I got on the tail of one of the Me 109s. He tried to outrun me in level flight. Then he tried to outclimb me and I used water injection. I was gaining on him in the climb when he found a hole in the 10/10 clouds and started to dive. I easily closed to 275 yards and started firing. I saw hits on wings, engine, cockpit and tail. At the same time I saw a fire start at the wing roots. As I pulled up I saw the E/A spin several turns." The plane went into the overcast in flames.

A total of 740 bombers were dispatched to strike at targets in southern Germany on March 16. Weather again affected the mission and the bombers bombed their secondary targets of Augsburg and Friedrichs-

hafen, Germany. The Luftwaffe was aggressive and began its attacks in the Chalons, France, area. The action was continuous for the fighters of VIII FC, and during the day they deducted another seventy-seven fighters from the Luftwaffe's inventory.

The twin-engined fighters were up in the fray as well as their cousins from the NJGs (the night fighters). The 4th Fighter Group encountered a number of them in the target area and downed thirteen Me 110s. The German craft attempted to flee, but as usual the American fighters camped on their tails and sent them spinning down to their destruction.

Lt. Quince Brown was leading a flight in 78th A Group, giving withdrawal coverage to the bombers of 1st ATF, when he sighted a crippled B-24. He stayed with this bomber for about ten minutes when he sighted some activity down below. Leaving two other flights of P-47s to protect the B-24, he went down to 5,000 feet and sighted three Me 109s in the traffic pattern at an aerodrome one mile west of St. Dizier, France. Throttling back and skidding from side to side to get a good deflection shot, he narrowed the gap to about 350 yards and opened up. The 109 took the full brunt of the blast and crashed to the left of the runway.

Brown then pulled up and immediately sighted a Junkers Ju 88 parked on the far side of the field. He proceeded to set it on fire. As he departed the airfield, he fired into two more parked aircraft.

Brown led his flight out of the area on the deck and then took them up to 7,000 feet. At this point two FW 190s bounced the P-47s from nine o'clock. The Thunderbolts broke into them, and all aircraft wound up in a left-hand Lufbery. Several times one of the 190s attempted to break and climb out, but Brown hit his water injection, caught them and they would break

Capt. Quince L. Brown and his P-47 Okie *were star attractions in the 78th FG. Brown pioneered ground strafing in the Eighth AF on a high-speed flight heading home on the deck.* USAAF

73

down once more. The wingman finally broke right and went into the clouds while the leader made a break and attempted to outrun the Jug. Brown then closed rapidly and sent the 190 crashing into a small creek.

Brown headed for home but once more met with enemy opposition. Two Me 109s took the P-47s into another turning contest. Once more the wingman broke and made it into the clouds while Brown and the leader had it out: "This leader was trying to outrun me just on top of the clouds. The E/A threw out lots of black smoke in the chase. I was drawing 54 inches of Hg. without water injection. At first he pulled away from me, but in about two minutes I could see I was closing on him. He then saw a hole in the clouds and went for it. I cut across to head him away from the hole and he turned away. In the turns he was making, I was catching up with him so he started some violent maneuvers, turning, zooming, skidding and diving, to get away from me as I approached firing range. I took a few deflection shots but didn't see any hits until I took a shot of about 25 degrees. At the time he was making a slow turn to the left. I saw strikes, producing smoke from engine and wing roots . . . He was headed almost straight down into the clouds, smoking very badly from engine and wing roots."

Once more Brown headed for home since his gas was low, and his wingman called in a 109 on his six o'clock position. Fortunately, after the break, Brown's element leader was able to get on the tail of the 109 and drive him off.

Lt. Col. Gabreski led 56th B Group on penetration support and thirty-plus single-engined fighters were encountered. The Thunderbolts were a bit late getting to the bombers but the E/A were quickly broken up and chased out. Most of them broke through the overcast as usual and the P-47s were forced to go down and hunt them out. Gabreski and his wingman, Flight Officer McMinn, proceeded to do so and Gabreski downed two 190s for victories fifteen and sixteen. McMinn also downed one of the 190s and, as Gabreski closed his combat report, "A good time was had by all."

The Mustangs of the 357th Group encountered large numbers of enemy craft in the target area, among them a large formation of Me 110s. As Capt. Montgomery Throop of the 363rd Squadron put it: "I took [the formation] to be P-38s there were so many around. They were heading for the bombers at about 24,000 feet. When they saw us they poured on the coal, belched black smoke and started to break formation. The pickings were so good it took me a few seconds to make up my mind which to chase." Needless to say, he chose one and commenced to shoot it down. The Mustangs of 357th downed six of the 110s and an additional six single-engined fighters in the target area.

The 355th Fighter Group's Mustangs sighted forty-plus fighters (mostly Me 109s) in the vicinity of Augsburg, Germany, and in combats that took place during most of their escort accounted for seventeen E/A for the loss of two of their own. Top scorer of the day was Lt. Thomas Neal who, strangely enough, had to leave the bomber stream due to a lack of oxygen supply. His flight had dropped down to about 12,000 feet and kept the bomber stream in sight, but then the German fighters began to drop down through the thin cloud layer in the vicinity of the Mustangs. Neal managed to latch onto the tail of an Me 109G and send him crashing. As he broke off he sighted three other 109s in a tight Lufbery with a P-51 in pursuit. As he closed, one of the 109s broke toward him and spun out. The enemy aircraft recovered and Neal got in behind him. Once more the 109 spun out, but this time he was too low to recover. He smashed into the ground.

Neal then latched onto a 109 passing under him that had been previously damaged by Lt. Lenfest. The left oleo strut was hanging down about fifteen degrees and he still had his belly tank. As the 109 leveled out, Neal gave him several long bursts which culminated with the E/A seeming to almost stop in midair and then dive straight into the ground and explode.

For good measure, Neal got in a good burst at a locomotive in the area and had the satisfaction of seeing the steam rising high in the sky as he scampered for home.

On March 18, weather improved and the bombers set out to strike aircraft manufacturing and component factories in the south of Germany. Oberpfaffenhoffen and Friedrichshafen targets in addition to aerodromes at Lechfeld and Landsberg were hit with primarily fair to poor results. P-38s of the 20th Fighter Group met sporadic enemy opposition on penetration escort with the 1st Air Task Force and managed to destroy seven enemy aircraft. Maj. F. C. Franklin was leading the group and had dispatched one flight down to destroy two Me 110s taking off from an aerodrome near Ulm. While engaged in covering, Franklin sighted another 110 making ready for takeoff and then getting airborne. As the German craft began to climb, Franklin dived down and sent him crashing.

The 4th Fighter Group met stiff opposition in the target area and downed a dozen of them. Two Me 109s fell victim to a colorful young man who was classified a maverick but was destined to become a high-scoring ace of the "Blakesleewaffe"—F/O Ralph ("Kid") Hofer. He almost did not return from the mission, however. After he had downed his two 109s, he bounced a third but lost him in the clouds. He then set course for the target area and encountered another pair of 109s. He gave chase climbing at full throttle when his prop ran away. Hofer set course for Switzerland and prepared to bail out. After he was already over the neutral country and had begun to climb out, the roar of the prop suddenly returned to normal. Hofer took a glance at his fuel gauge, figured that he could probably make it back to England and proceeded to do so, landing with about six gallons to spare.

Both the 357th Group and the 355th Group Mustangs were slated to give target area support of the 2nd Air Task Force. Due to an error in timing, cloud cover and flak, however, the B-24s' wings were scattered all over the place. Lt. Col. Everett Stewart was leading the

355th and decided that his Mustangs would give general support to any bombers that seemed to need help. Southwest of Munich he sighted a squadron of Me 109s approaching the bombers from the rear. The P-51s were up-sun in perfect position for a bounce. Stewart called for his pilots to pick a target and headed down. Stewart closed fast and went in firing, obtaining strikes from one end of the fuselage to the other. Suddenly the 109 blew, and aircraft parts were all over the place, with some of them causing damage to Stewart's wing. All total the P-51s took six down out of the squadron.

Lt. Richard A. Peterson of the 357th Group chased an Me 109 down to the deck and proceeded to work it over from stem to stern. The 109 seemed to level off with its landing gear about halfway down. Peterson fired again and got more strikes. The E/A then slowed to about 200 mph and dived at the ground, hitting on its belly and bouncing back into the air. It shed its right wing and proceeded to roll itself into a heap. Peterson then observed the pilot extracating himself from the wreckage and running off into a nearby forest.

The 56th B Group didn't run into trouble on withdrawal support, but Lts. Joe Powers and D. E. Stream did some fancy maneuvering to down two FW 190s. The P-47s had broken escort and were in the vicinity of Cambrai, France, when two FW 190s were sighted. The P-47s took off after them and chased them to the deck. There, Powers closed on one of them and shot him down at zero feet.

There were now three Thunderbolts left chasing the lone FW 190. Powers closed on the 190, hit the tit and nothing happened. He was out of ammunition. He informed his wingman of the predicament and told him to stay behind the 190 and that he would turn it for him. Powers pulled up above and abreast of the E/A and then dove on him. The 190 turned into Powers, but in doing so struck the top of a hill tearing off large sections of cowling and pieces of the wing. One wheel came down and the prop flew off. At this time Stream opened fire and the German bailed out. His parachute opened just as he hit the ground.

A sign of things to come took place on March 21 when Maj. James Clark took forty-plus P-51s of the 4th Fighter Group on a long-range strafing mission. The Mustangs swept far south to the Bordeaux area where the 336th Squadron turned port and the 334th and 335th Squadrons turned starboard. Ten minutes later Maj. George Carpenter, commanding officer of the 335th, saw an airfield at Landes de Bussic and both squadrons dove and began strafing runs across the field.

The 334th made its firing pass and was bounced by five FW 190s as they pulled up from strafing. They quickly countered the German attack and gunned down two of the 190s, one by Clark and the second shared by Lts. Archie Chatterly and Nicholas Megura. The remainder of the 334th continued to attack other targets.

The run on the airfield by the 335th was led by Major Carpenter who reported: "I was leading Green-

Lt. Col. Everett Stewart served as an outstanding fighter leader in three different units: the 352nd FG, as CO of the 355th FG and finally as CO of the 4th FG. E. Stewart

One of the Mustang pilots of the 357th FG that ran up an early victory total was Lt. Richard A. Peterson, shown here with his crew chief and his P-51 Hurry Home Honey. Kramer

Maj. George Carpenter was one of the old-timers and top scorers of the 4th FG. Carpenter scored 13.83 in the air and two on the ground before becoming a POW on Apr. 18, 1944. Jackman

A Luftwaffe 190 pilot makes a hasty exit in one of the heated air battles of March 1944. USAAF

belt Squadron on a fighter sweep . . . Ten minutes after arriving in the target area I saw an aerodrome southwest of us and immediately dived to attack. We approached . . . from the north. I picked an FW 190, gave it a 3 or 4 second burst and saw it catch fire as I passed over it. As I approached the field I noticed several dummy twin-engined E/A outside the boundary."

A few minutes later Mustangs were seen attacking another airfield which was located about 100 miles north of Bordeaux, and Carpenter led them through a flak-filled sky to attack. He and his wingman, Lt. Charles Anderson, teamed up to destroy a Ju 52 parked on the east side of the field. As they pulled up and away from the field, Carpenter saw an FW 190 at eleven o'clock and slightly below him: "I opened up to about 50–55 inches of mercury and slowly closed on this E/A even though he seemed to be trying to outrun me. At about 300 yards I gave him a short burst of 1–2 seconds and hit him with an effective concentration in the fuselage. This FW 190 fell off into a dive and crashed in a field a few seconds later. The pilot did not bail out."

Moments later, Carpenter and Anderson were at 1,500 feet when Anderson broke around to three o'clock after 190s flying at the same level. Both planes had their gear down and were preparing to land when Anderson shot down one of them. The second Focke Wulf pilot pulled up his gear, climbed and met Carpenter at about thirty degrees off head-on. Carpenter fired a deflection shot into the 190's fuselage and saw the stricken fighter burst into flames as it passed by him. Anderson then finished it off with a burst from his guns and saw it crash near the airfield.

The 336th Squadron came down on the aerodrome at Evreux and strafed many soldiers doing work on the airfield. A blister hangar was shot up and an Me 410 was destroyed by Major Goodson.

The Mustangs had a field day shooting up all the military targets in the area, and they encountered a considerable number of enemy planes in the air including a Feisler Storch observation plane which was downed by Capt. K. G. Smith and Lt. J. H. Brandenberg. When the tally was added up at the end of the day, the P–51s had destroyed nine enemy aircraft on the ground and shot up myriad military ground targets, including personnel. Twelve E/A had been caught in the air and shot down; however, the cost had been heavy. Seven Mustangs had not returned from the mission and one pilot returned painfully wounded. Of the seven, two proved to be KIA, four became POWs and one successfully evaded and returned to England. Regardless, it emphasized the fact that if the fighters had to get down on the deck to destroy the Luftwaffe, the cost was going to be very high.

The effect of the Allied air offensive was beginning to show some results. When the Eighth Air Force returned to Berlin on March 22 with a force of 688 bombers and 817 fighters in perfect bombing weather, the Luftwaffe was virtually absent. Only thirty-six enemy fighters were observed that day and they avoided combat. Obviously the German fighter force was being worn down by the incessant attacks, and they were trying to rest their pilots and rebuild their aircraft strength.

The next day the target was Brunswick, and this time the Luftwaffe was able to put up a defense force. The German fighter controller directed the bulk of the fighters at the 1st Task Force, and numerous air battles broke out in the target area. The 4th Fighter Group found themselves in action as soon as they made rendezvous with the bombers. Within a few minutes the Mustang pilots had claimed 11-0-3, with Capt. Duane Beeson getting his fifteenth and sixteenth victories. Maj. Jim Goodson and Capt. Don Gentile each claimed two Me 109s in the fight. The 4th scored twice more that day for a total of thirteen E/A destroyed.

Col. Glenn Duncan, CO of the 353rd Fighter Group, had decided early in 1944 that in view of the fact that the Luftwaffe wasn't coming up to fight, the correct approach to the problem was to go down after him on his airfields. Several strafing and bombing missions against the enemy during February had strengthened his belief despite the loss of some outstanding pilots, including Maj. Walter Beckham.

Duncan presented his idea to Maj. Gen. William Kepner, commander of VIII Fighter Command, and on Mar. 15, 1944, sixteen volunteers—four pilots each from the 353rd, 359th, 361st and 355th Fighter Groups—reported to Duncan for training in the art of ground strafing. In typical fighter pilot procedure it was deemed that they should have a name duly representative of themselves, their mission and their sponsor, so they became known as "Bill's Buzz Boys." Officially, they were the 353rd C Group and were based at Metfield, home of the 353rd. The purpose of the unit was solely to strafe enemy aerodromes within a 300 mile radius of Metfield.

The initial mission of the new group was staged on March 26 when Duncan led the twelve Thunderbolts, four carrying two each M-4 frag clusters, against targets in France. Airfields at Chartres, Chateaudun, Anet, St. Andre de L'Eure and Beauvais/Tille were attacked. Claims were one twin-engined aircraft destroyed, one Me 210 probably destroyed and four damaged. In addition, hangars, gun emplacements, a flak tower and a water tower were strafed. One P-47 flown by Lt. Kenneth Williams of the 355th Fighter Group did not return. He was later reported as POW. Three remaining planes suffered slight damage and two had moderate damage.

"Bill's Buzz Boys" provided escort to bombers the following day, but returned to Metfield without making any strafing attacks. However, the 4th Fighter Group turned in the most outstanding strafing performance to date. They had finished their escort for the bombers and were attacking airfields in the south of France when the 334th and 336th Squadrons spotted

Unusual photo of a 357th FG P-51 flying off the wing of a B-17 over the English countryside. M. Olmsted

some seventy-five enemy aircraft on Cazau aerodrome, which the bombers had missed. The Mustangs roared down with a vengeance and proceeded to destroy twenty-one of the enemy aircraft on the ground and caught another in the air. The 335th destroyed an additional two enemy fighters in the air in the vicinity of Bordeaux. Unfortunately, their lone loss was one of their most outstanding pilots, Lt. Archie Chatterly, who bailed out near Tours after being hit by flak.

The 56th Group also lost two of its top leaders and aces on March 27. Maj. Gerald Johnson was flying with the 56th A Group when he was hit by flak and forced to belly in his Thunderbolt between Isigny and Carenton in France to become a POW. Maj. Walker Mahurin was flying escort to the bombers with 56th B Group when he attacked a Dornier 217. Mahurin managed to score hits on the twin-engined German craft, but at the same time the gunner of the Dornier put telling shots into the P-47. Mahurin was forced to bail out between Bonneval and Voves, France. Mahurin eventually made his way back to England after a successful evasion.

The heavies of the Eighth Air Force went after the Luftwaffe's airfields in France again on March 28 and created another great strafing opportunity for one of the fighter groups. This time it was the 355th Group under the leadership of Lt. Col. Gerald Dix. Dijon aerodrome was attacked four minutes after the final

bombs had been dropped, and the Mustangs used the smoke and dust from the explosions as a cover to make their initial passes. The strafing runs surprised the stunned Germans to the point that it was not until the fourth or fifth pass across the field that the light flak began to come up. It was estimated that there were some seventy-five planes on the field and the Mustang pilots claimed to have destroyed twenty-four of them, probably destroyed one and damaged thirty-one. Top scorers were Maj. Edward Szaniawski with four and Lt. B. D. Johnson with three. Not a single P-51 was lost.

On March 29 the 4th Fighter Group encountered a number of E/A on the way to Brunswick, Germany, and then sighted another thirty coming in from a different direction. To break up the assault the 4th bounced both formations, and numerous dogfights ensued.

Capt. Don Gentile was flying Blue One in Shirtblue Squadron when a gaggle of seven or eight FW 190s were bounced underneath the bombers at 18,000 feet. He closed behind a 190, fired and saw many strikes around the cockpit. The 190 rolled over to port slowly and went down vertically.

As he began to level out, Lt. John Godfrey called a break as two 190s were on Gentile's tail. Gentile broke hard left and blacked out. When he recovered, there was an FW 190 right in front of him. Gentile fired from 300 yards, and the pilot bailed out.

A familiar visitor at 66th FW bases was the Wing CO Brig. Gen. Murray C. Woodbury and his P-47 Piccadilly Pete. Kramer

Lt. John Godfrey had started down with Gentile, but discovered that his engine had cut out due to failure to change the fuel selector valve. Once this had been accomplished he sighted five FW 190s with two Mustangs hot after them. Godfrey dumped flaps and opened throttle in an upward spiral turn. At this time he observed one of the 190 pilots bail out. He later learned that this was Lt. Charles F. Anderson's victim.

Godfrey joined in the chase down to the deck. He finally latched onto one, fired five or six short bursts and the 190 blew up at zero feet. Godfrey tagged onto a second FW 190, closed and got good strikes, and when last observed it was smoking badly.

F/O Fred Glover had observed Godfrey's first victim getting clobbered on the deck while going full bore. He was approximately 100 feet higher than the pack and heading for the lead 190 that was pulling off to the left. As he crossed over he observed a Mustang shooting at a 190. This P-51 pulled right up in front of Glover and forced him to go under. This left the 190 right in front of Glover. Glover opened fire, then saw the left gear of the 190 drop and it crashed into the trees.

The Mustangs turned at this point and sighted a Heinkel He 111 crossing in front. At this point Godfrey opened fire on the Heinkel and got good strikes before breaking away. Glover then fired the balance of his ammunition at the He 111, and it was later seen to belly into a field. While attacking the Heinkel, Glover had been forced to break by a 109 attacking from behind, but this 109 was hit by Maj. Carpenter and also made a belly-landing.

After his initial two kills, Gentile joined another Mustang which was immediately attacked by two Me 109s. Gentile called for the Mustang to break but apparently it didn't receive the transmission. He broke into the 109s, scaring them into the cloud cover. The Mustang escaped. Gentile then came under attack from another 109. He broke to port to escape. The 109 chose not to follow, and as the enemy started to disappear, he reversed his turn and wound up astern of the 109. As he began to fire, the 109 began to stream glycol and the pilot bailed out.

Lt. Col. Everett Stewart was leading the Mustangs of the 355th Group in the target area when fifty-plus enemy aircraft were sighted fifteen miles to the south, headed for Brunswick to intercept the bomber stream. The P-51s held their formation in an attempt to make the enemy think that they were part of the intercepting force until the Mustangs could move in fast. The tactic seemed to work and the P-51s were right on the enemy fighters when they dropped tanks. Stewart's left drop tank refused to release and he was only able to close on his FW 190 with difficulty. He fired two or three bursts at his target and saw some strikes before the E/A split-essed and headed down.

After the encounter Stewart was south of Brunswick, still trying to shake off the left drop tank. Finding himself over an aerodrome, he circled at 8,000 feet hoping to find something taking off or landing. Here he was joined by another three P-51s from the 355th. As they swept over the airfield, they sighted some trainer aircraft attempting to get in and land. Stewart gave one a burst, overran it and watched it crash into a fence.

A second pass caught another Me 108, igniting its engine. The aircraft crash-landed and began to burn. The three P-51s then proceeded to strafe the aerodrome and damaged another three aircraft parked on the field.

As the Mustangs climbed from the aerodrome they sighted an FW 190. Stewart did his best to latch onto it, but handicapped with the drop tank he could not close so he turned it over to Lieutenants Lenfest and Kaminski.

The final tally for the day gave the 355th twelve FW 190s destroyed in the air in addition to the two trainers destroyed by Stewart and two trainers destroyed on the ground.

Col. Glenn Duncan led "Bill's Buzz Boys" that day on a strafing mission against a number of aerodromes in the vicinity of Dummer Lake. In Duncan's words, the activities were as colorful and dramatic as a Sunday drive in the country: "We preceded the bombers by a few minutes and arrived at Dummer Lake on time. The cloud layer was 6/10 to 8/10 at about 5,000 feet making it almost ideal for ground work. As planned, the three flights went to designated aerodromes previously picked for their importance. I took my flight of four down on Bramsche Aerodrome. We began our dive from about 10,000 feet from out of the sun and hit zero feet about two miles from the field. I pulled up to about 150 feet as I crossed my check point on the edge of the drome and began squirting a few bursts. No matter how hard I looked I could not see any E/A parked or hidden. The only thing of interest was a light flak tower on the northwest side of the field that shot to beat hell but couldn't figure the correct deflection for 400 mph on a P-47. We four pulled up to about 5,000 feet on the far side of the field and surveyed the situation. A little bit of flak followed us but was not too great of a bother.

"We had turned left trying to pick up another available target when we saw an aerodrome off to the right. Due to the close proximity of the drome and our position, I called to the rest of the flight and told them to stay up and go around to the edge of the field as I was going down. I passed across the front of the hangar line and saw many twin engine and single engine aircraft parked on the drome. I lined up two of the twin engine and let go. The first one lit up quite well but never did blow up or catch fire while I was coming on it. The second one took in quite a number of strikes and consequently caught fire. There were single engines dispersed in a line across the field from these two and I was able to pick up many of those in my sights and get a few hits on each. There were about 5 or 6 of the single engines that I could see at the time. However, it is very hard to pick out a great number of objects going along lickity split. I pulled up from this and joined the flight dodging the flak that was coming up . . . One of my pilots seemed to be the center of interest of one group in the flak tower and made him so mad that he dove down

79

on them and silenced them. The flak died down a bit after this and in turning I saw a B–17 sitting on its belly in an open field. It seemed to be in good shape except for the belly landing and I pulled around and went down on it. As I was going down flak starting coming up from unseen places and caused me to go down a bit lower than I anticipated. I got plenty of hits on the B–17 and saw a good fire start on the inboard engine.

"I again assembled my 4 ships and pulled up to 5,000 feet heading out. I looked back and the B–17 was burning fiercely . . . It only took a short while for us to pick up another aerodrome . . . a staff car was speeding across one end of it and there were several T/E and S/E E/A parked . . . I called for flights to go down and believe me the boys were really flying good this day . . . The staff car caught quite a lot of .50 caliber from both the man on my left and myself at which time my guns ran dry . . . The four ships came out of this in good shape but when we pulled up one of the boys said he had been hit. I throttled back and we all got together . . . One of the boys had been hit in his gas tanks . . . he consequently ran out of gas about 40 miles off the English coast being picked up safely by air-sea rescue . . . I am sure that the Hun is licking his wounds very deeply after this affray into his so-called superior race's backyard. My claims are 1 T/E destroyed, 1 T/E probably destroyed, 5 unidentified E/A damaged, 1 Me 210 damaged, 1 B–17 destroyed."

Total for the "Buzz Boys" was six destroyed on the ground, five probables and nine damaged.

During March 1944 the Allies had gained complete aerial superiority over the Luftwaffe. The VIII Fighter Command alone had destroyed a total of 406 enemy aircraft in the air and 100 on the ground. Morale was at an all-time high and these deeds really showed it.

For the enemy it had been a horrible experience. First, many of the Luftwaffe's best pilots were killed or injured during the furious air battles that had taken place over the Reich. Second, the ever-increasing strength of the US Army Air Forces made the German position more desperate. Finally, the arrival of the P–51 Mustang with its extremely long range left the Luftwaffe no sanctuary in which it could recuperate.

During the month, VIII Fighter Command also made a decision concerning aircraft markings. The 56th FG had been the pioneer in this change when each squadron painted the noseband of their P–47s in a squadron color. They did so in the thought that the Germans might mistake the Jugs for the brightly painted Focke Wulfs and give them an advantage at the time of encounter. The "Wolfpack" had been marking their planes like this since January, and since it seemed to work other units began to do the same. In late March the 4th FG adorned their Mustangs with bright red noses, which became well known by friend and foe alike. As other groups decided to do the same, VIII FC decided to step in and institute a standardized system. Each Group was assigned a different nose marking so they would be easily identifiable in the air. The second most important thing about the markings was that they were definite morale builders. The groups came to be proud of their markings, and this intensified the friendly competition between the various groups for accomplishment when they sighted each other over enemy territory.

Spring 1944 found the air war in Europe undergoing a dramatic change. The targets were deeper into Germany, and the average distance from England to where opposition was encountered increased to 350 miles. The long missions were beginning to seriously hinder the Thunderbolt groups because a large part of the German fighters were now out of their range.

By April 1944 the Luftwaffe's fighter command was beginning to hoard its planes and did not send them into action unless the advantage was in its favor. More dependency was put on the flak batteries to defend the targets, and many additional batteries of guns were added to already intensive flak areas.

Chapter 8

Hunting the Luftwaffe High and Low

Faced with the Luftwaffe's new combat strategies, VIII Fighter Command was forced to make a decision regarding its tactics as well. The decision was to go down to the ground after the Luftwaffe. To do so the groups were assigned targets in France and Germany and the mission was to find and destroy all the enemy aircraft situated on these dispersed airfields. This order included all fields used by German combat units, depots and training bases. The order was not easy to carry out because many of the bases were not charted and had to be found by exploring various target areas. Second, strafing attacks on airfields were extremely dangerous because of numerous flak batteries guarding them. A third factor in the new mission was pilot preparation. The Americans had been trained for high-altitude escort, and these new low-level sweeps required some retraining. The most obvious change was in navigation, in the use of maps and in fighter control. Each pilot found it necessary to be prepared to fight it out alone and find his own way back to base.

The plan was put into action on April 5 when eleven fighter groups were dispatched to strike German airfields. Bad weather over the assigned target area kept eight of the groups from attacking, but the other three were able to wreak havoc on the enemy. The 4th FG struck at several fields in the Berlin area and came away with forty-five victories. Stendal aerodrome was strafed by the 336th Fighter Squadron under the leadership of Major Goodson, and it was there that best results were obtained. Very little flak was encountered and the Mustangs claimed twenty-five-plus enemy aircraft destroyed in their strafing passes. The aerodrome west of Brandenburg was another story, though. Out of a flight of four P-51s attacking a line of Ju 88s, two were downed including the 334th Squadron's high-scoring ace, Capt. Duane Beeson.

One of the more prominently engaged pilots of the 355th Group's 354th Squadron was Capt. Walter Koraleski. The Group had been assigned aerodromes in the vicinity of Munich and Augsburg, Germany. Upon arrival Koraleski and his flight sighted a Dornier 217 flying low and away from an aerodrome. Immediately the Mustang pilot went after it, but two other P-51s made passes on the E/A before he could get to it. However, the German was still full of fight and Koraleski had to put the gunner out of commission on his first pass. As he pulled up to get ready for another pass, another Mustang came in and gave the Dornier a squirt. Koraleski then proceeded to make his second pass, which was successful in setting the left engine on fire. Once more he pulled up to see what was going to

happen and another P-51 got his shots in before the Dornier crashed to earth.

Koraleski headed back for the aerodrome but en route sighted a lone Me 109. The two met in a head-on pass and then went into a Lufbery maneuvering for a shot. The Mustang pilot finally pulled his nose through, and just as he was about to hit the trigger noted that the E/A was taking hits. Koraleski pulled to one side as Lt. Woody raked the hapless 109 with his .50s. Woody finished his pass, and Koraleski took over raking the craft from stem to stern at a distance of fifty yards. The 109 straightened out and made a belly-landing in a field.

Koraleski returned to the enemy aerodrome and made a strafing pass, damaging a Dornier 217 and an Me 110 on the ground. As he pulled up from his pass he sighted a biplane trainer in the air. Koraleski put a burst into the craft which started down immediately. It pulled up just above the ground where Woody put a finishing burst into it, causing the wings to just fold up and crashing the plane to the ground.

Koraleski and Woody encountered two more training craft in the air which were immediately attacked and downed with a minimum of effort. Koraleski made one more pass at the aerodrome. Woody took a flak hit, which fortunately was not fatal, as he pulled up and headed for home.

Capt. Walter Koraleski shared in three victories and damaged two E/A on the ground in the big Luftwaffe airfield attack on Apr. 5, 1944. 355th FG Assn.

The 20th Fighter Group was also out on a strafing mission with Lt. Col. Rau leading. The P-38 formation had just begun to let down into an overcast southwest of Hanover when Rau's wingman, Lt. Jack J. Yelton, took a hit. Yelton was momentarily knocked out and was down to 1,500 feet before he was able to recover. The Lightning pilot pulled out just above the treetops and surveyed the damage. The canopy was smashed, the instrument panel was riddled and both engines were throwing oil and running rough. Yelton was bleeding from superficial cuts on his face and neck. With no compass and no sun, Yelton had to guess on a heading. Flying at approximately 2,000 feet Yelton found himself in a maze of German airfields. In the next ten minutes he was able to down two enemy aircraft. The first was an FW 200 which he caught in the traffic pattern and shot down in flames from 400 feet. The second was a Focke Wulf 190 that was cruising along low and happy. The 190 pilot took a long burst, pulled up to 700 feet and bailed out. Yelton then sighted a large city in the distance which he took to be Berlin. Deciding he was headed in the wrong direction, Yelton made a 180 degree turn but at that time both engines failed. The Lightning pilot decided to bring in his craft deadstick on a German airfield. As he lined up with the runway he sighted two Me 110s lined up for takeoff. Yelton stated that he "must have just gone nuts," for he chose to crash his P-38 into the 110s. A violent crash took place in which Yelton was thrown upward from his cockpit. He came down landing on his back, breaking both shoulders. All three aircraft involved were completely destroyed. Yelton finished the war in German hospitals and prisoner of war camps.

On April 8 the bombers of Eighth Air Force set out to strike five Luftwaffe installations in northwestern Germany and two aircraft factories in the Brunswick area. While the B-17s encountered no enemy aircraft, the largest single-engined force ever met intercepted the B-24s in the Brunswick area. The ensuing battle cost the Luftwaffe eighty-eight planes in the air. Strafing attacks by the escorting fighters accounted for another forty enemy craft. Twenty-three of the attacking US fighters were lost in the day's action.

The savage attack on the B-24s, which was intercepted by the 4th, was vividly described by Lt. Willard W. Millikan: "I heard Upper report 100 plus coming towards the bombers from the northeast from 1030 to 11 o'clock to the bombers. I was still 3 or 4 miles from the bombers but I saw the Hun easily because there were so many of them. They came down like a tremendous swarm of insects, and the whole bomber formation lit up as they fired at the attacking fighters and the cannon shells began bursting all around the bombers. With the first attack about 6 B-24s plummeted out of formation. The Huns were keeping good formation and there seemed no end of them, but I thought I saw several knocked down by the bombers in the first attack. In the meantime I had been pulling up fast on the bombers and by the time I reached them, coming in from 5 o'clock to them, the first swarm of 30 plus had pulled out from beneath the bombers and were making a climbing port turn.

"I closed in as fast as possible with my section and attacked the rear aircraft, a Me 109. I was not closing fast until I pushed everything forward and dived slightly. I waited until I was about 300 yards and opened fire. Immediately he broke left and I followed using plenty of deflection. Apparently I was using too much for I let it fall off and immediately got strikes on the port wing, engine and cockpit. By this time I could no longer hold deflection so I went right on past him. A part of the port side of the cowling was tearing off and the 109 slowly rolled up on its back, just hung there, then stalled and spun. It crashed in the forest below near a B-24 which had been hit and exploded.

"I called to my section to make a port climbing turn and the three of us reformed. Almost immediately I saw a Mustang doing violent evasive action with an Me 109 on his tail. I attacked again but couldn't get behind him so I laid off three rings deflection and was lucky enough to hit him with hard strikes all over the engine and cockpit and full length of the fuselage. Flames poured out of the engine and the aircraft fell like a stone and crashed in another forest.

"Again reforming the section I climbed up a bit and at 12,000 feet I found a Mustang having a hard time with an Me 109 carrying a belly tank. This character was winging around shooting at everyone with no apparent regard for the guy on his tail. The Mustang could not get in a position to shoot but could stay with the 109. I again attacked but had so much speed that I could not match the 109's turns. He broke into my attacks as well as the other Mustangs and broke away and down full bore towards Brunswick where there was a tremendous pall of black smoke and haze. I followed behind the other

The 355th FG lost its outstanding Thunderbolt ace, Capt. Norman E. Olson, on Apr. 8, 1944, when he fell to flak while strafing. 355th FG Assn.

Mustang and when the 109 would shake him I would come in and shoot. I got a few strikes on a deflection shot. Shortly afterwards the other Mustang got a few strikes on the 109, but the Jerry still fought hard. All this time my two wingmen were staying with me and doing a beautiful job of covering me. Once when the 109 was turning to the right with the Mustang on his tail I broke away to the left to do a tight turn and come down on the 109's tail. He reversed his turn, pulled up and around toward me so I sank the stick and used full rudder just in time for I could see the tracers from his cannon go past my tail. Immediately I came around and again he broke giving me a 90 degree deflection shot. I laid off deflection and began firing, and let the deflection fall off as I closed right up to him. At about 150 yards I hit him all over the engine and wings, flames poured out and a great amount of debris and so forth came streaming off. Immediately, I broke away to miss this nice stuff and did not see him bail out. My wingmen saw him bail out just in time for his chute to open."

Capt. Don Gentile and Lt. Louis Norley also got three victories apiece while Maj. George Carpenter downed two FW 190s. All total the 4th Group claimed thirty-two destroyed in the air.

The 354th Group of the Ninth Air Force was in the thick of the fight over Brunswick, too, claiming twenty of the German fighters for a loss of four of their own. Capt. Jack T. Bradley and Capt. Don Beerbower led the 354th scoring with three kills apiece.

The 355th Group was also heavily engaged and managed to down several German fighters before they headed for home. Capt. Emil Sluga had already shared one Me 109 with his wingman, Lt. Harrington, when he latched onto a second 109 at about 3,000 feet. As he closed he called Harrington to come in, as all but one of Sluga's guns were jammed. In view of the fact that he was already in a good position, Sluga decided he would go ahead and attack with one gun. Closing from 400 to fifty yards astern he scored good hits on the E/A. As he pulled up to avoid overrunning the aircraft, Sluga called for Harrington once more but Harrington was unable to spot the E/A just off the ground. Sluga began to close in again and noted that the craft was getting lower and lower. It then dawned on Sluga that the 109 was going to belly in at about 200 mph. The 109 finally struck the ground, went through a fence and finally stopped in a mangled condition. The pilot was not seen to emerge from the aircraft.

The P-38s of the 20th Fighter Group found their most productive role of the air war when they attacked the aerodrome at Salzwedel, Germany. Some twenty-five German aircraft were left in flames or otherwise destroyed as the P-38s made repeated attacks. Lt. Col. Rau, leading the group, left three aircraft in flames in three passes and then led the 79th Squadron in strafing German barracks in the area. Two other flights from the squadron caught over 300 German soldiers in drill formation and undoubtedly diminished their numbers considerably before leaving them.

As the 79th Squadron headed for home it was attacked by six Me 109s. Rau reported: "I broke left and saw 6 Me 109s. I had zoomed up to about 4,000 feet and saw a Me 109 at 2,000 feet zooming up after a P-38 that was above me, and pulled right up in front of me. I gave him a long burst, smoke poured out and the plane burst into flames. The pilot was probably killed and the plane continued up and crashed into the P-38. Both planes went down in flames."

On the morning of April 9 the heavy bombers of the Eighth Air Force were dispatched to strike targets deep in Germany and Poland including Poznan, Tutow and Gdynia, Poland, and Mariembourg, Belgium. The weather was such that a large number of the B-17s and B-24s aborted the mission and returned to their respective bases. However, the bombers that chose to plow on did attack their targets, some with great success. Enemy aerial opposition was quite spotty. While some of the bombers encountered no opposition, others were set upon by ferocious single-engined aircraft which cost them heavily. The length of the mission and lateness of the bombers assembling and getting off on the mission caused rendezvous to be missed and a number of the fighter escorts were not able to remain in areas to provide withdrawal support. A total of eighteen B-17s and thirteen B-24s were lost.

Capt. Robert S. Johnson was flying with the 56th A Group over Denmark when the B-24s that his squadron was escorting were bounced by a formation of FW 190s. Although Johnson was unable to release his belly tank he and his wingman, Lt. S. D. Hamilton, rolled over and went down to attack fifteen-plus FW 190s. Johnson reported: "They had dived down and were coming up from the rear and beneath the Libs. We got on their tail and began tangling. Some rolled to the deck. I fired a short burst at one and broke into two FW 190s on my tail. These two went on to get on Lt. Hamilton's tail as I tangled with two more FW's. I got rid of these two and began to look for more targets. I saw Lt. Hamilton on the water northwest of Kiel turning with two FW's on his tail. One FW would turn with him and the other would pull out and make head-on passes. He called for help and I told him to keep turning and hold out that I was coming as fast as I could. I still had the belly tank on and was at 18,000 feet. I went down but was going so fast I couldn't get on one of them. I fired at one making head-on passes to scare him off and they broke off Lt. Hamilton's tail. Lt. Hamilton hit the one making head-on passes and he burned and went into the sea, 1,000 feet below. I watched it as Lt. Hamilton got on the other. Then the other FW got on me. I gave throttle and outclimbed the FW 190 in a spiral to the left. He dropped his nose as he stalled and I rolled over and got on his tail. Lt. Hamilton had also hit this one in the left wing tip. The FW could break into me every time I tried to line up on him. I fired several times at him seeing strikes twice. He turned inland and I got on his tail again and was firing and hitting him as he bailed out."

The 352nd Fighter Group flew a mixed aircraft mission with the 328th Squadron flying P-47s and the 486th and 487th flying their new P-51s. Little aerial opposition was encountered so the new Mustangs were given an initial tryout strafing. The 487th destroyed eleven enemy aircraft on the ground while the 486th got an additional four. The 328th Squadron, on its last P-47 mission, encountered three FW 190s and destroyed one of them.

The IX Fighter Command's 354th Fighter Group was providing the last force of returning B-17s with withdrawal support when they encountered a determined attack by fourteen FW 190s in the vicinity of Kiel, Germany. The Mustangs of the 354th accounted for ten of the Focke Wulfs, two of which were credited to Lt. Robert L. Shoup. This P-51 pilot had already accounted for one FW 190 when he and his wingman, Lieutenant Weber, went after another 190 which was attacking a crippled B-17 attempting a crash-landing. The gunners in the rear of the Fortress apparently had already bailed out as a few chutes were present, and the 190 was receiving no return fire from the bomber.

Shoup and Weber came in at approximately 400 mph attacking the 190 at about 300 feet. Shoup fired two quick bursts as the German fighter opened fire on the Fortress. Shoup observed strikes on the 190's wing roots and several pieces flew off. At about the same moment the B-17 slipped off on the left wing and crashed into the ground. The FW then turned sharply to the left and Shoup slid under and outside to keep from overrunning. By this time Weber turned inside Shoup

and fired at the E/A. Many of his tracers passed between the FW and Shoup's nose, causing Shoup to have to maneuver up and over. As Shoup pulled back inside to renew his attack he began to overrun, and as he slowed he found himself directly over the Focke Wulf. Apparently, the German pilot didn't spot Shoup who was only ten feet or so above him. Shoup throttled back and homed in on the tail of the 190 and opened fire. Strikes were scored immediately and the German fighter dipped its nose toward the ground, pulled up and then nosed over violently, struck the ground, bounced and hit again tearing the wing off.

Following the attempts at Thunderbolt high-level bombing using a B-24 as bombardier in the fall of 1943, work had gone forward to provide the fighters with a higher speed bombardier aircraft. The obvious choice was the Lockheed P-38. A new P-38J had been modified with a plexiglass nose, and a Norden bombsight had been installed for the use of an airborne bombardier. The only drawback was the possible vulnerability of the aircraft because it was stripped of its armament to provide a cabin for the bombardier. In a novel adaptation of camouflage, the P-38s of VIII Fighter Command were ordered to paint white bands around the noses of their aircraft and remove any paint forward of the band to give a uniform appearance of all their aircraft.

The initiation of the so-called "droop snoot" Lightning came on April 10 when the 55th Fighter Group under the leadership of Col. Jack S. Jenkins took off laden with one 1,000 pound bomb and one drop

A "droop snoot" P-38 is readied for a mission. The guns had been removed from the Lightning's nose and replaced with a plexiglass nose and bombardier. J. Ilfrey

tank each and set course for St. Dizier aerodrome in France. Upon arrival at 20,000 feet, the aerodrome was found to be cloud covered so the P–38s proceeded to Coulommiers. On arrival, two squadrons of Lightnings formed up in bombing formation while the third squadron provided top cover. On "bombs away" by the bombardier in the lead aircraft, the other Lightning pilots dropped their bombs and were successful in getting a good strike pattern across the airfield. Jenkins then proceeded to take his P–38s down to strafe the target. His first pass was spoiled by a fogged-up windshield, so when the second run was made the ground gunners were out of their shelters and fully alerted. Unfortunately, both Jenkins and his wingman fell victim to their fire. Jenkins managed to belly in and became a prisoner of war.

The 20th Fighter Group had set out on its first droop-snoop mission the same morning, but after finding its target covered by clouds it turned back, dropped its bombs in the English Channel and returned to base. A second mission that afternoon proved to be quite successful, however. Twenty-five 1,000 pound and two 500 pound bombs were dropped in a good concentration on the airfield buildings.

The next day, strikes were launched against targets in Germany and Poland. Approximately 819 fighters from VIII FC were up to support the mission and found themselves occupied by both aerial action and strafing attacks. Most of the aerial action again went to the longer ranged Mustang groups. The 357th FG really blunted the attack of their adversaries when they destroyed twenty-three and damaged another ten E/A.

The Mustangs of the 357th Group bounced a large formation of German single-engined craft just after they had made a pass at the bombers and were in a shallow dive. This enabled the P–51s to get in firing position immediately, chase the German fighters to the deck and proceed to down the majority of them. The biggest problem encountered by the Mustang pilots during the encounter was they were in turn bounced by a formation of P–38s while they were in the process of attacking the Luftwaffe. As Lt. William C. Reese reported: "I attacked again (a Me 109) from astern. While I was closing, 4 P–38s attacked me. I broke to the left and the P–38's zoomed back up." Reese then attacked the Me 109 head-on. The 109 broke to the right while Reese chandelled to the left, which brought him in position to attack the 109 once more. This time he put telling strikes in the enemy craft, which proceeded to crash. The P–38s were not encountered further.

Two other Mustang groups participating in penetration support for the 3rd Task Force—the 352nd A and the 355th—ended the day with a near-tie for victories. The 352nd A claimed 23-2-17 of which three were aerial victories, and the 355th claimed 23-0-17. Eight of the 355th FG's victories were in the air, two of which were scored by Lt. Col. Everett Stewart, CO of the Group. The 4th FG rounded out the Mustang victories with seven in the air and two on the ground.

With the strafing attacks against German airfields

on the Continent increasing, VIII FC decided to draw up a more formal plan of action. This plan assigned to each fighter group a certain area in Germany, and each group had the responsibility of attacking the airfields within its own sector. The codeword for these missions was to be "Jackpot," and the letter A would designate targets in northern Germany and B in the southern sectors of Germany. The benefits of this new plan were as follows: First, and foremost, it enabled the pilots to become more familiar with the targets in their area, therefore they could learn the defenses of each location and plan their attacks accordingly. Second, it prevented the same targets from being attacked by more than one group. This was important in that it helped prevent midair collisions resulting from uncoordinated attacks or firing on friendly aircraft. Also, if a second group hit an airfield right after an attack, it would most likely suffer losses because the flak gunners were on full alert.

Meanwhile, the aerial assault against Germany continued and on April 13 the Eighth Air Force headed to targets in Schweinfurt, Oberpfaffenhofen and Augsburg. It was the first anniversary of operations against the Germans for the 56th and 78th FGs and before the day was out both groups added to their victory lists. Two of the 78th's victories were scored by Lt. Alwin Juchheim of the 83rd FS to bring his total to six. The victory list for the day was topped by the 355th with 27-2-16.

The success of the 355th FG was best expressed by Maj. Claiborne Kinnard who led the mission: "This is one report that I would like to write a story about because from beginning to end it was a hell of a good show! Seldom do all things happen like you want them

Col. Harold J. Rau, CO of the 20th FG, his P-38 Gentle Annie, dog and crew. Rau led his Lightnings in many of the big air battles in the spring of 1944. USAAF

to. Even a slip up at the target turned out O.K. This was a combination escort and strafing mission. I was leading the Group and when I gave the bombers the weather over the target we were on time and they were on time. Just as I was turning to R/V with them I saw seven 109's right under me climbing up. I called 'Blowball Leader' to take care of them which he did pronto and to wait there until we got back. I took the other two squadrons on over and we picked up the bombers on time and escorted them to the target at Oberpfaffenhofen. The bombers were flying as briefed and as we reached the target I worked back to the last box and we went down with the bombers.

"I went over the field at 6,000 feet to get a good look at the situation and plan my runs and also to see if they would throw up any light stuff that could be spotted. Things looked too good to be true! All the south and east side was clear and literally covered with airplanes. The field was so over-crowded that about 40 Do 217's without props were pushed out in a couple of clearings behind the south hangar. On the southeast part of the field itself about twenty twin-engined jobs were sitting there like ducks.

"I let down in a turn and came in on the deck from southeast to northwest. The smoke made the proper approach very easy. I pulled up to about 400 feet and picked out a JU 88 that looked operational, as on a

Maj. Claiborne Kinnard, here boarding his Mustang, led the 355th FG on its picture-perfect mission of Apr. 13, 1944, resulting in claims of 27-2-16. USAAF

previous mission on a nearby field where there were some Do 217s without props, you couldn't set one on fire with a blow torch. I cut loose on it and he blazed up.

"After pulling up I decided to have a general look at the situation at close quarters. Near the hangar line on the northwest side were about six or eight twin-engined aircraft, two of which the bombers had hit and on my right near the east hangar were fifteen or twenty more twin-engined aircraft, four or five of which the bombers had hit. I was approaching the hangar line then and gave the hangar and a couple of 217's in front a blast just for fun. As I pulled over the hangar I looked back and boy, what a sight. About five guys behind me were making their run. I saw two blaze up from somebody's guns. There was smoke and fire all over—guys firing, pulling up, dodging each other, some going up, some down—boy, it was better than any movie ever made!

"I hit the deck again and steamed around for a south to north run. On the way I passed over two heavy gun batteries and couldn't help but laugh because the gunners were just standing there with the guns too big to use. As I reached the field I pulled up again and picked out a 217 right on the south edge of the field to give me an easy double on the pass. One of the other guys had the same idea because just as I was getting ready to fire the 217 blew up so I picked out a Ju 88 just off to the left and had to fire in a pretty steep bank but when I opened up, much to my surprise I got him dead center and he blazed up."

Two more passes by Kinnard destroyed a third Ju 88, a Dornier 217 and damaged a Dornier 217. Kinnard continued: "By this time I was heading for all the 217's parked behind the hangar. I was too low to do any decent shooting but gave them a squirt mainly to get some pictures. By this time the gunners had come out of their holes and tracers were flying around so I called everybody out. I picked a spot about thirty miles away that looked healthy and we all corkscrewed up to 14,000 and headed for the bombers. On the way to the bombers I saw a big aircraft stooging around about 2,000 feet below a big patch of cirrus and off to the side of the clouds. As we began to close on him I saw seven unidentified aircraft disappear into the cirrus at our two o'clock. I called everybody to watch out, that it looked like a trap. I had five ships with a little to no ammunition and the other flights were out of sight. Sure enough, as we closed on the big aircraft the 190's half rolled over the edge of the cloud on our tails. We wheeled into them and they broke for the deck—thank goodness. We then caught the bombers and escorted them on out along with the P–38s which I sure was glad to see."

For Capt. Don Gentile of the 4th FG, it was his last mission. With 21.83 aerial victories and six destroyed on the ground, he was going home. However, his last mission turned out to be his most embarrassing. As he returned to Debden he decided to put on a show for the press which had their cameras running. As he made one of his legendary low passes over the field Gentile realized, too late, that he was too low and his Mustang *Shangri-La* bounced off the turf and crash-landed. Gentile was unhurt, but *Shangri-La*'s fuselage was broken in half by the impact.

April 15 was the day that VIII Fighter Command decided to try its first full-scale Jackpot mission. More than 600 fighters of the VIII and IX Fighter Commands were up for the mission. The objectives were airfields in France and the low countries, and plenty of targets were found. During the day the pilots destroyed at least forty E/A on the ground and another eighteen in the air. The 352nd FG had a good day. The 486th FS led by Lt. Col. Luther Richmond struck at Vechta airfield in Germany, and caught ten FW 190s taking off. Richmond gunned down one of the 190s but his ship was hit by flak almost immediately and he, too, went down. His men pressed the attack and double victories were scored by Lts. Alton Wallace and Martin Corcoran. Lts. Henry Miklajcyk and Murdoch Cunningham each

downed one. In an attack on Planthenne airfield, Lt. William Furr of the 328th flamed an Me 110 on the ground.

The 56th Fighter Group also enjoyed a good day. The A Group strafed Flensburg aerodrome in Germany where they destroyed eleven He 111s and damaged another four. The attack was not without loss, however. Maj. Leroy A. Schreiber, CO of the 62nd Squadron and high-scoring ace with fourteen aerial victories to his credit, was hit by flak and spun in from 700 feet.

B Group caught a flight of ten FW 190s in the air west of Hamburg, Germany, and shot down four of them, but Capt. Charles Harrison was shot down. Their strafing mission was thwarted when their selected aerodrome was found under attack by another fighter group.

The triumphant end of Capt. Don Gentile's tour came to a most embarrassing close. In his final pass for the newsmen,

Gentile got too low, bounced off the turf and crash-landed. USAAF

Capt. Gerald Brown of the 55th Fighter Group had been involved in a Jackpot mission near Halberstadt, Germany, when he sighted a Focke Wulf 190 flying fifty feet off the deck. Brown lined up on him immediately and after a short burst the 190 flicked over and went into the ground. About five minutes later Brown pulled up over a small hill and sighted a Heinkel He 111 flying at ninety degrees to him at an altitude of 200 feet. The sight of the P-38 apparently was too much for the German pilot, who proceeded to attempt a crash-landing immediately. The right wing sheared and the plane went skidding across the landscape. The destruction of these two aircraft made Brown the first P-38 ace of the 55th Fighter Group.

Even though the mission brought fifty-eight new victories, it was a costly one. The weather had allied itself with the enemy on this day and thirty-three US fighters were lost, at least nineteen of which were due to weather. Heaviest hit was the 364th FG which lost seven of its Lightnings.

The fighters returned to escort duty to Germany on April 18 on a mission that was to be particularly costly to the 4th FG. They were to escort bombers to the Berlin area. Shortly after rendezvous, a mixed group of German fighters attacked their charges. The 4th struck into the Me 109s and Focke Wulf 190s, destroying three of the E/A before driving them off. Maj. George Carpenter of the 335th FS scored two victories before he, too, was shot down. He later described combat as follows: "I bounced a squadron of Me 109s and was flabbergasted when the plane I was attacking did not go down. I flew past him and he swung over on my tail and let me have it. I took violent evasive action then, but I had been hit. I deliberately spun down to a low level, smoking badly but no body wounds. There I found myself in a head-on battle with a 190. He didn't hit me and I didn't hurt him but I found my engine temperature was up in the red. I was smoking badly so I bailed out rather than taking a chance on catching fire."

Carpenter did in fact down two of the three planes he attacked and these victories were confirmed for him

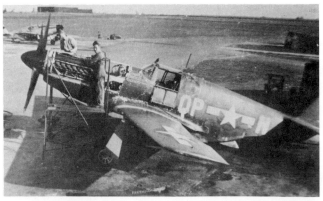

Fourth FG mechanics at work on Lt. Nick Megura's Mustang Ill Wind. *The devotion of the ground crews to their pilots and aircraft was unsurpassed.* L. Schmidt

by Lts. Goodwyn and Hunt. Carpenter became a POW and ended the war with fourteen confirmed victories. Also shot down that day were Lt. Lloyd Henry of the 335th and Capt. Vic France of the 334th FS. France, a 334th ace, was killed when he flew his plane into the ground while attacking 109s caught in the landing pattern at Genthin airfield in Germany.

The Mustang groups continued their mastery over the Luftwaffe on April 19. While escorting bombers attacking Kassel, Germany, four P-51 groups combined for sixteen victories. The 357th FG was first to engage the enemy fighters and downed five of them near the target area. About this time the 352nd A Group, the 4th FG and the 355th FG assumed the escort responsibility, and within minutes all three groups were involved in combat. Pilots of the 352nd claimed three kills, with two of the victories going to Lt. John Thornell of the 328th FS. Of the remaining eight victories, three were claimed by the 355th FG and the last five by the 4th FG. Unfortunately, the battle cost the 4th FG another of its aces; Capt. Charles Anderson of the 335th FS was killed in action. Anderson had 10½ aerial and 5½ ground scores to his credit at the time of his death.

Three days later, the 4th FG returned to the Kassel area and resumed their flailing of the German fighter forces. They were escorting the bombers on the way to Hamm, and as the force passed over Kassel a sharp-eyed pilot of the 4th spotted a gaggle of twenty Me 109s forming up far below at 4,000 feet. The scarlet-nosed Mustangs dove to the attack and a swirling dogfight that took place from 4,000 feet down to the deck sent seventeen of the Messerschmitts to their doom. High score went to Lt. Willard Millikan of the 336th FS who downed four Me 109s, and runner up Lt. John Godfrey also of the 336th, with three.

Millikan's combat was marked by excellent maneuvering, shooting and mutual support. Millikan stated: "When we reached 10,000 feet we sighted the E/A (20 Plus Me 109s) off to our left at 9 o'clock. Our squadron approached them and flew alongside the circle, my section between Horseback and the Huns. Our three sections were all well up, very nearly abreast, and were compact, thus preventing any lagging. I watched the 109s as we flew along and presently one detached himself to attack my section. I called a break to port into his attack and the flight did a beautiful job of breaking and staying together. The Hun kept up his attack and turned steeply to come in on my No. 4's tail, so I pushed everything forward and dropped flaps to turn inside him. Through the early stages of the turn he outturned me, but I pulled up and corkscrewed inside him and laid off a deflection shot which hit him hard enough to cause him to flick out of his turn. He started to split-ess but my shots forced him to turn back the other way. Immediately I managed to get a few scattered strikes and he began to skid and slow up and prepare to bail out. I was closing rapidly so I dropped full flaps and throttled back completely. I was still overshooting him though as I skidded and raked him without using my sights. Finally I had to break away over him and he bailed out.

". . . Pulling up and around to port I reassembled my section and then I saw a Me 109 chasing a Mustang and I jumped him. I had to use a lot of deflection again, blacking out in one of the turns. Luckily I hit him in the turns and caused him to jink trying to avoid my fire and I hit him pretty well again causing him to start smoking and go into a steep dive . . . My wingman confirms this one as destroyed. I had to break away for a Me 109 was coming at me and I could not see what happened. Fortunately for me my No. 3, Lt. Norley, was on hand and did a good job of shooting the devil out of the Me 109 and the Hun went straight in. He was pulling enough deflection on me to shoot me down a dozen times.

"Turning on around I pulled up on another Hun and managed to clobber him in pretty good shape after turning and pulling and doing awful things to the engine. I got strikes with a deflection shot and I would have to pull my nose through, fire a short burst, let off my turn so I could see the Hun, and then pull through again. I managed to get scattered strikes this way and the Hun half rolled and went straight in.

"By this time things were certainly mixed up and it seemed we had been fighting for hours. Fires were burning everywhere and all the fighting had taken place from 8,000 feet on down to the deck. Pulling around again I sighted another Me 109 and I tackled him but he put up an amazing demonstration of aerobatics, and I soon found myself alone. I again laid off deflection and hit him and he straightened out and slow rolled. I shot again and hit him just as he rolled out of it. Immediately he rolled on his back and plowed into the ground at a flat angle. He was burning pretty well and I must have hit the pilot. I started to follow when he half rolled but realized I was only 1,500 feet up and I recovered right over the tree tops.

". . . Good wingmen are at a premium and without them we could not do much . . . I would not have made it home without Lt. Norley's timely clobbering of one Hun and the ready assistance of my own wingman. Every man had countless opportunities to break away and attack, but wingmen stayed on and did their job, which is the only way the Huns Lufbery can be broken up."

Lt. Ray S. Wetmore, one of the up and coming pilots of the 370th FS, 359th FG, had finished his strafing run when he sighted two aircraft about five miles away, flying line astern. Wetmore reported: "As I joined them, the lead ship made a gentle turn to the right making it easy for me to catch them, and to join in formation with the lead ship, about twenty yards to the right of him. It suddenly dawned on me that I was flying beside a FW 190. He evidently saw me at the same time for he made a sharp turn away. I immediately got on his tail, but we were so low that I was unable to get him in my sight, since he was weaving. He pulled slowly away from me and I started firing at 300 yards. I gave him a long burst and noticed strikes around the wing roots and fuselage. He pulled up to 1,500 feet, jettisoned his canopy and bailed out."

VIII Fighter Command continued its reign of terror over the Germans on April 24, claiming another 124 confirmed victories, sixty-six in the air. The bulk of the aerial victories again went to the long-range Mustangs. During the target support phase, pilots of the 355th and 357th FGs guarding the bombers of the 1st Air Task Force destroyed forty-two enemy fighters.

The 357th Group sighted a gaggle of enemy aircraft positioning themselves to attack the bombers in

One of the rising stars in the spring of 1944 was Lt. Ray S. Wetmore of the 359th FG. USAAF

Lt. Fletcher Adams of the 357th scored a double and a triple in April 1944 to run his score to seven. M. Olmsted

Lt. George G. George of the 357th FG married a Blackpool girl and flew Blackpool Bat, *a colorful Mustang.* M. Olmsted

Capt. Robert E. Woody and his crew chief, Sergeant Gertsen. Woody downed four E/A and shared a fifth over Munich on Apr. 24, 1944. R. E. Woody

the Munich area. As the 362nd Fighter Squadron swooped down to attack a formation of Me 109s, they sighted some eighteen Me 110s and Me 410s flying above and in loose formation. Leaving the other squadrons to go down on the Me 109s, several sections of the 362nd climbed up after the twin-engined fighters. Still clinging to the traditional Lufbery for mutual protection, the 110s and 410s began their circle. The Mustang pilots were well versed in tactics to oppose this maneuver. They would choose the aircraft with the least protection to the rear, dive down, put in some good bursts, pull out to the side to observe results, then pull back up to dive down on another victim. Capts. Fletcher E. Adams and John B. England got three apiece in this manner. Another four twin-engined fighters were downed by other members of the squadron.

When attacked, the single-engined aircraft performed the usual split-ess and most of them headed for the deck where the P-51 pilots had a field day. A number of the 109 pilots appeared to be quite inexperienced, and most of the victims were shot or driven into the ground from low altitude.

The 355th also encountered large formations of Me 109s coming in from the northeast in the Munich area. Capt. Robert E. Woody was leading Yellow Flight of the 354th Fighter Squadron when the call for help came in from the bombers. The Mustangs were flying at 23,000 feet and as they closed on the bomber formation some fifteen to twenty contrails of E/A were sighted at

28,000 feet. The P-51s climbed to the attack. Woody sighted a flight of five Me 109s at one o'clock to him attacking the bomber box at eight o'clock to the Big Friends. Woody positioned himself on the "tail end Charlie" of the formation and closed to about 300 yards. Soon after he opened fire the 109 went down in flames.

Woody expected the rest of the enemy formation to break immediately, but they didn't seem to notice and continued to bore in on the bombers. He resumed his attack, picking the next 109 in line and sent it down. In one of the first of the classic "clay pigeon" shoots that escort pilots would encounter, Woody downed four consecutive 109s while the others flew on as if nothing was happening. Woody's wingman, Lt. Boulet, put a burst into the sole survivor of the five before Woody pulled in and finished it off. Woody had scored an unprecedented 4½ kills for the day. All total, the 355th Fighter Group sent twenty Me 109s down for the loss of four of their own.

While these victories were being scored in the air, several other fighters came in low to administer the second part of the old "one-two" punch, destroying scores of German planes on the ground. The 56th B Group claimed 16-0-11 and the 352nd claimed 28-0-24 during strafing attacks on several airfields. All of the 352nd claims were made by the 486th FS. Capt. Robert C. MacKean was seen to destroy five E/A before he hit a high-tension wire. High scorer, however, was Lt. Edwin Heller who destroyed seven planes: four Me 110s, two Ju 88s and one Ju 52.

The Lightnings of the 20th and 55th Fighter Groups were back out on droop-snoot missions on April 27 and 28. On the twenty-seventh the 20th Group received a scare as they lined up on an alternate target at Albert/Meaulte, France, when some of the pilots mistook a formation of P-47s for FW 190s, causing a premature drop. The 55th was more successful when they dropped their bombs on the airfield at Roye/Amy, France, from 17,000 feet.

The following day the 20th Group P-38s bombed the airfield at Tours, France, while the 55th Group went to Chateaudun. Following their bomb drop, the 55th Group Lightnings provided cover for the Thunderbolts of the 56th and 353rd Fighter Groups' strafing attacks.

The bombers returned to Berlin on April 29 and while the bombing results were fair to good, the escort-to-bomber relations were a fiasco. The 3rd Division leading the mission had trouble assembling, and when enemy territory was reached, the bomber stream was so badly strung out that effective escort was impossible. Faulty navigation put another bomber formation forty miles south of their briefed position, causing them to encounter concentrated attacks from Luftwaffe fighters while unescorted. Seventeen B-17s fell victim to this tragic navigational error.

B-24s from the 2nd Division were badly behind schedule. The Liberators made it to the target without stiff opposition, but coming off the target late caused them to have to fend for themselves until Thunderbolts picked them up at Dummer Lake. They lost twenty-five Liberators to German fighters before the Thunderbolts intervened. The escorting fighters were able to down only fourteen enemy fighters in limited action, but the Germans downed thirty-eight B-17s and twenty-five B-24s. Once more the dire necessity of proper escort had been strongly confirmed.

VIII Fighter Command closed out the month flying fighter sweeps over France. In addition, they flew a few strafing attacks and escorted bombers that hit airfields in the Paris area.

As they did before, the Luftwaffe ignored the fighter sweeps, but rose in great numbers to intercept the bombers. The 357th Fighter Group intercepted a number of FW 190s and Me 109s and downed nine of them. Capt. Clarence Anderson's section had six FW 190s come through them head-on, but Anderson used twenty degrees of flaps and full throttle to pull around on their tails. The action came about so quickly and apparently, according to Anderson, "scared the hell out of them as they all hit the deck." Anderson latched onto and got numerous strikes on the craft before he overran and had to pull up. As he positioned himself for another strike a blue-nosed P-51 dived down right in front of him, pulled up immediately and apparently never even fired. However, it was a scare enough for the badly damaged FW 190 pilot. He pulled up and bailed out.

It was quite obvious to everyone as April 1944 drew to a close that VIII FC's new aggressive fighter tactics had really paid dividends. The Command had claimed 825 enemy aircraft during the month, of which 493 had been destroyed on the ground. It also showed that the faith in the P-51 was more than warranted, as the Mustang claimed more than three quarters of the month's victories. The job had not been cheap, however; it had cost 163 aircraft, sixty-seven of them new P-51s. Strafing had paid off, but at a high cost. To illustrate the point, only one of 100 fighters sent on

Always a highlight at any Eighth Air Force base was the appearance of the Maj. Glen Miller dance band. E. Stewart

escort were lost as opposed to three out of 100 on strafing attacks.

Gen. Adolph Galland, Chief of the Luftwaffe Fighter Forces, reported to Air Marshal Goering that Luftflotte Reich (Defense of Germany) had lost thirty-eight percent of its fighter pilots in April and Luftflotte 3 had lost twenty-four percent of its strength. Altogether, the Luftwaffe had lost 489 pilots while training centers were only able to furnish 396 replacements. Galland proposed that all fighter pilots in staff positions be returned to combat duty, that night fighter pilots be transferred to day fighting duties, that two fighter Gruppen be returned from the Eastern Front and that ground attack units return all pilots with more than five aerial victories to their credit. Fighter units on the Eastern Front were ordered to return fifteen veteran pilots

to the west when they had received their quota from training schools. The day bombing offensive and the American fighter forces were, indeed, placing the Luftwaffe fighter forces in dire circumstances.

Even as the Eighth Air Force had been carrying out its destructive attacks against the Luftwaffe and Germany's industry, preparations were being made for the invasion of the Continent. Part of the preparation was the growth of the Ninth Air Force which would be the tactical air force supporting the ground forces following the invasion. As their new units arrived some base changes were required. To accommodate these new units, three VIII FC groups were forced to move. The 55th FG moved to Worningford, the 56th FG to Boxted and the 353rd FG to Raydon.

Mustang of the 363rd FS, 357th FG over England. At this period all aircraft were still painted olive-drab with white spinners and ID stripes. O'Brien

Chapter 9

Clearing the Path

During the first few days of May 1944 the Eighth Air Force assisted the Ninth Air Force in striking tactical targets in Europe. From May 1 through May 6 they struck at Crossbow and Noball targets in occupied Europe. These rocket-firing bases were a real menace, not only to English cities but also to the invasion build-up, and their destruction was a high-priority mission. Also on the first of May, the 339th Fighter Group under the command of Col. John B. Henry flew its first mission with VIII FC. The 339th was another new P-51 Mustang group and was based in Fowlmere.

Even though the Luftwaffe had lost its superiority it was still a fighting force to be reckoned with. While it could pick and choose its time of battle, the German fighter forces still continued to do their utmost to defend strategic targets in the Fatherland. On May 8 the bombers headed for targets in Brunswick and Berlin, and well over 200 enemy fighters rose to meet the challenge. The 1st Air Task Force headed for Brunswick was met by a large fighter force. In the vicinity of Enschede, Netherlands, a force of seventy-five enemy fighters attacked the bombers head-on and the 359th Fighter Group charged in to break up the assault. In disrupting the attack the 359th knocked eleven E/A out of the sky, with Lt. Robert Booth claiming three of the victories. The 352nd FG picked up the escort over the target area and flew into a hornet's nest of activity. Just as they made rendezvous with the bombers, a force of 100–150 Me 109s and FW 190s attacked the bombers.

Lt. Col. John C. Meyer, leading the 487th Fighter Squadron, took his section of eight Mustangs to attack a formation of fifteen-plus FW 190s that had just made a pass through the bombers. Meyer made an ineffective pass at one of the FWs but was attacked by two more, so he broke off and turned into his attackers. These two continued on through the undercast after firing at Meyer. He followed them on down but lost them in the undercast. Sighting no enemy aircraft, he joined up with Captain Hamilton, and the two Mustangs proceeded to shoot up a locomotive before pulling back up to seek the bomber stream.

Meyer and Hamilton sighted a formation of fifteen FW 190s still laden with belly tanks headed for the bombers. The two Mustangs closed on the unsuspecting 190s. Meyer fired a short burst from 250 yards, causing an explosion that blew the whole rear of the fuselage off the 190. Meyer overshot, pulled up into the sun, looked back and saw a number of E/A on the tail of Hamilton. Meyer dove back down to the rescue. As he closed in on the tail-end Focke Wulf, the enemy pilot bailed out.

The two Mustangs climbed back up, and were joined on their way by Lt. John Thornell of the 328th Squadron. At 15,000 feet the pilots sighted three Me 109s above them. As they climbed to attack, the 109s headed for the deck. The Mustangs gave chase and as they headed through a hole in the clouds, a burst from Lt. Thornell's .50s blew up one of the 109s. The two remaining 109s broke; Thornell took after the 109 on the left and Meyer took the one on the right. Meyer made some good strikes on his opponent as he attempted to chandelle back up into the clouds. The 109 came out of the clouds in a tight spiral, and continued on down to crash.

Thornell shot his Me 109 down but became separated from Meyer and Hamilton in the chase. As he headed for home he was bounced by another Me 109. Thornell outflew the German and quickly got on his tail. Believing that he was out of ammunition, he called

Lt. Bob Booth of the 359th FG already had three P-47 victories when he got a triple flying a Mustang on May 8, 1944, to become an ace. USAAF

for help. Meyer had trouble spotting Thornell, but when he finally sighted him he called to him and told him to "chew his tail off, you're close enough." Thornell tightened his turn inside the 109 and the pilot promptly bailed out.

Lt. Carl J. Luksic of the 487th Fighter Squadron became the first Eighth Air Force pilot to down five E/A in one day. Luksic had gone down to attack a formation of enemy aircraft in the Brunswick area but lost his first target in the clouds. Luksic stated: "Red, 4, Lt. O'Nan, then called in another 109 which I did not see and I told him to get him and I would follow. While he was chasing this 109 I saw on my left 5 or 6 190s which I immediately turned into. Lt. O'Nan at this time was engaged with the 109. I put down 10 degrees of flaps and started queuing up on one of the 190s. I fired very short bursts from about 300 yards, 15 degrees deflection, and observed many strikes on the canopy and fuselage. He immediately pulled up and rolled over and the pilot bailed out and the plane went straight in from 1500 feet. Captain Cutler, 486th Squadron saw this one take place.

"At this time, in this vicinity there were three chutes, one from the E/A that I had shot down, one from the E/A that Lt. O'Nan had shot down but I do not know where the 3rd came from.

"I then broke away from one shooting at me and got onto another 190's tail and gave short bursts but did not observe any hits. However, the pilot evidently spun out as he went straight into the ground from 800 feet or so and blew up.

"I was then joined by two P-47s but lost them and finally joined up with two of our own Group, Captain Cutler and his wingman. He started down over Brunswick to strafe a drome, but observing much ground fire and flak I pulled away and lost them. I then saw another plane which I thought to be a P-51. I closed on it to about 25 to 30 yards and identified it as a Me 109. I gave

a short burst but don't know if there were any strikes and found myself riding his wing as I was at full throttle. He was about 200 feet off the deck and when he looked at me he pulled up, jettisoned his canopy and bailed out. I then went down and took a picture of the plane which had crashed into a small woods, right on a small fire flame. . .

"I then started to climb back up when I was rejoined by my wingman, Lt. O'Nan, and Red Leader, Captain Davis. We started back up toward the bombers when off to our left at 9 o'clock low we observed about 20 to 25 Me 109s in close formation going down through the clouds. The three of us immediately turned in to attack and came down on them through the clouds. I found myself directly astern of a 190 with a 109 flying his wing in close formation. I evidently was unseen as I got in a very successful burst at the 109 and observed numerous hits on wings, fuselage and tail. He was about 800 to 900 feet and after catching fire went straight into the ground.

"I immediately kicked a little right rudder and got in another successful burst at the 190 and observed numerous hits on its left wing, engine and canopy. The 190 went into a tight right spiral and crashed into the deck from 1000 feet.

"At this point there were about 15 or more E/A in the vicinity and they started aggressive tactics and since I was alone and they were making head-on passes at me I had to take violent evasive action. I evaded in the clouds."

Capt. Robert S. Johnson was flying with the 56th A Group north of Brunswick when he sighted bombers under attack. As he took his flight in to cover, he noted

Lt. Carl J. Luksic of the 487th FS, 352nd FG was the first Eighth AF pilot to become an "ace in a day" when he scored five victories on May 8, 1944. USAAF

Capt. Robert S. Johnson, shown here with his last P-47 Penrod and Sam, *scored victories number 26 and 27 on May 8, 1944, to close out his combat career. USAAF*

an Me 109 diving away at three o'clock. Attempting to outdive the heavy Jug was a foolish tactic for the Luftwaffe pilots, but, strangely, they continued to try it. Johnson gained on the 109 steadily in the dive. He began to fire at 400 yards and the 109 attempted to evade by rolling, but it was futile. The fifty-caliber slugs took their toll: the wing broke off and the 109 exploded.

East of Hanover, Germany, Johnson's number three man called out two FW 190s diving at three o'clock, so Johnson told him to go after them. He then called a warning to the Thunderbolts not to go under the clouds, but it went unheeded. Then a P-47 appeared, coming out of the clouds with four FW 190s on his tail. Johnson told the pilot to climb and turn if he couldn't make the clouds. He did as instructed and Johnson and his wingman began to get in position to help him. Johnson was going in the opposite direction to the chase so was able to make head-on passes at them, getting rid of the last two and getting hits on the nose of the second one, which rolled over trailing a bit of smoke. Johnson attempted to get back to the P-47 which seemed to tire of staying in the turn with the 190. The ill-fated Thunderbolt pilot straightened out, took hits in the engine and was forced to bail out. The FW 190 that Johnson had hit in the head-on pass was seen to catch on fire and explode. These two victories marked numbers twenty-six and twenty-seven for the top-scoring ace.

Capt. Roy Spradlin of the 364th Fighter Group sacrificed himself for his wingman on withdrawal support. He and Lt. Adrian Parsley were protecting straggling Big Friends when they sighted several Me 109s. The two P-38s chased them down below the overcast but lost them. There they sighted a train which they proceeded to strafe, blowing up the locomotive. As they recovered, an Me 109 was sighted flying "fat and happy" at 1,000 feet. Spradlin hit him with two good bursts and sent him down in flames.

As the two Lightning pilots headed for home they spotted another duo of Me 109s breaking out of the overcast. As they pulled up, the P-38s went after them. Spradlin caught his victim and shot him down; Parsley made short work of the other 109. The P-38s were then attacked from behind by a 109. Spradlin told Parsley to get in the overcast, which he did. When he broke out he was all alone. Spradlin did not return from the mission.

During the next three days the Eighth Air Force turned its eyes to targets in occupied Europe, but on May 12 they focused their attention back to targets deep in Germany. Once more the Luftwaffe was up in force with most of the activity taking place during penetration.

This mission saw the initiation of the "Zemke Fan," whose performance consisted of the group flying to a designated point from which it dispersed in three fan-like formations, which covered a 180 degree area. While the three forces were equally portioned, an extra flight was maintained in the center. This made a central force available to any point on the arc where enemy opposition was met in force.

Zemke had moved out with two other P-47s to scout an area north of Frankfurt when they were bounced by seven Me 109s. These German pilots proved to be top-notch opponents as Lt. Col. Preston Piper and Lt. W. D. Johnson, who had accompanied Zemke, were both shot down. Zemke managed to escape by outspinning and outdiving the enemy. On the way out he was attacked by another flight of four Me 109s and only barely managed to escape again.

South of Koblenz, Germany, Zemke spotted four enemy aircraft circling at 15,000 feet. The Thunderbolt pilot was flying at 20,000 feet and his first thoughts were to bounce the Messerschmitts but as he watched, these four were joined by several other Me 109s and FW 190s until a force of thirty had accumulated. It seemed that this unit was assembling in force to strike the bombers, so Zemke began to climb to stay above them while he called for assistance over the radio. At the end of fifteen minutes he was flying at 29,000 feet where he was joined by Lts. Robert J. Rankin and Clem C. Thornton. Rankin had already downed two Me 109s in an earlier battle and was eager for more combat.

Zemke told Rankin and his wingman to cover him while he dived down to attack the formation of thirty E/A. He picked out an Me 109 that was on the outside of the formation and took a sixty- to ninety-degree deflection shot at him. The German aircraft flew through the pattern and an explosion was seen over the entire length of the fuselage. Zemke nearly rammed the 109, but succeeded in climbing over him. He looked back to see the 109 going into a spin, the engine bursting in flames and the pilot bailing out. At that moment Zemke got a call from Rankin to "break left, there's a 109 on your tail." Zemke then made a pass at four Me 109s, did a half roll and outran them.

May 12, 1944, saw the inaugural "Zemke Fan" mission by the 56th FG and also marked a five-victory classic combat mission by Lt. Robert J. ("Shorty") Rankin. USAAF

Rankin reported: "As Colonel Zemke pulled up from his attack I called him and said I was going down to attack. I got behind 2 Me 109s and fired on the one on the left, got good hits, greyish black smoke came back and landing gear came down. I moved over on the next one. I got many hits from dead astern and the E/A smoked badly and his landing gear also came down. I had both of these Me 109s in front of me going down in 50 degree angle smoking and landing gear down. I saw both E/A crash into the ground very close to each other and explode . . .

"I was coming around in a turn to the left about 15,000 feet with many E/A still circling below. I was getting into range of two in formation and one ahead slightly above when for no reason, all three pilots of these aircraft bailed out. All the chutes opened. I didn't fire, my wingman didn't fire, neither did Colonel Zemke. There were no other Allied fighters in this area at all. I couldn't figure this one out for all three Me 109s seemed to be in no trouble. I make no claim on these.

"I was still climbing to the left when I got on 2 more Me 109s. I got in a very tight circle with them and fired a short burst at each. I was unable to observe results as deflection blacked out the E/A. I claim these 2 Me 109s damaged. Just after this I got 1 Me 109 coming up from the box of E/A and climbing up underneath Col. Zemke. I called for him to break and turned to get on the Me 109's tail. I managed to turn with him, fired a short burst, got a few hits and this E/A started down with very little smoke coming back. One landing gear came down at about a 20 degree angle. I broke into two more Me 109s which were coming in on my wingman. As I turned I saw the pilot bail out of the E/A I had just fired on. We circled with the 2 Me 109s until my wingman had to break down and away. I kept circling with the 2 Me 109s while my wingman came up and fired at one of the E/A head-on. I saw hits with glycol and smoke pouring out. The pilot bailed out as the Me 109 started down. I confirmed this Me 109 for Lt. Cleon Thomton. We circled with the one remaining Me 109. I got on his tail, fired a short burst when my tracers came and I ran out of ammunition. I closed to 50 yards dead astern and could only take a nice picture."

All total the 56th Fighter Group accounted for eighteen German fighters that day. The 4th got ten in the air and the 352nd destroyed another ten.

The 357th Group accounted for fourteen German fighters in heavy fighting northeast of Frankfurt. The flight led by Capt. C. E. Anderson, Jr., was attacked by a flight of Me 109s, and they went around and around for about five minutes. Then two P-47s came in to join the fight but one of them fell to the guns of an Me 109. Anderson lined up on this E/A, but before he could fire the pilot bailed out. Capt. William ("Obie") O'Brien's flight was also engaged and O'Brien managed to down one of the 109s. The pilot successfully bailed out. O'Brien vividly described him as a "Pilot wearing blue flying suit and blond headed."

Col. Glenn Duncan, leading the 353rd Group, managed to down one Focke Wulf 190 but later met with a near-tragic encounter: "I saw 4 P-51s chasing something so flew over to investigate and took a left turn over them. I had just about found out that it was an Me 109 but too late. Another one came from behind me and laid in several nice close 20 mm, two in the right wing root knocking out the flap wheel, which burned out, and aileron, two in the right elevator and several in the fuselage and prop. These things give you a start for a while but you can usually bring a P-47 home. P.S.: This is no way to be used as an advertisement for the [P-47], though. Well, we got home to learn that two of the boys shot the Jerry so-and-so down. I claim one FW 190 because I saw him strike up and go down burning . . . Also claim one P-47 to be repaired."

The 78th Fighter Group, which hadn't had much opportunity to score of late, chipped in with another five. One of the 78th victories was scored by one of its more aggressive pilots, Capt. James Wilkinson. His encounter occurred just after his 82nd Fighter Squadron bounced some FW 190s which were attacking the bombers. He reported: "After the E/As made their pass they broke down and southward followed by all four flights of our squadron. In the ensuing dive I overtook one straggling 190. I fired three short bursts from 200 yards astern observing numerous hits around the cockpit and wing roots, after which he caught fire and went down out of control and dived to the deck. No parachute was observed. I continued to follow about 30 E/A southward to near Mannheim at full throttle but was unable to overtake them as my aircraft had been seriously damaged by the belly tank which hit my tailplane when I jettisoned it at the onset of the engagement. Inasmuch as I was unable to overtake the E/A I fired several bursts at extreme range in the hope that I could cause them to turn." Wilkinson's victory was his fifth.

The massacre of the Luftwaffe continued May 13 and pilots of the VIII FC claimed forty-seven of the fifty-eight aerial victories scored during the mission. The bulk of the action was seen by the 1st Task Force and it began just as the 356th FG was breaking off its escort near Kiel, Germany. The unit broke off as the 352nd FG arrived to take their place, and as they made their turn three gaggles of forty Focke Wulf 190s were seen lining up to attack the bomber stream. All three squadrons of the 356th quickly swung into action, downing nine of the FW 190s. One of the Focke Wulfs fell to Lt. Ray Withers of the 360th FS who also performed a heroic rescue during the encounter.

Withers, leading Blue Flight, saw his squadron leader turn to meet the German fighters and followed. By then forty Focke Wulfs had passed over the 360th FS, twenty of which turned and headed to cut off Blue Flight. Withers saw a 190 lock onto the tail of Lt. Charles Adams' P-47 and called for him to break. Too late though—the German opened fire and scored hits all over Adams' Thunderbolt destroying the instrument panel, gun sight, one stabilizer and wounding Adams. Withers hauled his P-47 into a wingover turn and went after the 190, opening fire at about 500 yards and observed hits on the wings and tail section. Flames then burst out under the stricken 190's fuselage and it went into an uncontrolled dive.

As Withers pulled his P–47 back up, he took shots at two other 190s and drove them off. This action broke up the enemy attack. Then he set about reassembling the flight and locating Adams who was last seen heading for the deck. Within a few minutes Adams radioed that he was in serious trouble and was going to jump. Withers called to him to hold on. Adams was soon spotted mushing along at a very low speed, and Withers slipped in beside him, throttled back and began escorting his crippled friend back to base. Because of Adams' inability to climb and the distinct possibility of his engine failing, the two could not head out over the North Sea, so the pilots were forced to fly over the entire Frisian Island chain where they were exposed to fire from German flak. Several times during the flight Adams radioed that he was going to have to jump, but each time Withers was able to reassure him. Finally Adams brought his crippled P–47 back to a safe belly-landing in England.

While this was going on, the 352nd FG was continuing the escort and they, too, ran into large numbers of enemy fighters. Numerous fights broke out in the vicinity of Neubrandenburg, Germany, that lasted for nearly half an hour. The 352nd pilots destroyed fifteen of the enemy fighters but lost one of its up and coming aces, Capt. Frank Cutler, when his plane collided head-on with a 109. At the time of his death, Cutler was credited with 7½ aerial kills and another three destroyed on the ground.

The 355th Fighter Group, with Lt. Col. Gerald J. Dix leading, attacked the Me 410s of II/ZG 26 as they queued up to attack the Fortresses of the 96th Bombardment Group. These Me 410s had been modified to carry a BK, 50 mm cannon in the nose. This weapon enabled the aircraft to lob heavy projectiles into the bomber formations while they were far out of range for the fifty-caliber guns of the Big Friends.

As Dix and his wingman, Lt. Morris, lined up on a pair of Me 410s, the E/A went into evasive action and two of them collided. The Messerschmitts disintegrated and fell to the ground in pieces. Dix and Morris chased two more Me 410s through a hole in the clouds. As they closed on the enemy craft one of them broke right. Dix called his element leader to take this 410 while he concentrated on the other. Dix then got good strikes on the 410 which he continued to follow down until he saw it crash to the ground. Altogether, the Mustangs of the 355th shot six of the Me 410s from the sky. The 357th Group caught another flight from II/ZG 26 and downed

Capt.– G. J. DIX
CREW CHIEF– S/SGT– J.A. ESTRADA

Lt. Col. Gerald J. Dix led the 355th FG in a combat against the Me 410s of II/ZG 26 that was so successful the Luftwaffe unit's combat potential was finished. 355th FG Assn.

Mustangs of the 354th FS, 355th FG in formation. With their conversion to P-51s in April 1944 the scoring of this unit took a big upswing. 355th FG Assn.

Capt. James Wilkinson of the 78th FG became a Thunderbolt ace when he downed a Focke Wulf 190 on May 19, 1944. H. B. Slater

three. This, coupled with the aircraft that were badly damaged in the combat, ended the operational participation of this group of Me 410s.

After an eleven-day pause in the attacks on Berlin and Brunswick, the Eighth Air Force resumed its assault on May 19. Berlin was the primary target of May 19, and 578 B-17s of the 1st and 3rd Bomb Divisions were designated for the attack while the 2nd Bomb Division sent 390 of its B-24s to strike at Brunswick. For its part in the effort, the VIII FC dispatched fourteen of its fighter groups to escort the bombers to and from the targets while IX FC furnished another five.

The Luftwaffe reacted in strength to the challenge and struck hard and continuously against the bomber formations. Pilots of VIII FC reported numerous encounters during the entire mission and they scored heavily against the German fighter forces. The final count showed that the escort had claimed seventy aerial kills and another seven on the ground.

The intensity of the enemy opposition on the mission is exemplified by the report made by Capt. James W. Wilkinson who was leading a flight from the 82nd Fighter Squadron of the 78th Fighter Group. With only three P-47s (one member of his flight had aborted), he attacked members of the first gaggle of enemy fighters from the rear. Before they completed their attack they were in turn attacked by a second force of enemy fighters. The Thunderbolts immediately turned into this force and their attack, coupled with the presence of more P–47s above caused this second wave of attackers to break up. By this time only Wilkinson and one other P–47 were left flying together. They positioned themselves on the lead box of bombers from whence they sighted a third gaggle of E/A climbing up to attack. Wilkinson dove to the attack once more and again they were successful in breaking it up. During this maneuver Wilkinson lost contact with the Thunderbolt flying his wing, so he was now alone. Wilkinson picked out a single Me 109, which he clobbered, and the pilot went over the side. Wilkinson headed for home.

The 357th Fighter Group, led by Maj. Irwin Dregne, met a gaggle of seventy-five-plus E/A headed for the bombers and thwarted their plan of attack. As they chased the single-engined fighters toward the deck, they sighted another flight of forty to fifty Me 109s and FW 190s on their way up. Dregne singled out an Me 109 and shot him down.

Lt. Robert W. Foy had downed one Me 109 when he was almost involved in a midair collision with a green-nosed P–51. Foy then sighted two Me 109s spiraling down so he split-essed and went down after them. While in his dive he sighted two other Me 109s coming down from ten o'clock high to make a head-on pass on

Lt. Robert Foy of the 357th FG got his scoring career off to a big start on May 19, 1944, with a triple. M. Olmsted

him. At this time the two 109s that he had been diving on sighted Foy and immediately broke to the left. This caused the lead ship of the duo to crash into the outside 109 of the two that were attempting the head-on pass. The wing of one 109 was sheared off while the 109 making the head-on pass lost his prop. Foy then went

B–24s of the 491st BG leave Achmer airfield burning. While very successful, the Liberators were not able to hold the tight *formations typical of the B–17s, which made them more susceptible to fighter attack. USAAF*

into a Lufbery to combat the remaining two 109s which wound up on his tail. Fortunately, Foy was saved by another Mustang which happened along in time to shoot one of the 109s off his tail. The other 109 split-essed and fled.

Lt. John H. Oliphint of the 359th Group helped break up a formation of Me 109s attacking the Big Friends and had chased one of the E/A getting good strikes on it all the way: "I caught him red handed from about 800 feet and started cutting his bottom out where it had previously been smoking and leaking. This set him on fire, so closed to about 300 feet where the bottom blew completely out as I chopped up and down the left side of the belly fuselage, cockpit and engine. The fire blew gas and oil all over me and pieces chipped my wings and tail. As I pulled out of the mess my prop sliced off the left stabilizer though doing little damage to me. I then found myself flying pretty close formation. The canopy of the Me 109 was splintered, the engine dead and on fire from nose to tail. The plane was all to pieces, the pilot flopping around dead in the fire that blazed in the cockpit. I expected it to blow up any time so I pulled away . . ."

For the 356th Fighter Group the mission was a real success for two reasons: its scoring and its experiment, which gave the Luftwaffe pilots who encountered Green Flight of the 360th Fighter Squadron something to think about—the Superbolt.

Up to this date the pilots of the 356th were facing some difficulty in countering attacks by German fighters, who seemed to always enjoy the altitude advantage. The German radar would pick up the approach-ing formations and the Luftwaffe could time their takeoff to climb to approximately 35,000 feet and posi-tion themselves for attack just as the bombers were arriving in the sector. The stream of B–24s normally operated about 25,000 feet and were vulnerable to the German attack. The escort fighters were also at the same disadvantage since they, too, flew at 25,000 feet or so. Only six days before, the 360th FS was hit from above and it nearly cost the life of Lt. Charles Adams. As a result of that attack, Green Flight leader, Lt. Ray-mond Withers, got permission from his commanding officer, Capt. John Vogt, to modify the P–47s in his flight to Superbolts.

The Superbolt was the brainchild of Vogt and Withers, and their idea, Withers related, was "basically to lighten the aircraft and improve its performance. To do so we removed 4 of the 8 machine guns and limited the remaining guns to 200 rounds each which reduced the plane's weight considerably. Then we removed the paint from the leading edge of the wings and tail sur-faces and waxed the remaining painted surfaces there-by adding another 6–8 mph to its top speed. The last change was to use a higher octane fuel which permitted higher manifold pressure and better supercharger per-formance. With these modifications the P–47s flew quite well at 35,000 feet."

The mission of May 19 was the Superbolts' debut. On this mission the 356th FG was escorting the B–24s to attack on Brunswick. In the vicinity of Hanover they encountered a gaggle of at least forty enemy aircraft. Twelve more Me 109s were above them at about 35,000

Lt. Ray Withers of the 356th FG came up with the original Superbolt. This aircraft was stripped of four .50 caliber guns and carried only 200 rounds of ammunition for the remaining four guns. Leading edges of the wings were highly waxed. R. R. Withers

feet. While the remainder of the squadron joined in the engagement at bomber level, Withers led his flight of Superbolts up to attack the high flight of Messerschmitts. His four planes charged into the German formation at 32,000 feet and scattered them. Withers relates the encounter, which earned him the Silver Star, as follows: "Green Flight climbed to 32,000 feet where we engaged 8–12 Me 109s making contrails and went into a climbing orbit with two of them. The front E/A broke and my second element followed it. I closed on the rear 910 very rapidly and fired at about 250 yards, observing strikes on the cockpit and canopy. Immediately on firing my plane did two snap rolls and spun. I recovered at 25,000 feet and climbed in a spiral to 31,000 feet, at which altitude the other three men in my flight were in a climbing orbit with a 109. I climbed into the orbit and closed to approximately 150 yards at 35,000 feet. I fired from almost dead astern and the E/A began to disintegrate and smoke badly. I flew through oil and the pieces from the E/A. The bottom of the fuselage was torn all open and a heavy gray smoke was pouring from it. The E/A went into a spin and Vortex Green 4 (Lt. Clifford Walters) followed the plane down to 5,000 feet. The E/A spun continuously to the left and right, and at 5,000 feet straightened out momentarily, then flipped over on its back and went into a vertical dive through the clouds. After this combat the flight headed for home at 28,000 feet and crossed out near Ijmuiden at 1410 hours. Green Flight was carrying only four guns and had no difficulty in outclimbing and outmaneuvering the enemy at this altitude. I claim one Me–109 destroyed and one Me–109 damaged."

The Superbolt had done its job quite effectively on this mission and demonstrated to the Luftwaffe pilots that superior altitude might not be their "trump card" any longer. However, as it turned out the Superbolts were used only on a few missions because the Germans realized that they could now be engaged at high altitude and began to change their tactics.

With the invasion of occupied Europe drawing ever closer, the Eighth Air Force decided to turn its attention to the German rail and transportation systems on May 21. These strafing missions were appropriately named Chattanooga, and each fighter group in VIII FC would strike the same areas they had been assigned for airfield strafing.

As the fighters from fourteen fighter groups, 552 in all, arrived over their respective areas in Germany they found targets everywhere. Like big birds of prey, the Thunderbolts, Lightnings and Mustangs swooped down and ripped apart targets all over the Reich. The German railway system paid a terrible price. Ninety-one of its locomotives were destroyed and another 134 were damaged by the fighters. In addition to the locomotives and rail cars, they shot up or bombed numerous bridges and trestles, stations, switching stations and so on along the tracks. Trucks and staff cars along the highways received the same treatment and many of them were left as smoking hulks along the roads. Even though the German transportation system had been the primary

target, the pilots also found and destroyed over 100 enemy aircraft on the ground. Twenty more German aircraft were shot out of the air. For the young 339th Fighter Group it was like a turkey shoot. They caught a formation of seventeen enemy planes and sent thirteen of them down in flames within a matter of minutes.

Nineteen-year-old Lt. Chris J. Hanseman of the 339th's 505th Squadron caught a Junkers Ju 88 flying on the deck between Leipzig and Dresden in Germany. He initially got in a deflection shot and closed astern. He and Lt. Reid both got strikes on the aircraft, set both engines on fire and sent it crashing into the ground. Hanseman then sighted three biplane trainers at 500 feet. Closing rapidly he opened fire on the rear aircraft and sent it down in flames. Immediately, he opened fire on the number two aircraft. This plane attempted to get away by sideslipping, but Hanseman sent it crashing too.

Maj. John H. Lowell of the new and latest P–38 unit to enter combat, the 364th Fighter Group, led a section of Lightnings of the 384th FS strafing German airfields at Parchim, Ludwigslust and Hagenow. Lowell managed to flame three Ju 52s and a Ju 88 on his strafing runs while other members of his section were successful in destroying another five enemy aircraft. Regretfully, one of the flight leaders, Maj. Andrew Chilton, was hit by flak and killed just after setting a Ju 88 on fire at Hagenow aerodrome.

Lt. Chris ("Bull") Hanseman of the 505th FS, 339th FG. This aggressive young pilot became the first teenage ace of the Eighth Air Force. J. Starnes

The 55th Fighter Group flying Lightnings led all others in the destruction of locomotives. Armed with a 20 mm cannon as well as fifty-caliber machine guns, the P-38 packed a powerful punch and on this day destroyed twenty-three locomotives and damaged fifteen. Right behind them was the yellow-nosed 361st FG, which had recently converted to Mustangs, with 23-0-5.

The 352nd FG also had a busy day and hit targets of all types. An excellent example was the mission flown by Lt. Robert Powell of the 328th FS. Flying his P-51B *The West By Gawd Virginian,* Powell destroyed two He 111s and damaged two more, shot up a freight train and damaged a factory. The most unusual claim of the day for the 352nd were the twenty-five cows strafed by Lt. Edmond Zellner of the 328th FS.

This attack marked the end of VIII Fighter Command's pre-invasion strafing missions. These missions, which began in February of 1944, had been extremely successful in clearing the way for the invasion of occupied Europe. During the period from February 20 through May 21 VIII FC pilots had destroyed over 1,500 enemy aircraft, nearly 1,000 locomotives and numerous other installations, factories and storage facilities. Now that aerial supremacy had been gained and the enemy's transportation system was seriously damaged, the only real decision for General Eisenhower and his planners was when to attack.

There was still plenty of interdiction work to be done before the invasion force set sail, however, and on May 22 four VIII FC groups mounted fighter-bomber attacks against bridges in Belgium. The 78th and 356th FGs skip-bombed bridges in Hasselt, Belgium, and the 56th FG dive-bombed a railroad bridge in Hasselt.

The 356th FG had a very aggressive Thunderbolt pilot in Lt. David Thwaites who became an ace in May 1944. D. Thwaites

Among those tangling with the Luftwaffe that day were the 56th Fighter Group which downed twelve E/A. Lt. Col. Francis S. Gabreski of the Group scored his twentieth, twenty-first and twenty-second victories on this mission. The Group once more utilized the new Zemke Fan tactics. As Gabreski led his section out on a vector that took them some twenty miles east of Bremen, Germany, two locomotives were seen puffing along through a hole in the clouds and Gabreski sent one flight down after them. While the other flights orbited, a well-camouflaged aerodrome was sighted. Some sixteen FW 190s took off from the field, so Gabreski took his charges down from 20,000 feet to engage.

The fight took place at about 3,000 feet. Gabreski took his flight in astern of eight FW 190s and observed his first victim burst in flames as it took a telling burst from his .50s. He immediately slid behind a second 190, hit the gun tit and observed smoke streaming from the E/A. The canopy flew off and the German pilot went over the side.

At this moment Gabreski was attacked by two FW 190s. He made a couple of orbits with the 190s before he was able to break away and outclimb the enemy craft. Gabreski then assembled another six members of his squadron and as they completed forming up they sighted twenty-plus FW 190s headed across the aerodrome below. The flak batteries began to throw up a barrage at their own aircraft until one of the 190s fired a green recognition flare and the flak abruptly ceased. This was the signal for the Thunderbolts to go down and attack.

The six P-47s dived down and caught the 190s from the rear, and Gabreski immediately sent one of them crashing to earth. As he attempted to line up on a second 190, Gabreski noted another Focke Wulf off his left wing sliding back to get on his tail. Gabreski cut throttle, drew back on the stick and nearly stalled out. But his gamble paid off, the 190 overran and Gabreski slid in on its tail. The German pilot went into a tight turn and formed up with another five 190s out in front. Gabreski made about three turns with the E/A, but then broke up in a steep climbing turn. He was then attacked from above by another 190, but Gabreski just kept climbing and turning and managed to join up with some friendly fighters at about 10,000 feet.

Gabreski spotted another lone 190 on the way home, dived down, made a stern attack, scored a few hits and the enemy craft rolled off streaming smoke, but Gabreski didn't have the ammo or fuel to pursue. He accepted claiming a probable, climbed back up and continued the route homeward.

The Eighth Air Force launched a massive attack against marshaling yards and airfields in France on May 23. A total of 1,045 bombers escorted by 562 fighters dumped 2,283 tons of bombs on these targets. No planes were lost to enemy action which was a real tribute to the manner in which the fighters had driven the Luftwaffe deep into its own territory.

On May 24 the Eighth Air Force sent attack forces to occupied France and to Germany. The target in Germany was Berlin, and the German controllers sent

Eighth AF fighters went after enemy transportation in a big way before D–Day. Here, a train gets a good "hosing down." USAAF

up over 200 fighters to intercept the American force. A number of bombers were lost due to bad weather. Clouds were stacked up and so separated some formations from their escort. The 4th FG providing penetration support engaged forty enemy aircraft in the Hamburg-Lubeck area and after a series of dogfights, sent eight of the enemy fighters down in flames. Two of the victories went to the 334th FS's flamboyant ace Lt. Ralph ("Kid") Hofer. These were the thirteenth and fourteenth victories for the former Golden Gloves champ. Hofer had scored his first kill on his first mission and had taken a steady toll of the Luftwaffe ever since. A bit of a rebel, he often wore his number 78 football jersey into action and had a real penchant for getting into trouble. Nevertheless, he was one of the more proficient pilots in the group and had the score to prove it.

By the time the 3rd Task Force entered the area, the Luftwaffe was still trying to do battle with the American air fleet. The 352nd FG and the 339th FG, which were flying penetration support for this task

Lt. Ralph ("Kid") Hofer, a young, flamboyant ace of the 4th FG. His Mustang Salem Representative *and his football jersey became well known in fighter circles.* K. Rust

force, also got their chance to battle the Luftwaffe and claimed another twelve victories between them.

Maj. Donald Larson led the 339th Fighter Group against the sixty to seventy bogies that they encountered over Berlin. Larson downed three single-engined fighters and damaged another in the combat. In the melee, Larson wound up separated from his flight and crossed the whole city of Berlin all alone while flak and 20 mm seemed to burst all around him.

Lt. Harold Everett of the 339th's 505th Fighter Squadron was not so lucky. Everett and his flight went after the formation of German fighters and he sent one of the E/A down in flames in short order. With his attention fully on his target, he did not see the FW 190 sneaking up behind him until he began taking 20 mm hits, which exploded his left fuel tank and blew off the

Capt. Jack Ilfrey of the 20th FG with his P-38 Happy Jack's Go Buggy. *Ilfrey had been a Lightning ace in North Africa and came to the Eighth AF to command the 79th FS.* J. Ilfrey

entire upper surface of the wing and most of the left aileron. Another shell took out his radio, and hit his armor plate with such force that it broke his shoulder.

Flying for his life, Everett threw his plane into violent twists and turns in a futile attempt to break away from the Focke Wulf. Suddenly he found himself in a massive Lufbery with a gaggle of FW 190s. One of the 190s crossed his sights and he raked it from stem to stern, setting it on fire. The pilot bailed out. By now the Mustang pilot had taken more 20 mm hits in his engine, and it began to burn. Everett released his canopy and bailed out as the P-51 entered a spin. The war for Everett was over. He spent the balance of the conflict as a German POW.

Capt. Jack M. Ilfrey barely missed going down that day. He was leading a flight of P-38s with the 79th Squadron of the 20th Fighter Group when they tangled with thirty or more Me 109s in the vicinity of Eberswalde, just outside Berlin. The enemy was engaged, and a large Lufbery began with Ilfrey pulling a tight right turn to keep the Me 109 on his tail from getting a shot at him. As he tightened his turn he was able to get a good burst in on an Me 109—sending it down in flames.

After hitting the Me 109 he reversed, pulling into a tight left turn. He completed a 360 and straightened out to see an Me 109 at one o'clock coming in almost head-on. The 109 crashed into Ilfrey's right wing and tore up the outer three or four feet. Ilfrey went into a spin but managed to recover and climb back up to the bomber stream. Limping along, the Lightning pilot managed to make it back to base long after his squadron mates had returned and reported him as missing.

The four victories scored by the 352nd FG took place over Perleburg-Berlin. Shortly thereafter they dove to the earth and turned their guns on ground targets and destroyed eighteen locomotives. The ground strafing was costly with two pilots lost to flak, including Lt. Carl Luksic of "five in a day" fame.

By mission's end the fighters had claimed a total of 33-7-6 victories against ten losses.

May 26 marked the first operational mission by the VIII FC's newest group, the 479th. The group was based at Wattisham and was flying P-38s. On this date Maj. John Lowell, on loan from the 364th FG, led the new group of thirty-four P-38s on a sweep over Holland and Belgium. They didn't get to fire their guns but did learn what it was like to be shot at when the flak batteries opened up on them.

Primary targets for the bombers on May 27 were marshaling yards and industrial targets on the French-German border as destruction of lines of transport was continued in preparation for D-Day. The only fighter groups that encountered intense enemy opposition were the 352nd and 357th who met fierce and experienced single-engined fighters in the Strasbourg, France, area. The 352nd downed thirteen fighters for no loss and the 357th accounted for twenty Luftwaffe opponents but lost four P-51s. The balance of the escort made strafing runs on German rolling stock; specifically locomotives on the way home. The 55th Group perforated twenty locomotives.

Lt. Glennon T. Moran of the 352nd had already downed one Me 109 when he encountered an old pro who was climbing up to engage the bombers: "He saw me at about the same time and we turned into each other. We fought for about 20 minutes and it was necessary for me to put down combat flaps three times in order to turn with him. At about 15,000 feet I hit him with a short burst and he started smoking. However, he continued to turn and dive and climb. He led me down to the deck and between some hills. As he came to a fairly clear spot over a small village I was able to hit him again. My deflection was 10 degrees, my range 250 yards. He started to burn and as I pulled up over he exploded and crashed in the village."

Capt. Clarence E. Anderson of the 357th FG got his second victim of the day by dogged determination: "I singled out No. 2, he dove and pulled up in a left climbing turn. I pulled inside and overshot—he straightened out and I pulled up to 100 miles per hour watching him as he tried to get on my No. 2's tail; he stalled and I went after him—he repeated with another left climbing turn. I overshot again and the same thing followed and the third time I made up my mind I wouldn't lose him—so as he pulled up for the third time I fired. I was in prop wash going almost straight up in a left climbing turn. The first tracers went over his right wing. I skidded my nose over and strikes appeared all over—an explosion occurred—I slid alongside and fire was breaking out. It rolled over and went straight in."

When the bombers struck at the oil refineries and aircraft factories in central Germany on May 28, they were attacked by over 400 single- and twin-engined fighters over the Magdeburg area. Part of the German force kept the escort fighters well occupied and the balance hit two combat wings of B-17s and downed seventeen of them. The attackers did not go unpunished, however. The 4th and 352nd FGs each downed 7½ enemy fighters over Magdeburg and the IX FC's 363rd FG claimed another fourteen. When the day was over, fighters of the VIII and IX Fighter Commands had downed sixty enemy fighters in aerial combat at a cost of twelve of their own.

The 78th FG lost its top-ranking ace, Capt. Alwin Juchheim, when his P-47 collided head-on with a Mustang over Magdeburg. At the time, Juchheim had eleven aerial victories and 4½ ground victories to his credit. The Mustang pilot was killed but Juchheim survived the impact and parachuted to captivity. Years later he commented on the incident by saying, "By all rights I should have been a dead man, too—surely someone was watching over me that day."

On May 29 the bombers once more went after the vital German oil targets, this time flying deep into the Fatherland to strike synthetic oil refineries at Politz. Fighter opposition was heavy and determined. The green-nosed P-51s of the 359th Fighter Group met a force of forty to fifty Focke Wulf 190s in the vicinity of

Malchin, Germany, and later they broke up heavy attacks on the Liberators in the Stettin area.

Lt. Ray Wetmore downed one FW 190 and then received a call to break as he was attacking another enemy aircraft—a 190 was on his tail. Wetmore glanced back and noted that the 190 was still some distance out so he continued to close on his target but got no strikes. He then broke left and entered a fight with the 190 that was attacking him. The two fought all the way down to the deck with neither pilot being able to get in a shot at the other. Wetmore then scored with a forty-degree deflection shot and saw the canopy come off the Focke Wulf as the pilot dropped his gear to attempt a landing. Wetmore gave the 190 another burst as the pilot rolled over and bailed out. His chute opened and he landed in the middle of an aerodrome below.

The P-51s of the 361st Fighter Group also had a very good day. They broke up several attacks of both single- and twin-engined fighters which resulted in the destruction of twelve E/A in the air. On the way home another seven were destroyed on the ground at Neuhausen aerodrome.

Maj. Ralph J. White had led the 401st Bombardment Group which bombed the Focke Wulf assembly plant at Sorau, southeast of Berlin, and they had rallied off the target and were heading for home. White reported: "At 1329 hours, in the vicinity of Woldenberg, Germany, four Me 410s appeared, flying parallel to our formation and in the same direction, at a speed I estimate at 200 MPH. They were approximately 1,500 yards away, flying echelon to the left, and were looking us over. We had been watching them come up and at first I had thought they were B-17s because of their perfect formation. At that particular time, there were no friendly escorting fighters around and I expected them to start lobbing rockets into our Group formation.

"Approximately 20 seconds before the Me 410s were parallel to us, I observed a single P-51 Mustang fighter [Lt. Dale F. Spencer of the 361st Group's 376th Fighter Squadron] coming up on the Me 410s from slightly below and to their rear. He seemed to be throttled back and was not observed by the Me 410s who were intent upon our formation. When the P-51 was still slightly below the 410s and within 100 to 150 yards behind them, he started firing. I could see the bullets hit the planes.

"The rear Me 410 burst immediately into flames and one chute came out. The other three started a diving turn to the right. They had turned scarcely as much as ten degrees before the P-51 got the second one, which burst into flames and one chute came out.

"By this time the other two were diving very steeply, still in echelon. They had lost about 3,000 feet when the third 410 was hit and my ball turret gunner reported on interphone that the third chute came out.

"The P-51 by then was right after the remaining 410 and got him on what seemed to me to be a deflection shot. I could see the bullets striking his wing. He crashed by a lake, no opportunity to bail out."

Eighth Air Force heavies attacked a large variety of German targets on May 30, including aircraft factories at Dessau, Halberstadt and Oschersleben, marshaling yards in France and Belgium and an oil refinery at Mersberg. The 352nd Group fought seventy-five to 100 enemy fighters in the vicinity of Magdeburg and claimed 13½ destroyed. Their up-and-coming ace, Maj. George E. Preddy, downed two Me 109s and shared another with his wingman, Lt. Bill Whisner.

The big scorers for the day were the Mustangs of the 357th Fighter Group which got eleven single-engined fighters and seven twin-engined fighters in a dogged air battle that went from 30,000 to the deck in the Magdeburg-Bernburg area. Capt. William R. ("Obie") O'Brien was leading Cement White Flight of the 363rd Squadron when nine contrails were sighted coming down: "They went down under us in a string and we split-essed down on their tails. I got #9 man in the string by a damn lucky deflection shot. I pulled my nose past him till I couldn't see him and cut loose. At this point the surprise was mutual, as he came out from under my nose trailing glycol and black smoke . . ." O'Brien then latched onto number eight man, chased him down to the deck: "I throttled back, got slowed up behind him at 450 to 500 yards, held a deflection and shot his fuselage all to hell. Held same deflection and got nose hits . . . canopy came off. I pulled up, rolled over on my back and watched him go straight in."

Capt. Clarence E. Anderson of the 357th FG became an ace in May 1944 and went on to become a top scorer with 16½ aerial victories. USAAF

Unfortunately, the 357th Group lost their ace, Capt. Fletcher Adams, that day. His flight was homeward bound and in the vicinity of Celle, Germany, trying to catch up to the bombers when they were hit by four Me 109s out of the sun. Lt. Gilbert O'Brien stated: "I was first aware of them when I saw tracers and felt strikes on my ship. Broke straight down immediately and called for the rest of the flight to break. As I broke, I looked up and saw Captain Adams' ship start to trail white smoke. I then pulled up and made a tight 360 degree turn to the left to clear my tail. I chandelled back up and saw a 109 firing at Lt. Norris' tail." O'Brien fired a burst past the nose of the 109 which caused him to break combat with Norris. O'Brien then chased the 109 to the deck where he sent it down in flames.

Norris also downed one of the Me 109s in the combat, and Lt. Arval J. Roberson managed to down the other two. Although they accounted for all four 109s that came out of the sun, Captain Adams apparently had been killed in the initial attack.

The highlight for the last day of May for the fighter pilots was the dive-bombing of Gutersloh aerodrome by the 56th and 353rd Fighter Groups. Col. Hubert ("Hub") Zemke flew as leader of the high cover for the groups that did the dive-bombing. Lt. Col. Gabreski's P-47s had completed their bombing, and the 353rd under the leadership of Col. Glenn Duncan were making their bomb runs when Gabreski called Zemke and told him of the approach of a gaggle of fighters from the southeast. Zemke told Gabreski not to call him (the high cover) the enemy, but Gabreski replied, "There are a lot more than twelve of them."

Zemke took his Thunderbolts to investigate and identified them as FW 190s. Zemke sent one flight of P-47s down to make a pass while he called the 353rd and told them to scatter. Zemke and his flight now followed a formation of twenty FW 190s that were out of range, and they pressed on to close the gap. The 190s skirted a couple of German airfields to avoid flak, but finally, as the P-47s continued to gain on them, they arrived over Gutersloh aerodrome. Zemke called Gabreski and Duncan for reinforcements, but Gabreski's flight were low on fuel and Duncan apparently never got the message.

Now aware that there would be no reinforcements, Zemke took his flight down on a fast and furious pass on the formation of FW 190s. To quote Zemke: "It is interesting to note that this combat consisted of but one pass at terrific speed by four aircraft. It was enough to cause twenty enemy to split and run like a flock of chickens hit by a car. All my ammunition was shot in one pass of less than two minutes, which is inconsistent with the life of gun barrels but everyone in two fighter groups returned home from a dangerously low mission." Zemke broke out of the fight, having downed two of the FW 190s and damaging a third.

Chapter 10

Overlord Air Supremacy

By June 1, 1944, the path to invasion had been cleared by the combined air forces of the United States and Great Britain. While General Eisenhower wrestled with his final decision—the date of D-Day—the Allied Air Forces were concentrating on targets along the coastline of Europe. Their last preinvasion task was to isolate the battlefield. During the first few days of June the Hawker Typhoons of the 2nd Tactical Air Force and the Ninth Air Force's medium bombers demolished the German radar systems along the coast, and seriously hindered Field Marshal Rommel's ability to detect an approaching invasion fleet. While the tactical bombers struck at the German radar system, the heavy bombers were attacking German installations in the Pas de Calais area. For three days bombs rained down on these positions and the thundering explosions could be heard as far away as London. Smoke and debris drifted across the Channel to Folkstone, England.

While these operations were being carried out, the P–38 groups of the VIII and IX Fighter Commands were busily preparing their Lightnings for the invasion. During the evening of June 4 these units were issued cans of black and white paint and ordered to paint their aircraft with the now-famous zebra stripes around the wings and fuselage. The P–38s were the first Allied aircraft to be adorned with the "Invasion Stripes" because they had been chosen to fly top cover for the invasion fleet during its trip across the Channel. The Lightning had been picked for this job because the invasion planners felt that its silhouette was so distinctive that shipboard gunners were less likely to mistake it for enemy aircraft.

During the final preinvasion hours the Allied Air Forces devoted their attention to targets in the actual invasion area. Throughout the night and early morning of June 5 and 6, Allied bombers rained over 9,200 tons of bombs down on the fortifications along the coast of Normandy.

Earlier in the afternoon of June 5 the invasion fleet began its historic voyage across the Channel under its protective umbrella of P–38s. The 77th and 79th Fighter Squadrons of the 20th Fighter Group were given the honor of flying the first mission. These two squadrons led by Lt. Col. Herbert Johnson and Maj. Delynn ("Andy") Anderson respectively, took off at 1651 hours and made rendezvous with the fleet at 1726 hours. For the next hour and a half they patroled above the mass of ships and then were relieved by the next two squadrons. This aerial umbrella continued in relay fashion for the next twenty-four hours.

Meanwhile, the Thunderbolts and Mustang groups of the Eighth and Ninth Air Forces were working feverishly to prepare for their D-Day assignments as they, too, were painting on invasion stripes. The task of these single-engined fighter groups was designated as follows: The Ninth Air Force's fighters were to fly high cover over the beaches while the RAF fighter-bombers acted as close support. The VIII Fighter Command had the responsibility of protecting both the bombers attacking targets in the invasion area and the troop carriers carrying the airborne assault force. In order to keep enemy planes away from these formations, the VIII FC assigned nine of its groups to patrol areas to the east and west of the beachhead. Two other groups, the 4th and 355th, were assigned to cover areas to the north and northeast of the invasion front.

The single-engined fighters began taking to the air at 0300 hours on June 6—D-Day. Taking off in the predawn darkness and forming up was a new experience for most of the fighter pilots and all did not go

Mustangs of the 376th FS, 361st FG prepare for a D-Day mission sporting their new invasion stripes. USAAF

The P-38 Lightnings were assigned landing beach cover on D-Day by virtue of their unique silhouette. USAAF

Lt. Russ Westfall's P-47 of the 56th FG ready for D-Day with invasion stripes and drop tank. USAAF

well. VIII Fighter Command's first D-Day loss came at Bodney, the home of the 352nd Fighter Group. Lt. Robert Frascotti of the 486th FS took off on an incorrect heading and smashed into Bodney's new control tower and was killed instantly.

The 4th FG took off from Debden without incident and flew to their assigned patrol area near Rouen, France, only to find that a very heavy cloud cover prevented them from pinpointing any targets. Changing winds along with the clouds drifted the Group to an area east of Paris. They finally started back across the Channel from various points near Calais. Only one pilot, Lt. Ralph Hofer, found anything to shoot at and his targets were two locomotives. The Group lost one pilot, Lt. Thomas Fraser, who disappeared shortly after they entered the cloud formation over Rouen.

The early morning mission flown by the 4th FG was fairly typical of the early missions of D-Day. The Luftwaffe was just not there, and the absence of the German air force was most welcome to the assault forces attacking the Normandy beaches.

Lt. Shelton Monroe of the 4th did manage to down an FW 190 around noon with some assistance from the flak batteries at the airfield near Evreux, France. After shooting up a troop train he and his flight sighted three FW 190s at 6,000 feet and gave chase. They then sighted another seven flying down at 1,000 feet, headed for the aerodrome. They chose to bounce the seven, but this led them into a flak barrage over the aerodrome. As Monroe was getting into position on the tail of a 190 it was hit by flak in the cockpit area, causing the pilot to pull to the right. Monroe then got in a good burst and the 190 continued to dive into the ground.

Lt. Col. Gerald Dix was leading the 355th Group when bandits were reported north of Chartres, France. Upon investigation, a flight of ten Ju 87 Stuka dive-bombers were sighted. When the German bomber pilots spotted the Mustangs they panicked and attempt-

Maj. Howard ("Deacon") Hively and his Mustang were one of the few to encounter enemy aircraft on D-Day. His 334th FS P-51s downed four FW 190s over Evreux airfield. AF Museum

ed to crash-land in the closest available spots. Dix dove down and set one on fire that had just landed. As he pulled up he sighted two more bombers and managed to put a burst into one of them before he overshot. The Mustangs destroyed eight of the Stukas before breaking combat.

The 357th Squadron encountered another formation of Stukas about the same time and shot down

This P-47 from the 350th FS, 353rd FG with shiny invasion stripes reflecting over the English Channel. USAAF

another seven. Lt. Wayne James got on the tail of one, dumped thirty degrees of flap to slow down enough to get a thirty-degree deflection shot. He got hits immediately and the German pilot bailed out about 300 feet. James then chased another formation of four Ju 87s and managed to damage two before he latched onto the number three aircraft in the formation. He scored two good strikes on this one and the pilot set the aircraft down in a pasture and immediately scrambled for cover. James made another pass at the Stuka and set it on fire.

Lts. Peter McMahon and William Mudge of the 339th Group's 505th Squadron happened along during the Stuka massacre and managed to get in their own licks. McMahon successfully downed two of the Ju 87s and Mudge downed a third.

In an unusual sighting late on the afternoon of D–Day, Capt. William Maguire of the 353rd Fighter Group sighted a balloon in the vicinity of St. Helier, an island northwest of Granville, France, at an altitude of 16,000 feet. This he immediately dispatched. On his way home he sighted a train. Four passes by him and his flight exploded ammunition in the cars and completely destroyed the entire train.

On its second mission of the day the 4th FG also encountered enemy action. The 334th FS led by Maj. Howard ("Deacon") Hively headed back across the Channel to the Rouen area to take another look for targets in their assigned area. Near Evreux, the Mustangs caught a German troop train and damaged it heavily in a bombing and strafing attack. Moments after leaving the train the 334th caught a formation of ten FW 190s preparing to land at Evreux aerodrome, and shot four of them down. In the air battle Lieutenant Siems' P–51 was damaged by 20 mm fire, but he made it safely back to England.

The 4th's good luck ran out for the day. Two of the 336th FS's pilots were lost to flak on a fighter sweep to

Thunderbolt of the 83rd FS, 78th FG being made ready for a mission. Close examination shows the wobbly invasion stripes painted in great haste. J. Ethell

the Rouen area during the late afternoon. The evening mission suffered the most. On this mission, which was led by Colonel Blakeslee, seven pilots were lost. The tragedy began at 1840 hours when Blue Flight of the 335th was attacking a truck convoy. Intent on their ground targets, the flight never saw the fifteen enemy fighters boring in on them. Within a few seconds all four pilots of Blue Flight were dead. Two hours later the same fate was in store for three pilots of the 334th. Shortly after Maj. Winslow Sobanski asked his wingman Lt. Ed Steppe to check his plane for any damage caused by the wires he had hit, the two pilots were ambushed and killed by enemy fighters. The last loss of the day was Maj. Michael McPharlin. McPharlin had been a member of the Eagle Squadron and an early member of the 4th before being transferred to the 339th FG. Because of that, he wanted to fly the long-awaited D–Day mission with his friends in the 334th. His loss is a mystery. He was heard by the controller telling Major Sobanski that his engine was acting up and that he was turning back. He was never heard from again.

By day's end VIII Fighter Command had flown 1,873 sorties and had claimed twenty-six enemy fighters, but at a cost of twenty-six of their own. Other VIII FC groups that scored against the Luftwaffe on June 6 were the 56th, 78th and 352nd.

On June 7 the VIII Fighter Command continued its format of patrols and fighter-bomber missions over the Continent. Enemy opposition was again light, but several engagements did occur. The 56th and 353rd FGs ran into the heaviest opposition and between the two of them claimed twenty-three enemy fighters. Fighter losses for the day were twenty-two, with the 355th FG losing five.

The 78th FG was able to bring down three more enemy fighters in a dogfight near Montdidier, France. The group was engaged in dive- and glide-bombing targets in a marshaling yard when the fight broke out. Red Flight of the 84th FS had just hit a railroad siding when Capt. Ben Mayo noticed the 84th's Yellow Flight and White Flight were being attacked by a swarm of Me 109s. Mayo described the encounter: "About this time Shampoo White and Yellow Flights were having a big scrap with a bunch of Me 109s in the area, so I headed northeast looking for them. I had been flying for about five minutes when I saw a Me–109 about nine o'clock on me, flying in the opposite direction. I made a sharp 180 degree turn and got on his tail, although I was way out of range. He obligingly made a 90 degree climbing turn to the right and I cut him off, using water injection and closing to about 800 yards. I started firing short bursts as I had only about 75 rounds left in four guns. He hit the deck and I was steadily closing when he decided to climb up into the clouds. He started a climbing turn to the left and I held the trigger down, figuring it was now or never. Just as he reached the cloud base, I saw his canopy fly off and pieces fly off his right wing. He started to spin to the right and continued same until he hit the ground, at which point he blew up. My wingman, who had been behind me throughout this rat race, now pulled up alongside and informed me that I still had my right wing bomb! I dropped it in the Channel on the way home. I claim one Me-109 destroyed."

Lt. Sam Wilkerson of the 361st Group was an early scorer that morning. His flight had just pulled up from shooting up a train in the vicinity of Vendone when he sighted a big Heinkel He 177. Return fire from the German aircraft forced Wilkerson to take evasive action, but he managed to put telling shots into the bomber which crashed into a forest at Marchenoir.

Col. Hubert Zemke's 56th Group formation had been scattered when they were bounced from above by fifteen German fighters. Zemke got fleeting bursts at two of them but with no result. He sighted two unidentified over Dreux, France, but on the bounce he found that they were two of his own. He ordered them to join up but apparently the order was misunderstood or they were low on fuel, for they headed for home.

"South of Paris, the four FW's did a right turn to head west enabling me to cut off considerable distance," reported Zemke, "my altitude being about 27,000 feet, theirs being approximately 20,000 feet."

Zemke continued: "Again somewhere over Chartres, France, they conveniently did a 180 degree turn and headed east. This last turn put me almost directly over them and the attack was started. All flew in a company front as we do. As I drew to a point 2,000 yards in the rear of the four, the leader did a 45 degree turn to the southeast and everyone began to cross over. I picked out the last FW 190 and opened up on a 20 degree deflection shot, hitting him squarely after about 50 rounds. He went off spinning in flame, straight for the earth.

"The remaining three completed the turn and flew a three plane company front. The element leader was picked out next with me flying about 300–400 yards in the rear. I opened up on him from directly astern flying straight and level. It is definitely recalled that he rocked his wings and I would rock my wings in return. He probably thought I was his wingman, who I had just shot down in the cross over turn and was saying over the R/T 'Hans, you bastard, move up in line abreast and stop flying in back of me.' At any rate, I fired and fired at this pilot to finally tag him with a decent concentration and he nosed over to go straight down.

"This left two FW's still flying line abreast and unconcerned, so I slid over in back of the Flight Leader and opened fire. My tracers showed just as I hit him and the jinx was up for he immediately began kicking rudder to roll back over on his back and I swung over on the last man to shoot at him as he went down. No hits were seen but I claim a damaged on the Flight Leader. Both were seen running like mad in a steep dive so I climbed and came screaming home."

Meanwhile, Col. Glenn Duncan was leading the 353rd Fighter Group dive-bombing railroad installations and other communications targets. In the Compiegne, France, area, Capt. Gordon Compton tacked onto the tail of an Me 109 that had attacked Lt. Biddy, one of his flight members. The 109 dove for the deck with Compton and Duncan in hot pursuit. They both put in good bursts and the 109 bellied into a cleared field.

Duncan reported: "The jackpot came when we were forming up to set course and I looked over and saw a Ju 52 lumbering along the top of the trees. It was just getting dark under the clouds so it made a pretty setting for the coming scene. The JU was going so slow that I pulled down flaps to turn in behind him. It worked well except that I forgot to release them and fly level. When I pulled up and was in position for a sure kill on the first squirt, the strikes were all 200 yards behind. I pulled one ring lead—still the strikes in the trees were 50 yards behind. Boy, my head was up—the flaps were causing me to fly nose down. Well, I said, to hell with that, so I squeezed the trigger and pulled the nose up until strikes came into the Ju 52. He went down quick then. Such a beautiful sight—flames and blood all over the place. He ruined a nice section of woods when he crashed. I am hoping that he had a lot of infantry square heads on board going to see the invasion."

The Luftwaffe put up over 100 fighters on June 8, and numerous battles took place. Of the thirty-one victories claimed by VIII FC pilots, the young and eager 339th FG took top honors with eleven. The 56th Group came in second with seven. Unfortunately, for the third day in a row VIII FC suffered high losses. Twenty-two of its planes were lost over France.

Lt. Archie Tower and his wingman, Lt. Opitz, of the 505th Fighter Squadron had become separated from their squadron during a dive-bombing mission. In the early morning darkness they dropped down to 1,000 feet and noted four lights blinking on an airfield below. As they started for the airfield they sighted a squadron of FW 190s just above them. As the first 190 peeled off, Tower hit him good with a sixty-degree deflection shot. Opitz saw the craft crash.

Maj. Archie Tower, a highly successful ground strafing pilot of the 339th FG. J. Starnes

The two pilots then hit the deck to escape the heavy flak coming up from the airfield, but Tower then sighted a Dornier 217 flying ninety degrees from them on the deck. Tower gave him a long burst from 300 yards that flamed its left engine. Opitz then put a burst into the craft that sent it crashing into a hillside.

Lt. Billy G. Edens of the 56th Fighter Group was on his way home when he sighted two Me 109s taking off from an aerodrome at St. Andre de L'Eure. Blue Leader, Lt. Mark Moseley took the flight down to attack. Moseley lined up on one E/A, hit it good and the pilot bailed out. Moseley then pulled up on the element leader and downed him too.

During this time other enemy craft had been taking off and an Me 109 was closing in on Moseley. Edens maneuvered in on the 109's tail, opened fire at 500 yards and closed to 100. The 109 went into a dive, burst into flames and exploded. Now a second 109 went after Moseley and once more Edens came to the rescue. This time Edens didn't open fire until he had closed to 100 yards. The German craft broke sharply to the left, spun in and exploded. An FW 190 crossed in front of Edens in a climbing turn at about 300–400 yards' distance. Edens gave him a deflection shot. Although Edens did not see strikes, the Focke Wulf seemed to hang in the air for a moment and then fell off on its left wing, crashing and exploding.

The days following D-Day climaxed the combat career of 352nd FG ace, Lt. John Thornell. His final victories ran his score to 17½ in the air and two on the ground. USAAF, H. J. Whitely

On the morning of the tenth the 368th Fighter Squadron of the 359th Group was briefed for a most unusual mission. They were to provide escort for four photo reconnaisance P–38s to the Antwerp, Belgium, area. It was the job of the 368th pilots to keep E/A in the area from intercepting the mission while the recce boys got right down on the deck and braved the flak. Capt. Wayne N. Bolefahr led the squadron in over the Scheldt where the four P–38s came under a staggering barrage: automatic weapons emplacements and heavy guns all along the winding coasts and rail lines greeted the American flyers with a wall of lead. Captain Bolefahr decided it was time for him to get involved. Dropping down into the flak he proceeded to machine gun every emplacement and at the same time drew the flak away from the recon aircraft. Four miles north of Antwerp, Bolefahr's aircraft took a staggering amount of hits and went in from 100 feet. His sacrifice paid off; the P–38s made it back home with the desperately needed photos.

Since the invasion, the Luftwaffe had been forced to move reinforcements to the area and more intense opposition began to be encountered by the Allied fighters. The 78th Fighter Group felt the brunt of the increased activity, losing five of their number on the tenth. Their P–47s were caught in the middle of a dive-bombing attack by a mixed flight of FW 190s and Me 109s. Later in the day four more of the Group's planes went down from enemy action and two others were lost in a midair collision. The 78th did gain a partial revenge for their losses by downing nine of the enemy's fighters. High scorers for the day were Lts. Don McLeod of the 83rd FS and Luther Abel of the 84th FS who downed two each.

By now, many of the P–38 pilots were getting bored by flying the protective umbrella over the invasion fleet and wanted to get a crack at the Germans, too. Col. Harold Rau of the 20th FG decided to end his Group's boredom by leading them on a little ground strafing. Leading the Group's 55th FS Rau headed for France to look for targets. They headed inland at Granville on the Cotentin Peninsula and within minutes sighted targets. For an hour and forty minutes the P–38s of the 55th FS flew up and down the roadways and strafed several convoys. One pilot claimed eight ammunition trucks destroyed as well as a motorcycle and its riders. Other pilots of the 55th teamed up to claim twenty trucks, two horse carts, another motorcycle and numerous German foot soldiers. The Group's war diary for the day ended with this comment: "Morale was noticeably higher tonight for though the pilots appreciate the great importance of their sea patrol work there's nothing a fighter pilot likes better than drawing blood from the enemy."

The Mustangs of the 328th Fighter Squadron had flown a general area support mission with the bombers in France, and were patroling their assigned area at 17,000 feet during the morning when Lt. John F. Thornell and the remaining two members of his flight sighted forty Me 109s with bombs about to dive-bomb

Lt. John Thornell's P-51 Patty Ann II. H. J. Whitely

Allied positions near Bayeaux, France. They immediately attacked and although one flight of E/A continued their bombing operation, the majority of them dropped their projectiles and turned in to meet the attack. Thornell managed to maneuver onto one of the 109s and got him with a deflection shot. There were still about thirty enemy fighters trying to get the Mustangs, but they kept turning into the 109s and outturning them. Thornell managed to pull his nose through on a second victim and flamed it. All this time his tail had been protected by Lt. Charles Bennette. Three 109s had locked onto Bennette's tail but he managed to hold out until Thornell flamed his second victim. Bennette then broke into the clouds, did a 360, came out and latched onto the tail of a 109. He got strikes all over the craft which emitted much smoke and split-essed into the clouds. Bennette had to break off due to other enemy aircraft on his tail. He then pulled up, fired at three more E/A and broke for home.

After bombing railroad tracks west of Evreux, France, Lt. George Doersch of the 359th Fighter Group and his wingman, Lt. Paul Bateman were scouting the countryside for motor convoys when they spotted an Me 109 on the tail of a Mustang. Doersch latched onto the 109, but the E/A took such violent evasive action that few hits were scored. The 109 then zoomed down over the town of Evreux in the hope that Doersch would give up the chase. The E/A was now streaming coolant and the Mustang pilot just held on waiting for another shot or for the 109's engine to overheat. As Doersch fired again, the 109 pilot bailed out.

Lt. George Doersch, 359th FG ace, his crew chief and his Mustang Ole' Goat. *"Pop" Doersch, as he was known to fellow pilots, was one of the outstanding leaders of the "green-nosed" group.* G. Doersch

Lt. Chris Hanseman of the 339th Fighter Group had made one strafing pass on a German airfield near Laigle, damaging a Ju 88, and then headed north. Hanseman sighted another airfield with a dozen Me 109s in the landing pattern. He slipped in behind the single 109 that was flying as top cover. The Mustang pilot opened up at 300 yards, dumped twenty degrees of flaps and pulled right in on the enemy's six o'clock. Another burst was sufficient and the German pilot bailed out. Hanseman had his fifth aerial victory and the 339th FG had its first ace plus another first—the Eighth Air Force had its first teenage ace!

By June 11 the invading Allied armies had firmly established themselves along the Normandy coast so the need for the sea patrols by the Lightning groups was ended. Protection of the sea lanes now became the responsibility of Royal Air Force Fighter Command and the Allied Tactical Air Forces operating from forward bases in France.

Relieved from those duties the 20th Fighter Group now turned its attention to engaging the enemy. A strafing mission was laid on for the day, but heavy cloud cover over the Granville area aborted the mission. Another of VIII FC's Lightning groups, the 55th, did get the chance to engage enemy aircraft and downed three of them against two losses.

As the fighter units of VIII Fighter Command continued to attack truck convoys and railroad facilities throughout France, they began to meet heavier and more determined opposition from the Luftwaffe. On June 12, the 353rd Fighter Group was involved in vicious combat not once but twice with the forces of JG 3 in the area of Evreux and Dreux. The Group made an early morning takeoff to attack ground targets in the area. Upon arrival the 352nd Squadron under the leadership of Lt. Col. Bill Bailey went after a truck convoy; the 351st Squadron under the leadership of Colonel Duncan took off after rail targets, while the 350th Squadron of Capt. Dewey Newhart zeroed in on a truck convoy near Dreux.

Newhart took his flight down first through a cloud formation at 2,000 to 3,000 feet while the other two flights stayed above as top cover. As soon as Newhart's flight made its pass he called for the other two flights to come down. As they dropped through a hole in the clouds they were attacked by more than thirty Me 109s at about 2,500 feet coming from a nine o'clock position some 1,000 feet higher than the P–47s. The Thunderbolt pilots began dropping their wing tanks and bombs at the same time. The fight was on! Unfortunately, the 109s enjoyed more than a numerical advantage; they had altitude, position and surprise on their side. Six P–47s, including Captain Newhart, were shot down in the fight. Lt. James Ruscitto was able to down one of the Messerschmitts and damage another in his vain struggle to break out of the trap. Lt. Benjamin damaged another 109 in the combat.

The 352nd Squadron successfully attacked a truck convoy and as they pulled up to recover, they were bounced by fifty Me 109s. In a sharp fight, two P–47s

were lost while the Thunderbolts accounted for two E/A and damaged another. Lt. Harold Miller was one of the victors: "I chopped my belly tank and pushed everything to the firewall. The Me 109s did likewise and the fun began. Several passes were made head-on. I shook several off my tail and on recovering from a double snap, split-essed. Drawing 70 inches of Mercury and 2200 RPM I pulled in behind a 109 on another P–47's tail. I pulled a 40 degree deflection in a right turn and started firing at about 250 yards and closed to almost line astern at 100 yards and his left wheel dropped; a few seconds later the right one dropped. I kept firing and he slowly leveled out and rolled up and over the left . . . He rolled again and continued in an inverted dive . . . I then broke into a cloud as 3 Me 109s were trying to claim me."

Colonel Duncan heard over the R/T that the 350th was in a big fight so he dropped his bombs on a railyard and headed for the action. He sighted six Me 109s as he entered the area and maneuvered into firing range of the rear two: "(I) managed to grab onto tail end Charlie. I made a couple of turns with him and shot a good deflection shot. I scored hits and saw the glycol smoke come out. He immediately straightened out of the turn and started down. I was about to follow but the four Me 109s had come in by this time. Then the fun started; brother believe me, they can turn when they have a good pilot. I could hear the rat-tat-tat of the machine guns (and they weren't mine). Thru my mirror I could see him squinting down the gun barrel and cussing his poor deflection shooting. This went on for about five years of my future life that I will never live, then I started really working. I flipped over at 1,000 feet and went down. He must have thought that he had finished me off because he gave me about two seconds to get up into the cloud. Oh, why didn't I go into the cloud to begin with? Well, you try it when the boys are turning deflection on you and let me know how . . . back to the 109 I shot. I happened to see him auger into a bunch of trees . . ."

Duncan joined up with two P–47s and gained some altitude. As they passed over Evreux aerodrome he sighted two Me 109s diving across the field. The pair split, with Duncan taking the E/A on the left. A good deflection shot left the 109 smoking and the pilot bailed out.

Duncan continued: "By this time the other boys were having a big go with the other Me. I saw him coming in time to turn into him. As he went past I saw the stripes on the fuselage designating him as a leader or superman or somthin'. Well he figured that he had enough so he began climbing. He gained about four thousand on the initial acceleration by my ole 47 with both balls out and water in kept behind him. We went from zero up to 20,000 feet. The 109 just over and ahead of me all the time. However, at about 18,000 feet I began to overtake him—guess his engine began to boil water. That was his second mistake when he thought that he would put the nose down and go home. I ran the IAS up to 500 and caught him at 3,000 feet. I shot a long

114

burst as he went into the cloud. Well, I figured that having gone this far I wouldn't leave now, so into the cloud after him. When I came out there he was pulling up. He went into a loop and then changed his mind probably thinking that I would spin so made the loop into an Immelman. He had had it then. Strikes began to appear and I was in good range and he let go the canopy—then bailed out . . ."

The loss of eight top-notch fighter pilots infuriated Duncan so he set up a "grudge" sweep in the same area that afternoon. This time the P–47s were led by Lt. Col. Ben Rimerman. The sweep seemed to be drawing a blank until the Thunderbolts were about ready to call it quits. Then about forty-five Me 109s passed over the American formation. The 109s chose to go into a Lufbery above the P–47s. The Americans began to pick off the stragglers in the circle and then some of them chose to make head-on passes into the circle. This tended to break up the German defensive maneuver and planes began to break for the deck and combats went down to just off the ground. When the fight was over the Jug pilots of the 353rd had downed nine of the 109s while losing none of their own. In a small way some vengeance had been gained.

The next few days saw more attacks by the VIII FC fighters against enemy targets on the ground. The 357th Group enjoyed a particularly good mission on the sixteenth when Lt. Col. Thomas Hayes led them in an attack on the railyards at St. Pierre and Poitiers, France. The attackers were set up in flights of four. The first flights went in and dropped auxiliary fuel tanks two thirds full while the second flights came in strafing and set the gasoline on fire. As the Mustangs pulled away they observed enormous fires and billowing smoke from the ammunition-laden freight cars.

Missions in support of the invasion front continued for the next several days, but on June 20 the Eighth Air Force again turned its attention to targets in Germany. The 1st Task Force struck at Hamburg and met no real opposition, but it was a different story for the 2nd Task Force attacking Politz and Ostermoor. Numerous enemy fighters were seen and engaged by the bomber escort. The first major engagement was fought by the 355th FG.

Maj. Henry Kucheman, leading the 355th, positioned his Mustangs on the up-sun side of the bomber stream. As he watched he noted that the P–51 group on the other side of the bomber stream had turned to a point in front of the second box of bombers. Kucheman took his Mustangs toward the other group and began to orbit. As they made this maneuver, one of his pilots called out forty-plus twin-engined bandits attacking the bombers from the rear. This formation of Me 410s had come up from astern and below the other group of P–51s. The Mustangs of the 355th immediately dropped their tanks and dove down to the attack. The interception was successful in breaking up the attack on the bombers as the Me 410s began to break their formation and seek refuge on the deck, and the 355th shot down five of the 410s.

When Kucheman took his formation down to attack, Capt. Bert Marshall, who was leading a flight in the 354th Fighter Squadron, had difficulty getting rid of his drop tanks. They finally fell away and as he hurried to catch up with his flight, he encountered the formation of Me 109s that were chasing after the P–51s. He sighted one Mustang with a 109 on its tail and succeeded in getting hits and driving it off the P–51's tail on the first pass. After overshooting, Marshall came back down and finished off the 109.

Once more Marshall went hunting for his flight. On the way he saw a 109 on its way to earth. He managed to give it a fleeting burst, but it was already done for. He then sighted a P–51 involved in a three-ship Lufbery Circle with a 109 on its tail. Marshall went in with deflection shooting that ranged from thirty down to five degrees. The 109 never pulled out of his dive after taking strikes all over the aircraft.

The fighting continued as the 4th FG began its portion of the escort. They claimed ten aerial victories and destroyed two more in a strafing attack on Neubrandenburg aerodrome, Germany. Two of the 4th's pilots were lost, one of whom was Maj. Jim Goodson, one of the group's highest scoring aces. At the time of his loss, Goodson had been credited with fourteen aerial and fifteen ground victories. Like so many other outstanding pilots of VIII FC, Goodson fell victim to ground fire as he strafed Neubrandenburg.

The action continued as the 3rd Task Force struck at other targets in Germany. The 352nd FG claimed four in the air and two on the ground. While the missions over Germany were going on, other groups of

Lt. Col. Thomas Hayes had flown in the Pacific before he came to the 357th FG as CO of the 364th FS. He and his Mustang *Frenesi* became well-known Luftwaffe opponents. M. Olmsted

VIII FC were carrying out strafing attacks in France and they accounted for another eight enemy planes. All in all it had been a great day for the Command. Its pilots had destroyed 41-2-19 in the air and 18-0-18 on the ground against eight losses.

Throughout the spring of 1944 the bombers of the Eighth Air Force and the RAF had been striking at targets deeper and deeper in the Third Reich. By late June 1944, Eighth Air Force planners were ready to try the ultimate long-range mission—the shuttle to Russia. On these missions the bombers would bomb targets in eastern Germany, continue on to bases in Russia, bomb new targets in Hungary and then return by way of Italy and the Mediterranean. Fighter escorts for this mission were mandatory, and the obvious choice for this task was Col. Don Blakeslee and his experienced 4th Fighter Group. For the mission, the 4th was enlarged to four squadrons by the loan of the 352nd FG's 486th Fighter Squadron. The 486th was sent to Debden during the evening of June 20 to be briefed and to prepare their planes.

The weather didn't look good on the morning of June 21. A heavy overcast hung 200 feet over the field, and some of the participants doubted that they would be given the takeoff order. Their doubts, however, were short-lived as the weather officer assured them that good weather would accompany them throughout

Maj. Jim Goodson, a top-scoring ace of the 4th FG, was another who fell to flak while strafing. Goodson had 15 E/A on the ground and 15 in the air before he became a POW. AF Museum

Mustangs from the 486th FS assembled at Debden to fly with the 4th FG on the first shuttle mission to Russia on June 21, 1944. T. Ivie

the mission. With this assurance the mission was on, and at 0755 hours Colonel Blakeslee led forty-nine Mustangs of the 4th FG and sixteen Mustangs of the 486th FS out of Debden en route to Russia. In addition to the pilots, the 4th (and 486th) sent crew chiefs along to maintain the Mustangs. These key maintenance personnel flew in the B-17s and acted as waist gunners during the mission.

Once the planes broke through the overcast over England they found sunny skies for the flight across the Channel. However, as they crossed over the enemy coastline at Overflakke Island they again encountered a heavy cloud cover, and visibility was at a minimum. Nevertheless, Colonel Blakeslee's navigation was faultless and the rendezvous with the bombers was made over Lezno, Poland. The moment was described by Lt. Don McKibben of the 486th FS: "At exactly the briefed minute, the red-nosed ships of the 4th Group and our own blue-nosed planes swung over the bombers and began weaving out to the side and over the glistening B-17s. They had effectively bombed their target, Ruhland, and had reformed into two compact boxes. There's something dignified and majestic about a large formation of our bombers plodding through the sky, and knowing we were flying over territory never before visited by American aircraft, a certain pride was felt by all our boys. At the waist guns of some of those Big Friends our crew chiefs were keeping a nervous eye peeled for the enemy. We didn't intend to let the enemy get a crack at our crew chiefs."

The flight continued without incident for about another hour, but at 1240 hours the bombers were suddenly attacked by a gaggle of enemy fighters. The escort quickly bounced the enemy fighters, destroying six and damaging three others before breaking off. Four of these victories were scored by pilots of the 486th. McKibben told the story as follows: "Warsaw had passed under our wings 20 minutes ago when the 109s came. There were 15 plus of them and most of those never got to attack. The few that did attack never reformed because P-51s were hot on their tails. Lt. Northrop accounted for two, Lt. Whinnem nailed one, Lt. Heller got one, and Major Andrew damaged one. We were quite pleased with our showing as the three squadrons of the 4th FG tallied only one or two Huns for the loss of one P-51. The 109s did give us a break by delaying their attack until we had run our external tanks dry, so we didn't waste any gas." The 4th FG victories were claimed by Lieutenant Lang of the 334th and Captain Jones of the 335th. Lieutenant Sibbett was lost in the fight.

Because of the fuel situation, the pilots broke off combat and didn't pursue the escaping 109s. That is, all but the 4th FG's perpetual bad boy, Lt. Ralph Hofer, who continued right on after them. As they passed over the border into Russia, the pilots could look down and clearly see what the war had done to Russia. McKibben reported: "Soon we were over the marsh lands of eastern Poland and western Russia. Looking down we could see no activity from the armies we knew were clashing there, but as we penetrated into the old battlefield areas we could see that here indeed was the scorched earth of Russia. Now and then our course took us over what had been a Russian village but now was a cluttered heap of rubble. Tank tracks had chewed the earth and shell blasts had laid it bare."

Minutes later, Russian P-39s took up the bomber escort and the fighters turned and headed for their bases at Piryatin, USSR. Right on schedule, the Mustangs appeared over Piryatin at 1450 hours and Colonel Blakeslee radioed to his men, "Well, boys here's the end of a perfect mission." The landing didn't go perfectly, though. One of the first planes in had an accident at the end of the runway, and the rest of the Group had to circle for fifteen to twenty minutes while the plane was being pulled out of the way. When the damaged plane was finally removed, the remainder of the planes landed and all were accounted for except Hofer. Hofer was listed briefly as MIA, but later in the day he phoned in from an airfield at Kiev, Russia, and announced that he was okay.

During the evening of June 21 the bomber base at Poltava, USSR, was attacked by German bombers, and the fighter pilots expecting a similar attack at Piryatin spent an uneasy night in the slit trenches. The next day all the fighters were moved to alternate bases as a precaution against another nocturnal raid. The 486th FS went to Kharkov while the 4th FG was sent to Chugiev and Zaporozh'ye. For the next two days the pilots were treated royally and provided with excellent food, drink and entertainment by their Russian hosts. One of the most popular activities during these parties was trading. Many of the US personnel traded their Air Corps insignias for Russian red-star cap insignias. Maj. Howard "Deacon" Hively of the 334th FS got involved in some high-level "horse trading" and received a Russian general's belt with its large brass buckle complete with the hammer and sickle insignia. In exchange the general received "Deacon's" western belt and its silver buckle.

By June 25 the pilots were able to bring the planes back to Piryatin and prepare for the next mission. As soon as they arrived their crew chiefs began working on the planes so that they would be ready for the next leg of the shuttle. The 486th FS was three planes short, as gremlins invaded the Mustangs flown by Lieutenants Gremaux and Heller, and Lieutenant Brashear's plane had been damaged in a landing accident at Chugiev.

At 1409 hours on June 26 the Mustangs departed Piryatin to rendezvous with the bombers and head for the next target of the shuttle which was the oil refinery at Drohobycz, Poland. The target was hit with excellent results and the formation then headed for Italy. The fighters broke off escort at the Yugoslavian coast and flew across the Adriatic Sea to land at Lucera, Italy. This leg of the mission had been 1,100 miles.

The next day the Group was dispersed to three airfields. With no missions scheduled for the next several days, the flyers used the chance to enjoy the sun, the sights and some excellent food and wine.

Action resumed on July 2 when the Group went on a fighter sweep to Budapest, Hungary, with the 52nd and 325th Fighter Groups of the Fifteenth Air Force. The 4th FG was to sweep the target area before the bombers arrived, and then join up as part of the escort. However, just as the bombers arrived over the target a large force of enemy fighters appeared and the 4th FG went after them. Combat broke out everywhere and the dogfights ranged from 30,000 feet down to 10,000 feet directly over the city. The enemy pilots were quite aggressive and pressed their attacks hard. Colonel Blakeslee's force downed nine enemy planes in the fight, but the battle cost five of the 4th FG's planes and pilots and two of the 486th's. One of the losses was Lt. Ralph "Kid" Hofer, who many believe was a victim of Germany's greatest ace, Erich Hartmann. High scorer for the 4th FG was "Deacon" Hively with three, but he was hit and painfully wounded during the fight.

The next mission of the shuttle was on July 3 when the Mustangs escorted the Eighth Air Force bombers to Arad, Romania. The mission was without incident and all planes returned safely. The shuttle's final mission came on July 5. With Colonel Blakeslee in the lead, the Mustangs flew out of Italy. They crossed over the island of Corsica and rendezvoused with the B-17s over the Mediterranean, south of Toulon, France. From there

Capt. Don Bochkay led the 357th FG out to provide escort for the bombers returning from Russia on July 5, 1944. The Luftwaffe intervened and the Mustangs broke them up. Bochkay scored his sixth and seventh victories. M. Olmsted

Lt. Col. Francis Gabreski taxies out in his Thunderbolt shortly before he, too, went down on a strafing mission. USAAF

they escorted the Fortresses to the target—the marshaling yards at Beziers, France. The 4th FG and the 486th FS broke escort and headed for home without encounter, but for the groups sent out to England to relieve them it was a different story.

Of the sixty-five Mustangs that departed Debden on June 21, fifty-two returned to England. Five 4th FG and two 486th FS pilots and planes were lost. Six other planes and one wounded pilot had been left behind. This outstanding mission had covered over 6,000 miles and ten countries and resulted in total claims for the fighters of fifteen destroyed and four damaged. Their total operational time was twenty-nine hours and fifteen minutes.

VIII Fighter Command sent out 139 P-51s and eighty-nine P-47s on July 5 to pick up and escort the B-17s returning to England from the shuttle mission. While the bombers dropped their bombs on the marshaling yard at Beziers, the fighters fought with relatively strong opposition. The 357th Group encountered more than fifteen single-engined fighters in the vicinity of Rouen and downed four of them. Capt. Donald Bochkay sighted twenty-plus FW 190s below, climbing. Two flights went down to attack, but Bochkay held his flight back looking for top cover and sure enough he spotted six more 190s just above. Bochkay took his flight up into them and gave the formation a spraying burst. The 190s, which were carrying drop tanks, got rid of them immediately and headed for the deck. Bochkay dived down on the tail of one and downed him. He then climbed back up. Spotting two more 190s on the deck, he dove on them, but was in turn attacked by a 109 from his left. Bochkay feinted a break into the 109 which pulled up into a right-hand turn. Bochkay turned with him, fired and got strikes all over him, sending the 109 straight down.

Lt. Col. Francis Gabreski was leading the 56th Group and the mission had been primarily uneventful until escort was broken. At that time small flights of Me 109s and FW 190s began to show up in the area, and various flights from the 56th bounced them. Gabreski made a couple of attacks, but lost the first one in the clouds. The second time another P-47 beat him to the target. Finally he spotted three Me 109s on the deck. As he attacked, two dove away and so Gabreski went after the single. After about three turns the German dived for the deck, with the Thunderbolt closing on him all the time. The 109 then racked over into a hard turn to the left. Gabreski gave him two rings of deflection and got hits all over him. The 109 leveled off and was then really clobbered before the pilot bailed out. This was Gabreski's twenty-eighth aerial kill, but little did he know that it would be his last.

Chapter 11

Summer Support and Jets

VIII Fighter Command's headline story during the last ten days of June and early July was, of course, the shuttle mission to Russia. However, the battles over the beachhead continued as fierce as before. From June 22 through 28 VIII FC aircraft struck primarily at targets in France. On June 24 these rampaging fighters destroyed thirty-one enemy aircraft during strafing attacks on German aerodromes in occupied France. The following day VIII FC fighters again escorted the bombers to Noball targets in France, but on this occasion the Luftwaffe rose to challenge them in the air. The 361st FG had an early morning appointment with the German fighters. Just prior to their rendezvous at 0700 hours with the bombers near Caen, fifteen enemy fighters were spotted below them at 8,000 feet.

Col. Joe Kruzel leading the 361st described the battle: "At about 8,000 feet [I] was able to identify the mess as a scattered jumble of P-38s, 109s, 190s and flak from 5,000 feet to the deck . . . It was difficult to determine the exact number of P-38s and E/A present as they were very low and scattered over a fairly large area, flying in ones and small groups of two and three." Kruzel latched onto a 190 that was chasing a P-38, and although he was hampered by his gunsight bulb burning out, he destroyed the Focke Wulf right on the deck.

Lt. Jack Crandall was being chased by two Me 109s when he finally decided to turn and fight it out with them. The three went into a Lufbery and when Crandall began to outturn them, they broke and climbed. He got on their tails and shot down both.

One of the scorers for the 55th FG was a veteran Pacific ace, Maj. John D. Landers. He positioned his flight under a formation of some forty bandits and when they were attacked from above and broke for the deck, Landers and his flight tacked onto individual E/A as they came down. Landers downed an FW 190 and damaged an Me 109 while the other members of his flight were credited with two 109s and a 190.

On the afternoon of June 27 Maj. Kenn Gallup was leading the 350th FS of the 353rd FG flying top cover while the balance of the group was dive-bombing an aerodrome. Someone called out a bandit in and out of the clouds near Epernay, France, so Gallup went down to investigate. He sighted an Me 109 which suddenly flicked into a small hole in the clouds. Gallup followed in hot pursuit and began firing: "I closed to about 30 yards, he [was] trying to pull up into the clouds, with 8 fifties helping him. Seeing that was doing him no good, he leveled out with oil flying from his ship, and smoking. I pulled in beside the ship to see if it was a woman pilot but could not tell. The pilot jettisoned his canopy, then threw off his helmet and over the right side he went. My #2 man saw the pilot sitting on the wing before jumping. The plane proceeded on down to explode in a small clump of trees. The pilot's chute opened and I hope to meet him again if he continues to act so stupid about flying an airplane."

On June 29 the Eighth Air Force dispatched its bomber force to strike numerous targets in Germany; VIII FC sortied 779 fighters to act as escort. The Luftwaffe made an attempt to defend Leipzig by sending up at least seventy-five fighters, but these Messerschmitts were unlucky enough to find themselves in airspace occupied by the 357th Fighter Group.

Lt. Col. Thomas Hayes flew one of the new P-51Ds with the bubble canopy while leading the 357th Group. Southwest of Leipzig they encountered large formations of Me 109s and FW 190s. In the ensuing air battle that lasted some forty minutes, the Mustangs downed twenty-one E/A for the loss of one P-51. Hayes put his new Mustang through a real test when he went into a turning match with a Luftwaffe pilot who was a real veteran. After about five minutes of turning, Hayes finally managed to pull his nose through and get strikes on the enemy craft which then broke for the deck where Hayes finished him off. Although the new mount was victorious, Hayes was the first of a number of Mustang pilots who deemed that the P-51D was not the same quality mount as the old B-model.

Lt. Col. Joe Kruzel was another leader who had seen action in the Pacific before coming to the Eighth AF. He eventually commanded the 361st FG. U. L. Drew

Capts. Clarence Anderson and Robert Foy were both successful in downing three of the E/A. Anderson singled out each of his and sent them down. Foy got his first in a Lufbery and then shot the second off the tail of another Mustang. He went into a Lufbery with the third victim, and when he finally got strikes on the 109 it split-essed and headed for the deck. Both planes went down in screaming dives. Foy started pulling out when his air speed reached 550 mph. The Mustang leveled out about 3,000 feet, but the 109 continued on to crash into the ground.

While the engagement was taking place, the 339th FG sighted another group of at least thirty enemy planes over Naumburg, Germany. Several flights of the 339th turned and waded into the German formation and then shot eight of these enemy fighters out of the air. Lt. Col. Harold Scruggs, who was leading the 339th Group, had downed two FW 190s and damaged another when he met with an old pro: "This one didn't dive away and we went into a dogfight that lasted for about ten minutes. Every time I got on his tail he would dive into a cloud; another trick was to dive below the cloud, pull up into it, chop throttle and as I went past under the cloud he would drop down behind me. At one time I was directly behind him at 50 yards. I fired and got strikes on both sides of the fuselage but he didn't go down. He broke as I overran him and we came at each other head-on, both firing. My gas was getting very low so I pulled up into cloud and headed for home."

After completing their escort, the 339th then turned their guns on ground targets. In their strafing attacks they destroyed two locomotives and damaged fifty rail cars.

When the day ended the VIII FC had claimed 34-0-9 aerial victories and 16-0-8 ground victories, and their excellent results brought high praise from General Kepner.

The fighter groups of VIII Fighter Command celebrated the Fourth of July by attacking aerodromes and communications targets in France. The 56th Group flew a dive-bombing mission that morning and was slated to dive-bomb Conches, France, aerodrome that afternoon. Cloud cover made it impossible to accomplish this, so the Thunderbolts set out to seek suitable alternate targets. A marshaling yard was finally spotted through a small hole in the clouds, and two flights went down and took care of fifteen to twenty freight cars. Other flights attacked some trucks and another small marshaling yard. Group leadership was then turned over to Maj. Lucian Dade who was directed to bomb Evreux marshaling yards. En route, several aircraft were sighted on an auxiliary airfield at Conches. When the 62nd Squadron dropped down to attack, a formation of ten Me 109s was sighted in the vicinity of the aerodrome. As the P-47s continued their run, another eighteen Me 109s were sighted at 2,000 feet in a javelin formation. The Jug pilots salvoed their bombs and the fight was on.

Lt. George Bostwick quickly lined up on one Me 109 which he sent down with one burst. He then did a 180 into a formation of eight 109s pursuing him. The 109s kept going and he latched onto two more on the deck. As he chased them, one broke right giving him an excellent deflection shot. Number two down! As Bostwick pulled off to the right he found himself directly astern of a third 109. Pressing his attack to fifty yards he scored hits all over the E/A. The pilot bailed out, bounced off the tail plane and went down entangled in his chute shrouds.

When the fight was over, the Thunderbolts of the 56th claimed twenty enemy aircraft destroyed and twelve damaged. The only loss was Lt. Sam Dale, who was last seen under attack by eight FW 190s on the way home.

The P-38s of the 55th Group led by Major Giller didn't get into any aerial combat, but they had a field day with the railroads. Before returning to base they had destroyed thirteen locomotives, eighty-one freight cars, thirteen oil cars plus a few miscellaneous buildings.

On July 6 the planes returned to escort duty for the bombers going to Germany, and flew an uneventful mission. This was not the case on July 7, however, as the Luftwaffe put up its strongest force since May. The targets for the day were German aircraft and oil facilities, and the Luftwaffe fought doggedly to protect them. In pitched air battles that continued across Germany, thirty-seven bombers and six fighters were lost to enemy fighters. The Germans paid dearly for those victories, though, as VIII FC fighters claimed 75-1-19, and the bomber crews claimed another thirty-nine. This mission was probably the proudest to date for VIII FC's P-38 groups. Up to this point in the war the VIII FC Lightning groups had not enjoyed the wide victory-loss ratio recorded by the Mustang and Thunderbolt groups. Even as this mission was being flown, plans were being formulated to convert these groups to Mus-

Coming into his own in July 1944 was Lt. George Bostwick of the 56th FG. He downed three fighters and damaged another on July 4 for a gala Independence Day. USAAF

tangs. The Command's two oldest P-38 groups were escorting the 1st Task Force whose targets were Lutzkendore, Halle, Bernburg and Aschersleben.

The enemy's assault began northwest of the target area, but the two P-38 groups quickly shattered the attack and in doing so claimed 26½ victories. The 20th FG was led by Lt. Col. Cy Wilson. Their diary entry records the encounter as follows: "Hell broke loose in the target area when 50 Me-410s with approximately 100 Me-109s and FW-190s stacked in layers as top cover made aggressive and determined attacks on the bombers. Twenty of the fighters bounced the 55th Squadron and in the resulting battle 3 Me-109s were destroyed for no loss. The 77th Squadron bounced Me-410s and enemy fighters as they prepared to attack the bombers. Two Me-410s and 2 FW-190s were destroyed and 2 FW-190s and one Me-109 damaged. In this engagement a barrage of accurate fire from Me-410 barbette guns caught Captain Jimmy Morris and he bailed out over the target. Captain Morris was the Group's leading Ace having destroyed 10⅔ planes; 7⅓ in the air and 3⅓ on the ground."

The 55th FG had its greatest aerial victory of the war with 19½ aerial victories for no losses. Maj. John D. Landers, with three kills, reported: "[We] had to escort some cripples back home. In the vicinity of Bernburg in support of the heavies . . . we had the good fortune to meet 20 to 30 Me 410s. Flying at 21,000 feet—180 degrees to the track of the bombers, who were headed north—we observed a large formation of these twin-engine enemy aircraft approaching our lead box of bombers at 19,000 feet.

"I led my flight in on the tail of the 410s but was unable to make an immediate attack because of some P-51s who insisted on acting like enemy aircraft and making apparently hostile—though actually playful—attacks on our formation. In the meantime my second flight became engaged with an umbrella force of Me 109s up top.

"After convincing the 51s that we were in no mood to play games, I again turned my flight into the 410s and at about 800 yards, almost dead astern, started firing on the nearest enemy aircraft. One of his engines immediately began smoking, and as he pulled out of the formation I continued firing. For a few seconds I diverted my attack to another 410. One of his engines also started smoking and he slipped out of formation attempting to regain control of his ship. By this time the combat had taken us to an altitude of about 3,000 feet. The attempts of these enemy aircraft to get control of their crippled planes was of no avail, because when I last saw them they both headed straight into the deck and exploded.

"I now turned my attention to the rear of the formation. I started firing at 350 yards, again dead astern, and closed to almost 100 yards, observing strikes all over the fuselage and canopy. At this point the Hun pulled up, rolled over on his back and smoking badly, crashed into the earth . . .

"The Huns stayed in a very tight formation throughout the rat race and only broke formation to crash into the ground or jump out of their planes. During the course of the battle I saw nine Me 410s crash into the ground and three chutes. We observed fire from their rear guns only when we were above their level and none of my ships were hit."

The Mustangs that were involved in this fight primarily came from the 355th Fighter Group and were being led by Lt. Col. Claiborne Kinnard. Kinnard had split his squadrons and had taken the 354th and positioned himself in the middle of the "U" where he could watch both sides of the bomber stream. Kinnard saw the large gaggle of approaching E/A and took his flight forward at full throttle as the 20 mm shells of the enemy began to burst into the B-24 formation. He had wanted to wait for his full squadron to attack, but time was of the essence: "I called the flight to hang on and I did a kind of half roll on the back of the formation. I wanted it to look good to the other Me 410s so I waited till I was about 75 yards from one and held the trigger down till after he blew up.

"To keep from overrunning the pack I ducked out and swung back for another pass. According to my number three man parts of the 410 hit my number two man, Lt. Huish, and he went spinning down. Evidently the bluff worked because when I swung around for another pass the 410s were going down away from the bombers and the rest of the squadron was coming in on them.

"I called Lt. Cross, my number three man, to stay on my wing and we would look for their top cover. I had no sooner said that than about thirty Me 109s appeared right in front of my nose, passing 90 degrees to me and going straight for the 410s. I called him to keep my tail clear and we would try to bluff them, too. As I swung in on the nearest man a couple split-essed out but I caught one real good and he blew up and believe it or not, damned if they didn't panic and start down.

"By this time, according to Lt. Cross, I had a 109 on my tail, so I broke violently and pulled away. I then told Lt. Cross to take over and I would fly his wing. He decided on the 410s and we went after them. By this time the other escort fighters were showing up all around and when we got to the 410s there were about twelve or fourteen P-38s and P-51s chopping away at the back end. Lt. Cross moved in and I saw him set a 410 on fire from engine to engine. About this time I lost him in the melee and I pulled out to the side and called him to come back on my wing as the whole works was turning into me. Things were getting pretty cramped so I picked out the closest Me 410 and fired about a 4 second burst from about 400 yards. I didn't see any strikes but he peeled out of formation and started for the deck. About this time we were over an airfield at about 5,000 feet and they were really throwing 20 mm and 40 mm at us. I overran the 410 going down so I essed to get behind him. I saw he was on one engine. I figured he was easy meat so I took plenty of time swinging around on his tail. As I made the turn in for the kill I saw a ship coming in from 90 degrees headed for me. At first I thought it was Lt. Cross but when he passed by I saw it was an Me 109. By this time I had swung back for another pass. Here he came again from the other side but went on by. By this time we were right on the trees and I was ahead of the 410 again. I pulled up in a kind of loop and started shooting nearly straight down. I saw hits in the ground in front of him but before I could change my lead I had to pull out. I felt pretty disgusted by then and made a swing around for a final pass looking for the 109 but could not find him. The 410 must have decided to try to get me because he started a steep turn and had nearly gotten around to meet me head-on when he caught a wing in the trees and burst into flames.

"I pulled around to get a picture still looking for the 109. About this time it dawned on me that maybe the reason I could not find him was because he was sitting right under my tail. To say I panicked is putting it mildly! I hit the deck, taking violent evasive action and let out a yell for Lt. Cross to come over to where the fire and smoke in the trees was. We got together pretty fast and came home."

The 355th Group accounted for twelve twin-engined fighters and two single-engines that day for the loss of only one of their pilots.

Capt. Fred Christensen was leading the 62nd Fighter Squadron of the 56th returning from their escort

Capt. Fred Christensen of the 56th FG. Christensen ran up a score of 21½ aerial victories including six Junkers 52 transports on July 7, 1944. F. Christensen

Capt. Fred Christensen's P-47 Rozzie Geth II. *F. Christensen*

duties when he noted activity over Gardelegen aerodrome. As the Thunderbolts dropped down to lower altitude, they discovered a dozen Junkers Ju 52 tri-motored transports in the landing pattern. The P-47s joined in immediately and Christensen managed to down six of the big aircraft. All total they got ten out of the twelve, with Lt. Billy G. Edens getting three of them.

The primary loser of what was otherwise an outstanding day was the 353rd Fighter Group. Col. Glenn Duncan, flying his P-47 *Dove of Peace*, led the group giving penetration support to the bombers. He was en route home when he took the 351st Squadron down to strafe enemy aircraft on Wesendorf airfield. He destroyed a Heinkel He 111 but was hit by intense light flak on the north side of the field which severed his oil line. Duncan pulled up and did his best to nurse the big Jug home, but he was finally forced to belly it in near Nienburg some fourteen minutes later. Before he left his aircraft he radioed, "I am okay, will see you in three weeks." Although the famed leader was never captured by the Germans, it was April of 1945 before he rejoined the group. In the interim he fought with the Dutch underground. His final claim gave him 19½ in the air and 6⅞ on the ground.

Eleven days later while escorting bombers to Peenemunde and Zinowiz, Germany, the 352nd FG encountered a large force of German interceptors and decimated it. The group had swept its assigned area and was en route to rendezvous with the bombers when the combat ensued north of Warnemunde, Germany, from 30,000 feet down to the deck. The enemy force was composed of approximately forty Me 410s and Ju 88s with a top cover of twenty Me 109s, and was obviously heading toward the bomber stream when the blue-nosed Mustangs tore into them. The German twin-engined fighters paid a terrible price for being there; thirteen were shot down and eight more were damaged. The 109s flying top cover didn't fare much better, as eight were destroyed and four were damaged. The 352nd lost two pilots in the engagement. The 487th FS's Maj. George Preddy had his biggest day to date with three kills, one probable and two damaged. Right behind him was Lt. Charles Ellison, also of the 487th, with three victories.

Preddy was leading the 487th Fighter Squadron when the enemy formation was sighted: "I made a right turn up sun of the enemy formation which consisted of a mess of Ju 88s with many Me 109s as top cover. I took my flight of three, Lts. Vickery, Greer and myself to attack the Ju 88s, about 50 in number, while the rest of the squadron dealt with the top cover. As we approached the formation I saw a single Me 109 ahead of me and attacked it from quarter stern. I opened fire at 400 yards and drove up his tail. The E/A was covered with hits and went down burning and falling apart.

"I continued on to attack the Ju 88 formation and opened fire on one of them knocking off many pieces and setting the plane on fire. Lt. Greer then called a break to the right as an Me 109 was pulling up on my tail

from below. After we broke the 109 stalled out and went back down. During this maneuver Lt. Greer became separated. Lt. Vickery and I then made a 360 and launched another attack on the main formation and I damaged one with a few hits and drove up the rear of another, getting hits all over the ship. I believe the pilot and crew were killed as the E/A began smoking badly and went down out of control with parts of the ship falling too. I broke off the attack and pulled out to the side before the third attack on the formation. I came in astern again. In this attack I plastered one Ju 88 causing both engines to burn and the E/A disintegrated. I damaged a second getting a few hits. I was out of ammunition, or so I thought, though later I learned that my guns on one side had a stoppage and I had been hit in the engine from the rear gun positions in the Ju 88s. My ship was covered with oil sprayed from the E/A which had been shot down, so I set course for home with Lt. Vickery."

The fighters returned to Germany on July 19 and scored another decisive victory over the Luftwaffe. The count was 17-0-4 in the air and 36-0-15 on the ground. The 352nd FG had another great day and claimed eight of the aerial victories. The ground strafing leader was the 78th FG which destroyed 20-0-9 twin-engined fighters, and two locomotives. Each of the Group's three squadrons had picked a different airfield and struck hard at their targets. Maj. Norman Munson of the 82nd FS was the individual high scorer with three, but was shot down by flak after making several passes over the field. His plane was seen to catch fire and then crash and explode. Maj. Ben Mayo led his squadron over Eutingen airfield and claimed 2⅓ victories, and his squadron accounted for four more.

Unfortunately, the 78th FG wasn't able to enjoy their victory because a tragic accident at Duxford later in the day consumed the Group with grief. A B-17 from the 95th Bomb Group came to Duxford so its pilot, who had been previously stationed there, could visit some friends. The big plane naturally encouraged curiosity and its pilot was soon persuaded to give some rides. The incident is described in the 78th FG records as follows: "He took aboard his two friends, pilots from the 84th FS, and eight EM of the base, besides two of his own crew. They 'buzzed' the drome, at breathtaking altitude for a bomber, circled, and then came across the field into the hangar line at all but naught feet. Many personnel were out watching by now and all sensed a seemingly unavoidable crash as the bomber drew close to the hangars with very little gain in altitude. The bomber did lift over the hangar—but caught its wing on the blinker light mounted on the hangar roof, shearing off a wing and a stabilizer. The stricken bomber rolled over, dropped its stabilizer in front of the Officers' Club, its wing on the Officers' Mess roof and then crashed into the end of the barracks occupied by some of the 83rd's men."

Upon impact the B-17 exploded and all fourteen men in the plane and one man in the barracks were killed. A raging fire broke out in the barracks and took three hours to bring under control.

July 19 also marked the beginning of the end of the P-38 Lightning era in the Eighth Air Force. Its oldest users, the 20th and 55th FGs, had been training with war-weary P-51s for several weeks, and were now ready to try their new mount. The 55th FG flew its first P-51 mission on July 19, and the 20th first tried their new wings on an operational mission on July 20. On this mission the Group was split into two groups: group A was the 77th and 79th Squadrons flying P-38s, and group B was the 55th FS in Mustangs. The new plane was an instant hit with the 55th, and they came back singing its praises: "Flying P-51s for the first time in combat the 55th FS led by Lt. Col. Wilson made rendezvous with B-24s returning from Dessau at Limburg at 1159 hours and escorted them uneventfully to the Dutch Islands where the boys withdrew at 1314. Already what prejudices the 55th boys had in favor of the P-38 have drifted away and they are now convinced they have a real fighting machine with which to carry on the war. As Colonel Cy (Wilson) once said, 'as soon as we get rid of those ice wagons and start flying fighter planes, we'll murder the Hun.'"

The Colonel was quite right in his assessment. Although the Lightning had proved itself an outstanding aircraft in other theaters of the war, it was not a suitable aircraft for the conditions encountered at high altitudes over Europe. The 20th FG, for example, had flown 138 P-38 missions to date and claimed eighty-three aerial victories and thirty on the ground, but they had lost eighty-seven pilots in the process. Many of these losses were due to mechanical failures. Both the 55th and 364th FG fared worse than the 20th FG with the P-38. Each of those groups lost more pilots and planes than they brought down. The third Group to be converted to Mustangs was the 364th FG, which made the transition on July 29, 1944. Only the 479th continued using the Lightning for a while longer.

The heavy bombers were back on track after industrial targets in Germany on the twentieth. While the Luftwaffe did not intercept in great force, there were some incidents of note. The 355th Fighter Group was providing the 1st Task Force with target support when twenty-five Me 109s made diving six o'clock attacks on the rear of the bomber formations and also attempted to gang up on the usual stragglers. Lt. Robert Peters of the 358th Fighter Squadron spotted an FW 190 making attacks on a B-17 that was already on fire along the left wing. Peters turned sharply to get after the 190 and in so doing lost his wingman. However, he caught the Focke Wulf by surprise and hit him good before the E/A began taking evasive action. The 190 split-essed for the deck and the two almost went into compressibility. A burst from the guns of the P-51 seemed to break the speed and the 190 took more hits. The pilot jettisoned his canopy and bailed out a few seconds later at about 3,000 feet.

Peters spotted another 190 flying along on the deck and had no trouble closing on him. Apparently the German pilot never saw the Mustang until he was hit. Two good bursts sent him crashing into the ground.

During the last encounter, Peters spotted the airfield that the 190 had been headed for and noted that other FW 190s were lined up on the field as well as some twin-engined aircraft scattered about. The Mustang pilot came in low over the trees hoping to shoot up some 190s, but he had miscalculated and had come over the wrong side of the field. However, he was able to line up on a Heinkel He 111, gave it a shot and saw it burst into flames. On his second pass he missed his position once more but found a Junkers Ju 88 under a camouflage net neatly set up. A burst from the fifty-calibers took care of it. As he turned to make another pass he noticed a Dornier Do 217 flying just over the treetops. Peters moved into position behind him and three short bursts set the left engine smoking. The Dornier pilot did his best to get back to the field but Peters put another burst into the smoking engine. Now flak was coming up fast and furious from the field and Peters swerved away to avoid it. The Dornier continued in to a forced landing just short of the woods on the east edge of the airfield. As it hit, the left engine burst into flames and the left wing then exploded near the root.

With all the excitement going on at the field, Peters nearly made a fatal mistake. While watching the action below an FW 190 crept up on his tail. A burst of cannon gained his attention and he broke for the deck and pulled into a tight left turn. A tight 360 pulled him into position on the Focke Wulf's tail but he was out of ammunition so he headed out of the area while remaining on the deck.

Peters later climbed back up to 21,000 feet and sought shelter under the wing of a crippled B-17. They enjoyed each other's company until they reached the Leipzig area where intense flak was encountered. Peters finally dove down to 14,000 feet and headed for home alone.

The 56th Fighter Group escorted the 4th Force of bombers over central Germany. After an uneventful escort, they spotted an airfield identified as Bassinheim, near Koblenz, and Lt. Col. Francis Gabreski, leading the 61st Squadron, called for one flight to go down and strafe. Lt. Praeger Neyland leading the flight called to say that there was seemingly little flak around the place and that several He 111s and Me 110s were scattered around. Gabreski then ordered each flight to go down in turn to shoot up the airfield. Gabreski made two passes and on his second pass he got too low and fouled his propeller on the top of a small knoll. He called in that he "had had it" and proceeded to belly-in his P-47 about a half mile from the field. He jumped out and ran into a nearby wooded area and the squadron went down and destroyed his aircraft. Gabreski remained loose for five days but was then captured and spent the rest of the war in a prisoner of war camp. Gabreski had twenty-eight aerial victories and three on the ground to his credit when his combat tour was brought to an abrupt end.

The first German jets were observed and reported on July 28 by pilots of the VIII Fighter Command. On that date five Me 163 rocket-powered aircraft were seen in the air near Merseberg by pilots of the 359th FG. The 163s started toward the B-17 formation as if they were going to attack, so the 359th attempted to cut them off. As soon as the German pilots saw the Mustangs heading in their direction they turned and dove away at speeds that were estimated between 500 to 600 mph. The 359th's commanding officer, Col. Avelin Tacon, tried to follow but lost the speeding rocket-planes in the sun.

VIII Fighter Command had known of the existence of the German rocket-powered Me 163 and the jet-powered Me 262 for some time, but the appearance of the new aircraft caused quite a stir in the entire Eighth Air Force structure. Major General Kepner, CO of VIII Fighter Command, issued a TWX alerting all fighter units of the initial operations of the Me 262 and concluded it with the following: "It is believed we can expect to see more of these aircraft immediately and that we can expect attacks on the bombers from the rear in formations or waves. To be able to counter and have time to turn into them our units are going to have to be in position relatively close to the bombers to be between them and our heavies. It is believed these tactics will keep them from making effective, repeat effective, attacks on the bombers. Attention is called to the fact that probably the first thing seen will be heavy, dense contrails high and probably 30,000 feet and above approaching rear of bombers. Jet aircraft can especially be expected in Leipzig and Munich area or any place east of nine degree line."

Ironically enough, the first successful engagement with one of these new rocket-planes was fought the next day by the plane the VIII FC was doing away with—the P-38. On that date the Eighth's last P-38 group, the 479th, was returning from an escort mission to Merseberg when the engagement took place. Capt. Arthur F. Jeffrey, flight leader of the 434th FS's Yellow Flight, and his flight were escorting a straggling B-17 from the target area. At 1145 hours as they were passing over Wesermunde an Me 163 made a pass at the Fortress. Jeffrey and his wingman went after him and the 163 pilot started evasive maneuvers. As the 163 continued weaving, Jeffrey closed in and opened fire, and saw numerous strikes on the little German fighter. The Messerschmitt then climbed to 15,000 feet while trailing smoke. At 15,000 feet the 163 circled to the left and Jeffrey hit it again with a good deflection shot, then followed it down in a vertical dive. Jeffrey pulled out of his dive at about 3,500 feet because he was entering a solid overcast. The 163 was not seen to pull out and Jeffrey was awarded a confirmed victory. While this engagement was going on, a second Me 163 was seen shooting past the lumbering B-17, but Jeffrey's second element was unable to engage it. Postwar records fail to confirm Jeffrey's kill but if he didn't down the bird, he really burned its rear.

Capt. Art Jeffrey's P-38 Boomerang *of the 479th FG. Jeffrey encountered an Me 163 on July 29, 1944, and put telling hits into the rocket-powered craft which was last seen going down "balls out." B. McDonald*

The same day, the 339th Fighter Group was also escorting the bombers to Merseberg. Their Mustangs had successfully broken up an attack of enemy fighters, with one flight of the 505th FS winding up below the overcast. Lt. Ed Ball reported: "The flight then spotted two Ju 52 transports on the ground about four miles northwest of Naumburg parked in a meadow along a row of fairly high trees. We went down to strafe them and on the first pass, Lt. Chris J. Hanseman, who was flying Number Two position evidently pressed his attack too far, catching a wing in the ground and cartwheeling over the trees into a field. His plane caught fire and scattered over a wide area." The brilliant combat career of the Eighth Air Force's first teenage ace had come to an end.

On a more successful note, two members of the 20th Fighter Group found that their new Mustangs certainly held them in good stead. Lts. Louis W. Adams and Rex Moncrieff were returning early from an escort mission due to rough-running engines when they sighted more than fifty Me 109s near Gutersloh. The two pilots made an attack from dead astern and Adams shot down two of the 109s while Moncrieff accounted for one. About this time another gaggle of fifty Me 109s was sighted above. Both pilots ran "balls out" for home in a chase that lasted for some twenty minutes.

A later photo of Art Jeffrey (now a major) with his P-51.
A. Jeffrey

Chapter 12

Sweeping Ahead

VIII Fighter Command spent the first two days of August 1944 attacking targets in France. Little aerial opposition was encountered and only three victories were claimed. In direct contrast to the lack of targets in the air, the pilots found numerous enemy vehicles and installations on the ground and ripped them apart with devastating strafing and bombing attacks. As in many strafing missions, the cost was high. Ten of the fighters did not return.

The Eighth Air Force returned to Germany on August 3 and struck at targets throughout the Fatherland for the next three days. An immediate increase in aerial opposition was noticed, and during the mission on the third, six enemy fighters were downed. This was only a small preview of what was to come during the next two days.

Fifteen fighter groups of the VIII Fighter Command headed to Germany on August 4 as escort for more than 1,000 heavy bombers attacking industrial targets. The first bomber task was to strike oil refineries at Bremen and Hamburg, and it was met by a large force of enemy fighters determined to blunt the attack. Escorting the 1st Air Task Force were the pilots of the 339th, 78th, 56th A, 356th A and 353rd A Fighter Groups. The 339th FG was the first to encounter enemy fighters and in a series of engagements the Mustang pilots sent nine enemy fighters down in flames. Two of the 109s destroyed were claimed by Maj. Donald A. Larson, but he too went down a few minutes later after a midair collision with Lieutenant Burns. The other seven victories were shared by eight pilots. The 339th then strafed an enemy airfield crammed with twin-engined planes, destroying six.

While the 339th FG was engaged in its air battle the 356th FG was approaching Hamburg. When it arrived at a point about twenty-five miles southeast of the city, pilots observed at least twenty-five Me 109s making contrails at an altitude of 35,000 feet. The order to drop tanks was given to the Group's three squadrons, and they climbed to meet the Messerschmitts. Contact was made at 35,000 feet and the 356th successfully boxed in the German formation. At this altitude the 109s could easily outturn the standard P–47s, but the 356th had a number of its four-gun Superbolts on the mission and they were able to stay with the Messerschmitts. These Superbolts struck at the center of the German formation, and caused the Germans to make a fatal error. The enemy formation went into a steep dive to the deck in

Thunderbolt from the 361st FS, 356th FG off on a bombing mission in the summer of 1944. K. Miller

P-47s of the 351st FS, 356th FG outbound with drop tanks. By the summer of 1944, mixed formations of olive-drab and natural silver-colored aircraft became common. USAAF

an attempt to escape, but the heavier Thunderbolts easily overtook them. Individual dogfights broke out everywhere, and when it was all over fourteen 109s had gone down. Three pilots—Maj. John Vogt and Lt. Westwood Fletcher of the 360th FS, and Lt. Howard Wiggins of the 361st FS—each claimed two of the 109s. Fletcher managed to score his victories in a most unorthodox manner. He chased two of the Messerschmitts down to the deck and followed after them at treetop level. The first 109 was forced into a large oak tree, and the second was forced into the ground where it bounced a couple of times, then exploded. Fletcher scored two victories without firing a shot!

The 109s that the 356th encountered were the top cover for another group of enemy fighters that were attacking bombers near Hamburg. These E/A were apparently so intent in their attack on the Forts that they did not see the Thunderbolts of the 353rd A Group coming in after them. The 353rd completely disrupted the enemy attack and in doing so downed fourteen of their planes.

The opposition encountered by the 353rd was very ineffective and seemingly inexperienced. Lt. Harrison Tordoff, who downed two Me 109s, commented that "they seemed more interested in getting away than shooting me down."

In a late afternoon mission, Lt. Col. Bill Bailey led thirty-four P-47s of the 353rd Fighter Group and Col.

Hub Zemke led thirty-four P-47s of the 56th Group on a strafing mission directed at Plantlunne aerodrome. Although the 353rd Group lost one aircraft to flak, they were successful in destroying twenty-four enemy aircraft on the ground. The 56th Group lost no aircraft and destroyed six E/A on the ground. This mission was so successful that Zemke nominated the 353rd Group for a special commendation for their beautifully organized attack and excellent strafing job.

By day's end the VIII Fighter Command claimed 38-1-5 aerial victories and another 15-0-5 on the ground during the bomber escort missions to Germany, plus the strafing and dive-bombing attack on Plantlunne which accounted for an additional 30-0-5. On this one day, VIII FC destroyed eighty-three enemy aircraft and damaged many more for a loss of sixteen of their own!

The Eighth Air Force maintained its momentum by returning to Germany on August 5 with 1,500 bombers escorted by nearly 600 fighters. Its targets were the oil refineries and tank and aircraft production centers in northern and central Germany. The weather was good for bombing and recognizing this, the Luftwaffe was again up in force. The 1st Task Force striking at Magdeburg met stiff opposition. The 20th FG was the first of the escort fighters to encounter it, and this occurred shortly after they had crossed the enemy coast. Sixty 109s were spotted and Major Anderson dispatched the 77th and 79th Fighter Squadrons to intercept them. The enemy pilots showed no real inclination to do battle with the Mustangs boring in on them and tried to split-ess away. Three of the Messerschmitts and probably a fourth didn't get away as Capt. Merle Gilbertson and Lts. Ernest Fiebelkorn and Harold Binkley of the 77th FS each scored a confirmed victory. The 479th FG picked up where the 20th left off and claimed another five victories. Their first two kills were claimed by Capt. Raymond Carter of the 435th FS. A third 109 was destroyed a few minutes later when Lt. C. V. Moore and Capt. George Sykes of the 435th chased the German down to the deck and then Sykes dispatched him with a well-placed burst. Intent on his quarry, Moore never saw the second 109 which sneaked in and opened fire. They went into a Lufbery with Sykes falling in behind and trying to shoot the German out of the pattern, but it was too late. Moore's P–38 spun in and exploded as it hit the ground. The German got away. The 479th's final victory of the day was scored by Capt. Clifford Moore and Lt. Melvin Mickey of the 436th FS. Each of them downed a 109 in a dogfight which took place over Stendal, Germany.

Capt. John Godfrey of the 4th Fighter Group wound up on the deck after chasing an Me 109, so he and Capt. Otey Glass proceeded to shoot up some trains. After this strafing Glass was out of ammunition so they began to climb, but Godfrey spotted a small airfield with ten Junkers Ju 52 transports on it. Even though he had no ammo Glass orbited at 2,000 feet as top cover while Godfrey went down to strafe. Godfrey made head-on passes in order to set the Ju 52s on fire. He was successful in destroying three of the tri-motored craft in this manner.

Maj. George Preddy of the 352nd FG, after his return from the mission of Aug. 6, 1944, when he shot down six Me 109s. USAAF

As they headed for home Godfrey sighted an Me 109 while they were flying at 15,000 feet some twenty miles north of Osnabruck. Godfrey split-essed down to 8,000 feet to attack and although he had only two guns working, he managed to send the Messerschmitt down in flames. Once more Glass had to fly impotent cover, but fortunately all went as planned.

The escort for the 1st Air Task Force was replaced by the 352nd and 361st FGs for the return trip. Even though the 20th and 479th FGs had worked over the 109s earlier, the Germans continued to press the attack, and both the 352nd and the 361st went into action. The 352nd brought down five E/A near Hamburg, and the 361st closed out this air battle by claiming 5-0-1 in the air near Rotenburg. The Group also observed a flight of Me 163s in the air as they crossed the Dutch-German border, but could not catch the speedy little planes.

The final tally for VIII FC on this mission was 29–1–9 in the air and 4–0–6 on the ground. The mission cost six fighters.

Aug. 6, 1944, was a notable day for VIII Fighter Command for two reasons. First, it was the date for their second shuttle mission to Russia and second, the 352nd FG's Maj. George Preddy flew a truly outstanding fighter mission during his Group's trip to the Brandenburg area.

The 352nd was part of the escort for the 1st Air Task Force when they attacked aircraft production facilities near Brandenburg. As the force arrived in the vicinity of Hamburg, 30 Me 109s were seen stalking the bomber formation. Preddy was leading the 352nd FG on this mission and ordered the attack on the enemy fighters. Anxious to do battle, Preddy went after a flight of six 109s and opened fire. He reported the encounter as follows: "I opened fire on one near the rear of the formation from 300 yards dead astern and got many hits around the canopy. The E/A went down inverted and in flames. At this time, Lt. Doleac became lost while shooting down a 109 that had gotten on Lt. Heyer's tail. Lt. Heyer and I continued our attack and I drove up behind another enemy aircraft getting hits around the wing roots and setting him on fire after a short burst. He went spinning down and the pilot bailed out at 20,000 feet. I then saw Lt. Heyer on my right shooting down another enemy aircraft. The enemy formation stayed together taking practically no evasive action and tried to get back for an attack on the bombers who were off to the right. We continued with our attack on the rear end and I fired on another at close range. He went down smoking badly and I saw him begin to fall apart below us. At this time four other P-51s came in to help us with the attack. I fired at another 109 causing him to burn after a short burst. He spiraled down to the right in flames. The formation headed down in a left turn keeping themselves together in a rather close formation. I got a good burst into another one causing him to burn and spin down. The enemy aircraft were down to 5,000 feet now and one pulled off to the left. I was all alone with them now so went after this single 109 before he could get on my tail. I got in an ineffective burst causing him to smoke a little. I pulled up into a steep climb to the left above him and he climbed after me. I pulled it in tight as possible and climbed at about 150 MPH. The Hun opened fire on me but could not get enough deflection to do any damage. With my initial speed I slightly outclimbed him. He fell off to the left and I dropped down astern of him. He jettisoned his canopy as I fired a short burst getting many hits. As I pulled past, the pilot bailed out at 7,000 feet.

"I had lost all contact with friendly and enemy aircraft so headed home alone. CLAIM: Six (6) Me-109s."

The remaining pilots of the 352nd FG claimed an additional six enemy fighters. Doubles were scored by Capt. Henry Miklajcyk of the 486th FS and Lt. Charles Cesky of the 328th FS.

At 0930 hours on the morning of August 6, seventy-two P-51s of the 357th Fighter Group took off from Leiston aerodrome bound for Russia. Their assignment was to escort B-17s which were bombing industrial targets at Gdynia, northwest of Danzig and continue on to Piryatin in Russia. This was the second shuttle mission flown by the Eighth Air Force, and the 357th had to make ready in very short order since they were only given thirty-six hours to prepare.

Crew chiefs and some selected maintenance men were aboard B-17s as waist gunners in order to transport them to the Russian base. The bombers encountered some flak over the target but there was little to oppose the escorting P-51s. Some twelve Me 109s and FW 190s were seen, and combat took place over the Gulf of Danzig and intermittently to north of Brest-Litovsk Lt. Robert M. Shaw sighted two Me 109s attacking the last box of bombers and went down to intercept. He latched onto the tail of one of the 109s and

got several hits before the Messerschmitt broke right, split-essed and headed downward. Shaw hung on to the 109 and several more bursts brought about a stream of smoke emanating from under the cowling and the enemy craft went into a spin. Little did Shaw know that his victim was Hauptman Gunther Schack who had 174 victories to his credit.

The Mustangs of the 357th arrived at Piryatin and set down on the metal strip runway. There were no hangars or permanent buildings present except for a small wooden control tower. Living quarters consisted of pyramid tents which were fitted out with sleeping bags. Food was primarily GI rations served by sturdy, attractive Russian girls who were to be strictly "left alone."

On August 7 the Mustangs escorted the bomber force which attacked an airfield near Krakow, Poland. Some enemy opposition was encountered and three enemy aircraft were destroyed. The following day the 357th shuttle group headed for Italy. En route the bombers attacked targets in Romania where the Mustangs destroyed one E/A. The 357th landed on one of the numerous airfields near Foggia, Italy, where they spent a couple of days.

On the tenth the Mustangs escorted a group of C-47 transports carrying wounded out of Yugoslavia. This proved to be a welcome, uneventful mission. On the morning of August 12 the fighters and bombers departed Italy en route to their bases in England. The Big Friends dropped their bombs on Toulouse airfield in France with good results. A lone Ju 88 was downed by Lt. Merle Allen.

During August 7 and 8 the VIII FC supported bomber missions to France or made fighter-bomber attacks on rail targets in France. On August 8, the 4th

P–51 parked on the field at Piryatin in Russia. The Mustangs encountered little enemy opposition during their shuttle mission duty. M. Olmsted

FG parted company with the rest of VIII FC and participated in a mission to Norway. Thirty-eight of its Mustangs escorted thirty RAF Beaufighters on a shipping strike. The Beaufighters attacked fourteen ships off the Norwegian coast near Verhaug with torpedos, sinking four and damaging several others. One Beaufighter was downed by defensive fire. After completing the shipping strike the 4th, less its Blue Section, headed toward German airfields in Norway for some strafing. At Stavenger-Sola aerodrome they blasted one Ju 88 into flames before heading on to other airfields. After checking three other airfields and finding no other targets the 4th set a course for home. As Maj. Leon Blanding led his charges back to the coastline, the German flak batteries unleashed a vicious barrage. One of the first planes hit was Blanding's, and the burst that hit the canopy severely wounded him in the head. Two other Mustangs were hit and crashed. Their pilots Capt. Frank Jones and Lt. Robert Fischer were both killed. These losses, coupled with the loss of Lt. Tom Underwood earlier in the mission, had made the Norwegian excursion a very expensive one for the 4th.

Eighth Air Force launched a massive strike on industrial targets in Germany on August 9, but weather conditions over the Continent prevented the bombers from carrying out their planned attacks. For their fighter escorts, though, the mission was an entirely different story. The Luftwaffe had scrambled hundreds of its fighters and was prepared to do battle. The 20th FG's assignment was to escort B-17s to targets in the Munich area. They had rendezvoused with the Fortresses near Brussels, but as the weather worsened all but one of the bomber groups turned back. With one bomber forma-tion to escort, the 20th's leader, Maj. Jack Ilfrey, decided to make a broad sweep around Munich looking for enemy fighters. As they approached Ulm the first enemy fighters began to appear. The 79th FS was the first to attack when its Red Flight jumped a gaggle of thirty FW 190s. In a swirling dogfight that went from 16,000 feet down to the deck, Red Flight destroyed seven German fighters and damaged three others. Less than five minutes later Capt. Bob Meyer led White Flight of the 79th in a bounce against fifteen more 190s and succeeded in destroying seven of them and damaging two. Meyer was credited with two destroyed and one damaged. About thirty minutes later the 55th FS saw about fifty Me 109s following the bombers and attacked. They quickly destroyed two more enemy fighters, and with these two final victories the 20th FG completed its most successful mission to date. It returned to King's Cliffe with 16-0-6 victories against no losses.

The 364th FG followed closely on the 20th's heels with ten aerial victories, and then added twenty-four ground victories to that total.

The Mustangs of the 364th Group swept the areas of Beckingen-Regensburg and Kaufbeuren, Germany, on the way to the target and then proceeded to strafe airfields in the Munich area. One flight of the 385th Fighter Squadron under the leadership of Capt. Fred McClanahan sighted an airfield at Gaukenigshofen with many aircraft on it. There was a dummy airfield site about two miles away and the initial letdown brought the P-51s in on the wrong field but this was quickly rectified. McClanahan destroyed two E/A. The balance of his flight accounted for twelve more,

Lt. Col. John H. Lowell of the 364th FG aloft in his Mustang. The 364th FG exchanged their P-38s for P-51s in July 1944.
USAAF

132

Mustangs of the 364th FG get ready to take off on an escort mission. USAAF

the majority of which were twin-engined fighters—Me 110s and 210s.

Maj. George Ceuleers leading a flight in the 383rd Fighter Squadron took his Mustangs down on strafing attacks against two aerodromes and was on the way home when he sighted another field southwest of Munich. Ceuleers led his flight in and bounced fifteen to twenty FW 190s in the traffic pattern. The 190s broke and scattered dogfights took place all over the area. Ceuleers managed to get shots off at three 190s and saw one do a double snap roll at low altitude before it spun into the ground and blew up. The 384th Squadron was also involved in the fight and Lts. John J. Gawienowski and Frank Kozloski chased a 190 between the hills over a river bed until it finally crashed. Just after the 190 crashed, a training aircraft was seen heading balls out in the other direction. The Mustangs did a quick 180 and tacked onto its tail. After a series of passes against the wily little opponent it, too, smashed into a hillside.

While the Mustang groups were raising hell at high altitudes the P-47s were finding targets galore on the ground. The 78th FG turned its guns on the German rail systems and destroyed twenty-one locomotives and damaged numerous rail cars, and the 356th FG added another seven locomotives to the total. The 479th FG, still flying P-38s, found tempting targets on German airfields near Furth and destroyed seven enemy planes by strafing.

As a whole, August 9 was a very successful day for the VIII Fighter Command as its pilots claimed thirty-nine aerial and twenty-four ground victories and damaged another twenty-nine enemy aircraft against a loss of only three.

In order to support the operations in Normandy and to prevent the reinforcement of German ground units in that area, VIII FC dispatched seven fighter groups to France on August 10. They were to attack truck convoys and rail targets between Paris and Ger-

man depots in Belgium. One of the groups participating was the 479th FG and the mission was to cost them their commanding officer, Col. Kyle Riddle. The 479th's sector was the rail lines from Vesoul to Melun, France. As they roared down the rails, targets were spotted and their first target, a train, was destroyed near Oulchy LeChateau. Shortly afterward Riddle led his men to a marshaling yard where they were met with a barrage of light flak. As they passed over the target, Riddle's left wing burst into flames and his plane dropped to a dangerously low altitude. Riddle was then able to straighten his stricken P-38 out long enough to pass over the crest of a small hill and then belly it in. After his plane came to rest Riddle scampered to safety, and watched his unit carry out its attack. One more of the Group's Lightnings was brought down and its pilot killed, but in spite of their losses the 479th destroyed nine locomotives and more than 100 rail cars.

These interdiction raids continued through August 14 and then, on August 15, the Eighth Air Force turned its attention to Luftwaffe control stations and airfields in Germany, France, Holland and Belgium. The first strike force, which was composed of RAF Lancasters and Halifaxes escorted by four groups from the VIII FC, encountered no opposition from the enemy. However, for the second strike force, which was attacking targets in the Cologne, Frankfurt and Wiesbaden area, the situation was totally different. The 364th FG encountered a number of enemy fighters in the vicinity of Frankfurt and engaged them in several air battles.

The 364th, with Lt. Col. Jack Dale leading, was providing target area support in the Frankfurt area when its flights and squadrons were bounced by a mixed force of Me 109s and FW 190s. These fighters seemed to be doing their utmost to get most of the escort to abandon their mission and go off chasing enemy aircraft. Dale took the 384th Squadron and skirted the flak over Frankfurt to the north keeping a

133

gaggle of enemy fighters in view. When they began to queue up in the area where the bombers would rally after coming off target, Dale took his fighters to the attack: "I gave chase at 3,000 RPM and 67 inches of mercury in a slight dive, closing on the gaggle while they were attacking the last group of the last wing. The 383rd Squadron had just entered a fight with a gaggle. As I did not immediately see the Huns, I instructed Lt. L. A. Johnson to assume the lead and I would follow him. He had executed his first pass, picking off a tail-end Charlie, when I saw an FW 190 making a bounce on a burning B-17. I bounced this E/A at 22,500 feet with my wingman. The 190 split-essed to the left, did a rollout to his left and headed for the deck at a 50 degree dive. I had no trouble keeping up with him and opened fire with a one and a half second burst, at about 200 yards and ½ radi lead observing strikes on the fuselage. He took evasive action right and left and I gave him another burst at slightly reduced range, from dead astern. Finally at 2,000 feet he rolled to the right, with smoke pouring out and wheels flopping down. He dove into a patch of woods, exploding when hitting the ground."

The 364th accounted for ten enemy aircraft in scattered air battles while losing none of their own.

The 3rd Task Force also encountered enemy activity, and the 479th FG accounted for another three aerial victories, one of which was claimed by Capt. Arthur Jeffery. The Group then headed for deck and claimed another 4-0-3 enemy planes on the ground and then shot up an antiaircraft battery for good measure.

The Command's tally for the mission was 22-0-11 but it was at a cost of six of their own.

The Eighth Air Force returned to Germany on August 16 to strike at industrial targets and airfields. The Luftwaffe met them with a strong defensive force, and engaged several of VIII FC's units. The first battle took place over Eisenach when the 20th FG waded into a mixed force of over ninety Me 109s and FW 190s attacking the bomber formation. The 77th FS led by Lt. Col. Cy Wilson destroyed six of the enemy fighters and damaged one. Two of the victories were claimed by Wilson and the story was told by the Group historian as follows: "Lt. Colonel Wilson first picked out an FW-190, got on its tail and fired until the pilot bailed out. He then swung over and blasted at a 109. The canopy flew open and another pilot decided it was better to live than die for the Fatherland. Again the Colonel started after the planes but this time his Mus-

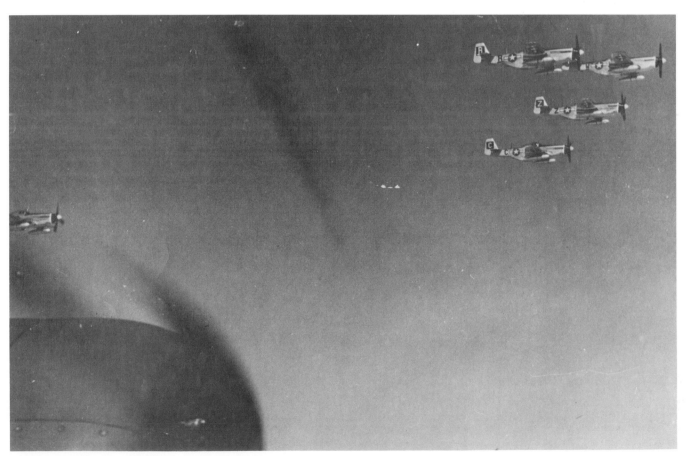

P-51s of the 79th FS, 20th FG in a photo taken from a B-17. This scene portrays the greatest morale booster the bomber crews experienced.

134

tang refused to put out and he lost all his power much to his disgust as he had his heart set on destroying five today."

Lt. Col. John B. Murphy, leading the 359th Fighter Group, and his wingman, Lt. Cyril Jones, were headed west at 27,000 feet at Bad Lausich, southeast of Leipzig, positioned to the rear of a box of B–17s. Murphy sighted a long, dense, white contrail, about half a mile long, climbing toward the bombers. Due to its speed and altitude advantage Murphy knew that there was no way he could overtake it. At the same time he noticed a straggling B–17 at 25,000 feet which was headed northward to Leipzig all alone. Murphy figured that this Fortress would become a likely target for the German jet. The jet made a pass at the bomber formation and went on down to attack the straggler. Murphy couldn't beat him to the Fortress but he wasn't far behind. He scored a few hits, but had to pull up sharply to the left to keep from overrunning and placing himself in front of the jet.

As Murphy pulled off to the left his wingman, Lieutenant Jones, closed the gap. After taking the hits from Murphy, the now identified Me 163 split-essed with Jones right behind. Jones fired one burst and missed, but increased his deflection and saw the canopy of the aircraft shattered as his hits took effect. As Jones passed behind the jet he hit jetwash and did a hard turn to get out. At that time Jones blacked out and on recovery was unable to see the Me 163 which had been headed straight down with what was apparently a dead pilot at the controls. German records later confirmed that this was true and that the pilot was Lt. Hartmut Ryall of I/JG 400.

After Murphy pulled up into his chandelle he sighted another Me 163 off to his right. He started down and was able to overtake it as the jet was making shallow diving turns. Murphy held his fire until he closed to 750 feet and then held a continuous burst while observing strikes all over the fuselage. Parts flew off and a big explosion took place, and Murphy picked up the odor of chemicals as he flew through the debris. FW Herbert Stratznicki of I/JG 400 had fallen under the guns of the Mustang pilot.

Jones' statement regarding the Me 163 was as follows: "While the 163 has its jet [actually a rocket engine utilizing chemical propellents] in operation it would be impossible for the P-51 to overtake it, but with the jet off or expended, it seems to be slower than the P-51. It is difficult to judge the speed of the jet with its power off and its speed seems to change very quickly . . . It climbs at an almost vertical angle, faster than conventional aircraft at level flight, with its power on. It also has very great acceleration with power on and a fast gliding speed immediately after using its power."

Two other Mustang groups, the 339th and the 355th, combined for another sixteen aerial victories and the VIII FC finished the day with another overwhelming victory over the Luftwaffe. It had destroyed thirty-two enemy fighters against three losses.

There were three noteworthy events that took place on August 18. One was that command of the 479th FG was assumed by Col. Hub Zemke. After a long and successful tour with the 56th FG and its P-47s, Zemke went after the opportunity to command a Mustang unit. On this date the group still was flying P-38s but it was due to convert soon. The second event of the day which did not escape notice of the entire command was the daring rescue of Capt. Bert Marshall by Lt. Royce Priest.

Quite a number of the fighter groups were assigned to fly sweeps against rail targets north and west of Paris. The 355th Group, led by Captain Sluga, was so designated. The squadrons split up and met with varied success against marshaling yards in the area. While the 357th Squadron flew top cover, the 358th accounted for several direct hits on the rail yards and also destroyed three staff cars and a bus in the area. Lt. Brien was downed by flak but eventually managed to make his way back to England. Sluga was hit by flak and had to bail out over the Channel where he was picked up by a mine sweeper and returned to England.

The amazing feat of the day came about after Capt. Bert Marshall, commanding officer of the 354th Squadron, was hit by flak which caused him to lose his coolant. When it was apparent he wasn't going to make it home, Marshall reported over the R/T, "My plane has been hit by flak, I'm gonna belly in."

Lt. Royce Priest got on the R/T and told Marshall, "Land in a road, coach. I'll land and pick you up."

Marshall protested, but once he had bellied in, Priest began to look for a place to set down. He finally found a field about three quarters of a mile away that looked good and brought the Mustang in. Marshall ran as quickly as possible to get there, but the course was difficult and he had to slow down to a fast walk to make it. Priest had turned the Mustang and taxied out of that field, across the road and into another that looked promising.

Capt. Bert Marshall and Lt. Royce ("Deacon") Priest of the 355th FG reenact the tight cockpit fit that was used in Priest's pickup of the downed Marshall. B. Marshall

135

Priest stood up in the cockpit, threw his parachute on the ground and called for Marshall to "Get in!" Marshall protested but there was no time for lengthy conversation. After a reasonable amount of profanity Marshall got in the seat and Priest sat in his lap. Priest then taxied back across the road, lined up with his improvised runway and gave the P–51 some throttle. The canopy came back and hit him on the head, but Marshall grabbed it and pushed it closed as they raced forward. Suddenly, a hay stack loomed ahead, but Priest hauled the stick back and they just managed to clear it. The trip back to Steeple Morgan was uneventful, but the control tower operation was really shook up when Priest told him he was coming in with two men on board. Priest's daring rescue was acclaimed by VIII Fighter Command, and he was awarded the Distinguished Service Cross for his feat.

The third major event of the day was the daring and devastating strafing attack on Nancy-Essey airfield in France by the 479th Fighter Group. The Group, led by Colonel Zemke, was to provide escort for the B–24s assigned to bomb the airfield. As the airfield came into sight the Liberators dropped their deadly cargo on the northern, eastern and southern parts of the field and achieved excellent results. The 436th FS continued on as bomber escort while the 434th and 435th FS turned and prepared for a strafing run. The first two passes were made by Zemke and seven pilots of 434th FS. When very little flak was seen, Zemke called for the rest of the planes to join in the attack. At least seven passes were made over the field and the explosive firepower of the P–38s turned the remaining undamaged German planes into flaming wreckage. When the attack started more than seventy planes were seen on the field, and when it ended, forty-three were destroyed and twenty-eight more were damaged. Twenty-eight of the Group's pilots shared the victories, and only one pilot was lost in the attack. The P–38 flown by Lt. P. W. Manning was seen streaking over the field at 100 feet altitude when it took a flak hit directly in the cockpit. The big fighter shuddered, rolled over and crashed into the main street of Nancy.

Aug. 18, 1944, had been a day of bad timing and misfortune for the 4th Fighter Group. Late in the afternoon Captain MacFarlane led a dive-bombing/strafing mission to France. As the formation approached Les Andelys it went down to 4,000 feet and split into attack formations. Not seeing much rail traffic, the Mustangs began looking for targets of opportunity. Finally some rolling stock was spotted and the planes bombed, but just as they pulled up they were bounced by Me 109s, and three Mustangs went down under enemy guns.

Col. Hub Zemke with his P–38 in which he led the 479th FG on a number of successful missions. Zemke fell victim to *extremely bad weather and became a POW on Oct. 30, 1944.* USAAF

Twenty minutes later the Group was again attacked, this time by over fifty enemy aircraft. In this battle six more Mustangs went down and five pilots died. The 4th did claim five aerial victories during the two engagements, but that was small consolation for the loss of nine of their friends. Two of these pilots evaded and later returned to Debden, one became a POW, and six were killed.

Six days later the 4th headed to Germany on an escort mission to Misburg, and then picked up the returning bombers at Merseburg for the homeward flight. On this leg of the mission the pilots from Debden got the opportunity for a little revenge for their losses on the 18th. The first two victories were scored by Lt. Ted Lines who caught a couple of 109s trying to sneak in and attack some stragglers in the bomber formation and shot them both down in flames. As they approached Nordhausen several pilots of the 336th FS saw an airfield filled with Ju 52 transports and went down to strafe. The strafing attack was deadly and successful, and eight of the tri-motored craft were set ablaze, but as in so many of these low level missions casualties were suffered. In this case it was fate that caught up with Capt. John Godfrey. He had already destroyed four of the E/A and his wingman, Lt. Melvin Dickey, claimed another three. Somehow there was a mixup, and Godfrey's Mustang was hit by Dickey's gunfire and another of the 4th's great Aces was now out of the war. Godfrey survived the crash landing but became a POW shortly afterwards. The final tally for the day's mission for the 4th FG was ten victories.

VIII Fighter Command returned to Germany on August 25 and escorted the bombers attacking industrial targets throughout the country. The 20th FG was assigned to escort 180 B-17s of the first Division from the western border of the Jutland peninsula to Pennemunde and out again. On the way back to England the 55th Fighter Squadron saw some seaplanes in the waters of Kubitzer Bay and Lt. Col. Wilson sent the 55th down to look the situation over. What they found was a combined seaplane base and airfield crammed with at least eighty camouflaged aircraft. The pilots quickly went into an attack formation and struck at the base. One pilot was downed by flak, but thirty enemy aircraft were destroyed and another twenty-one damaged in the attack.

The 434th FS of the 479th FG had a highly successful day. The squadron was part of the escort that was escorting B-24s striking at Wismar, Germany. Just before the formation reached its target area a large gaggle of at least forty Me 109s was spotted. The sixteen Lightnings of the 434th charged into the German formation and scattered them over the sky. Then in a series of dogfights five enemy fighters were shot down, two others were credited as probables and one other was damaged. Capt. Robin Olds led the pack in scoring, claiming three Me 109s, and the other two 109s went down under the guns of Capt. ("Cap") Duffie. All of the 434th FS made it home safely in spite of intense German aerial opposition and heavy ground fire. The unit

reported the flak over Rostock, Germany, as follows: "Rostock threw up heavy flak, light flak, small arms, and the kitchen sink at the battling P-38s and Me-109s from the deck to 4000 feet."

While the P-38s of the 479th were fighting it out with the Luftwaffe, they also became involved with the Mustangs of the 361st Fighter Group. Capt. Martin Johnson, Jr., sighted the fight going on down below and dropped down to join in. Johnson stated: "I singled out one E/A and just as I was positioning myself for an attack my wingman and I were in turn attacked from the rear by several P-38s. Consequently, I was detained in going through with what was to be that Jerry's fate and broke into the P-38s shaking them. I again picked a sparring partner and for the second time I became the picture in a P-38s gunsight and had to change my plans. At this time 2 Me 109s singly made head-on passes at me with all guns blazing. Most discouraging, Me 109s in front of you and P-38s behind, all shooting. Finally, I had to shake the P-38s a third time and then picked out my third would-be victim and the real scrap started. He was definitely a 'hot rock.' When I first encountered him he was giving a P-38 one hell of a battle. I took him on just as he had gained the advantage of the P-38, who quickly pulled out and left me with the 109. For several round abouts all I could get was a 90 degree deflection shot and this is where I made my mistake. The Jerry kept his belly tanks on throughout the fight. We went through some of the most violent and beautiful, to say the least, maneuvers I've ever seen performed in an A/C. I kept firing at him every chance I could and on 3 different occasions he led me down and across the city of Rostock and the airfield there at 2,000 feet. They really threw up the flak then. Finally I got on his tail to stay and with only one gun firing I managed to get my last burst into what appeared to be his cockpit. He then went into a spiral from about 4,000 feet and at about 2,000 feet he went over on his back and went straight in."

August 26 was spent hitting at coastal targets in France and the low countries and it proved to be a costly day for VIII FC as ten of its planes went down. The following day the Eighth Air Force returned to Germany and the bad luck continued for VIII Fighter Command as eleven planes were lost. One of the losses was the commanding officer of the 20th Fighter Group, Lt. Colonel Cy Wilson. His group had been assigned to escort bombers which were to strike at industrial targets in eastern Germany. Bad weather over the target areas prevented bombing, so the bombers split up into small groups and looked for targets of opportunity. When this occurred the 20th covered the bombers attacking Esbjerg airfield on the western coast of Denmark. As soon as the bombs had been dropped, the 55th and 77th Squadrons led by Wilson went down to strafe. Unfortunately, the German flak gunners were at their post and were firing an intense and extremely accurate barrage. Three planes were hit immediately, and their pilots began looking for the right place to put them down. Wilson and Lt. Alphonso Kent of the 55th FS both pulled up and headed to sea, then bailed out about ten miles offshore. Both men were rescued by Danish fishing boats within minutes, but the third pilot, Lt. Anderson, also of the 55th, tried to belly-land in the sea and went down with his Mustang. A few moments later the Group lost a fourth pilot when Lt. Ed Doering of the 77th FS lost his coolant and had to jump. To add insult to injury, this raid which had cost the 20th its commanding officer and three other pilots, added only one enemy plane destroyed to the Group's tally. The pilots did continue on over Denmark for a little while longer, and took out their frustration on rail and highway traffic.

Later in the day VIII FC dispatched 316 P–47s on a fighter-bomber attack on targets in eastern France and western Germany. In these raids the Thunderbolt pilots claimed 14-0-4 enemy planes destroyed or damaged on the ground against one loss.

On the ground the Allied dash across France was in full swing. By August 28 the First and Third US Armies had crossed the Marne River on a ninety-mile front between Paris and Chalons and were pushing toward the Aisne River. With this rapid movement the demands

on the VIII FC and Ninth Tactical Air Force for ground support missions were increasing. On August 28, VIII FC responded by dispatching 796 fighters to support the ground troops. In Field Order 538 a large force of 606 planes were sent on fighter-bomber attacks on rail targets in Holland, Belgium, eastern France and western Germany. It was another costly mission for VIII FC as nineteen of its planes were lost. Its planes claimed 19-1-0 aerial victories and another 11-0-8 on the ground. The planes dropped 8,216 tons of bombs on enemy installations and then followed up with strafing attacks which destroyed countless other enemy installations and facilities. The enemy's rail systems suffered heavily in these strikes: 189 locomotives and 260 rail cars were destroyed, and over 1,000 locomotives and rail cars were damaged. Five of VIII FC's losses were suffered by the 4th FG and one of them was a 335th FS ace named Maj. Pierce McKennon. Three of the pilots that went down were killed and one became a POW. McKennon was able to evade capture and eventually made it back to Debden.

The 353rd Fighter Group was one of the more successful units that morning as they destroyed twenty-

Thunderbolt of the 353rd FG loaded with bombs. The "Slybird" Group excelled at bombing and strafing. USAAF

two locomotives, sixty-six freight cars, thirty-three trucks and various other targets of opportunity. One of the pilots who had been in on the loco busting was Capt. James Ruscitto who was leading Blue Flight in the 350th Fighter Squadron. Ruscitto knew he was about out of ammunition, for he had seen tracers signifying the end of the belt was near when he had finished strafing. However, he sighted an Me 110 with wheels and flaps down over an airfield just outside of Wavre, Belgium. The 110 was at twelve o'clock to him so he headed for it. As he crossed the boundary of the airfield, light flak opened up and one 40 mm shell almost took the left aileron off his Thunderbolt. He kept going, closed the distance to the Me 110 and fired. He got hits in the wing and then was out of ammo. Still in pursuit he followed the Me 110 which proceeded to let down for a crash-landing. The E/A hit the ground and his right gear, which had still been down, caused him to spin to the right and one wing broke off while the rest of the aircraft skidded into a clump of trees.

Ruscitto had to pull up sharply to avoid hitting a church steeple and at that time he sighted another Me 110 at only about fifty feet high. He called for his wingman to "shoot him down as [I] am out of ammo." Ruscitto had not noticed that his wingman had pulled off to one side to avoid the flak over the airfield. The Thunderbolt pilot decided that he would "bluff" the E/A and he pulled right in on his tail. The enemy pilot apparently hit the panic button, for he continued down and crash-landed the aircraft, which bounced back into the air about sixty to eighty feet and then slammed back onto the deck which wrecked the plane completely.

During the second mission of the day about 190 fighters were sent out on fighter-bomber missions against targets in northern France, Holland and Belgium. It was during this mission that the pilots of the 78th FG were introduced to the plane that instituted a new beginning in aerial warfare. At the time of the encounter the 78th was engaged in attacking ground targets near Brussels. A flight of eight of their P-47s led by Maj. Joe Myers was flying top cover when the unidentified plane made its appearance. From his altitude of 11,000 feet Myers looked down and caught sight of an unusual aircraft moving along at a surprisingly high speed. Deciding to investigate, Myers led his flight into a steep dive and went after the mysterious plane. His P-47 built up tremendous speed in the dive and gradually overtook the German plane. As he drew closer Myers realized it was a new twin-engined jet fighter, and tried to get it lined up in his sights. However, the German pilot had seen his approach and began taking wild evasive maneuvers. The plane twisted lower and lower toward the earth and suddenly the Me 262 crash-landed. As Myers flashed over the 262 he caught a glimpse of its pilot running to get away from his damaged plane. Almost simultaneously he saw the jet being hit by a hail of fifty-caliber gunfire from Lt. M. E. Croy's P-47. Even though neither of them had fired a shot at the Messerschmitt in the air, Myers and Croy shared the credit for the first Me 262 destroyed in combat. In addition to the victory over the new jet fighter, Lt. Col. Jack Oberhansley claimed a Ju 88 in a separate aerial action.

The first encounter with the new German jet had been successful, but it was a clear and ominous warning that the battle of the skies was not over yet. The VIII FC would now have a new and powerful adversary, one which if not checked, could rip the heart out of the bomber formations as they lumbered toward their targets deep in Germany.

Bombed-up P-47s of the checker-nosed 353rd FG taxi out for takeoff. USAAF

Capt. Gerald E. Budd's Thunderbolt Roger The Lodger
*undergoes servicing. The 78th FG was another unit that kept
its Jugs into the fall of 1944.* USAAF

As August ended, Allied troops had pushed across France and into the low countries as a result of the ground war. However, in the early days of September a dramatic change took place. The rapid movement and sledgehammer blows to the enemy, which had highlighted the Third Army's drive across France, suddenly was grinding to a halt. The reason: Patton had outrun his supply lines. D-Day planning had called for US armies to halt and regroup at the Seine River before pursuing the Germans deeper into their own territory. No one could have foreseen the devastating breakthrough Third Army was to make, and so the prearranged plans had to go by the wayside in order to keep the enemy off balance and from regrouping. Patton's fuel crisis reached a peak during the first five days of September, and his armored legions were forced to stop.

Even with the front becoming static, VIII FC continued its interdiction raids against German positions and facilities in the occupied countries. If anything, these missions increased in importance because of the need to keep the German ground forces from regrouping and resupplying. On the first day of September, VIII FC sent its four Thunderbolt groups to Belgium to seek out and destroy rail and highway targets. Throughout the day these pilots inflicted fearful losses on enemy transportation facilities. More than 100 locomotives and 500 rail cars were destroyed or put out of commission by these roving raiders. Highway vehicles were not spared either, as nearly 400 vehicles, including fifteen tanks, were damaged or destroyed. Not content with the damage they had caused on the ground, the 78th FG bounced a formation of German aircraft and shot down five of them.

The Eighth Air Force struck in several directions throughout the day on Sept. 5, 1944, and VIII FC destroyed a record number of enemy planes on the ground. Of the 143 E/A destroyed on the ground that day, the 479th FG laid claim to fifty-two. The Group flew two missions during the day and worked over several German airfields. On the first mission with Lt. Col. Sidney Woods leading, the 479th strafed the fields at Bad Nauheim, Mershausen and Ettinghausen and claimed twenty-seven planes destroyed. On the second mission, Captain Duffie took the Group back to the Hanau area, and paid a return visit to the fields they had strafed that morning. In this attack twenty-five more enemy planes were torched and scores more were damaged.

VIII FC pilots not only found and destroyed the enemy's aircraft on the ground, but they worked over the Luftwaffe in aerial combat, too. The 55th FG joined in the scoring when they intercepted a flight of enemy training planes, and easily shot fifteen of them from the air. Right behind them was the 56th FG with nine aerial victories and over seventy on the ground.

In a most unusual combat, a flight of Mustangs from the 343rd Fighter Squadron of the 55th Fighter Group got involved with sixteen German training planes over Goppingen aerodrome. The P–51s were escorting the bombers en route to Stuttgart when Lt. Bill Allen called in aircraft taking off from the aerodrome. Lt. William H. Lewis, leading the flight, took his charges down to investigate. As they approached, they sighted a gaggle of sixteen single-engined and a few more twin-engined training aircraft heading north on the deck at not over fifty feet. The Mustangs passed

140

Two of the Mustang pilots from the 55th FG that got into the big training plane shoot-up on Sept. 5, 1944, were Lts. William

H. Lewis (left photo) and William Allen (right photo). Each was credited with five of the craft. USAAF

south of the airfield and attacked out of the sun from a five o'clock position. As the Mustangs drew within firing range some of the aircraft began to attempt crash-landings. Some of the pilots did fire a few bursts at the aircraft in the air, but most of the firing was done on crashed aircraft on the ground. When the P–51s finished making their strafing passes, fifteen of the aircraft had been destroyed. Lewis and Allen were officially credited with five destroyed, Lt. Ted Hoffman with four and Lt. William Perez with one.

The 56th Fighter Group was involved in two very successful strafing missions during the day. The morning mission led by Maj. Lucian Dade arrived in the area northeast of Koblenz, Germany, at about 1110 hours and began flying strafing attacks on Merzhausen aerodrome where some twenty-five E/A were sighted. The 62nd Squadron was successful in destroying nine of them despite some opposition from light flak. The 63rd Squadron then set out after targets on the autobahn when they were bounced by six or seven Me 109s.

Lt. Cameron Hart met one of the Messerschmitts head-on. Hart pulled up the nose of his Thunderbolt and the two craft closed on each other firing. Hart kicked his Jug around hard, seeking his opponent, but it was long gone. Hart sighted another 109 and by using water injection was able to pull his nose through and get some strikes. At this instant the 109 reversed its turn. The P–47 pilot then was able to close from astern and a good burst sent the 109 crashing into the ground.

Hart then engaged another 109 and was able to get on its tail but ran out of ammunition. The 109 was not aware of this and went down in a dive with the heavy Thunderbolt right behind. Hart pulled out at just above a hilltop, but the 109 was nowhere to be seen. In all probability it went on into the ground, but Hart had to settle for a probable. All told the pilots of the 63rd managed to down six of the 109s.

The 62nd Squadron had gone on to strafe Limburg aerodrome and got another six E/A on the ground to wrap up a very successful mission for the 56th Fighter Group.

Lt. Col. Dave Schilling took the 56th Group on its second strafing mission of the day that afternoon. The Thunderbolts arrived in the Hanau area northeast of Frankfurt at 1745 hours, and the 62nd and 63rd Squadrons proceeded to strafe Gelnhausen aerodrome. Schilling described what may be termed a classically efficient strafing attack: "I told my Red and Blue flights to orbit the field while I took my flight across the field to draw out any flak that might be around. On our first pass, we came across the field from East to West along the South side of the aerodrome. My No. 2 man and I were the only ones to fire on this pass, silencing flak positions on the east side of the field on the way in. I also fired at two FW 190s located near the SE corner of the field and raked my fire through a blister hangar near the center of the South side of the field, as I strafed the whole South side. Lt. Rotzler, my wingman, also strafed the entire length of the field, damaging some FW 190s which were lined up just in front of the hangar on the West side of the aerodrome. The flight then dropped to the deck and pulled up about two miles from the field.

"The flights' second pass was made in the same direction over the southern hangar line. Lt. Rotzler destroyed an FW 190 camouflaged under a tree, and Lt. Albright blew up a Ju 52 in flames in the SE corner.

"The third and fourth passes were made the same as the second. This time I destroyed an FW 190 E of the large hangar near the SW side. Lt. Rotzler destroyed an FW 190, and Lt. Daniel destroyed an FW 190 in the same area.

"I then called in that the flights could change their direction of attack due to the smoke and the availability of the target and to come in from the South to the North along the W. side of the field. Three passes were made in this direction by my flight.

"On my sixth pass I saw two planes in the hangar near the SW corner of the S side of the field and concentrated on them. Lt. Albright spotted another one in the hangar and destroyed it. The hangar burst into flames from my attack and burned to the ground, destroying everything in it. Lt. Rotzler destroyed an FW 190 in the SW corner on his 5th pass. On his 6th pass he suspected flak firing from the hangar on the W side of the field. Raking his fire down the entire length of the building, he scored many hits on the planes inside. On his 7th pass, Lt. Rotzler destroyed what he believed to be a Me 109 on the N side of the field."

When the strafing attack ceased the P-47s of the 62nd and 63rd Squadrons had destroyed a total of forty-seven enemy aircraft.

Other P-47 Groups joined in the destruction by striking at German rail facilities and doing tremendous damage. The 78th FG had a particularly successful day with 25-0-9 locomotives, and hundreds of other rail and highway vehicles destroyed or damaged. Their losses were two planes and pilots.

Another outstanding leader and Eighth Air Force ace fell to ground fire on Sept. 8, 1944. Maj. Quince L. Brown of the 78th Fighter Group was leading his flight when he sighted aircraft on Vogelsand airfield. Lt. Richard L. Baron related: "Brown called and said he was going to go over it and investigate. He made a steep turn and we ended up in string formation. He went over first and I saw tracers going at him, so I hit low for the deck. I looked up and saw several strikes on his plane. He pulled up sharply as we got across and I pulled up alongside. I saw his plane shake and his canopy come off. He then bailed out at about 1,200 feet. His parachute opened and I saw him land in a field. He than ran and lay down in some tall grass."

With this report from Lt. Baron the men of the 78th had high hopes that Quince Brown would either be able to evade the enemy or in the worst case, that he would become a prisoner of war. Such was not to be his fate, however. Brown was captured but was killed by a German Schutzstaffel (SS) officer who was prosecuted after the war.

On September 10 the VIII FC again returned to Germany in great strength and dealt the Germans another hard blow. In two separate missions the Command dispatched 640 fighters, 519 of which escorted bombers striking industrial targets in Germany. These pilots were able to claim six aerial victories and seventy-three more on the ground. Four of the aerial victories were claimed by Capt. Ted Lines of the 4th FG. He scored his first three victories when he jumped a flight of seven Me 109s near Schirmeck. In the battle, Lines' Mustang was hit by light flak, and he had to evade two of the 109s which were eventually driven off by two unidentified P-47s. In spite of the close call, Lines wasn't through hunting for the day and shortly afterward caught a Ju 188 over Kaiserslautern, Germany, and sent it down in flames.

VIII FC's second mission of the day was a strafing mission on airfields and transportation facilities in Germany. The 356th FG strafed areas east and south of Cologne and claimed seven locomotives and numerous rail cars, and the 353rd hit at targets in the Munster-Gutersloh area with similar results. The 78th FG, which strafed at targets east and south of Darmstadt, leveled the heaviest blow at the enemy and also suffered the highest casualties. Striking at several airfields, the 78th destroyed thirty-eight enemy aircraft and damaged another twenty. Eight of their own were lost in these attacks. High scorer was Lt. Robert Bosworth of the 82nd FS with four destroyed. He was closely followed by several other pilots who claimed three apiece.

Colorful takeoff line-up of Thunderbolts of the 350th FS, 353rd FG. USAAF

A 353rd FG Thunderbolt fully armed. This P–47 carries two 500 lb. bombs, 4.5 in. M–10 rockets, eight .50 caliber machine guns and its range is enhanced by a 150 gallon auxiliary fuel tank. USAAF

The targets for September 11 were the industrial and petroleum industries throughout Germany, and the Eighth Air Force was to meet the largest defensive force the Luftwaffe had put up since the previous spring. Not only did the Germans put up large numbers of interceptors, but they also apparently had worked out a new defensive plan. Large numbers of their fighters were encountered all along the penetration route, and a second large force was met in the target areas. The 1st Air Task Force hitting the Chemnitz machine works and oil plants at Ruhland, Bohlan and Baux felt the first blow, and its fighter escort had a real turkey shoot. In three separate air battles the 55th FG, the 339th FG and the 352nd FG claimed twenty-eight, fifteen and fourteen aerial victories respectively.

Lt. Col. John L. McGinn was leading the 55th Group when they sighted a gaggle of fifty-plus E/A. Two of the Me 109s seemingly made an overanxious pass at the escort before the gaggle was ready to attack the bombers. As the two broke, McGinn was on one of them immediately. This first 109 broke away so McGinn

latched onto another 109, set him up in the K–14 sight and blasted him.

By this time the entire group had swung back and met the gaggle of E/A head-on; combats ranged from 26,000 feet to the deck. Before the fight was broken off, the pilots of the 55th had accounted for twenty-six of the enemy while losing four of their own.

The 339th FG had to split up into squadron strength to cover the bomber formations which had become scattered. When they reached the vicinity of Jessa the 505th FS broke escort to pursue some E/A headed toward Munich. In an area twenty to twenty-five miles southeast of Munich, they observed a number of E/A scattered throughout airfields along the autobahn and went down for a strafing attack. In these attacks the 505th claimed more than twenty E/A destroyed before heading for home. About an hour later the 503rd FS encountered over 100 enemy fighters in the vicinity of Annaburg and went after them. The E/A were in two gaggles of fifty and were concentrating on the bombers when the Mustangs hit them. The 503rd shot down fifteen of the German fighters but could not completely break up the attack on the bombers. As a result, twelve of the B-17s also went down in flames. The 339th FG lost two pilots during the mission. Lt. Staggers was brought down by flak while strafing, and Lt. Jones was shot down later by an Me 262. Lt. Francis Gerard of the 503rd FS was the Group's high scorer with four victories.

Gerard was flying number three in his flight which was taking the heavies to Grimma, Germany. Four contrails were sighted ahead and below but his flight leader decided these must be decoys and that they had best maintain their formation with the bombers. Action was not long in coming, however.

Gerard related: "We stayed in the up-sun position and about 10 minutes later we sighted a large gaggle of E/A about 5 o'clock to us and going 90 degrees across our tail. We dropped tanks and started after the E/A who were in a slight dive and traveling at high speed. I didn't gain at first but as they made a 90 degree turn on to the bombers I started to close and fired some short bursts to distract them; they took no evasive action but continued straight at the bombers.

"I took the tail-end Charlie and he exploded after a short burst. Coolant and flames streamed out behind him and my wingman, Lt. Mayer, saw him spin with his wheels down and pieces flying off.

"Just before we reached the bomber formation I got on the tail of a 190 and he exploded after a short burst. Captain Robinson confirms this kill.

"I then damaged a Me 109 but in the confusion of diving through the bomber formation, dodging chutes and debris, I didn't see what happened to him.

"I started after another 109 going down but had two more coming in on my tail so pulled up in a tight turn. My G-suit came in very handy here and in two or three turns I was on their tail. I gave the nearer one two or three short bursts and he blew up and started down. I followed him in a steep dive and saw him spin into the ground.

"While going down Major Aitken passed me on the tail of another 109 and he was getting strikes all over the E/A. I pulled up as my speed was excessive and bounced another 109. I chased him a while before getting in position for an attack but when I did close he blew up at the first burst. He went into a crazy spin and I pulled up into a tight turn to clear my tail and look for other E/A. I saw my 109 hit the ground still spinning.

"I saw six more 109s break for the deck and rolled after them but only had 110 gallons of gas left so broke off the attack, climbed to 15,000 feet and started home.

"My G-suit was invaluable and I never want to fly combat without one."

The 352nd FG followed right behind the 339th with fourteen victories, and Lt. Col. John Meyer led them with four victories. It took Meyer only 587 rounds to down three Me 109s and one FW 190.

In the colonel's report he noted that most of the enemy seemed to be inexperienced and even hesitant in putting their aircraft into violent maneuvers. In the course of his combats, Meyer ran out of ammunition and was forced to outrun two Me 109s who attempted to bounce him on the way home.

The desperate enemy defense continued as the 2nd Task Force made its way to the target area. In simultaneous but separate air battles the 364th, 4th and 359th FGs continued the savage pounding of the enemy fighter forces.

All squadrons of the 359th Fighter Group encountered massive enemy attacks. They managed to break up large gaggles of 109s and 190s attacking the 100th Bomb Group, but not before a number of the B-17s had been shot down or damaged. Several of the damaged failed to make it back and once more the "Bloody Hundredth" suffered high losses. A number of Mustang pilots, not only from the 359th but also from several VIII Fighter Command groups, noted that the Luftwaffe fighters were flying excellent VIII FC formation to attempt to fool the escort as well as the gunners in the bombers.

Lt. Cyril Jones of the 359th's 370th Squadron led his flight after two Me 109s but when they were unable to close, they went down after two E/A taking off from Gotha aerodrome. These, too, got away, however. Another airfield was sighted south of Gotha and strafing runs were made, but most aircraft on the field were found to be dummies. Jones did strafe a Heinkel He 177 which burst into flames.

As Jones pulled up he sighted two Me 109s headed toward him. He and his wingman, Lt. Buchanan, latched onto them immediately. One of the 109s appeared to be damaged and dove into the ground trying to escape. Jones lined up on the other 109, scored hits and as he overshot, Buchanan got a burst into it. The E/A crashed into the field wiping out a number of the dummies on the field.

Jones continued on to Gotha airfield where he strafed and damaged two Junkers Ju 88s and two Me 210s on the ground. As he left Gotha he sighted two more Me 109s. A long burst took care of the first which cartwheeled across the ground. Blue Two and Blue Three tacked onto the other 109 which Jones later came after. He made two 360s with this aircraft and sent it crashing into some buildings.

The 359th Group downed twenty-five E/A during the heated combats and destroyed another eight on the ground, while six of its Mustang pilots failed to return to base.

The 364th Group, which was continuing along the same track of bombers as the 359th, encountered two gaggles of fifty-plus enemy fighters in the vicinity of Sangerhausen. The Mustangs attacked immediately and some of the German fighters went into a climbing Lufbery. However, the P-51 pilots were able to get above them and dive down to cut the 109s and 190s out of the formation and drive them to the deck where they could be disposed of. Eleven of the German fighters fell to these attacks. The remainder of the German formations stuck together as the inexperienced pilots were reluctant to attempt to fight. After downing an FW 190,

Capt. Cowan Hill found himself in the middle of a formation of some forty German aircraft. Rather than bring immediate attention to himself, he stayed with them until they reached an airfield at Frankfurt and proceeded to begin their letdown. At that time Hill peeled up and departed for home at full throttle.

The 4th FG had two encounters with the Luftwaffe and claimed a total of 8-1-2 in the air and 4-0-3 on the ground. In their first encounter the red-nosed Mustangs caught a group of enemy fighters trying a stern attack on a bomber formation and sent five of them down in flames. Later they caught another small formation and destroyed three in the air before going in for the strafing attack, which netted them the ground victories.

It was an extremely expensive victory for the 4th FG, as five of their own planes went down. Two of the pilots were killed in action and the remaining three became POWs.

The 3rd Task Force assigned to strike targets in Hanover, Misburg and Magdeburg was also greeted by the Luftwaffe defenders. The largest force of Messerschmitts was encountered by the 355th FG in the vicinity of Kassel.

Lt. Henry Brown was leading Falcon Blue Flight of the 354th Fighter Squadron when the interception was made. His flight encountered twenty Me 109s which went into a Lufbery. Brown went after a flight of four and immediately hit the leader who was flying a bit higher than the others. Using his new K-14 gunsight he took a large deflection shot and could hardly believe his own eyes when the 109 burst into flames and exploded.

Brown fell back into the Lufbery and shot down another 109. At this time he was attacked by two Me 109s. Brown turned into the 109s and they split. One tried to follow, but the Mustang pilot got on his tail and all but ran him into the ground.

Lt. Joseph Maisch, Jr., headed for home with his flight leader who developed engine trouble but finally made Maisch understand that he had wanted him to take over the lead, not turn back to cover him. Maisch headed back looking for the flight but instead sighted five flights of four Me 109s flying impeccable American-type formation attacking some B-24s. Maisch tacked onto the last flight of four and downed two of them before he found himself all alone and headed west.

The Luftwaffe showed renewed strength on September 11, and its pilots fought with real determination against the overwhelming forces sent out by the Eighth Air Force. The German pilots managed to bring down approximately forty bombers and fifteen Mustangs, but they did so at a prohibitive cost. VIII FC pilots had their biggest victory of the war to date in this battle. They destroyed 116 enemy fighters in aerial combat plus another forty-two on the ground for a grand total of 158-7-69.

The mission also included the third shuttle mission to Russia. This time it was the responsibility of the 20th FG to escort the B-17s to the targets and then on to Russia. The shuttle force escaped the attention of the Luftwaffe but encountered another tough foe—weather. A huge cloud formation was encountered and nearly blocked the way to Russia. Colonel Rau decided to scout ahead, and found some gaps in the cloud layers at 22,000 feet. The Mustangs dropped to this altitude and continued on toward Russia while the bombers plowed on through the clouds at 25,000 feet. As they came out of the weather front the 20th was somewhat scattered, but Rau quickly reformed his Group and resumed his escort to Russia.

The Eighth Air Force returned to Germany on September 12 and found the Luftwaffe up in strength. The escort fighters for the 1st Task Force ran into numerous gaggles of enemy fighters. The 336th FS of the 4th FG attacked fourteen enemy fighters near Frankfurt and destroyed five of them. Moments later, pilots of the 334th FS downed two more and the 335th FS claimed one for a group total of eight.

The most successful encounter by the 1st Task Force was made by the 352nd FG. In a series of air battles, the "Bluenosers" from Bodney destroyed thirteen enemy planes in the air. The 486th FS led the assault with eleven of the victories. Lt. Earl Lazear, Jr., was the high scorer with three, and Lt. William Gerbe was second with two. The two remaining victories were scored by pilots of the 328th FS. One of them was scored by one of the Squadron's rising young stars, Lt. Charles J. Cesky. This victory raised his total to 4½. Cesky related it as follows: "Before we were able to jockey into position both E/A fired rockets at the bombers, then pushed their noses down trying to evade us. The flight leader, Lt. Stott, took the one nearest to him and I and my wingman, Lt. Lambright, started after the other one. Almost immediately after the E/A fired its rocket I began shooting. Hits were observed on

Lt. Henry Brown, 355th FG, and his P-51 The Hun Hunter from Texas. *Brown became the top-scoring ace of his group before he was downed strafing. 355th FG Assn.*

145

both wings and wing roots, after which his left wheel dropped about six inches. Upon closing in to within 30 yards, I moved my sight well out on the left wing knowing I couldn't hope for my left guns to score any hits. As it turned out my right guns scored hits around the wing root and a little out on the E/A's right wing. At this time the E/A went into a spin to the right. I circled over him to 12,000 feet and watched him until he crashed into a wheat field and exploded."

The 364th A Fighter Group also encountered a large number of gaggles attacking the bomber formations and made some interesting observations. One squadron of the 364th sighted fifteen to twenty fighter contrails above the bomber stream. As the Mustangs climbed to attack, the enemy craft split-essed and headed for the deck. At this time the Germans loosed a vicious attack by some 200 FW 190s on the poor and strung-out formation of B–17s. Attacks were made from all sides and below, and the bombers took very heavy losses before the escort could come to the rescue.

The men of the 364th noted that this was their second straight mission where German fighters had chosen to make contrails above the bombers in order to get the escorting fighters to climb up to them. When the escort made its move toward them they split-essed for the deck, taking a number of the escort with them. At this time another force of enemy fighters who had been flying below and to the rear of the bombers would make their attack.

The Mustangs of the 361st encountered two gaggles of German fighters and found these pilots to be experienced and aggressive. Lt. Bill Kemp was leading Yellow Flight of the 375th Fighter Squadron when they sighted ten Me 109s coming in at ninety degrees to the bomber stream. Upon sighting the escort they did a 180 degree turn away from the P–51s, dropped their belly tanks and once more reversed their course and came

back at the Mustangs. Initially, combat commenced in a big Lufbery, but then fights began to break up and scatter all over the area. Kemp shot two E/A out of the Lufbery and then chased a third down to the deck where he put in his final burst at only fifty feet above the ground. The Group destroyed fourteen enemy planes.

For the second straight day the Luftwaffe fighter force had put up a large and aggressive defense. However, they again suffered heavily at the hands of the ever-growing and ever-improving VIII FC. On this date, fifty-four enemy planes were shot from the skies and twenty-six more were destroyed on the ground.

Heavy air action continued on September 13 and it was the 3rd Task Force bombing the synthetic oil plants at Merseberg and Lutzendorf that caught the bulk of it. In fact, all of VIII FC's aerial victories of the day were scored by two of the fighter groups escorting this task force.

Both heated combats by the 55th and the 357th Fighter Groups took place on the way home. The 338th Fighter Squadron of the 55th Group made initial contact with about a dozen Me 109s. When they called in that they were in a fight, the 38th Squadron rushed back to join in. However, as the 38th sped toward the rear of the bomber stream they sighted contrails of eight more Me 109s up high that had hoped to jump them from above. Lt. Merle Coons took his flight up to meet them head-on. They made a halfhearted head-on pass at the Mustangs and then attempted to pull back up into the sun, but the P–51 tore into them and split them up.

By this time the third squadron of the 55th, the 343rd, had joined in the fight. Although the E/A were

Lt. Bill Kemp and Betty Lee II *of the yellow-nosed 361st FG. Kemp won a Distinguished Service Cross in July 1944 defending the bombers and climaxed his career with three victories on Sept. 12, 1944, making him an ace with six victories.* U. Drew

Lt. Charles J. Cesky was one of the 352nd FG aces whose star would rise in the fall of 1944. S. Berlow

146

scattered, Lt. William H. Lewis spotted two Me 109s headed for a B-17. He peeled off and made his attack out of the sun and fired on one of the 109s until he overran the craft. As he passed the E/A it was smoking, spinning and headed downward.

The excellently coordinated attacks of the three squadrons from the 55th Fighter Group resulted in the destruction of sixteen enemy aircraft while not one of the attackers was able to break through to attack the bombers. Two Mustangs of the 55th failed to return from the mission.

The 357th Group encountered two gaggles on the way out. The first was composed of fifteen to twenty Me 109s south of Nordhausen. Capt. John B. England was leading the 362nd Squadron in the interception. He picked out a target, and as he sped down at 400 mph he went into a tight turn to line up on the 109. Thanks to the K-14 gunsight and new G-suit he was able to get good strikes while in a six-G turn. The E/A went down burning and out of control.

About twenty minutes later England took his flight in to attack another eight Me 109s. He singled out one and took him to the deck where he finished him off. England then did a 180 and sighted another enemy craft. This was a most skillful opponent, and he and the Mustang pilot went round and round in a Lufbery for about five minutes, each seeking to bring his guns to bear on the other. England finally got a few strikes and

one of his wheels dropped. This killed his speed and England overshot. At this time Lt. Fuller, the wingman, pulled in and got more hits on the 109. England returned and was still putting bullets into the craft when it crashed into a hillside.

The 357th scored fifteen kills that day but lost five of its own.

Lt. Merle Coons of the 55th FG in the cockpit of his P-38. Flying a Mustang named Worry Bird, *he became an ace in the fall and winter of 1944.* M. Coons

Chapter 13

Flak Busting

While the Eighth Air Force was flying these missions deep into Germany, General Eisenhower's Supreme Headquarters was busying itself in finalizing plans for Operation Market-Garden. This plan called for British and American airborne forces to make parachute landings behind enemy lines in Holland. It was hoped that this assault behind the battlefront would break the stalemate in the west and allow the ground forces to bypass the Sigfried Line and strike directly into Germany. The landings were to begin on September 17 and if they were to have any chance of success, the enemy's flak batteries would have to be silenced. The flights of C–47s and gliders carrying the paratroopers would be very vulnerable targets for the enemy's defenses in the Arnhem-Nijmegen area of the Netherlands. It would be utter suicide for the airborne troops to attempt a landing without first neutralizing the flak guns.

The job of neutralizing these guns went to the Thunderbolt groups of VIII FC. Their task: flak busting, a dangerous and most unenviable job. In effect, the pilots of the 56th, 78th, 353rd and 356th Fighter Groups

were to become decoys for the German flak gunners. To accomplish this, 200 P–47s were dispatched ahead of the transports on September 17 and flew at altitudes of 2,000 to 2,500 feet over the C–47s' course. As soon as enemy gunners opened up on them the P–47s would dive and attack. One of the Thunderbolt groups taking part in this mission was the 78th, and their historian described the action as follows: "The method of attack was this: A flight went down to between 2,500 and 2,000 feet and 'stooged' around to draw enemy fire, then the group went down and dive-bombed and strafed the guns. Fragmentation bombs (260 pounders) proved most effective in knocking out the guns. About ten to fifteen minutes after our attack began, all the German gun positions, with the exception of one battery just south of Nijmegen, stopped firing completely. After that the Group stayed in the area looking unsuccessfully for more ground gun targets. Then they returned to the coast and picked up the C–47s and gliders and flew along with them until they were cut loose and landed. The Group's intention was to neutralize any incipient

Formation of 61st FS Thunderbolts over England. The 56th FG faced one of its greatest challenges and suffered its highest *casualties on flak-busting duty in Holland in Sept. 1944.* P. Conger

ground fire, but they reported no firing on any gliders or tugs. Several flights went with C–47s carrying paratroopers, and of these C–47s some 10 to 12 were knocked down by gun positions which could not be located by Group pilots."

As can be seen from this account, things did not go as planned and it was obvious that both the forces on the ground and the forces supporting them from the air would have a rougher time than was anticipated. The German strength on the ground was much higher than intelligence had stated, and the antiaircraft forces were thick. On September 17 heavy fighting was encountered on the ground and the commanders were calling for more supplies. The next day a force of B–24s was sent in to drop supplies. The Thunderbolts preceded the Liberators to the drop zone and were greeted by heavy ground fire and hazy weather. The weather was so bad that their vision was seriously impaired. As a result they became easy targets for the ground gunners. The 56th FG, which was operating in the Arnhem area, suffered its worst day of the war. The Wolfpack lost sixteen of the thirty-nine planes it dispatched to the Arnhem area. Fortunately, eight of their pilots were able to guide their crippled planes down in areas occupied by Allied forces and escaped capture.

In direct contrast to the fate suffered by the 56th FG, the 357th FG encountered a large force of enemy fighters at high altitude and scored an impressive victory.

Maj. Thomas L. Gates was leading the 357th Group over the drop zone when a gaggle of German fighters was sighted. The bogies were some 2,000 feet higher than the Mustangs, so Gates turned the group to intercept and called for them to drop tanks as soon as they were clear of the gliders below them. The first bunch of Me 109s continued to climb into the sun and as soon as it appeared that they were not going to drop down to do combat, Gates led his charges into the Me 109s. Following a head-on pass, Gates managed to get on the tail of one of the E/A and flamed him with two bursts.

Gates and his wingman then climbed back up to 10,000 feet where they sighted five more 109s being bounced by some P–51s. One of the E/A made a break for the deck and Gates went after him. When they came over an aerodrome the enemy craft went into a steep turn. At that time Gates noted that there were American markings on the aircraft but its overall paint job was the same as on the 109s. Closer observation confirmed that it was a P–51 Mustang in German camouflage. Gates swung wide to avoid the light flak from the airfield and at that time the P–51 leveled out and headed out of the area at full throttle.

Of the 357th pilots scoring a total of twenty-six kills for the day, the most successful was Lt. Gerald E. Tyler who was credited with two Me 109s and an FW 190.

The 356th FG also enjoyed a great deal of success on September 18. They had again been assigned the thankless job of flak busting, and during sixty minutes of patroling the Nijmegen, Netherlands, area they destroyed a total of thirty-five flak batteries.

The Eighth Air Force again split its forces on September 19, sending formations into Germany and to the invasion area in Holland. The 1st Task Force heading for Germany ran into heavy cloud cover and the bombers were forced to strike at targets of opportunity. One of the escort groups was able to attack a small gaggle of enemy fighters and score some confirmed victories. The 55th FG caught four Me 109s on the deck and shot three of them out of the sky. The fourth enemy fighter escaped but only after his plane was heavily damaged.

The 2nd Task Force striking at marshaling yards in Germany encountered no aerial opposition. Over Holland, however, it was a different story. The 3rd Task Force, which was covering the invasion front, encountered numerous enemy fighters and won another decisive aerial victory. The 364th FG met more than thirty E/A near Wesel, Germany, and claimed 4-0-3 while losing one of its own planes. The force that struck the day's decisive blow at the enemy was again the 357th FG. In four separate air battles the Group claimed 18-1-1 victories for the loss of five of their own. Seven of the Group's pilots claimed two victories apiece. In two days the 357th had destroyed forty-four enemy planes against seven losses for a ratio of nearly 7:1.

The Luftwaffe remained unusually aggressive for the next few days and on September 21 it decimated the formations of Allied transport planes operating in the Arnhem, Netherlands, area. Because of a very heavy cloud cover only two US fighter groups were operating that day, the 56th and the 353rd. It turned out to be an active and successful day for the Thunderbolt pilots. The 353rd downed six enemy fighters over Nijmegen, and in another air battle northeast of the city the 56th FG massacred a formation of FW 190s. In that dogfight the Wolfpack claimed fifteen enemy fighters against a loss of three of their own. Scoring honors went to Col. Dave Schilling who claimed three.

Schilling had been patroling in the vicinity of Lochem, Holland, when he sighted an FW 190 and an Me 109 some 700 yards ahead of him. He flamed the 190 as it went into a sharp left turn. He then sighted a P–47 with an FW 190 on its tail about two miles to the north. As he climbed toward the combat the 190 pilot apparently sighted the Thunderbolt and tried to climb away but to no avail. Schilling made some good strikes from 700 yards and the pilot bailed out.

Schilling caught another FW 190 at low altitude which attempted to turn with him. A four-second burst from forty-five degrees sent the Focke Wulf crashing to earth.

Two days later the Germans were still putting up great numbers of fighter aircraft over the invasion area, and the aerial melees continued. While the dogfights went on above them other Thunderbolts continued the flak busting mission in support of the transports trying to resupply the beleaguered invasion forces. The 78th FG was particularly successful. They destroyed or damaged twenty-four flak positions, and shot up a German truck convoy. High above them the 353rd FG again tackled the Luftwaffe and defeated them handily.

The Thunderbolts of the 353rd Group were nearly at the end of their endurance when the Microwave Early Warning (MEW) controller called in bandits approaching from the northeast. As they turned, the P–47 pilots sighted a gaggle of thirty Me 109s followed by ten to fifteen FW 190s. As the Jugs turned to give combat most of the 109s broke for cloud cover at about 7,000 feet and some of them went into a defensive Lufbery. Some of the FW 190s headed for the deck but a few were aggressive and stayed to do combat. After several indecisive head-on passes with the E/A, Capt. Bill Price mixed it up with a 190 that chopped throttle and reefed up his craft into a tight chandelle. This surprised Price who overshot. A turning, weaving and circling dogfight went on for about ten minutes. When Price finally hit the 190, it was so low that it went in without a chance for the pilot to get out.

The P–47 pilots of the "Slybird" group accounted for nineteen E/A in the fight, with Lt. Bayard Auchincloss taking top honors with three victories.

It had been a heroic effort at Arnhem-Nijmegen, both on the ground and in the air. Allied forces had fought hard to gain a foothold in Holland, but the German ground forces in the area were too strong. The withdrawal of the British paratroopers had to begin. VIII FC had played a vital role in this ill-fated adventure, and had done an excellent job in its support role. It, too, paid a high price in the invasion. Seventy-three of its planes went down, of which forty-five were manned by the hard-working Thunderbolt pilots that had drawn the difficult and extremely dangerous job of flak busting.

The cost of Operation Market-Garden had been extremely high to the ground forces, as well. The British airborne division, which landed at Arnhem, suffered the loss of 6,600 out of 9,000 men in this fiasco, and the two American airborne division casualties numbered 3,500. The total casualties for this operation were extremely high for the limited gains that were made. For this price the Allies had pushed a sixty-five-mile corridor into Holland which included some bridgeheads over the Maas and Waal Rivers—but the advance fell far short of what Field Marshal Montgomery had expected to achieve.

The VIII FC flew its last missions in support of the invasion area on September 26 and for the 479th FG it would be a day to remember. The group, which began receiving its first increment of Mustangs earlier in the month, was flying a mixed formation of thirty-one P–38s and twelve Mustangs on the mission. Their assignment was supporting the C–47s which were dropping supplies to US forces in the Nijmegen area when they received an MEW vector to the Munster-Haltern area. (The Microwave Early Warning was a radar technique that enabled radar operators at ground stations on the Continent to vector the US fighters to formations of enemy aircraft.) Near Munster they found a large formation of at least forty enemy fighters flying at low altitude and headed for Arnhem. Using their altitude advantage the 479th dove on the enemy and struck hard. Dogfights broke out all over the sky and lasted for at least fifteen minutes. When it was over, twenty-eight enemy fighters had gone down under the guns of the 479th and eight more had been damaged. Two pilots scored triples. Lt. Col. James Herren destroyed three 109s, probably destroyed an FW 190 and damaged another, and Lt. George Gleason destroyed three Me 109s and damaged a fourth. One P–38 was lost in the battle.

The fighters went back to escorting the bombers full force on September 27. The most successes scored by any fighter unit were chalked up by the 361st Group who provided escort for the Third Force which struck targets at Kassel, Germany. The Mustangs were sweeping under the bombers when about forty FW 190s attacked from above and to the rear. Lt. William Beyer was leading Red Flight of the 376th Fighter Squadron when the storm hit. Beyer tacked onto a flight of eight FW 190s and began to pepper the tail-end Charlie from 400 yards. He closed to 100 yards still firing and getting good strikes when the FW's pilot jettisoned the canopy before the plane entered a cloud layer. Beyer dropped down below the clouds and saw a parachute drifting down to his right.

Beyer now had only his wingman with him, but he proceeded to find another 190 whose pilot took him through some split-esses and tight turns before being hit and bailing out. Beyer then pulled up to 1,000 feet, spotted another FW 190 and gave him a short squirt. This pilot didn't tarry. He jettisoned his canopy and bailed out. Number three!

The Mustang pilot then sighted and began chasing victim number four. This pilot dropped flaps and chopped throttle hoping that Beyer would overshoot, but the P–51 pilot did the same. As the 190 pulled up into a turn he took the full impact from the Mustang guns and bailed out.

A 190 then came in making a pass on Beyer but Lt. Robert Volkman latched onto him. The pilot bailed out before Volkman could open fire, however.

Beyer spotted an FW 190 coming in from the south, pulled up into a steep climb, did a wingover and placed his Mustang on the tail of the 190. It went into a steep turn to the left, pulling heavy streamers. Beyer dropped some flap to stay with him and gave him a couple of short bursts to scare him. The 190 then dropped to the deck, skidding from side to side. The German pilot nearly hit a tree and then tried to lead Beyer into some power lines. Beyer pulled up sharply but the German went under the lines, but to no avail. Beyer pounced on him from above and closed up to seventy-five yards before he pressed the gun tit. The 190 crashed into a house and blew up. Number five!

The 376th Squadron accounted for seventeen of the FW 190s while losing only one of their own.

On September 28 the 479th FG scored another lopsided victory against the Luftwaffe while escorting bombers in the Halberstadt area of Germany. In this mission the Group claimed 13-0-6 victories against no losses, and saw to it that the P–38 Lightning closed out its service in the Eighth Air Force in a blaze of glory.

The 20th Fighter Group met sharp opposition taking bombers of the 1st Force to Magdeburg. Lt. Ernest Fiebelkorn encountered two gaggles of about thirty-five E/A each. Fiebelkorn took his flight to attack a gaggle of Me 109s which immediately went into a Lufbery. He managed to shoot down two of them and damage another before the majority of the 109s were lost in the clouds.

Fiebelkorn went down through the overcast to see what he could find and broke out over a German fighter aerodrome. Approximately seventy-five single-engined craft were parked in revetments and around the perimeter track. As he climbed back into the clouds, Fiebelkorn received a call from his wingman that he was pursuing two E/A on the deck. Fiebelkorn asked if he needed help, but was told no. Regardless, Fiebelkorn dropped back down over the airfield and sighted five enemy craft in the landing pattern. He immediately got on the tail of a 190 with its wheels down. A couple of short bursts sent it crashing into the outskirts of a small village. As he pulled up, Fiebelkorn saw an Me 109 pull up his gear as he took off across the countryside. The Mustang pilot dropped down to the grasstops and closed to fifty yards to fire what ammunition he had left. It proved to be just enough to send the 109 skidding into the ground where it blew up.

October 1944 was a month of dramatic changes in the VIII Fighter Command. The P–38 flew its last missions for the Eighth Air Force, and the Fighter Command itself lost operational control of its fifteen fighter groups. On October 10 the three fighter wings that had reported to VIII FC now reported to the Bomber Divisions of the Eighth Air Force. These Fighter Wings, the 65th, 66th and 67th, now reported respectively to the 2nd, 3rd and 1st Divisions. These changes were intended to simplify the chains of command, and facilitate easier planning of fighter escort missions. These changes did not put Headquarters, VIII FC out of business entirely, though, as they maintained control over the three fighter training organizations in England.

A third very noticeable change in operations during October 1944 was the absence of the Luftwaffe. The enemy had been quite active during September and had suffered heavy losses. As a result, the German high command apparently decided to stand down and rebuild its dwindling fighter force during October.

The absence of the Luftwaffe drove the US fighters back down to earth. Like earlier strafing missions, these took a toll of VIII FC aces. On October 3 the 355th Fighter Group—which had rejoiced at the rescue of Capt. Bert Marshall, Jr., by Lt. Royce Priest—was greatly chagrined at the loss of two of its aces in a similar rescue operation that failed.

Capt. Henry Brown was downed by flak while strafing an Me 110 on the ground near Nordlingen. Brown bellied in his Mustang on a nearby field. Maj. Charles Lenfest landed his P-51 close to Brown in an attempt to rescue him. However, Lenfest's aircraft

Lt. George W. Gleason scored a triple in a P–38 and added two more flying a Mustang to become a 479th FG ace in Sept. 1944 USAAF

became stuck in the mud while taxiing across a small creek to effect the rescue. Unknown to them, Lt. Al White had also landed in a rescue attempt and was not able to gain the attention of either pilot. Try as they may, Lenfest could not get his aircraft out of the mud and both pilots were captured. At the time of their capture, Brown was credited with 14.2 aerial victories and 14.5 E/A on the ground. Lenfest was an ace with 5½ aerial kills and two ground victories. Following the failure of the rescue a strongly worded memo came down from Eighth Air Force strictly forbidding further rescue attempts.

In spite of the general lack of enemy activity in early October, the fighter pilots did have a couple of big days in terms of enemy aircraft destroyed. These victories occurred during the last few days of VIII Fighter Command's operational control of the fighter groups. On the mission of October 6 the Luftwaffe made an attempt to defend its homeland against the Eighth Air Force formations and in the process lost nineteen of its fighters. In addition to these aerial victories, strafing accounted for another thirty enemy planes. The strafing claims were all made by the 20th FG and the victory was their biggest to date. Most of the kills were scored against flying boats found at Jasmunder Bay, Groszenbrode and Bievenow Ost. The bulk of the victories went to the 55th FS which claimed a total of 20-0-8.

The mission of October 7 accounted for another thirty-eight victories, twenty-nine of which were aerial victories. The high-scoring group was the 361st with eight.

Three of the victories on the October 7 mission went to the 78th FG. Because of its flak busting assignment during the airborne assault on Arnhem-Nijmegen, the group had not had much opportunity of late to battle the Luftwaffe. Beginning with this mission things began to change somewhat for the 78th, and during the next several days they claimed more victories. Their next kills came on October 12 when they escorted bombers to Bremen, Germany. Fifteen FW 190s appeared as the 78th passed south of Hamburg. A brief dogfight ensued and two of the 190s went down under the guns of Lt. H. H. Lamb and Maj. Richard Conner of the 82nd FS. Conner had also scored one of the victories of October 7.

On October 15 the 78th returned to Germany on a planned strafing mission in the Hanover area. As they passed over the aerodrome at Bohmte, Germany, the 83rd FS spotted a number of FW 190s far below them. In the initial attack, Lts. Bob Green and Julian Reems dove after a flight of two 190s and downed both of them in short order. No sooner had Green downed his first victim than another Focke Wulf appeared in his sights. He followed the German's evasive maneuvers and hit the 190 with a number of well-placed bursts. The pilot jumped and Green's second kill continued on down to a fiery crash. As he pulled up, light flak was following him but it was wide of its mark. As he continued his climb, Green spotted another flight of four FW 190s. He broke toward them about the same time another P-47 (Reems') was attacking the number four man. Green then went after the number three man who tried frantically to lose him. This time it took only one burst of fire as the German fighter rolled over immediately and went straight down and exploded on impact. Green then circled upward and saw Reems

dogfighting with a 190. The two of them joined up and jointly downed the German fighter. When the battle ended, seven Focke Wulfs were shot down. Green was top gun with 3½ victories, and Reems followed with 1½. The remaining kills went to Lt. Lloyd Eadline of the 83rd FS and Lt. Huie Lamb of the 82nd FS, who chased an Me 262 over its airfield and shot it down.

Highly notable amongst the victories of the 361st Group that day was the destruction of two jet Me 262s by Lt. Urban L. Drew. This was the first time any pilot had ever shot down two jets in one combat. It was very rare at this date to even see one!

Drew was leading the 375th Fighter Squadron when the call came that the 361st was in a fight. He dropped his Mustangs down to join in. As they arrived below the bombers the fight had been dispersed so he and the flight that he was now left with stayed with a formation of bombers until they arrived over Achmer aerodrome.

At that point Drew reported: "I spotted two A/C on the A/F at Achmer. I watched them for a while and saw one of them start to taxi. The lead ship was in take off position on the east-west runway and the taxiing ship got into position for a formation take off. I waited until they both were airborne and then I rolled over from 15,000 feet and headed for the attack with my flight behind me. I caught up with the second Me 262 when he was about 1,000 feet off the ground. I was indicating 450 mph and the jet could not have been going over 200 mph. I started firing from about 400 yards, 30 degrees deflection, as I closed on him, I observed hits all over the wings and fuselage. Just as I passed him I saw a sheet of flame come out near the right wing root. As I glanced back I saw a gigantic explosion and a sheet of red-orange flame shoot out over an area of about 1,000 feet.

"The other jet was about 500 yards ahead of me and had started a fast climbing turn to the left. I was still indicating about 400 mph and I had to haul back on the stick to stay with him. I started shooting from about 60 degrees deflection, 300 yards and my bullets were just hitting the tail section of the E/A. I kept horsing back on the stick and my bullets crept up the fuselage to the cockpit. Just then I saw the canopy go flying off in two sections and the plane rolled over and went into a flat spin. He hit the ground on his back at about a 60 degree angle."

Both of the pilots were members of the Erprobungskommando Nowotny which was the experimental unit that had been formed as the initial Me 262 fighter unit under the command of the famed Luftwaffe ace Maj. Walter Nowotny. Lt. Kobert was killed in the first 262 that Lt. Drew hit, but the pilot of the second Me 262, Oberleutnant Bley, managed to bail out. By the month's end, however, he lost his life in a crash following takeoff.

There was a second successful jet encounter the same day when Lts. Elmer Taylor and Willard Erfkamp of the 364th Fighter Group caught an Me 163 attacking a straggling B-17. Taylor was leading Yellow

Lt. U. L. ("Ben") Drew and his P-51 Detroit Miss *of the 361st FG was the first Eighth AF pilot to down two Me 262s in one day when he caught them on takeoff from Achmer aerodrome on Oct. 7, 1944. Drew received a belated Air Force Cross (in lieu of a Distinguished Service Cross) on May 12, 1983, for his feat.* U. L. Drew

152

Another view of Lieutenant Drew's Detroit Miss. U. L. Drew

Section of the 385th Fighter Squadron in the vicinity of Brux, Germany, when the Me 163 was sighted. Taylor made a wide pass from his position 2,000 feet above the E/A in order to come down on its rear. He started shooting from 1,500 yards, hoping to damage it and get it away from the bomber. Surprisingly, the jet apparently had its rocket engine shut off as the P–51 closed rapidly. Taylor chopped throttle to stay with the 163 and continued to fire as he closed to 100 yards. The Me 163 rolled over and dived straight down, emitting a trail of smoke. Taylor called to his element to follow it and Erfkamp and his wingman took off after it. Erfkamp fired on the 163 as it continued downward at speeds up to 500 mph. The German pilot finally managed to pull out of the dive and landed the craft in a grassy field.

After being shot down in the spring of 1944, Lt. Charles ("Chuck") Yeager had evaded the enemy and made his way to Spain and thence back to England. At his insistence he was permitted to fly combat again and even though he was only a 1st lieutenant, in the fall of 1944 he was leading the 357th Group on missions. On October 12 he led their P–51s on an escort to Bremen and was on the way out when he sighted a gaggle of about twenty-five Me 109s near Steinhuder Lake. The Mustangs dove out of the sun and Yeager lined up on the tail Messerschmitt of the gaggle. Just before Yeager

Lt. C. E. ("Chuck") Yeager of the 357th FG in his Mustang Glamorous Glen III *downed five enemy fighters in one combat on Oct. 12, 1944. Yeager went on to become the first man to surpass the speed of sound and win many other acolades as an outstanding test pilot. USAAF, M. Olmsted*

153

had a chance to fire at his first victim, the pilot went over the side and bailed out. Skidding behind another, the same thing happened. Two down and not a shot fired! The next two did stay long enough to get shot at and both went down in flames. Victim number five tried to chop throttle and break in behind the P-51 pilot, but Yeager wasn't having any of that. He, too, chopped throttle, hung behind the 109 and shot it down.

Chuck Yeager's Glamorous Glen III. M. Olmsted

Chapter 14

Battle of the Gaggles

By October 15, aerial encounters with German fighters had come to a virtual standstill. For the remainder of the month the German fighter forces were so conspicuous by their absence that many people began to speculate that the Luftwaffe was finished. Logic would certainly support that school of thought. The Luftwaffe had been thoroughly mauled during the first nine months of 1944, and the long-ranged escort fighters of the Eighth Air Force controlled the skies over Germany. However, Allied intelligence knew that in spite of the continuing bombing attacks, German aircraft production was increasing and the Luftwaffe was no doubt building up its strength for retaliation. The reply from the German fighter forces was not long in coming.

The mission of November 2 was a massive attack against the I.G. Farben petroleum facilities at Leuna in the vicinity of Merseberg. Even though the Eighth Air Force attempted several diversionary tactics, the Ger-man controllers were not fooled and assembled their defensive force over the target area. The first force to cross the Initial Point was the 3rd Air Division and they were met by a mixed force of over 100 Me 109s and FW 190s.

Mustangs of the 55th Fighter Group were flying at 31,000 feet when the Me 109s and FW 190s, flying in one gaggle—but in three distinct sections about 4,000 yards apart—were sighted passing over at about 32,500 feet. The P-51 pilots dropped tanks and began to climb at full boost up to 35,000 feet. From this position they initiated their bounce on the rear of the enemy formation that was beginning to attack the bombers. The attack broke up the concentration of enemy aircraft and many of them broke for the deck.

Lt. Robert E. Welch started climbing with his squadron when the call came over the R/T that a fight was on. As he climbed, he noted a box of bombers

Lt. Robert E. Welch of the 55th FG in Miss Marilyn II. *Note the olive-drab rear fuselage and bare metal lower cowl and wings.* USAAF

under attack at his eleven o'clock position. He dropped tanks and dove down but the enemy craft broke and rapidly dispersed. As he climbed back up he found himself in the midst of a big dogfight with an Me 109 on his tail. Both aircraft went into a turning match that continued down to 14,000 feet. Both pilots then came on in a head-on pass at just above stalling speed. Welch got in a good burst and the right gear of the 109 was seen to partially drop, indicating damaged hydraulics. The E/A then started down out of control and the pilot bailed out about 5,000 feet.

Welch followed the 109 down, and like many other victorious pilots, he found that it was nearly a fatal mistake. As he circled the parachute to the ground Welch found himself with two Me 109s on his tail, with all guns blazing! His reaction as he described it was: "I shoved everything to the firewall, said a prayer, unlocked my gyros and headed up toward the overcast. The E/A fired at me until I went into the overcast; very poor shooting with no deflection. I flew balls out on instruments for 15 minutes straight west and then broke out and joined up with three green-nosed P–51s."

In the course of his combats, Welch also observed a veteran Luftwaffe pilot neatly maneuver himself onto the tail of a Mustang. This P–51 was on the tail of the 109 and had every advantage. As the 109 started a flick roll the P–51 started to roll, too. The German pilot stayed on his back for half a second, not split-essing as the P–51 pilot expected. The enemy pilot quickly completed his half-roll with a snap, pulled the nose up in a steep climb, losing air speed, and then did a pushover forward, bringing him out directly on the tail of the Mustang which had completed a sloppy slow-roll.

Capt. Donald Bryan, shown here with blue-nosed Little One III *of the 352nd FG, joined the "five in a day" club on Nov. 2, 1944, when he accounted for five Me 109s and damaged two more.* D. Bryan

The diving attacks of the 55th Group Mustangs succeeded in breaking up the gaggles of E/A while their pilots accounted for seventeen of their number.

The major encounter took place about twenty minutes later and involved the 20th, 352nd, 359th and 364th FGs, escorting the 1st Air Division B–17s. First contact was made when Maj. George Preddy, CO of the 328th FS, spotted fifty E/A headed for the bombers. Moments later they saw other formations of German fighters, and the 352nd's squadrons split up and went after them. Preddy's 328th struck with a vengeance, and within fifteen minutes, twenty-eight German fighters had been shot down. The squadron's high scorer in the battle was Capt. Donald Bryan with five. Following close on his heels were Lt. Arthur Hudson with four and Capt. Bill Stangel and Lt. Charles Goodman with three each.

Captain Bryan led his flight into a diving attack on a gaggle of forty-plus E/A and managed to damage an Me 109 on his first pass. His number three man then called in another 109 on his tail, which Bryan managed to lose by snap-rolling. For the next ten minutes Bryan was in at least fifteen separate combats. During this period he made stern attacks on eight Me 109s flying in string formation. Each time he would attack the tail-end aircraft and sent most of them down in flames. His final claim was five destroyed and two damaged.

Capt. Stangel, onetime bush and RCAF pilot, stated: "I was leading Red Flight with Lt. Goodman #2, Lt. Cammerer #3, and Lt. James #4. We encountered about 100 plus E/A with the rest of the Squadron. I singled out one E/A and fired a short burst and overshot. I then climbed up to another E/A. Lt. Goodman informed me on return that the pilot of this E/A bailed out. Shortly thereafter I engaged another E/A. I overshot and saw Lt. Goodman fire upon him. This E/A started spinning violently with smoke coming from it. It continued to spin into the overcast which was at about 4–5,000 feet. Shortly afterwards we engaged another mess of E/A. I noticed an E/A on Lt. Cammerer's tail. I tried to turn into him, but unable to make this turn I called Cammerer to break. At this time I engaged another E/A. We started into a few quick turns and finally ended up making head-on passes at each other. Each time he would try to head away and I would close on his lead. At last we were closing directly head on. There wasn't time to roll either way so I dropped the nose a bit more and it seemed we were about to hit when I pulled the trigger with a short burst. I pulled up sharply and started a turn to the left. I saw this E/A pull up a bit, start to roll on his back and then dive vertically into the ground and explode.

"About this time another E/A passed in front of me. I fired a short snap burst and tried to tighten the turn to get on his tail. At the same time I dropped 10 degrees flaps. I was in a very tight turn and I looked back to clear my tail. Just to my left was a P–51, PE-E, with Lt. James as pilot. Also two E/As were closing on my tail. I pulled the stick right into my stomach and almost stood my aircraft on its tail. Lt. James tried to

Capt. Fred Glover of the 4th FG downed an Me 163 on Nov. 2, 1944. AF Museum

Capt. Louis Norley also shot down an Me 163 on November 2. AF Museum

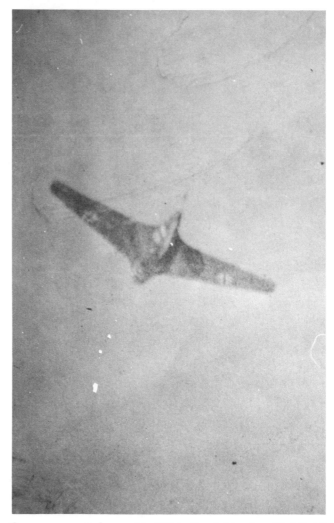

Gun camera catches an Me 163 in the sights of an Eighth AF fighter. USAAF

pull up with me and mushed between myself and the two E/As. The nearest E/A dropped a bit to clear Lt. James and collided with the second E/A. Both E/A went down, the pilot of one of them bailed out. Lt. James again formed on my wing and then we proceeded to climb to the bombers which were out of sight by this time." The two pilots had scored a total of five confirmed victories between them.

In addition to the 328th FS's twenty-eight victories, another thirteen victories were claimed by pilots of the group's 486th and 487th FSs. The 328th FS's score was a new record for victories scored by a squadron on a single mission. The victory was not without cost, however, as the 486th FS lost Capt. Henry Miklajcyk who was an ace with 7½ aerial and 5½ ground victories to his credit.

The 4th Fighter Group was sweeping in front of the bombers en route to the target and sighted about fifteen contrails headed for the bomber stream. Capt. Fred Glover leading the Mustangs dropped his tanks and headed for the E/A. As the aircraft, now identified as Me 163s, reached the altitude of the bomber stream they seemed to throttle back in an attempt to make their attacks. Glover dropped in astern one of the rocket-powered craft, gave it a good burst and the belly of the craft caught fire and exploded.

Capt. Louis Norley, also of the 4th, took his charges after the Me 163s and managed to get his new K–14 sight

Lt. Col. Robert Montgomery scored three of the 28 aerial victories that his 20th FG was credited with on Nov. 2, 1944. USAAF

Here is a hand of four aces, all from the 357th FG: left to right, Maj. R. A. Peterson, Maj. Leonard ("Kit") Carson, Maj. John B. England and Capt. C. E. Anderson, Jr. M. Olmsted

set on one of the craft at about 1,000 yards. The 163 began to dive, increasing its speed and began to pull away. Then the German pilot made the mistake of turning to port and leveling out. Norley closed and began firing on the 163, scoring hits, but he was traveling too fast and overshot. By this time the rocket craft was apparently out of fuel and Norley was able to come back for another attack. This time he closed to 400 yards, scored more hits and the 163 went down flaming to crash into a small village.

The 20th FG was also heavily engaged on the November 2 mission and it accounted for another twenty-eight aerial victories. Three of its pilots scored triples. One of them was Lt. Col. Robert Montgomery who downed two 109s and a 190 without the aid of his gunsight. Others scoring triples were Capt. John H. Tennant and Lt. Ernest Fiebelkorn.

When the final accounting for this battle was finished it turned out to be one of the Eighth Air Force's greatest victories of the war. During the course of the battle 136 enemy planes were destroyed, seven probably destroyed and twenty damaged. Allied losses were twenty-six bombers and eight fighters shot down by E/A. Another fourteen bombers and eight fighters were lost to other causes.

The number of enemy planes encountered on November 2 also revealed that the Luftwaffe had, indeed, been rebuilding its forces. Not only were larger numbers of conventional fighters such as the Me 109s and FW 190s encountered, but more and more encounters with jet-or rocket-powered fighters were being reported. Jet encounters were a matter of great concern to Eighth Air Force Commanding General James E. Doolittle, and he responded by increasing the number of escort fighters per mission.

The heavies went back to the Leuna petroleum complex near Merseberg on November 8. There were no concentrated attacks on the Big Friends, but on the way home they were attacked by Me 262s from Kommando Nowotny. Lt. James W. Kenney and Lt. Warren Corwin of the 357th Fighter Group were covering a group of unescorted bombers when they sighted an E/A making a pass at the B–17s. The aircraft was identified as an Me 262. The Mustang pilots saw the craft make a pass from ten o'clock and then a 180 degree turn and prepare to come back from five o'clock. At this time Kenney, with Corwin covering, made a pass on the jet. Kenney began firing from about 400 yards and observed a puff of smoke emit from the 262. The German pilot dove for the deck and Corwin split-essed. Kenney rolled down on the jet and got on his tail again. Kenney overshot twice, but the second time the 262 pilot went into a turn to the left and Kenney was able to close and get good strikes. The pilot, who was eventually identified as Capt. Franz Schall, Knight's Cross winner, bailed out at about 4,000 feet.

Lt. Edward Haydon of the 357th Fighter Group sighted another Me 262 in a dive south of Dummer Lake. He gave pursuit, pouring on full power, and managed to close but was overtaken by some P–51s from the 20th Fighter Group. The jet led the Mustangs over an airfield where they became the targets of intense ground fire. The Me 262 pulled back up through the overcast, and as reported by both Haydon and Capt. Ernest Fiebelkorn of the 20th Group, it flipped over on its back and crashed into the ground about four to five miles from the field.

The pilot of this Me 262 was the famed leader of the Kommando Nowotny, Maj. Walter Nowotny, 258 victory German ace, holder of the Knight's Cross, with

Oak Leaves, Swords and Diamonds. With his loss the jet unit was broken up and the jets moved from Achmer to Lechfele where they formed the nucleus of JG 7. It was never determined what caused the death of the German ace, for neither Haydon nor Fiebelkorn fired at the 262 though they are jointly credited with the destruction of the craft. It is more likely that he was hit by fire from the bombers or that he suffered power loss and encountered difficulties in maneuvering from the Mustangs that put him in a stall from which he was unable to recover.

For the next several missions the enemy fighters did not make an appearance, so on November 18 fighter sweeps were launched to find and destroy them on the ground. The 4th and 355th FGs were assigned the airfield at Liepheim, and when they arrived at the area tempting targets were found. Scattered over the airfield were at least twenty of the new Me 262 jet fighters and several 109s. The pilots of the 4th made four passes over the field and succeeded in destroying twelve of the jets and one Me 109. While the strafing attack was going on, Capt. John Fitch and Lt. John Creamer caught another Me 262 in the air and combined their firepower to send the German jet crashing to earth.

Despite the warning letter that had come down from Eighth Air Force Headquarters, there was another downed fighter pilot rescue. This particular feat was accomplished by a 20th FG pilot and there is no mention of it in the official records. On November 20, Capt. Jack Ilfrey of the 79th FS landed on a strip in enemy-held territory in Belgium and picked up his wingman, Lt. Duane Kelso.

Capt. Ernest Fiebelkorn of the 20th FG was one of the two pilots credited with the victory over top-scoring Luftwaffe ace and leader, Maj. Walter Nowotny. The other pilot sharing the victory was Lt. Edward Haydon of the 357th FG. USAAF

Ilfrey had led a flight of five P–51s escorting two photo recce P–38s to the vicinity of Magdeburg, Germany, where they accomplished their strike photo mission. On the way back, the Mustangs dropped down through the clouds and attacked targets of opportunity. Following one of the strafing runs Kelso radioed that he

Good close-up of a crash-landed Me 262. This photo was taken shortly after WW II, with aircraft in French markings. J. Cuny

had been hit. The P-51s were flying at 700 to 800 feet, and a small emergency landing strip was sighted. Ilfrey told Kelso to use his own judgment but if he desired, to go ahead and land.

Kelso went ahead and made a wheels-down landing and Ilfrey landed to pick him up. They were taking some ground fire so it was imperative that they get off immediately. Without delay Ilfrey got out of the cockpit, dumped his chute and he and Kelso climbed into the cramped cockpit. Ilfrey gunned the engine, roared down the strip, dumped some flap and lifted off, barely clearing the trees. After a short flight to Brussels, Belgium, they set down and remained there overnight.

When Ilfrey returned to King's Cliffe the next day, Group CO Colonel Rau was livid. Admonished for jeopardizing himself and his aircraft in the rescue, Ilfrey took a royal dressing down. Rather than getting Ilfrey recognition, the event was purged from the group records.

On November 21 the Luftwaffe again tried to put up a real defensive effort against a force of 700 bombers and 650 fighters heading toward Merseberg. Due to terrible weather the Germans had not properly assembled and vectored their fighters toward the bomber formations. Several of their formations were bounced by escort fighters before they could get organized.

The bulk of Luftwaffe pilots flying in the west at this time had so little instrument experience that the task of bad weather interception fell on JG 300 and JG 301, whose pilots had been the single-engined "Wilde Sau" night fighter interceptors. However, on this day, the controllers had been so confident that the bombers would turn back due to the weather that they had belatedly given the fighters the command to scramble.

The 352nd Group was covering the last box of bombers off the target at Leuna when they sighted a gaggle of more than fifty FW 190s on an interception course with their belly tanks still attached. Col. John C. Meyer told Capt. Bill Whisner to take a straggler that was on the starboard and rear of the FW 190 formation. Whisner closed on the 190 and just as the craft joined his formation, he came under fire from the Mustang guns. Whisner closed to 200 yards, and pieces flew off the 190 which fell into a spin, smoking and burning.

Whisner fired at one FW 190 after another through five more attacks that saw more pieces flying off, planes going down and in some cases pilots taking to their parachutes. In his last encounter of the day he shot a 190 off the tail of another Mustang with a good deflection shot that saw the Focke Wulf fly through his line of fire and be raked from nose to tail. The pilot ejected his canopy and hit the silk. Whisner was credited with five

Capt. W. T. Whisner with a Mustang named Princess Elizabeth. *Whisner did most of his scoring in* Moonbeam McSwine,

including five destroyed and two probables on Nov. 21, 1944. USAAF

160

Col. Everett Stewart and his ground crew pose by Sunny VIII, *his 4th FG Mustang. E. Stewart*

Col. Jack Jenkins, CO of the 55th FG, in his P–38 Texas Ranger. USAF

Teddy, *the personal aircraft of Maj. Michael J. Jackson, 56th FG ace who had eight aerial victories plus 5½ destroyed on the ground. M. Jackson*

Lt. Vernon Richards in Tika IV. *Richards had two in the air and 3½ on the ground with the 351st FG.* USAF

Hollywood High Hatter *was flown by Captain Paul Conger of the 56th FG.* USAAF

Ole Cock *graced the nose of Capt. Donovan Smith's 56th FG Thunderbolt.* USAAF

Hairless Joe *on Lt. Col. David Schilling's P–47.*
USAAF

Capt. Fred Christensen had "Boche Busters" on the nose of this Thunderbolt. USAAF

Maj. Bob Johnson of the 56th FG flew this P–47 named Lucky. *USAAF*

Iowa Beaut, *a P–51 of the 355th FG, was flown by Lt. Lee Mendenhall for this photo. USAF*

Capt. Don Gentile of the 4th FG poses in front of his P-51 Shangri-La. Gentile scored 21.83 aerial and six ground victories. USAF

Col. Donald Blakeslee in the cockpit of his P-51. Blakeslee was one of the great fighter leaders of VIII FC; his leadership made the 4th FG the top scoring American fighter group in World War II. USAF

Sgt. John Koval (left) and Sgt. Joe Di Fransa (right) load the four deadly .50s in the port wing of Lt. Col. Francis Gabreski's P-47. Their expert arming skills kept Gabby's guns firing, allowing him to become VIII FC's top aerial ace with 28 German aircraft destroyed. USAF

Capt. Fred J. Christensen, Jr., of the 56th FG. Christensen had a total of 21½ aerial victories at the end of the war. F. Christensen

Col. David Schilling in front of his P-47. Schilling scored 22.5 aerial victories and 10.5 strafing victories. USAF

Lt. Col. Francis Gabreski of the 56th FG ready for takeoff. Gabreski had 28 aerial victories and three on the ground before he went down in July 1944. USAAF

This 56th FG Thunderbolt shows the group's famous red nose. USAAF

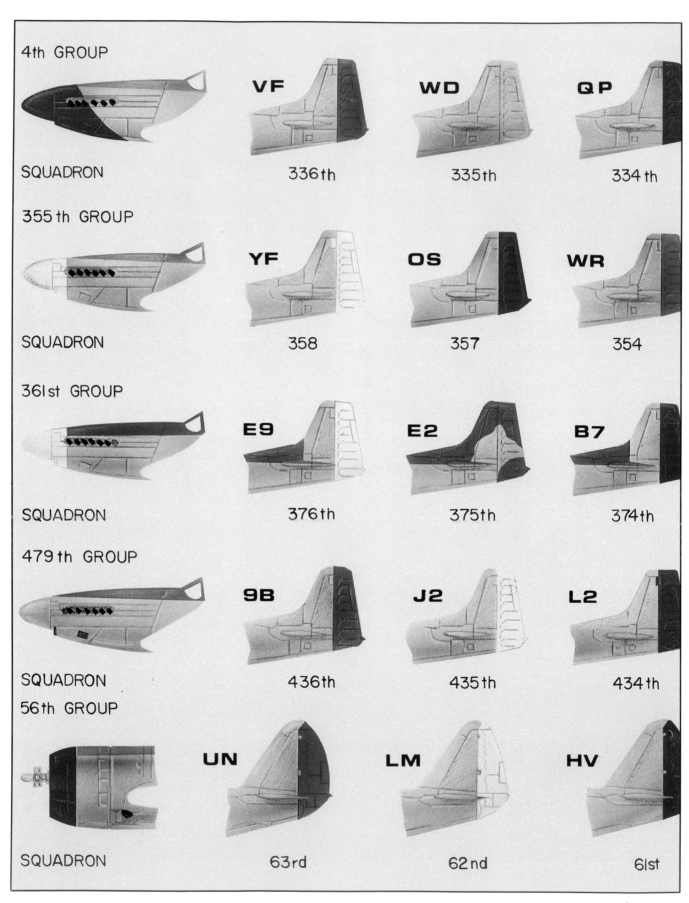

4th GROUP

SQUADRON

VF	WD	QP
336th	335th	334th

355th GROUP

SQUADRON

YF	OS	WR
358	357	354

361st GROUP

SQUADRON

E9	E2	B7
376th	375th	374th

479th GROUP

SQUADRON

9B	J2	L2
436th	435th	434th

56th GROUP

SQUADRON

UN	LM	HV
63rd	62nd	61st

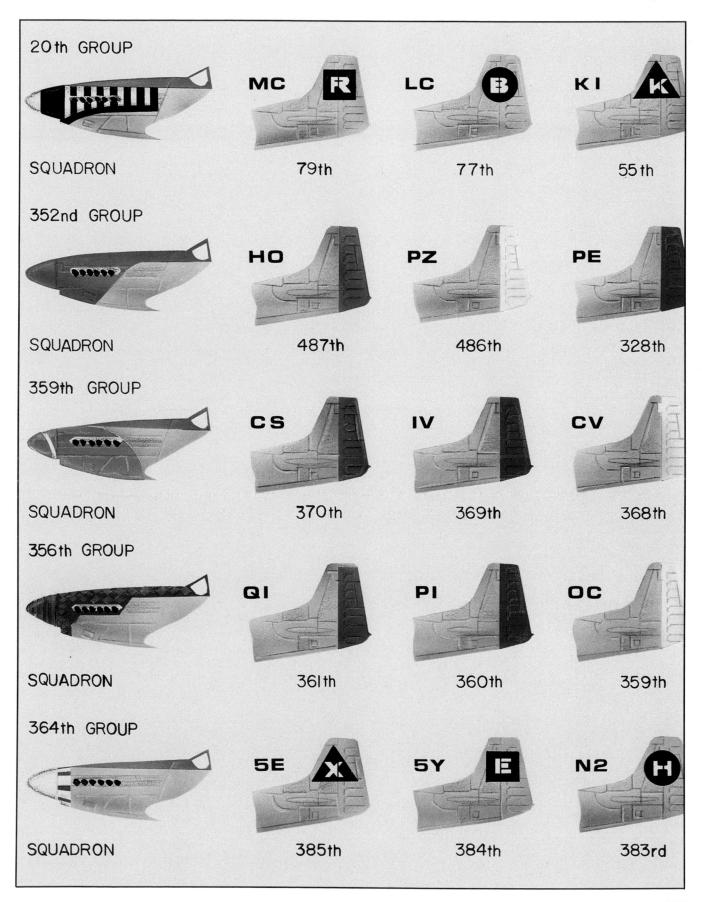

20th GROUP

SQUADRON

MC 79th   LC 77th   KI 55th

352nd GROUP

SQUADRON

HO 487th   PZ 486th   PE 328th

359th GROUP

SQUADRON

CS 370th   IV 369th   CV 368th

356th GROUP

SQUADRON

QI 361th   PI 360th   OC 359th

364th GROUP

SQUADRON

5E 385th   5Y 384th   N2 383rd

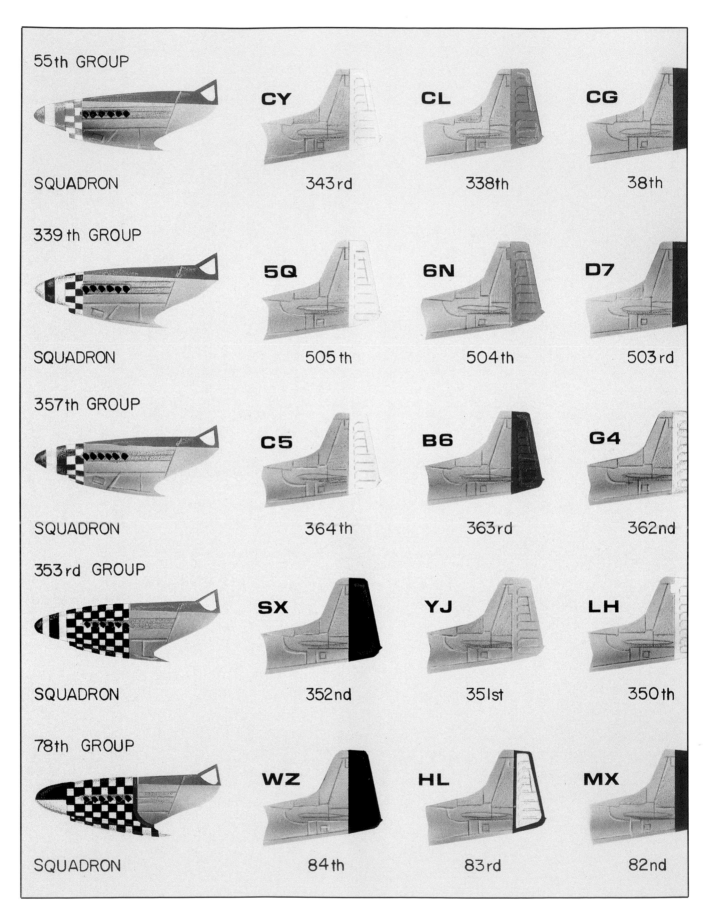

55th GROUP

SQUADRON   CY 343rd   CL 338th   CG 38th

339th GROUP

SQUADRON   5Q 505th   6N 504th   D7 503rd

357th GROUP

SQUADRON   C5 364th   B6 363rd   G4 362nd

353rd GROUP

SQUADRON   SX 352nd   YJ 351st   LH 350th

78th GROUP

SQUADRON   WZ 84th   HL 83rd   MX 82nd

FW 190s destroyed and two probables for the day.

Lt. Claude Crenshaw was leading a flight of P–51s from the 369th Fighter Squadron of the 359th Fighter Group, when the blue-nosed P–51s of the 352nd Group hit the Focke Wulfs. Crenshaw took his charges right in behind them and they proceeded to cut a swath through the enemy formation. One after another Crenshaw dispatched the 190s. Crenshaw claimed five of the 190s destroyed but only received credit for four. He did have some favorable comments to make about his new gunsight and G-suit, however: "The success of my encounter is attributable to the presence of Jerries as well as the superlative working of my K–14 gunsight and 'G' suit. The 'G' suit enabled me to make all the violent maneuvers necessary to protect myself and still be an efficient fighting force. Upon reaching my base I found that due to the weather conditions only three guns had functioned. The sight enabled me to fire short bursts with astonishing accuracy. I missed on only two bursts, one while firing at 90 degrees deflection, and the other while rolling with the E/A."

The majority of the FW 190s downed in these combats were from the all-weather JG 301 which lost twenty 190s that day. US fighters claimed sixty-eight E/A for the day. The Luftwaffe actually lost sixty-two, so the figures were relatively accurate. Fourteen escorting fighters did not return from their respective missions of the day.

Five days later when the Eighth Air Force went to oil installations near Hanover and the Hamm rail yards, they were met by another large force of Luftwaffe fighters. Try as they might to disrupt the massive Eighth Air Force strike forces, the Luftwaffe still was not up to it. The escort fighters charged into the German formations and ripped them apart.

However, the German controllers were still very effective at directing the fighters to any bomb group that drifted out of the formation; the result could be catastrophic. The B–24s of the 491st Group were caught alone by the FW 190s of JG 301 who shot fifteen of the Liberators from the sky before they were, in turn, all but massacred by the Mustangs. When the air battle that stretched for miles across an area of clear, blue sky ended, JG 301 had twenty-eight pilots killed or missing and another thirteen wounded.

This was high-scoring day for several different fighter groups. The 339th FG from Fowlmere destroyed twenty-nine E/A and were led by Lt. Jack S. Daniell who claimed five and became an ace-in-a-day. It was the biggest day of the war to date for the 356th FG which brought down twenty-one German fighters. They were flying a mixed force of P–47s and P–51s, since they were still in the process of converting to the Mustang. Their battle took place twenty miles northwest of Dummer Lake. The 356th claimed twenty-one victories against no losses.

Lt. George R. Vanden Heuvel of the 356th Fighter Group dove down on a formation of enemy fighters but when he pulled out of his high-speed dive, he found that he was alone. As he climbed along the bomber forma-

Lt. Claude Crenshaw of the 359th FG attacked a gaggle of FW 190s on Nov. 21, 1944, and was credited with four destroyed and one probable. USAAF

tion looking for someone to join up with, he sighted ten FW 190s ahead and they broke into him. Vanden Heuvel turned to meet the attack and managed to get on the tail of one of the 190s. A short burst which scored no hits also revealed that he had only one gun firing. While he was attacking the 190, other Focke Wulfs were making passes at him from either beam. Two FW 190s coming in from either side were on a collision course, so Vanden Heuvel dumped his stick and made a steep diving turn. The two FW 190s met almost head-on in a collision which was marked by a tremendous explosion and a falling mass of flame. Vanden Heuvel poured on the coal and slipped out of the area.

Capt. Wilbur Scheible also of the 356th Group attacked the rear of a gaggle of about thirty enemy aircraft and managed to get some strikes on an Me 109 before it dove away. Scheible latched onto the tail of a second Me 109 which immediately split-essed. Scheible, with his wingman Lt. Bob Cope holding on grimly, rolled over and dove in chase. Many strikes were seen around the canopy as the pursuit continued at a tremendous rate of speed. Scheible finally pulled out, blacking out from the Gs. Both of his wings were later found to have developed buckles in them from the strain. Cope observed the 109 continuing straight into the ground.

Two more 109s were sighted and in the ensuing dogfight Scheible managed to down one of them and damage the other. He then observed an Me 109 on the tail of this faithful wingman, Lt. Cope. As he turned his Mustang to the attack, the enemy pilot broke away from Cope's P–51 and went in a turning dive to the left. Scheible followed and fired until he shot the right wing off the 109.

Scheible then sighted an Me 109 attempting to sneak into Hesepe aerodrome but after closing on him, another aircraft came up from across the airfield. Scheible turned on it and then identified it as a strangely marked P–47. Scheible broke off, thinking the field was being strafed by Jugs, but on pulling up there were no other P–47s to be seen in the area.

Perhaps the most determined pilot to join the scorers of the 355th Fighter Group on November 26 was Lt. Jack Beckman. He had started out flying YF–R but had to change aircraft due to a flat tail wheel tire. He changed over to Mustang YF–I, took off and set course to catch up with the group. After five minutes, however, the electrical system went out and he started to return to base. Five minutes later the trouble seemed to clear up so he did another 180 and set out to catch his group once more. Beckman picked up the bombers at the coast and tried to find his outfit, but as the Initial Point for the bombers came up he sighted a gaggle of forty FW 190s, instead. When the last FW went below he bounced it and got a few hits before the 190s split-essed.

Beckman then sighted the big dogfight of the day and set out to find himself a target. He sighted a lone E/A about ten miles away heading for the Berlin area. Beckman flew at full throttle and managed to get within 700 yards of the FW 190, which continued to fly straight and level: "I closed to about 75 yards firing and seeing many strikes on the fuselage and wings. I got so close my guns were hitting on both sides of the fuselage in the wings. About this time my guns stopped dead . . . I thought the pilot was dead, so I slid out to the side a little and the E/A broke left. I had to follow, so we had a rat race for about ten minutes . . . Finally in desperation he started to dive and got up to about 350 mph and started a sharp pullout. As he did his right wing broke off."

Capt. John J. Hockery of the 78th Fighter Group took his flight into a gaggle of Me 109s and immediately sent one down in flames. Another Me 109 came across the top, and Hockery went after him. Hockery reported: "He led me down to the deck. He had Staffel Kapitan chevrons on the side of the 109. [This proved to be Lt. Heinz Sterr, 130 victory Knight's Cross winner, from IV Gruppe, Geschwader 54, who had just come from the Eastern front.] He led me down to an aerodrome and we went into a Lufbery at 1,500 feet right over the drome. The ground defenses threw up a lot of flak, but I kept trying to get in on the Me 109. I fired several deflection bursts, getting a few strikes. All of a sudden there was a big explosion on the E/A and his

Maj. Wilbur R. Scheible of the 356th FG almost lost his wings in a high-speed dive but still managed to come out of the Nov. 26, 1944, combat with three Me 109s destroyed and two damaged. USAAF

wing came off. He flicked into the deck. I believe his own flak may have shot him down. I broke away from the drome and started for home.

"I looked up and saw a fight above, so started up to get in on the fun. I got to 5,000 feet when I passed three FW 190s coming down. I bounced them and got in a rat race with them. They were better pilots than I expected and everytime I'd get on one's tail the others would fire at me. I tried to break for home and was holding my own until my water injection ran out. They started to catch me so I turned into them to fight it out. I managed to get on one and fired, getting strikes all over the wing roots and cockpit, but just at this time there was an explosion behind me. I lost part of my wing and crashed into a field. I got out of the ship just as two FW 190s started to strafe it. I saw a huge column of smoke and believed it was my last E/A I had hit. I was taken POW shortly after."

The fighter totals for November 26 came to 114 destroyed, three probables and thirty-one damaged, against the loss of nine fighters. The intensity of the air battle is evident, for when German Quartermaster records were checked after the war they showed that the admitted German loss for the day totaled eighty-seven.

When the Eighth Air Force returned to Germany on Nov. 27, 1944, it sent an escort force of 750 fighters. It was the largest force of fighter planes ever dispatched by the Eighth Air Force and it completely overwhelmed the defending Luftwaffe aircraft sent up to face it. The 357th FG caught a formation of obviously green and inexperienced pilots and virtually destroyed it.

The unit hit by the 357th Group was probably JG 300 which ran into what seemed to be an endless stream of Mustangs. Top scorer for the Group was Capt. Leonard ("Kit") Carson who was credited with five FW 190s. Carson likened the combat to shooting "fish in a barrel," as the German pilots took almost no evasive action and were picked off one by one as they continued to hold formation in the gaggle. Capt. Chuck Yeager and Capt. John England both chalked up four while Lt. John Sublett got a triple. Captain C. E. ("Bud") Anderson downed two FW 190s and later he and his wingman, Lt. Raymond Wolf, tacked onto two more 190s which they drove to the deck and rode down until they both crash-landed! The only loss to the 357th for the day was Lt. Frank Gailer who was downed by a Mustang from the 353rd Fighter Group.

A feat of daring and outstanding performance was turned in by Capt. Ray S. Wetmore and Lt. Robert York of the 359th Fighter Group. Wetmore's flight of four had been separated from the rest of his squadron after taking evasive action to escape flak in the Munster area. Wetmore related: "As we flew along trying to find our group to rejoin we spotted two large groups of enemy fighters. We estimated that there were at least 100 Me 109s in one group and at least that same number of FW 190s in the second group. All of the enemy aircraft had on belly tanks and appeared to have just formed in attack formation. They were looking for our bombers.

"We positioned ourselves behind them and above them and I got on the radio calling for help. I could contact the rest of my group so I began relaying the position of the enemy force, their altitude and direction of flight. I kept this up for more than 15 minutes, but no one else arrived. The enemy fighters kept changing course and it began to be more difficult to position ourselves so that we could still follow them and keep them from identifying us.

"To make things tougher, the fourth man in my flight called and said his engine was losing power and that he would have to abort. I ordered the No. 3 man in the flight to go with him for protection and that left just York and me and 200 Germans. It was a helluva lonely feeling, following that many enemy fighters and calling for help and no one turning up.

"Finally, the Germans must have gotten wise to us. They began to send flights of four ships climbing to get on top of the two of us. The flights would just sort of drop away from the main groups and begin to climb out to the side. I figured they were forcing our hand. I told the rest of my group over the radio that the enemy was wise to us and that York and I would have to attack alone. Just as we noticed several enemy flights in a good position for attack on top of us I called 'We're attacking now.'

"York and I dove beneath the top flights of the Jerries and picked out two planes in one of the flights in the main group of Me 109s. Both enemy planes we aimed at exploded in flames and then I lost York. When I got a glimpse of him about a split-second later, he was spinning down and I thought for sure that those flights from above had shot him down.

Capt. Kit Carson of the 357th FG stated that his five FW 190s downed in one combat were like "shooting fish in a barrel."
M. Olmsted

Capt. Ray Wetmore ready to taxi out in Daddy's Girl. *The top-scoring ace from the 359th FG, with Lt. Robert York as a wingman, broke up two Luftwaffe gaggles of more than 100 fighters each.* USAAF

"I turned into the Jerries coming down on us and took a long shot at one with a slight angle of deflection. He lighted up all over and went into a tumble, pouring black smoke.

"Then I spotted another one making a pass on me and I turned into him. We went round and round from about 30,000 feet clear on down to the deck. He seemed very aggressive and was damn good at the controls. Although I managed to catch up on him on the turns most of the time he was on my tail a lot, too.

"Once while he was firing, two 20 mm cannon shells plunked into the gun bays of my left wing and I thought he had me. I kept turning, though, and kept getting hits on him. I figured he would level off after he got down good and low. Finally, he leveled off and I lined him up for a finishing burst and my guns wouldn't fire. I was out of ammunition. I decided to pretend that I had some left and make a pass at him. I did and he pulled his ship up and bailed out.

"I felt good all over about this but didn't have time to feel that way for long. For the next 10 minutes I was busy as hell keeping some FW 190s off my tail. I managed to outmaneuver them and kept swearing at them because I didn't have any ammo left to take a shot at

them. I finally got clear and came home on the double."

Lieutenant York recalled: "We split those Jerries like flies and their belly tanks tumbled down through the sky like rain. After we got our first ones I then came up behind another one and gave him a long burst from dead astern. Strikes appeared all over his ship, smoke flew out and pieces began falling away. He went down spinning.

"The third one I got flew directly in front of me. He was about 800 yards away and apparently didn't see me. I closed fast and recall I was diving in a spiral. I pressed the trigger and saw hits on the canopy and at the wing roots. The Me 109 snapped over and as I passed him it exploded violently with a flash of red flame.

"I flipped up fast and got on the tail of a fourth and was firing away at him dumb and happy until I saw tracers scooting past me from some Jerry perched on my tail. I did a snap over and noticed that I almost piled straight into the plane ahead of me that I was firing at. It was the pilot climbing out. I went into a sharp dive to keep this one in the rear from firing again. I headed for a cloud and once in it straightened out."

York was later involved in a bounce on two other aircraft that turned out to be Mustangs. York, still tempered in the heat of battle, opened fire and damaged the Mustang of 353rd Group Leader Maj. Wilbert Juntilla, but fortunately Juntilla was able to make it back to home base.

Regardless of the damage done to their leader in a huge and confusing air battle, the 353rd also had an excellent day downing 21¼ enemy aircraft while losing only two of its own. Top scorer for the "Slybird" Group was Maj. Wayne Blickenstaff who was credited with four FW 190s. As he shot the enemy from the skies he noted, "The main gaggle continued merrily on its way, ignoring the fights that were going on to its rear."

The 352nd FG also joined in the action and claimed eighteen more enemy fighters during a twenty-minute dogfight. High-scoring honors were shared by four pilots: Capt. Ralph Hamilton, Lt. Ray Littge, Capt. Walter Starck and Capt. Bill Whisner, who each scored doubles.

With no more targets in the air the 352nd FG turned its guns to targets on the ground and strafed road and rail rolling stock in the Bielefeld to Minden and Minden to Osnabruck areas in Germany. These attacks netted them 16-0-15 locomotives, 7-0-21 rail cars and several trucks and barges.

November 1944 had taken a terrible toll on the German fighter forces. Although they had managed to build up a sizeable force during their standdown in October, once more the American escort fighters inflicted staggering losses. The I Jadgkorps made claims for 155 American aircraft downed during the month but had lost 404 of its own aircraft. The number of day fighter pilots lost during the month was 244. With ever-increasing numbers of American fighter planes escorting the bombers, the Luftwaffe was now absorbing losses from which there was no recovery.

For the next several days Eighth Air Force missions to Germany were virtually unopposed. The stillness was finally broken on December 2 during a mission to attack rail targets along the Rhine between Wiesbaden and Koblenz. The strike force consisted of 500 bombers escorted by 403 Mustangs.

The enemy fighters began to appear as the force was approaching the target area and a number of air battles broke out. The 20th FG was one of the escort groups to engage the enemy fighters and their encounter was described by the Group historian as follows: "Today's 8th Air Force effort was a modest one, just over 500 bombers were sent out to harry the German rail system along the Rhine between Koblenz and Wiesbaden, 40 miles to the south.

"The Group rendezvoused south of Liege at 1224 and escorted the bombers to the target area where unexpected excitement developed. Colonel Russell Guske, leading Walnut section, responded to a report of enemy fighters north of the target, located a gaggle of 15-plus Me 109s and FW 190s and attacked, personally accounting for one of the 109s destroyed. Lt. Eugene Planchak of the 55th, flying Walnut Yellow 3 position,

whacked two 109s down in quick succession, making himself the day's hero.

"Meantime, Captain Baker, leading 77th FS, was dispatched to take care of 30 more 190s spotted south of the target area making for the B-24s bombing Bingen. In the scrap that ensued Lts. Robert Murrel and James Garner knocked off a 190 a piece.

"A few minutes later, Lt. H. L. Brown, leading 55th Blue section, destroyed a FW 190 from a small gaggle that attempted to attack our bombers in the target area."

Another air battle developed in the vicinity of Hottenback, Germany, after pilots of the 4th and 361st turned to investigate a large formation of bogies. What someone had identified as P-47s turned out to be FW 190s and the dogfight began. When it was all over, five more enemy aircraft had gone down. Three kills were credited to the 361st and two to the 4th FG.

In other air battles that took place on December 2 an additional twenty-one victories were claimed, of which the 56th FG accounted for eleven.

Maj. Paul Conger was leading the 56th Group, whose mission was to fly a sweep ahead of the bombers, and depending on MEW control "Nuthouse" to lead them to the enemy fighters. The P-47s were in the vicinity of Koblenz, flying between two cloud layers at 20,000 feet, when they received a vector from "Nuthouse." First they were directed north and then south. Conger assumed that the bandits must be below the overcast and that they had missed them. Making a 180 degree turn the Jug formation went down through the overcast in a shallow dive where a bogie formation was sighted.

Conger reported: "As we closed in we stayed quite well hidden in the overcast for nearly five minutes until we could identify. Finally the gaggle became obviously Me 109s, carrying belly tanks. They still hadn't seen us so I called into the group to drop our tanks—and the fun was on."

Conger closed to 200 yards, dropped back to indicate 210 mph and let go with a two-second spurt on lead. The 109 took hits on the canopy and fuselage, and the leader bailed out. The formation held intact and took practically no evasive action. A skid to the right brought Conger behind a second Me 109 which he immediately dispatched.

Capt. Robert Foy was the leader for the 357th Group. His Mustangs sighted a small flight of Me 109s and while he dispatched some of his charges to attack them, Foy sighted a lone Junkers Ju 88. The aircraft was painted a pale gray and Foy was quite taken with the antenna regalia on the nose. He had contacted one of the Luftwaffe night fighters that had been rallied to go up and act as a daylight interceptor. Foy came in from astern, put one burst into the left wing and then one into the right wing. At this time the Ju 88 pilot dropped his flaps so Foy did likewise. Foy continued to follow the twin-engined craft down until it crash-landed in a field.

Nearly 550 heavy bombers of the Eighth Air Force escorted by over 800 fighters headed toward targets in

Two Mustangs from the 79th FS, 20th FG break out above the cloud cover heading for a rendezvous with the bombers. J.D. Bradshaw

Berlin and Munster on Dec. 5, 1944. The German early warning radar picked up the huge force as it headed toward the German capital and alerted its fighter forces. By the time the bomber stream was approaching its targets, huge formations of enemy fighters were there to meet them and a monumental air battle ensued.

One of the groups to engage the enemy fighters was the 356th FG. They found a large gaggle of over forty FW 190s in an area northeast of Berlin and hit them hard. When the fight was over they had destroyed thirteen of the Focke Wulfs. Two of the pilots, Capts. Wilbur Scheible and Donald Strait (who scored doubles in the fight), became aces.

Scheible described his encounter as follows: "After the lead box of B–17s bombed their target at Berlin we noticed formation contrails northeast of Berlin headed southwest to intercept the bombers. We attacked them northeast of Berlin before they reached the bombers. These E/A were FW 190s, about 40 in number. They were flying at about 28,000 feet and we attacked from the same altitude. I followed Captain Strait on the attack. Blue Leader [Captain Strait] exercised perfect judgement on the attack and his proper timing put us to the rear of the FW 190s and in excellent shooting position. I opened fire at approximately 700 yards on one FW. I saw no hits and increased my lead. I then saw hits on his wings, and I continued closing and hitting the 190. The FW pulled up and gave me about 30 degrees deflection at 300 yards and it seemed that all guns pinpointed on the cockpit. I gave him a long burst scoring a concentration of strikes in the cockpit. I'm quite certain that the long burst killed the pilot. The FW seemed to snap roll and do peculiar gyrations, black and gray smoke poured out and the 190 rolled over into a slow spin. I looked around and saw my wingman, Captain Hallmark, sticking to me like a leech. We cleared ourselves and saw another FW 190. I started firing at this 190 and closing at the same time. The E/A still had his belly tank and obviously he was trying to drop it. I saw many hits on the fuselage and cockpit and continued firing. This FW–190 pulled up to the left and rolled on his back, pieces of the 190 broke off and started flashing by me; I continued firing. Then gasoline and smoke poured back, the E/A snapped over on his back and went into an inverted spin. I then broke off to look around but the fight was over so we continued escorting the bombers home."

Pilots of 8th Air Force claimed eighty-seven confirmed victories on the mission. The scoring was pretty well even among the groups that encountered enemy fighters. Highest scoring was the 357th with twenty-two, followed by the 479th with fourteen.

Maj. Arthur Jeffrey of the 434th FS, 479th FG scored a triple on the mission to bring his total of aerial victories to nine. Lt. Richard Candelaria scored his first two victories.

Jeffrey ordered his squadron to drop tanks and follow him in an attack on a large gaggle approaching the bomber formation from below. In the dive, his gunsight bulb burned out and he flew right on through a formation of some fifteen Me 109s, most of whom broke for the deck. When he got his gunsight working, Jeffrey was right on the rear of a gaggle of about forty FW 190s. As he closed in on the left rear of the gaggle, he opened fire, hitting the belly tank on the 190 which immediately exploded.

174

Sliding over he brought his guns to bear on another FW 190, sending it down in flames. Not sighting any other E/A at his level Jeffrey dove down and found two more 190s stooging around aimlessly and proceeded to flame one of them. The balance of ammunition he used up on another 190 which went into evasive action but refused to go down. Jeffrey thought that he could close in close enough on his tail to scare the pilot into bailing out, but the German pilot was not bluffed.

The 357th Group spotted approximately 100 enemy fighters attempting to attack the B-17s of the 3rd Division that they were escorting. As the bombers were coming away from the target, Capt. Donald Bochkay and his flight, flying at 30,000 feet, approached head-on into about twenty FW 190s. The Mustangs dropped their tanks and pressed the attack. Bochkay met one and as the enemy pilot started to roll over and dive, he let go a good burst from 300 yards. The 190 took hits on the fuselage and the pilot bailed out. Bochkay slid over and met another 190 head-on and let him have a good burst as they closed. As the FW went underneath his nose, Bochkay noted a lot of smoke and the craft began to spiral downward. The FW's pilot was probably dead already, for the 190 continued down in an uncontrolled spin.

The Mustangs of the 357th were successful in completely breaking up the attacks of the enemy gaggles, and most of the enemy pilots opposed by this unit were very ineffective.

Maj. William Hovde who was leading A Group of the 355th ran into another of the green and inexperienced Luftwaffe units. Hovde took his group to the target and then to the north of Berlin to investigate the area. At about 1055 a gaggle of more than fifty German fighters was reported and the Mustangs dropped their tanks and headed for the fray. Hovde stated: "I swung in from five o'clock and 1,000 feet above to make an attack from six o'clock. Upon closing I called them all in as Focke Wulfs and to make a coordinated attack line abreast. These Jerries were carrying belly tanks and it wasn't until they were dispersed or shot down that they dropped the tanks. All appeared to be flying heads up and sound asleep.

"I attacked the Hun on the right rear of the gaggle and scored hits immediately. The ship went down in flames.

"Lt. Alexander, my wingman, called and said he had me covered and to take my time. I slid over to the left and picked out another. This one was well hit around the cockpit and wing roots. Either out of control or taking evasive action he did a wild chandelle to the left and collided with another FW 190. Both went down but I observed only one chute.

"I again slid over to the left and picked off another who went down burning. All strikes were well placed on wing roots and cockpit.

"Lt. Alexander called in to watch one back at four o'clock. He and I both did a tight 360 degree turn to port

Lt. Col. Don Strait, top-scoring ace of the 356th FG leading his flight home after an escort mission over Germany. USAAF

175

Maj. William J. Hovde of the 355th FG joined the "five in a day" group on Dec. 12, 1944, with five destroyed and one shared. He is shown here with his aircraft Ole IV and Russian inscriptions from the last shuttle in September. Hovde was one of the few pilots to name his aircraft after his dad. W. Hovde

with Lt. Alexander being out in front. I called and told him to take the Jerry as I had him covered. I saw strikes on the Hun as Alexander slid by him. Lt. Alexander called for me to finish him and as I had a good shot blew him up.

"Still flying Lt. Alexander's wing we jumped another FW. He got this one and I turned to get a 109 attacking Lt. Alexander. Hun half rolled down and I followed. I scored hits behind the cockpit and my tracers cut across his nose as he pulled the lead through. His courage or lack of it predominated and he bailed. The altitude was 12,000 feet and as I swung around I counted five parachutes; all brown ones.

"As I was out of ammunition, low on gas and generator out, I headed home. The Hun formation was very concentrated with no semblance of formation. Their front was of seven ships abreast and about six ships back in a horizontal plane. In depth it varied from two to three ships. The enemy was very herd-bound, and even after prolonged attacks did not break formation. I believe only the leader had a radio as evidently no alarm was given. It is my firm conviction that not one of this gaggle ever got to the bombers."

Some of the other Mustang pilots encountered German pilots who were obviously experienced and worthy opponents. Capt. Merle Coons of the 55th Fighter Group had downed an FW 190 when the following occurred: "I pulled up to kill my speed, I looked back to keep the E/A in sight, but found another FW 190 closing rapidly on my own tail. I split-essed and wearing a G-suit thought I would be able to pull out tight enough to black out the pilot of the E/A if he attempted to follow through. I continued to bring my pull out on over in a loop, expecting to get back on the E/A's tail; but was surprised and damned worried when I found him still following me though not yet drawing deflection. To add insult to injury he was still carrying his belly tank. I made two more loops with this E/A before another P–51 took him off my tail and on down to the cloud layer where he lost him."

Capt. Bill Tanner, of the 353rd Fighter Group, and his flight were attempting to bring home a crippled B–17 and were down at low altitude when they sighted a locomotive. They strafed the loco and pulled back to orbit the Fortress when all hell broke loose. Before they knew it the B–17 was attacked from out of the undercast by fifteen FW 190s and shot down. Tanner went into a sharp turn to the left and attacked the Focke Wulfs. His wingman, Lieutenant Cowen, flamed one of them but as Tanner lined up on his target and fired he saw tracers coming over his wing. As he broke hard, Tanner was hit by several pieces of metal that had broken off the E/A that he had just fired on.

Classic photo of Mustangs of the 353rd FG lined up for takeoff from their their base at Raydon. USAAF

The 190 that was on Tanner's tail was shot off by Lieutenant Deeds. Tanner then found himself in the middle of another gaggle of 190s that had been in a thin layer of cloud above. These 190s took out after Deeds who was attacking another 190. Tanner latched onto another Focke Wulf who flicked over and attempted a split-ess, but from 400 feet he couldn't make it. The 190 hit the ground and exploded.

Tanner now had three FW 190s on his tail, so he broke again and saw Deeds with a 190 on his tail. Tanner called for him to break, but Deeds' P–51 continued down taking hits and it crashed into the ground. Tanner was still in a tight climbing turn with the three 190s on his tail when he sighted Cowen who had another two E/A on his tail. He called for Cowen to break and finally managed to make the cloud bank and safety.

The tenacious attacks of the Luftwaffe fighter forces were turned back once more in a stinging defeat. They had lost eighty-seven aircraft while downing only five of the American bombers. Another seven bombers fell to flak. Seventeen American fighters failed to return to base.

Capt. Bill Tanner of the 353rd FG, one of the "Slybird" old-timers, did an outstanding job of saving a B–17 and his wingman on Dec. 5, 1944. B. Tanner

Chapter 15

Bastogne and Bodenplatte

During the next few days the weather over Europe deteriorated from bad to worse. It was the worst weather experienced in that part of the world in quite a few years. During this period battles with the Luftwaffe dropped off considerably, and the weather became the American fighter pilot's most dangerous enemy. The combination of heavy snows, icing conditions, thick clouds and extremely cold temperatures cost Eighth Air Force in excess of sixty fighter planes during the month of December.

The severe weather also served as a natural camouflage for the forces that Field Marshal Von Runstedt was massing in the Ardennes Forest in preparation for the counterattack which became known as the Battle of the Bulge. Under the cover of this horrible weather he struck with a fury on December 17, driving US ground forces back. Requests for air support went virtually unheeded during the first few days of this gigantic offensive, and US forces on the ground were being swept aside by columns of German panzers.

The Luftwaffe sent up hundreds of its fighters to support the attack and to protect Von Runstedt's lines of communication from our bombers. The weather limited aerial encounters during the first few days of the German offensive to small engagements. On December 18 the 4th FG was able to bounce seven enemy fighters in the vicinity of Dortmund, Germany, and shot down three of them. The 83rd FS, 78th FG followed suit the next day when they ran head-on into a small gaggle of Me 109s and FW 190s near Koblenz. The heavy cloud cover, which extended from 8,000 to 20,000 feet, had forced the Thunderbolts down to an operating altitude of 4,000 feet. As they cruised over the Moselle valley they happened upon the enemy fighters. Apparently, the opposing forces saw each other simultaneously and a number of dogfights broke out. When it was over, seven of the German fighters had exploded against the new-fallen snow. Four of the 83rd's pilots shared in the victories. Doubles were scored by Capt. Bob Bonebreak and Lts. John Kirk and Francis Farrington; Lt. Frank Fish claimed one confirmed victory and one probable.

On the ground, General Eisenhower was conferring with General Patton about Third Army's plan to turn around and strike at the enemy's flank. Within two days Patton had performed a military miracle. What it entailed was taking an entire army poised for an attack in one direction, turning it around and racing 125 miles to launch an attack within forty-eight hours. By December 20 some of Patton's troops were already in the Bastogne, Belgium, area helping the 101st Airborne Division resist a breakthrough. Although the Germans did succeed in surrounding Bastogne on December 22, they now had to contend with Third Army under Patton. It was at this time that Patton uttered his now-famous prayer for good weather. On December 23 his prayer was answered and the skies cleared. American airpower threw its might at the German forces in the air and on the ground.

Marshaling yards, communication centers and raillines at the rear of the battle zone were the bombers' targets for the day. The Eighth Air Force bombers dropped over two million pounds of bombs on their targets and the escort fighters had a field day against the Luftwaffe. The fighters destroyed 69–1–18 planes in aerial combat against a loss of seven of its own. It was the 56th FG that spearheaded the attack. They were dispatched on a sweep ahead of the bomber formations. En route to their assigned patrol area they received several vectors from the MEW controller, but all turned out to be false alarms. Finally, MEW directed them to another big target near Bonn, Germany, and this time it was the real thing.

Col. Dave Schilling was leading the 56th Group. The third time Schilling called and asked for MEW assistance, he was told, "Don't worry there is plenty straight east at 22 to 23,000 feet." About two minutes later Maj. Harold Comstock called in a large formation of Focke Wulf 190s directly below. About the same time, Schilling sighted another gaggle of approximately forty E/A flying south in a wide turn to his left, below and ahead of him.

Schilling told Comstock to engage the gaggle below while he took the 61st and 62nd Squadrons to engage the gaggle ahead. Schilling entered a diving turn to the left at full throttle to position his flight on the outside and to allow the other three flights to cross over inside in order to bring as many Jugs as possible line abreast to fire on the enemy. Schilling pulled up onto the rear of the gaggle and sent three Me 109s down in flames, one right after the other.

Only Schilling and his own flight remained, and they positioned themselves for another scrap. Calls came in from Comstock that he was in a hell of a fight, but as Schilling searched for the fight he spotted another gaggle of thirty-five to forty FW 190s 1,000 feet below. Once more Schilling brought his flight around to put them on the tail of the gaggle and this time he sent two 190s down to their destruction. Following the bailout of his fifth victim of the day, Schilling found himself alone. He joined up with a lone P-47 from the 63rd Squadron and together they began to shadow a gaggle

Col. Dave Schilling's Hairless Joe *being serviced. Note the rocket rails under the wing. Schilling downed three Me 109s* *and two FW 190s on Dec. 23, 1944, to run his air-to-air score to 22½.* USAAF

of forty FW 190s hoping to make another stern attack before they were discovered. This time they were not successful, however. Schilling's wingman was jumped by two FW 190s. Schilling directed him to do vertical aileron rolls and hit the deck, and almost immediately found himself under attack. Following his own advice he lost the Focke Wulfs and gathered his charges for the return home.

Maj. Harold Comstock took his P-47 formation roaring into a gaggle of FW 190s from out of the sun. Comstock made one pass right through the middle of the formation, damaging one E/A and sending the rest scurrying. Pulling up, Comstock made a head-on pass on another FW, shooting its engine all to pieces. The prop all but stopped turning and the pilot bailed out.

Comstock then found himself underneath another 190 whose pilot was unaware that a P-47 was just below. As he rolled out of his turn Comstock politely pulled in on his tail, fired from 200 yards, closed to 100 and watched as pieces flew off the FW in all directions.

Lt. Robert Winters of the 62nd Squadron shot down one FW 190 out of a gaggle and was closing on another which apparently chopped his throttle. Winters was too close to avoid a collision and as he kicked rudder and pulled on the stick, the right wing of the P-47 hit the left wing of the Focke Wulf. The 190 went down spinning, but the rugged Thunderbolt brought Winters home.

The 56th lost three pilots in the battle of the gaggles. One of those who went down, Lt. Lewis R. Brown, claimed another three FW 190s shot down and one probable when he returned from POW camp at the end of the war.

The 364th Fighter Group added another twenty kills to the day's total as they escorted the B-17s to their targets. Maj. George Ceuleers downed four Me 109s, taking three out of one gaggle and shooting the fourth off the tail of some other P-51s. Lt. James Fowle of the 384th Fighter Squadron also got four (the fourth bailed out before he could fire a shot). The green, young Luftwaffe pilots knew they didn't have a chance when they got a Mustang on their six o'clock position.

In an effort to provide up-to-the-minute air cover over the Battle of the Bulge, the 352nd FG was moved to Belgium. Their base was to be Y-29 at Asch, and living facilities were somewhat more primitive than the 352nd had been accustomed to. The Group was housed in tents and for the next several days the Arctic cold was their worst enemy. They were also visited each night for the next week or so by the Luftwaffe's "Bedcheck Charlie." Nevertheless, the 352nd quickly learned the tricks of survival at the front and went about their business. Lt. James Carter of the 486th FS had the following comments on Bedcheck Charlie: "Nearly every night for the first week or two 'Old Bedcheck Charlie' would fly over and raise a rumpus. The ack-ack

179

boys would have a field day, painting the sky with criss-cross patterns of flaming red. As soon as the alert sounded everyone would scramble out of the tents to stand in death-inviting openness and gladly watch the fireworks that ensued. Some of the more enterprising and intelligent individuals began digging foxholes, while the others drank cognac and happily shot holes in the tents with their 45s."

Pilots and essential ground crews of the 361st Fighter Group were also off to the Continent in December. The yellow-nosed Mustangs of the 361st were based at aerodrome A–64, St. Dizier, France. Although their quarters were not as snug as those enjoyed in England, the 361st was in permanent buildings; the officers were quartered in what had been German barracks and the enlisted men were quartered in a former German mess hall.

Continued clearing weather on December 24 allowed the Eighth Air Force to launch another massive attack against airfields and communication centers in western Germany. In fact, the mission turned out to be the largest air strike of the war. A total of 1,884 bombers escorted by 803 fighters dropped over ten million pounds of bombs on their assigned targets, while 502 RAF bombers along with the entire Ninth Air Force Bomber Command struck at targets in the Ruhr Valley. The Luftwaffe did not let the massive assault on the Fatherland go unchallenged, however, and a number of air battles were fought.

The fighting was fast and furious and the Germans paid dearly for their effort. Seventy of the seventy-five enemy fighters downed by Allied fighters were claimed by pilots of the Eighth. This time it was the 357th FG that led all scoring with a total of thirty-one. Their closest rivals in the day's scoring were the 55th FG with fifteen and the 359th FG with ten. Lt. Otto Jenkins of the 362nd FS, 357th FG destroyed four E/A on the mission, raising his total to 8½.

Jenkins slid in on the rear of a gaggle of FW 190s and finished off three of them in short order. Soon he sighted a fourth victim and positioned himself on its tail. Just as he readied himself to fire, Jenkins was fired on by another FW 190 on his own tail. Jenkins' wingman, Lt. Edward Hyman, pulled over and hit the 190 with a couple of bursts before it snapped over. The German pilot jettisoned the canopy and bailed out. Jenkins went back to the work at hand and downed his fourth FW 190 for the day. However, the enemy had done his work; Jenkins had taken hits on the left wing which caused him to call it a day and head for home.

Lt. Col. Elwyn Righetti was leading a six-ship flight of 55th Fighter Group Mustangs back from the target area when they sighted rail traffic in the vicinity of Frankfurt and Mannheim. Their strafing attacks destroyed five locomotives and about thirty goods wagons. While heading on out southeast of Munster, they sighted twenty FW 190s flying in four-plane flights in close train formation at three o'clock. All of the 190s were carrying belly tanks and apparently didn't sight the Mustangs before they, themselves, were sighted. As

Lt. James M. Fowle, 384th FS, accounted for four Me 109s on Dec. 23, 1944, to become an ace. USAAF

Lt. Otto ("Dittie") Jenkins celebrated Christmas Eve 1944 by downing four FW 190s. The 357th FG ace ran his score to 8½ in the air before his tragic death in a buzzing accident. M. Olmsted

the last flight of E/A crossed in front of them, the Mustangs turned in to get on the 190s' tails.

Righetti stated: "By this time the E/A were starting to turn and take other evasive action. I closed on the nearest 190, which was in a tight left turn, and fired a one second burst securing hits on the left wing tip and believe I saw pieces fly off. I turned with the E/A and as I did so, I saw two FW 190s directly ahead belly-in, one heading due west and the other northwest. Both raised large dust clouds as they hit, but they did not explode. Their airspeed was in excess of 150 mph. The E/A I was pursuing continued to tighten his turn to the left and when he reached a bank of 70–80 degrees, he snapped under and went straight into the ground from 800 feet.

"I completed my turn and observed my wingman, Lt. Griffith, in trouble with a 190 on his tail. I turned to engage this E/A and as I did so took short bursts at two other E/A which crossed my path and secured scattered strikes on both.

"Lt. Griffith was in a tight left turn and as I approached the 190 on his tail, I secured a good group of hits on the E/A. He apparently saw me and broke off into a climbing turn to the right. I followed, firing from about 300 yards and closing rapidly. I secured a scattered set of strikes all along the E/A and when he

reached 1,000 feet he rolled over on his back and went straight into the ground, crashing and exploding.

"Just after the E/A crashed, Lt. Griffith called that he was hit in the arm and that his engine was out. Due to the haze I could not locate him so I advised him to bail out. He stated that he was too low but was very calm as he wished me a Merry Christmas. I feel sure that Lt. Griffith was able to belly-in, as the terrain was suitable."

Christmas Day of 1944 saw no break in the fighting. It was ferocious on the ground and in the air. The German offensive had begun to bog down due to the lack of fuel and the thrashing it took from Allied air power on Christmas Eve day. So on the day that the Christian world sets aside to honor the birth of the man who was supposed to bring "Peace on Earth, Good Will to Men," the Germans launched a last-ditch effort to push the 101st Airborne Division out of Bastogne. While the "Screaming Eagles" were tenaciously defending their little spot of Belgium, the Eighth Air Force continued its harassment of the enemy's supply lines.

The bombers' targets were communication centers and rail bridges west of the Rhine. About 432 fighters escorted the strike force of 388 bombers to the targets, and again the Luftwaffe made a desperate effort to disrupt the strike. Battles broke out everywhere and

Lt. Col. Elwyn Righetti, the 55th FG strafing king, on his Mustang Katydid. *Righetti destroyed 27 E/A on the ground and 7½ in the air before being downed in April 1945.* Tabatt

eight of the twelve Eighth Air Force groups that were on the mission scored victories. These eight groups destroyed 46-6-8, against a loss of nine.

The 479th was escorting a box of B-24s, and the Group was divided into two formations. Shortly after rendezvous with the bombers, A Group was vectored to a position south of Bonn. Here they encountered a gaggle of more than twenty enemy fighters at 25,000 feet. The silver-nosed Mustangs of the 479th attacked the enemy formation and scored a few victories before they in turn were bounced by another gaggle of enemy fighters. While this was going on another section of A Group intercepted twelve Me 109s near Limburg, Germany. By now, B Group had located some of the E/A for themselves, and chased a formation of Focke Wulfs away from the bombers. When all of the shooting was over, the 479th claimed seventeen victories (fourteen were actually confirmed) and two probables. Lt. George Gleason led in the scoring with three, raising his total to ten confirmed victories. He was followed by Lt. Richard Spencer who claimed two FW 190s. The 479th lost four pilots in the air battles and one of them, Lt. James Bouchier, was involved in the incident that cost the 352nd FG its greatest ace.

The 328th FS of the 352nd FG led by Maj. George Preddy was on patrol when they received a vector to intercept a formation of enemy fighters near Koblenz, Germany. The squadron was flying at 24,000 feet when it arrived in the area, and within a few moments the enemy was spotted below them. Capt. Bill Stangel described the encounter this way: "When flying as White 5 to Major Preddy, we were vectored to intercept bandits who were intercepting big friends. This vector was given to a point SW of Koblenz. We were flying at about 24,000 feet when two bunches of E/A about 20 in

One of the last photos made of top ace Maj. George Preddy of the 352nd FG before he met a tragic death on Christmas Day 1944. S. Sox

each bunch were sighted down sun from our flight. One bunch turned and passed beneath us and Major Preddy with the flight attacked the second bunch. As I was number 5 I went into the bunch alone and singled out one Me-109, giving him a short burst. He split S'd, I followed, he jettisoned his canopy and I gave him another short burst just as he bailed out at about 6,000 feet. The E/A crashed into the ground and exploded. I turned away and shortly after engaged another Me-109 at about 7,500 feet. We started turning and every once in a while I would take a short burst even though deflection was great. I then gave him another short burst from the high starboard side and he went into a short dive. I followed; he then pulled up sharply, and he must have closed off his power because I overshot. I came around again and he bailed out as I was coming in for this pass. I passed just below him and circled until he hit the deck. The E/A crashed into a woods and exploded."

While Stangel was pulling his one-man attack, the other two elements of White Flight were also reducing the Luftwaffe's inventory. Preddy knocked two Me 109s from the sky in short order for his twenty-sixth and twenty-seventh aerial victories, and Lts. James Lambright and Ray Mitchell claimed one apiece.

Blue Flight of the 328th also tried to intercept the enemy formations near Koblenz. Capt. Charles Cesky who was flying as Blue Three went after an FW 190 but lost him in the overcast. When they could not locate the rest of the flight, Cesky and his wingman Lt. Al Chesser headed back to Asch. As they approached Maastricht, Cesky spotted a flight of four FW 190s flying about 500 feet above them. He pulled up and opened fire on the number three man who bailed out as soon as his plane was hit. In quick succession he downed the number two man and then the leader. Chesser took care of the last Focke Wulf. The squadron had now claimed eleven victories for the day, but the victories were about to become meaningless because of an impending tragedy.

After White Flight scored its victories near Koblenz, they were vectored to Liege, Belgium, to attack some reported low-flying bandits. Flying along with Major Preddy and Lieutenant Cartee was Lt. Jim Bouchier of the 479th FG. He had joined them after getting separated from his squadron. As the trio approached Liege the radio warned of intense flak but said it would be lifted when they arrived in the area. They were southeast of Liege when Preddy spotted an FW 190 flying right on the deck. Preddy went after him and chased the 190 at treetop level into the area guarded by the 12th AA Group. Cartee described what happened: "As we went over the woods, I was hit by ground fire. Major Preddy apparently noticed the intense ground fire and light flak and broke off the attack with a chandelle to the left. About halfway through the maneuver and about 700 feet altitude his canopy came off and he nosed down, still in his turn. I saw no chute and watched his ship hit."

Although his Mustang took some hits, Cartee got away but Bouchier was not as lucky. Forty-millimeter shells hit Bouchier's radiator and smoke started filling his canopy. He jettisoned his canopy and bailed out at 1,000 feet. Just before jumping, Bouchier saw Preddy's Mustang crash-land in a field. Bouchier made it down okay, but ground troops found Preddy dead in the cockpit. He had been hit twice by fifty-caliber machine gun bullets from a quad-fifty. A tragic error ended the career of one of America's most gifted fighter pilots.

The 4th FG also scored heavily against the Luftwaffe on Christmas Day. They engaged a group of enemy fighters near Bonn, Germany, and downed twelve of the E/A. Their victory was not without cost, either, as two of their Mustangs were downed. Lieutenant Poage was shot down and became a POW, but one of the Group's aces, Lt. Donald Emerson, was killed. Emerson scored two victories before German ground fire brought him down in Belgium.

The most frustrated man involved in the Christmas Day fracas was Maj. Gordon Graham of the 355th Fighter Group, who found himself in the middle of a gaggle of German aircraft and then discovered he had no wingman to protect him while he could have had a field day. As Graham related the combat: "I observed a gaggle of 75 plus FW 190s and Me 109s, approaching from five o'clock level to a group of bombers. The gaggle was about four o'clock to me and 3,000 feet below. I was flying at 27,000 feet. Prior to target time the three ship flight with me had gone down to bounce some 'bogies' and were at approximately 15,000 feet heading back toward my flight.

"I called a bounce, dropped tanks and went balls out for the gaggle. My wingman did not follow [unbeknownst to Graham at the time]. Immediately after calling the bounce my element leader called in 15 plus Me 109s, who were about 3,000 feet above us, covering the main gaggle. The Me 109s dived in to cut the three ships off and my second element leader turned in to them to engage them. I continued on into the gaggle to break up their attack on the bombers while they were still about 800–1,000 yards behind the bombers. As I was closing all the gaggle fired simultaneously at the "Big Friends." I closed rapidly and hit the gaggle in the middle and opened fire immediately, trying to break up their attack. They began to split-ess just before I hit them and just as I went through, they fired another long burst. I closed fast on one from dead astern and fired a long burst from zero deflection at about 250 yards, observing many strikes around the wing roots and pieces flying off. As I pulled up to go over him he either jettisoned his canopy or it came off and he was climbing out of the ship as I shot by.

"I closed rapidly on another FW 190 directly ahead and gave him a long burst from zero degrees at 350 yards. He fell off into a slow spiral to the left. I observed strikes on the wing roots, fuselage and around the cockpit. By this time I was through the main gaggle almost all of whom had split-essed. I observed a chute open and I believe it was the pilot of the first ship that I fired on. The second ship that I fired on was still in a slow, lazy spiral to the left and apparently this plane was out of control or the pilot was dead.

"As I looked back I pulled up and broke to the right. Three Me 109s were firing at me but they were back about 800 yards or more and their fire was breaking about 150 yards off my right wing. I called my wingman and he said that he wasn't with me. I picked out the nearest ship which was about 1,000 feet below me in a diving right turn and dove on him. He did two or three aileron rolls and I stayed on him but never got a shot. He rolled out and continued a diving right turn. I fired a long burst out of range as a farewell gesture before diving straight down. The Me 109s behind me were firing intermittently every time I looked around. About eight or nine more had queued up on either side, apparently waiting their turns! All of them were out of range, I believe, and their fire never came very close to me.

"I dove straight down and pulled out at 5,000 feet, pulling seven G's. My G-suit connection blew apart while I was pulling out. I ran through two flights of 353rd Group ships, I believe, who apparently thought I was leading a bounce on them, for they dropped tanks and turned into the ships pursuing me. I climbed back to 15,000 feet and headed home, wishing to hell I had had a wingman."

The stand by the 101st Airborne Division at Bastogne, Belgium, knocked the wind from the sails of the German offensive in the Ardennes. The fighting continued for days, but the momentum shifted to the Allies. The air fighting continued as well. On Dec. 26, 1944, the 352nd FG picked up where it left off the day before and destroyed another thirteen enemy fighters. This time it was the 487th FS that did the damage. Lt. Col. John C. Meyer was leading sixteen Mustangs of the 487th on a free-lance patrol and at 0945 hours the controller directed them to bogies southwest of Bonn, Germany.

Maj. Gordon Graham and his colorful Down For Double. *Graham lost his wingman during a Christmas Day bounce that almost cost him his life as well.* G. Graham

As they arrived in the area P-47s were dive-bombing targets on the ground, and the Thunderbolt pilots were unaware of the two flights of enemy fighters preparing to attack them. Meyer led his White Flight and Red Flight in an attack against the lead group of E/A and sent his Yellow Flight and Blue Flight after the German high cover. In the attack Meyer destroyed 1½ enemy planes, and his squadron-mates accounted for another eleven.

On December 27 the Eighth Air Force launched another large bomber force to strike at the marshaling yards and rail lines which were supporting the battle front. The 364th FG was in front of the bomber force. Its assignment was to sweep ahead of the bombers and drive off formations of enemy aircraft which were preparing to attack the bomber stream. The 364th found what they were looking for and in a series of battles destroyed 29½ enemy planes.

Capt. Ernest Bankey, Jr., was leading the 383rd Fighter Squadron of the 364th Group when the first gaggle of enemy aircraft was sighted. Bankey and his wingman took off after two FW 190s that had broken formation when the Mustang initially bounced them. Bankey got in a good deflection shot and his victim blew up. As he came off the combat, however, he found himself separated from his wingman.

Turning to the southwest, Bankey sighted three E/A heading northeast. He fell in behind them and discovered that they were FW 190s. After a running and turning fight about fifteen miles southwest of Bonn, Bankey was able to hit the trailing 190 and it went into a spin. At that time the leader of the 190s broke hard right and Bankey went after him, fired and felt an explosion as he passed over the German fighter. The third 190 had made good his escape, but there was a fire in the woods where the first FW had spun in.

Capt. Ernest Bankey, Jr., and Lucky Lady III *found German fighters in profusion on Dec. 27, 1944. The 364th FG Mustang pilot accounted for five of them and shared another.* E. Bankey

Bankey turned back to the west looking for some support, and attempted to climb up and join seven Mustangs some 5,000 feet above. As he climbed, two Me 109s crossed below and in front so Bankey dove out of the sun and fired a few long-range bursts. The two 109s split and Bankey hung on to the lead Messerschmitt. At about 800 yards he scored a telling burst on the craft, and it went into a shallow dive and continued on into the ground.

Bankey was still stooging around alone when he sighted twenty E/A flying on the deck in two groups of ten each. When they put their backs to the sun, the Mustang pilot swooped down upon them. As he closed on a straggler he noted that this formation was being followed by another twenty E/A also flying in waves of ten. Bankey opened fire at the straggler from 800 yards, but he soon let up on the gun tit, intending to wait until he was closer to continue firing. Before he could resume firing, the E/A exploded.

Bankey was soon joined by twelve blue-nosed P-51s from the 352nd Fighter Group. As they came in on the tail of the gaggle, Bankey joined four of them in a chase after two Me 109s. The leader of the 352nd formation downed one of the E/A and Bankey attacked the other. Opening fire at 400 yards, Bankey noted hits and the Me 109 began streaming coolant and went into a shallow dive to the right; one of the blue-nosed P-51s came in and finished it off. Low of ammo and fuel, Bankey broke off his combat and headed home.

Lt. Ernest Duderstadt of the 364th Group's 384th Squadron also lost his wingman after initial contact with the enemy, but went on to down two FW 190s and an Me 109 in intense dogfights that resulted in as many as eight FW 190s on his tail at one time. Fortunately, other Mustangs entered the area and the FWs gave up the chase. As a result of the violent maneuvering of the day, Duderstadt became another devotee of the G-suit.

Following closely behind the 364th was the 352nd. For the third day in a row the blue-nosed Mustangs were right in the thick of the action, and came away with 22½ victories.

The melee began when the 486th FS spotted a large force of enemy fighters southwest of Bonn, Germany. The "Angus" Squadron ripped into the German formation and knocked seven of the enemy fighters from the sky before the 487th FS joined in the attack. The 486th's assault was led by Lts. Dick Henderson and Bill Reese, and each of them scored a double victory. With the arrival of the 487th FS the tempo of the air battle increased, and the Luftwaffe lost another 14½ aircraft. Maj. William Halton enjoyed his best day of the war when he sent 3½ of the German fighters to their doom. In doing so he raised his aerial victory total to 7½. Right on his heels was Lt. Ray Littge with three victories, and Lt. Col. John Meyer and Lt. Marion Nutter each scoring doubles.

The Eighth Air Force closed out 1944 with a massive raid against German industrial and communications centers. More than 1,200 bombers struck at numerous targets, and in doing so attracted swarms of

German fighters. The most intense combat took place over Hamburg where a number of Focke Wulf formations tried to disrupt bombers of the 3rd Bomb Division attacking the oil refineries. In this engagement the 364th FG destroyed twenty-five enemy fighters.

Leading the 364th Fighter A Group was Maj. Sam Wicker. His unit was the assault force which had the task of ranging out in front of the bombers and breaking up the gaggles of German aircraft as they assembled to intercept the bombers. Wicker was about thirty-five miles south of Hamburg when three gaggles composed of fifty to seventy-five E/A each were sighted. Wicker entered into the most memorable combat of his career: "I don't believe they had seen us until now, if so, they believed us to be Me 109s because we were able to close in to about 600 yards before firing. I closed on the first gaggle of six 190s with my squadron (6 P–51s) and fired from 600 yards on what I believed to be a wingman. At this time they still had their drop tanks . . . I fired about a 3 second burst at this wingman and saw a concentration of strikes in the cockpit. There seemed to be an explosion and the canopy blew off. The pilot was wounded, the ship went out of control and spun in. The pilot tried to bail out but could not make it.

"Next I slid in behind the leader of the flight and fired 4 to 6 bursts into his left wing and engine. It smoked, but did not catch fire until about 5 seconds later at which time the pilot bailed out. By this time the rest of the pilots in the gaggle realized what was going on and split-essed for the deck. This gaggle did not reach the bombers.

"As I rolled to follow them down I took a quick look around and noticed the other two gaggles were being engaged. I only had one ship with me, my wingman. The other flight of four had split up and were on their way down after the FW 190s. My wingman and I singled out one 190 and went hell for leather to the deck after him. We pulled out at 1,000 feet and the 190 pulled back, straight up. Then we went into a Lufbery and he did things with that 190 that no ship was ever designed for. In my 10 months of combat I have never seen a better Jerry pilot. I hung on his tail but it was impossible to use the K–14 sight as we were pulling 7 G's. I was wearing my G-suit and did not black out but nevertheless I could not hit him. I fired on my back and in every position possible until I ran out of ammunition. Then I called my wingman and told him to take over and I would become his wingman. We changed positions and my wingman made one pass at him. He took evasive action by doing an Immelman and two snap rolls at the top, ending up on my tail. From that point on I did not see my wingman as I tried to shake the Jerry off my tail. I was out of ammo and low on gas as I tried to run for it but could not break combat. This fight was working west of Hamburg and down on the deck. I did a very tight loop, with flaps, on the deck and succeeded in getting on his tail. However, this was no good as I was out of ammo. As I was just about to break off and run for it again, I looked back and saw three more FW 190s in position and firing at me. This was too damn much

for me and I was sure I had had it. I used flaps at 120 mph and closed to about 25 yards on the lead 190 at which time he pulled up and tried to split-ess from six to 800 feet. He went in and exploded.

"At this time I saw tracers passing in front of my nose so I shoved the stick forward and kicked bottom rudder, doing what I think was an inverted vertical reversement. I redded out with a terrific headache and when I recovered I saw I had pulled 4 negative G's. This threw the three 190s off. I tried to run for an overcast but they caught me before I made it, so I turned with them a few more times and ended up on the tail of two of them. The wingman must have been a Junior Bird-man because he was so scared he pulled up and bailed out. I did one more turn, all the time working nearer the overcast. Then I broke off and pulled up into it and flew on instruments. I found that I had only 50 gallons of gas left and didn't know exactly where I was. I flew 245 degrees until I came out of the overcast. At this point I could see the Zuider Zee so I turned south to our lines. I crossed lines with only a few minutes of fuel left and saw a small field with Spitfires on it. I made a straight in approach, running out of fuel as I was taxiing to a parking area."

Lt. William Hess of the 364th also waded into several gaggles of FW 190s and managed to down three of them in combats that ranged from 20,000 feet to the deck. He traded six or eight head-on passes with one determined German pilot. Just as collision seemed imminent the engine of the 190 burst into flames, Hess

Maj. Sam Wicker was all packed and ready to depart the 364th FG when he encountered 60 plus FW 190s attacking the bombers on the last day of 1944. His four victories that day brought his score to seven. USAAF

dumped the stick and looked over his shoulder to see the 190 pilot jettison his canopy and bail out. Just for good measure, Hess strafed and destroyed a Ju 87 Stuka on the airfield at Luneburg on the way out.

On the same day Maj. Gordon Graham of the 355th Fighter Group (who had known such frustration on Christmas day without a wingman) had his wingman right with him but then his guns refused to fire! Graham and his squadron were providing close escort to the B-17s in the Hanover area of Germany when they sighted a gaggle of twenty FW 190s. Graham and his wingman, Lt. Robert Goth, bounced them, but when Graham pulled in on the stern of his target his guns refused to fire. He immediately called his wingman and told him to fire away. The 190 went into violent evasive action and Goth was unable to hit him. Graham looked back to see another 190 on his tail and was forced to leave Goth to turn into the E/A. The 190 split-essed and headed for the deck.

Graham hurried back to Goth and his 190, charging his guns all the way. He finally got them to fire and as he roared in over Goth, he gave the 190 a two- or three-second burst. The enemy craft shuddered under the impact of his hits and went straight down to crash.

As Graham and Goth climbed back up, Goth called to tell Graham that he had another 190 on his tail. Graham broke sharply to the left and the 190 went to the right after Goth. Graham racked the turn in, pulled through and dispatched the 190 with a thirty-degree deflection shot from 350 yards.

Lt. Col. John C. Meyer of the 352nd Fighter Group marked the last day of 1944 by downing the first Arado Ar 234 jet bomber to fall to US fighters. The blue-nosed Mustangs were flying area patrol in the vicinity of Euskirchen, Germany, when the first Ar 234 was sighted. Capt. Donald Bryan sighted the craft and got some hits on it before another E/A closed in on Bryan's six o'clock position, and Bryan was told to break by Meyer.

Meyer gave chase to the sleek aircraft with its slender, streamlined fuselage and jet pods under each wing. After chasing the jet for several minutes, Meyer caught the craft when it went into a turn at 5,000 feet just above the solid undercast. The Mustang pilot let go two bursts and the pilot of the jet released a canopy. Meyer lost the Arado momentarily but then sighted it headed straight down through the overcast.

The 78th FG scored only one of the Dec. 31, 1944, victories, but that victory was a Group milestone. Flying his last mission of his tour, Capt. Julius Maxwell caught an FW 190 pilot "napping" and blasted the 190 from the air. It was Maxwell's third and the 78th FG's 400th aerial victory. It was also the last victory they would score in their Thunderbolts; three days later the 78th turned in the last of its P-47s and became a full-fledged P-51 group.

On Jan. 1, 1945, the Luftwaffe High Command launched another offensive. This time it was their greatest strike since the days of the Battle of Britain. This aerial offensive was designed to destroy the Allied Tactical Air Forces in Holland and Belgium. It was felt that if these planes could be destroyed, the Ardennes offensive could be salvaged and if nothing else it would give the German ground forces an opportunity to regroup.

The offensive was called Operation Bodenplatte and it began in the early morning hours of January 1 when the Luftwaffe dispatched nearly 800 fighter planes. The attack was quite successful against some of the airfields, and the Allied Air Forces lost over 150 aircraft. Heaviest hit was the RAF which lost 120 planes. In addition to the 150 planes destroyed, the Luftwaffe pilots heavily damaged at least fifty more. The Luftwaffe paid a high price for its success, though. Nearly 300 German planes were lost in the attack. The day-fighter force lost 214 pilots, 151 being killed or reported missing, and a further sixty-three were taken prisoner. The tragic thing about the heavy losses was that many were lost to German flak; their batteries had not been properly alerted for the operation. The loss that hurt the Luftwaffe the most, however, was the loss of so many leaders and veteran pilots. Two Geschwader commanders, six Gruppe commanders, ten Staffel leaders and eighteen subunit commanders fell during the operation. This was truly the straw that broke the camel's back as far as Luftwaffe fighter forces went.

In the battle that is now known to the veterans of the 352nd FG as the "Legend of Y-29," the "Bluenosers" destroyed twenty-three enemy fighters. It was the Group's 487th FS that supplied all the punch, and their actions gained the squadron a unique honor. The 487th FS became the USAAF's only squadron in the ETO to win a Distinguished Unit Citation, an honor normally given to groups.

Jan. 1, 1945, was an extremely cold day in Europe, one that made soldiering a miserable existence. Nevertheless, the mechanics of the 352nd FG were up at 0530 hours to prepare the planes for the day's mission. The Group was on standby for a bomber escort mission scheduled at 1100 hours. By 0800 the planes were all serviced and the acting Group commander, Lt. Col. John C. Meyer, was ready to get his planes in the air even though they were not scheduled to fly at this early hour. He requested permission from 9th Tactical Air Command to fly a routine patrol over the battle area. Permission was granted and at 0930 Meyer led twelve Mustangs of the 487th FS into the air. Just as his wheels left the ground Meyer spotted fifteen enemy fighters headed toward his airfield.

Meyer's encounter report tells the story: "Immediately upon getting my wheels up I spotted 15 plus 190s headed toward the field from the east. I attacked one getting a two second burst at 300 yards, 30 degree deflection, getting good hits on the fuselage and wing roots. The E/A half rolled, crashing into the ground. I then selected another 190 chasing it to the vicinity northwest of Liege. On my first attack I got good hits at 10 degrees 250 yards. The E/A half rolled and recovered just on top of the trees. I attacked but periodically had to break off because of intense friendly ground fire. At least on three occasions, I got good hits on the 190, and on the last attack the E/A started smoking profusely and then crashed into the ground. Out of ammunition I returned to the field but could not land as the field was under attack. I proceeded west and was bounced twice by 109s and was able to evade by diving and speed. The squadron was engaged before it was ever formed, immediately after takeoff."

These two victories were Meyer's twenty-third and twenty-fourth aerial victories, and with his 13½ ground victories he had now achieved a total of 37½, the highest in the ETO.

Following Meyer off the field was Capt. Bill Whisner and he, too, encountered the enemy at low altitude. At 1,500 feet he ran right into thirty 190s and downed his first victim within seconds of the encounter. As he watched the 190 crash, Whisner felt his Mustang shudder under the impact of several 20 mm hits, and broke off quickly. His plane had taken some serious hits but Whisner stayed in the fight. Moments later he downed a second 190, and headed for another fight. This time the enemy fighters were Me 109s, and the 109 he chose had a pretty good pilot at the controls. Whisner reported: "We fought for five or ten minutes, and I finally managed to get behind him. I hit him good and he tumbled to the ground. At this time I saw 15 or 20 fires from crashed planes. Bandits were reported strafing the field, so I headed for the strip. I saw a 109 strafe the northeast of the strip. I started after him, and he

One of the victors in the 487th FS action on New Year's Day and recipient of the Distinguished Service Cross was Lt. Sanford Moats. T. Ivie

Maj. William Halton, shown here with his P-51 Slender Tender & Tall *and crew, was another of the 487th FS pilots* who distinguished himself in the New Year's Day air battle. 352nd FG Assn.

turned into me. We made two head-on passes, and on the second I hit him in the nose and wings. He crashed and burned on the strip. I chased several more bandits, but they evaded me in the clouds. I had oil on my windshield and canopy, so I came back to the strip and landed."

With his four victories, Whisner tied Lt. Sanford Moats for scoring honors. Right behind them in victories were Capt. Henry Stewart and Lt. Alden Rigby with three apiece, and Lt. Col. John Meyer and Lt. Ray Littge with two each. The remaining five victories were scored by Maj. William Halton, and Lts. Walker Diamond, Dean Huston, Nelson Jesup and Alexander

Sears. Distinguished Service Crosses for this action were awarded to Lt. Col. John Meyer, Capt. Bill Whisner and Lt. Sanford Moats. Maj. William Halton, Capt. Henry Stewart, Lt. Alden Rigby and Lt. Raymond Littge received the Silver Star.

In addition to the twenty-three planes destroyed by the 352nd over Asch, the 366th FG of the Ninth Air Force brought down twelve, and the antiaircraft gunners claimed seven for a grand total of forty-two. It was estimated that the field was attacked by fifty fighters and of that number eighty-four percent were shot down.

Credited with two victories in the big action over Asche, Belgium, on New Year's Day was 487th FS ace Lt. Raymond Littge. USAAF

Chapter 16

Running Up the Score

Aerial engagements on January 1 were not limited to the area of Asch, Belgium. Eighth Air Force pilots also claimed another 17-1-1 aerial victories while escorting bombers to targets in Germany. Five of those victories were claimed by the 4th FG's 336th FS during an engagement in the vicinity of Ulzen, Germany. Lt. Franklin Young claimed two of the German fighters, and one of his victories was over an Me 262 jet fighter.

For the next thirteen days the scoring fell off as encounters with enemy fighters were few and far between. On Jan. 14, 1945, it was an entirely different story, however. The fighters escorted a force of nearly 900 bombers to oil refineries and plants in central Germany. The weather was extremely clear for this mission, and visibility was almost unlimited as the 3rd Bomb Division strike force and its escort approached their target areas. Out in front of the B–17s were the P–51s of the 357th FG. Twenty miles northwest of Brandenburg, Germany, the pilots of the 357th saw a huge defensive force of Focke Wulfs with another force of Me 109s as top cover approaching them. As soon as the bandits were spotted, Colonel Dregne led his group to the attack.

Dregne and his squadron leaders had been studying tactics to combat the "company front" attacks of the German gaggles and this was to be their opportunity to spring their "mousetrap." Dregne was leading the 364th Squadron while the 362nd under the command of Maj. John B. England was farther back, followed by the 363rd under the leadership of Capt. Robert Foy. As Dregne took the 364th Squadron down, he noted that the gaggle of FW 190s of JG 301 was attacking in company front formations of eight aircraft abreast. Just above them as top cover was a large gaggle of Me 109s from JG 300. Dregne told his pilots to ignore the top cover and get into the 190s to break them up before they could attack the bombers. As the Mustangs roared into the attack the majority of the 190s reacted just as the P–51 pilots had hoped. They largely split-essed and broke for the deck. Dregne shot up one of the Focke Wulf's before he became embroiled in a big Lufbery with eight to ten 190s.

Capt. Chester Maxwell of the 364th sighted a separate gaggle of fifty FW 190s as the squadron flew to the attack. Rather than take time to get on the R/T, he dove to intercept this gaggle alone. As he approached, most of the formation broke to the left and the balance split-essed downward. Maxwell managed to tack onto one of the enemy and sent him down in flames.

Maxwell then climbed back up seeking his flight, but instead sighted a dozen 190s attacking the bombers from astern. As he bounced them the formation broke to the left. Maxwell hung on to the tail of one of the 190s, hit him with a long burst at 20,000 feet and it flopped down out of control.

Once more Maxwell climbed back up and this time he sighted a P–51 down at 6,000 feet with a 190 on its tail. Diving down, Maxwell positioned himself on the tail of the Focke Wulf and fired at him from sixty degrees. His aim was true and the German pilot bailed out. Then Maxwell climbed to attack a single 190 that was attacking the bombers. The German pilot split-essed, and Maxwell dove down in pursuit. As they passed 12,000 feet Maxwell looked back and saw a P–51 on his tail. Now confident that all was well at his six o'clock he continued his attack. The next thing he knew, he felt strikes on his plane and his canopy was shot off. The radio was out, the aircraft handled sluggishly and the coolant temperature began to rise. Maxwell observed a yellow-nosed P–51 close and take a look and then fly off.

Limping along, Maxwell knew that he had no chance of making it back to England. Two P–51s from the 357th pulled alongside him and looked him over but were unable to communicate due to Maxwell's radio being shot out. Keeping his rpm and manifold pressure to a bare minimum, Maxwell was able to limp into Antwerp, Belgium, where he bellied in on an English army parking lot.

Leading the 357th FG on their big day of Jan. 14, 1945, was Col. Irwin Dregne shown here with his Mustang Bobby Jeanne *and crew.* Kramer

As Colonel Dregne took the 364th Squadron into the fray, Maj. John England was positioning his 362nd Squadron to take on the German top cover before they could drop down to join the fight. The 109s hesitated before dropping down to engage and this gave the Mustangs of the 362nd time to close the gap before they were able to get into the fight. Some of the 109s chose to attack the bombers and a few of them got in some passes before they were attacked by the Mustangs.

England chased one Messerschmitt which sought to escape by diving and rolling. England went down with it, keeping his Mustang in a tight spiral until the German pilot made the mistake of leveling out and thinking that he was safe. England pulled up and began firing from 200 yards, closing to fifty. Before the Mustang pilot released the trigger, four feet of the left wing of the 109 broke off and the plane spun down to earth.

Lt. John Kirla was leading Green Flight in England's squadron and he quickly downed two FW 190s. He then sighted an Me 109 and attacked. The German pilot tried desperate evasive action: "He went into a very tight barrel roll going straight down. I fired a short burst getting strikes, and he straightened out. Then I really gave him the works, clobbering him all over. He flipped over on his back and started to burn. Pieces fell off the ship until, finally, just the framework remained. I laughed and commented to myself on the crazy contraptions they were sending up these days. There wasn't enough of this ship left to crash into the ground."

Kirla then sighted a P–51 going after two Me 109s that were attacking the bombers. The Mustang shot down one of them, but the other latched onto his tail. Kirla did his best to save the Mustang pilot, but he was too late. However, he did manage to get revenge by shooting up the 109 until he went down like a "falling leaf."

The man who sprung the mousetrap was Capt. Robert Foy, who took his 363rd Squadron in to the attack after the top cover of Me 109s had committed themselves. He turned and lined up on a Focke Wulf 190 and as he closed, opened fire. As soon as strikes began to register on the E/A the pilot jettisoned his canopy and bailed out.

Foy sighted another 190 below, so he split-essed and wound up on its tail. This E/A split-essed and went into a steep dive. As his airspeed reached 550 mph Foy decided it was time to pull out, and finally did at about 4,000 feet. Having accomplished a gradual pullout, Foy continued to observe the enemy craft until he dove into the ground.

Capt. James Browning was leading Yellow Flight in Foy's squadron, and as they entered the fray he sighted a gaggle of twenty-five Me 109s about 5,000 feet below and to the right. Browning took his flight down and drove right up on the rear of the formation. Browning shot down three of the 109s, one right after the other, and completely dispersed the enemy formation.

Capt. Robert Foy led the 363rd FS and scored his 12th and 13th victories on the January 14 mission. He is shown in the cockpit of his P–51 Little Shrimp. *M. Olmsted*

Browning then sighted a lone B-17 with a couple of aircraft orbiting above it. Closing the distance it became obvious that the vultures were 109s. One of them came down behind the Fortress and opened fire. There was no return fire from the tail gunner of the B-17, so the 109 continued to close. Browning gave him a burst from 900 yards in an attempt to scare him, but this was ineffective. Closing to 500 yards, the tracers from the Mustang's only operable gun struck the 109, and it went into a spin. Unfortunately, he recovered at 5,000 feet, but the attack on the B-17 was broken as the other 109 decided he was out-gunned and headed for home.

Although the 357th Group was scoring the greatest success that would ever be registered by an Eighth Air Force group, there were a few losses, too. Lt. William R. Dunlop's encounter report filed some months later related a survival that was miraculous. Dunlop's flight attacked a gaggle of Me 109s and he managed to thoroughly hose one of the enemy craft. The pilot went over the side. Dunlop reported: "The pilot came out the same side, barely missed my wing as I passed between him and the smoking 109. One fraction of a second later it felt as if my guns were firing without me pressing the trigger, and the controls went out, completely dead. I watched one of my left hand 50's blow thru the wing skin and my fuselage tank caught fire. The ship was in a drifting dive and going straight in. The pressure held me in the right of the cockpit and was powerful enough so that I couldn't raise my hand to release the canopy. Then everything blew—wings, canopy, tail sections and fuselage separated and seemed to blow in different directions. The canopy must have left first as I felt flame sucked in the cockpit, was conked on the forehead and then felt the cool air as I was blown from the rest. I landed still in the bucket seat with armor attached and shoulder straps neatly in place. The engine and one wing lay together about 50 feet distant and the pieces were still floating down all about. Another 100 yards distant lay the 109, ammo still popping."

As Colonel Dregne began to round up his forces for the journey home, Lt. Col. Andrew Evans, who had had a fantastic day with four victories, joined up on him as his wingman. En route home, Dregne sighted a lone Me 109 below. He dropped down and promptly shot the 109 down. It was his one victory for the day.

When all the claims for the day were tallied, the 357th had a total of 56½–0–4 with one ground victory for good measure. The 364th Squadron had 21½ kills, headed by Capt. Chester Maxwell and Lt. Raymond W. Bank with triples. Lt. Col. Andy Evans and Capt. John Kirla each shot down four. Capt. L. K. ("Kit") Carson scored three victories. The 363rd Squadron's score was headed by triples turned in by Capt. John Stern and Capt. Jim Browning. The exact confirmed score will never be known but it is a definite fact that JG 300 and JG 301, who were the 357th's primary opponents, suffered severe losses; sixty-nine of their pilots were killed or wounded that day.

Maj. John Elder led the 355th Fighter Group on a fighter sweep in the Munster area. They broke up a

formation of twelve Me 109s, downing five of them. Two fell to Lt. Newell Mills' guns. A short time later the Mustangs were vectored to intercept a formation of long-nosed FW 190s southwest of Dummer Lake. There Maj. Gordon Graham and Lt. George Kemper each downed two, and Lt. Mills downed another to give him a total of three for the day. Lt. Carl Decklar also downed one of the 190s to add to the 109 that he had shot down earlier.

The high Mustang scorer for the day was Capt. Ray Wetmore who scored 4½ of the 359th FG's total of seven. Wetmore and his flight were headed for a rendezvous east of Hanover when he sighted a bogie out in front practicing his lazy eights and chandelles as though all was at peace in the world. Wetmore and his Mustangs dropped their tanks and took off after the E/A at full throttle but were unable to catch him.

Shortly after, "Nuthouse" (MEW) called to inform them that bandits were taking off from an aerodrome twenty-five miles northwest of Dummer Lake. Just when the search seemed futile they sighted a formation of four FW 190s below. Wetmore and his flight made the bounce, catching the E/A on the deck. A long burst sent one FW down to an attempted belly-landing, which wound up as a complete destruct. The second Focke Wulf attempted to break when fired on but snap-rolled into the ground. There were now two 190s left so Wetmore told his wingman, Lt. Rueschenberg, to take one and he would take the other. Wetmore's burst from 300 yards sent the Focke Wulf into the ground. Rueschenberg attempted to get his 190 but his windshield frosted up and he couldn't see to use his gun sight. Wetmore cut off the E/A and both Mustangs put telling shots into it. The German pilot bellied in on a snow-covered field.

As Wetmore and Rueschenberg climbed back to altitude they spotted another pair of bogies. Just as Wetmore was starting his pass he was cut off by a red-checker-nosed P-51 which hit the German with many strikes. The German pilot bailed out. Wetmore closed to 400 yards on the other Focke Wulf and sieved it with his .50s; the pilot bailed out.

While the 357th FG was engaged with the enemy fighters at the front of the bomber stream, other battles began to develop behind them. The 20th FG was assigned to escort the 4th and 5th combat groups of the 3rd Division. The 20th was split into A and B Groups which were led by Majors Nichols and Gatterdam respectively. As the formation approached Berlin from the northwest, Nichols observed over 150 enemy fighters preparing to attack the bombers. He alerted his pilots, and the 55th FS led the attack on the enemy fighters just as the Focke Wulfs passed through the bombers. The 77th FS followed the 55th in the attack, and in a series of running battles that lasted from Wittenberge to Berlin, a distance of sixty miles, the two squadrons claimed fifteen victories against no losses. The attack was led by Major Gatterdam of B Group who scored two victories in the dogfight, both FW 190s. Three other 55th FS pilots, Lts. H. L. Brown, J. K.

Brown and J. D. Leon, also scored doubles in this engagement.

In a nearly simultaneous encounter, Nichols led the 79th FS against another gaggle of nearly 100 enemy fighters. In this engagement the 79th FS flamed another five German fighters and damaged three more. One of the victories went to Nichols who downed a 109 in the initial pass.

Most of the 78th FG's victories went to the 84th FS. The 84th provided area support for the bombers near Giessen. As they headed toward Cologne, MEW directed them toward a flight of twenty enemy fighters flying on the deck. Red Flight struck first, and in the initial attack three enemy fighters were shot down. Two of the E/A were claimed by Lt. Dick Spooner who shot down an Me 109 and then chased a Focke Wulf 190 into some high-tension wires. The third was an FW 190 flamed by Lt. Earl Stier. The remaining victories were claimed by Maj. Leonard Marshall, a 109; Lt. Louis Hereford, a 109; Lt. Frank Oiler, an FW 190 destroyed and a 109 damaged; Lt. William DeGain, a 109; Lt. M. T. Wilson, a 109; and Lt. Willis Lutz who downed an FW 190 and an Me 109 and damaged two FW 190s.

Lutz had the most unusual victories of the battle. He was left upstairs when the rest of his outfit dove to attack the enemy fighters because his tanks would not drop. When he finally got them off, he saw three planes

flying close to the ground and dove to join up, thinking that they were his squadron mates. Realizing he had made a bad mistake, Lutz checked his guns and found they would not fire, so he quickly turned from the formation. Two of the enemy fighters came after him and followed in a climbing spiral. During the climb Lutz recharged his guns, finally getting four of the six to fire, and turned in to his pursuers. He fired at one of the two FW 190s and chased it off.

Lutz then went after the lone 109 and downed it with a long burst. As the Messerschmitt smashed into the ground, Lutz went after the remaining FW 190 and set its right wing ablaze with a long burst. The 190 then flipped over at 100 feet and crashed into the ground. As Lutz pulled up from this combat two more 190s attacked him. His Mustang took hits in its left wing tip, and then the German fighters turned to try and finish him off. Lutz threw off their aim by turning sharply, getting on the tail of the second 190. He fired a short burst before running out of ammunition. However, that "dusting" was enough to scare the Focke Wulf away. Lutz then went after the remaining 190 and bluffed its pilot into turning tail and running for home. With the departure of the enemy fighters, Lutz decided it was time for him to head for home too. But the day's excitement was not finished for Lutz. Just as his Mustang passed over American lines, it was hit by a burst of

A formation of P–51s from the 360th FS, 356th FG looking pretty for the photo aircraft. via K. Miller

flak. Lutz climbed to a safe altitude and jumped. Faulty aircraft identification by American gunners caused a sour end to an otherwise sweet fighter mission.

The 78th FG's four remaining victories were claimed by Lt. Willard Warren who scored a double, Lt. Robert E. Smith of the 82nd FS and Capt. Peter Caulfield of the 83rd FS. Smith fought his duel at rooftop altitude and his victory was topped off with an unusual bonus claim. His report read: "I started chasing a FW-190 and it ducked into a fog bank over the city. We began a merry chase like a couple of airborne taxi-cabs careening around town a hundred feet off the ground. He pulled up for churches and tall buildings and every time the enemy aircraft appeared I fired. Finally he straightened out and flew right up a main street apparently intending to lead me over an airfield just northwest of the town, so that the ack-ack gunners could get in some shots at me. I caught him at this time and raked the entire plane up one wing and through the cockpit. As bullets smashed into the cockpit the left wing went down and he crashed and exploded into the gun site."

The 356th FG escorted B-24s of the 2nd Task Force to its target at Hallendorf, and saw no action until they were on the way home. At 1335 hours the controller notified them of bandits in the Dummer Lake area. The 356th left the bombers twenty miles south of Hanover, and Maj. Don Strait led them to the vectored position. Fifteen minutes later they sighted twenty FW 190s in a wide climbing and diving orbit from 10,000 to 14,000 feet. They immediately bounced the German formation and in a dogfight lasting fifteen minutes, destroyed thirteen Focke Wulfs and damaged at least four more. Four and one half of these victories were claimed by the team of Lts. C. T. Ashby and Clinton Burdick.

The two pilots cut a swath through the German formation and took turns downing the enemy fighters. Burdick's last victory was scored with only one gun. He had just broken off contact with a 190 that he damaged in a head-on attack when another appeared. Burdick reported: "I sighted White Leader [Lt. Ashby] flying above and to the right of me, still giving me protection, so I started after another 190 flying on the deck. I closed to very close range, about 100 feet and fired a burst, with only one gun firing, with about 20 degrees deflection. The FW 190 did a half snap to the right and went straight into the ground from about 20 feet."

It was an unusual engagement due to the German tactics, and the 356th FS historian recorded: "We are puzzled by the reaction of these FWs to our attack. Was this wide undulating orbit a preliminary maneuver to forming up? If so, how can we explain the climbing and diving? And why did they try to maintain this formation even after our flyers made the bounce? Perhaps it was a new form of German battle tactics. We shall probably never know for certain."

The Mustangs didn't have a total monopoly on the scoring during the air battles of Jan. 14, 1945. The 56th FG joined in the massacre of the Luftwaffe during a fighter sweep and claimed nineteen victories.

The 56th A Group, under the command of Maj. Paul Conger, flew a sweep ahead of the bombers en route to Magdeburg, Germany. In the vicinity of Stendal the Thunderbolts came upon a massive dogfight involving the 357th Fighter Group and many Me 109s. The P-47s entered into the fight and shot down three of the 109s, one of them falling to Conger's guns.

The 62nd Squadron of the 56th A Group was led by Capt. Felix Williamson, who was the high scorer of the battle, downing five of the enemy. The Jugs had just caught up to the bomber stream when enemy fighters made their appearance on the scene. Climbing to meet them, Williamson picked out a 109 and gave chase. The E/A pulled right up into the sun and the P-47 pilot lost him until he broke away to the left. As the 109 turned, Williamson turned inside of it, scored hits all over the left side of the aircraft and its pilot bailed out.

Williamson next sighted an FW 190 in a shallow dive. As he gave chase, the German went into violent evasive tactics. Finally, both aircraft were going straight down and the E/A was doing snap rolls. Williamson began to experience compressibility and had to struggle to pull out. When he finally managed to get out of the dive he sighted a fire on the ground which was later confirmed to be the 190 he had been chasing; it flew straight into the ground.

Williamson then pulled up and gave chase to another Me 109 but was cut off by another Thunderbolt. About this time two 109s dropped in on the other P-47's tail, so Williamson broke into them and fired head-on at one. Opening fire at 800 yards, he hit the

Lt. Clinton Burdick of the 356th FG had a definite goal in his combat tour—to become an ace as his father had been in WW I. Burdick fulfilled his goal in February 1945. He is shown on the wing root of his Mustang DoDo. USAAF

Capt. Felix D. ("Willie") Williamson of the 56th FG became a "five in a day" scorer on Jan. 14, 1945, but he had to dive into compressibility to do it. He is shown in front of his P-47 Willie. USAAF

E/A hard, and it slipped off into a falling turn to the right and then tumbled into the ground.

Williamson did a quick 180 and came back at the other 109 head-on. Once more, his aim was true; Williamson looked back over his shoulder to see the German pilot jettison his canopy and bail out.

Williamson's wingman, Lt. Withers, was still hanging on and called his leader to suggest that it was time to depart the area.

Before they departed they were attacked by two more Me 109s. Williamson called for Withers to break, and he reefed his craft hard to the left to try to get a shot. One of the 109s broke off and pulled up to join about ten 109s above. The other 109 continued to press the attack and managed to hit Withers who headed down smoking. Unfortunately, Lieutenant Withers crashed with his P-47.

Williamson did a wing-over and took a deflection shot at this 109 and registered many hits. The E/A began to smoke badly and finally caught fire, and the pilot bailed out.

Williamson was now all alone with about ten Me 109s above. He made a couple of turns, dropped the nose and headed down in a long dive before scooting for home on the deck.

The 56th B Group also met heavy opposition over Steinhuder Lake and downed ten E/A while losing none of their own. Doubles were scored by Maj. Mike Jackson and Lt. McBath.

When the day was over the fighter pilots of the Eighth Air Force had downed a total of 161 enemy

The FW 190D "long nose" became a formidable and well-remembered opponent of the Eighth AF fighter pilots from the fall of 1944 on. B. Garlich

fighters—a new one-day record which would remain unbroken. This incredible victory was gained at the cost of only sixteen US fighters. After this mission the pilots of the Eighth Air Force encountered fewer and fewer enemy fighters and had to turn their attention to targets on the ground.

For the rest of January there was very little opposition from the Luftwaffe. On the fifteenth the 357th Group, still heady from their great triumph, flew a mission against airfields in central Germany, and Lt. Robert Winks was able to catch an Me 262 trying to land at the aerodrome at Shongau. Winks marched right up his six o'clock and sent him down in flames.

The heavies went back to the oil plants at Magdeburg, Ruhland, Germany and Salzburg, Austria, on January 16, but there was no intercepting force. The 4th FG could find no aerial opposition so Maj. Fred Glover sent the Mustangs down to strafe the airfield at Neuhausen. The two initial passes went unopposed so the entire 336th Squadron was sent down. They destroyed twenty-nine E/A including a number of brand-new silver long-nosed FW 190s before departing. Four of the P-51s took damage from light flak, but they all made it back to England.

The heavies went back to central Germany on January 20 and once more the 357th Group was part of the escort. Lt. Roland Wright was flying Lieutenant Haydon's wing when they sighted an Me 262 near Heilbronn. The two pilots gave chase and the German pilot did his best to get the craft to Lechfeld aerodrome to land. As the Mustangs charged across the field to fire, Haydon was hit by flak and was forced to pull up and bail out.

Wright dropped down closer to the deck and continued his attack, firing a long burst. Good strikes were registered and the Me 262 went off the runway streaming smoke. As Wright pulled up and looked back, he could see the 262 burning fiercely.

Earlier, Lt. Dale Karger of the 364th Squadron spotted two Me 262s while strafing in the Munich area. The Mustangs started to climb and finally one of the 262s came almost head-on at Karger. The jet then started a slow dive toward Munich. Slowly Karger closed, and when the 262 made a long turn to the left, Karger cut him off and fired right into the cockpit. The pilot bailed out and the jet split-essed into the ground. With this victory, Karger's fifth, he became the second US teenage fighter ace of World War II.

On Feb. 3, 1945, there was a mixture of aerial action and ground strafing and the net results were 21-1-7 aerial victories and 17-0-11 ground victories. The aerial victories were scored by the 55th FG which downed twelve, and the 56th FG with the remaining nine.

Lt. Dale Karger of the 357th FG became the second teenage ace of the Eighth AF in January 1945 and went on to score 7½ victories in the air and four on the ground. He is shown with his P-51 Cathy Mae *and ground crew. D. Karger*

A gun camera sequence made by Lt. Bernard Howes of the 343rd FS, 55th FG when he got into the flight of Mistels on Feb. 3, 1945. The first photo shows two Mistels in flight, the second shows the Mistel pilot going over the side and the third shows the Ju 88 released from its FW 190, with Mustang right on its tail. USAAF

The 55th Group encountered some strange and unusual aircraft on its mission. Lt. Col. Elwyn Righetti was leading the group and split his squadrons to attack various targets of opportunity. Righetti sighted two locomotives through a hole in the clouds and dropped his flight down to investigate. As he neared the trains he sighted three "pick-a-back" craft. These were Ju 88s which had FW 190s attached to the top of the twin-engined aircraft. These aerial oddities were a weapons package consisting of the Ju 88 with a load of high explosives to be flown to a target by the pilot of the attached FW 190. Upon reaching the target the Ju 88 would be aimed nose down at its objective, the single-engined fighter would release itself and the pilot would be free to return to base.

Righetti positioned himself on the tail of the middle combo of a loose formation of three of the craft and opened fire on the Ju 88 portion. Both aircraft remained fastened and went into a steep dive. At this point Righetti overflew them but on turning back he observed a large explosion and the resulting burning wreckage where the two craft had gone in.

As he closed in on a second target the FW 190 pilot apparently cut loose from the Ju 88 which went into a diving turn to the left and crashed into a small hamlet. The FW 190, now free, snapped to the right and began evasive action. Righetti put a good burst into the 190 and it went down to crash straight ahead. Righetti then found himself under fire, apparently from another of the FW 190s that had released itself from its burden. The Mustang pilot broke away and headed out, having sustained only minor damage.

Lt. Bernard Howes also downed two of the FW 190s and one Ju 88 in the process of breaking up two of the combos. His wingman downed the second Ju 88 after it was released by the FW 190 pilot on whom Howes was firing. The fifth pick-a-back was credited to Lt. Richard Gibbs.

Lt. Dudley Amoss of the 355th was on his way home when he sighted two FW 58 twin-engined light transports. These aircraft were right above the treetops and doing their best to flee the P-51s. Amoss was quickly on top of them and poured fifty-caliber lead into them from directly astern. Both crashed into open fields.

While the other fighter units were assigned the task of escorting the Big Friends to Berlin, the 56th Group was free to sweep ahead of the bomber stream. Maj. Paul Conger was leading the group and as they reached a wooded area southeast of the big city, they sighted a formation of fighters down below. The Thunderbolts dropped down and identified them as fifteen FW 190s flying at 3,000 feet. These E/A had apparently just taken off from Friedersdorf aerodrome.

The aircraft went into a big Lufbery and Conger lined up on one of the 190s. Just as he opened fire on the craft, it opened fire on the P-47 flown by Lt. David Magel. Magel's Thunderbolt burst into flames and went down. Conger gave the victor a second squirt and as the 190 went into a steep diving turn its right wing tore off, the craft flipped to the left and went into the ground.

Conger then joined three other P-47s making passes on the enemy aircraft right down over the airfield where light flak was coming up in profusion. One P-47, in pursuit of a 190, broke off his attack due to the flak but Conger picked him up and bored in. The Jug pilot continued to close on the 190 and finally shot him down into the trees on the outskirts of Berlin.

Another heavy strike against Germany's petroleum industry was launched on February 9 with 1,200 bombers attacking a number of targets. The 479th FG was escorting B-24s striking at Magdeburg and ran into interference between Magdeburg and Dessau. The German fighters attacked shortly after bombs away, and the 479th went after them. The 479th was split into A and B Groups, and it was B Group that first sighted and bounced the sixteen enemy fighters. Moments later A Group joined the melee, and after a twenty-minute air battle ten of the enemy fighters were shot down. One of the 479th's planes also was shot down, and its pilot, Lt. C. B. Jarrell, was seen to bail out.

Capt. George Gleason led the scoring with a double, his eleventh and twelfth aerial victories. Two other pilots got their signals crossed and nearly collided, but each ended up with a victory instead. Capt. Norman Benoit of the 435th FS had just downed an FW 190 when he discovered another potential target, an Me 109. Benoit reported: "Later I found a Me-109 flying in and out of the clouds. I finally got him out into the open and closed on him and started firing at high deflection. The Me-109 pulled up flying straight. Just as I was squared away on him Lt. John Rogers, who was supposed to be flying my wing, dropped down on top of me, forcing me to break to avoid collision. So I watched

him [Lt. Rogers] shoot the Me-109 down. I had followed the 109 around and through the clouds for about ten minutes. The P-51 in the combat film of Lt. Rogers is me."

Viewing the event from a different perspective, Rogers stated in his encounter report: "I then found another P-51 from my squadron and joined him [Captain Benoit]. We stooged around for a while and found one lone Me-109. The other P-51 started after him and I saw him overshoot so I came in on its tail [the 109's] and after a couple seconds I saw many strikes, then fire broke out on his right side. He was about 3,000 feet when he went off on a wing and hit on his back in a small woods. The pilot did not get out."

Five days later the 479th returned to Magdeburg. Their mission was threefold, and this time the Group was divided into three forces. Colonel Riddle led A Group, Major Duffy led B Group and Lt. Keefe led C Group. The 479th historian reported the mission as follows: "Once again the heavy bombers we were assigned to escort headed for Magdeburg. 'B' and 'C' groups carried out their assignments without incident: 'B' group rode herd on the heavies into the target and out again; 'C' group escorted its PRU P-38 to the Stettin area, but on arriving there found that the area was overcast and returned home without taking pictures. 'A' group was vectored here and there after bandits with no success until they found themselves southwest of Berlin, where they sighted 15 Me-109s at 32,000 feet (our pilots were at 26,000) and climbed to attack. At the same time twenty FW-190s were sighted farther below. Evidently the 109s had been providing top cover for the FWs. The ensuing battle brought out the fact that the Germans were much more aggressive than usual, and may have been responsible for the loss of Lt. John Donnell. The whole attack took place on the fringe of Berlin itself. At one time when 'A' group became divided, one part of it sighted bandits and gave all-out chase without being able to catch up. It was later discovered that they were chasing the other part of 'A' group, and the race took them over Berlin and as far as to the Oder, where the Russians were then punching holes in the German defense line. The fight with the enemy fighters ended in claims of 10-0-3. The top scorer was Major Robin Olds with two Me-109s and one FW-190."

While A Group was disposing of enemy fighters, B Group was working on the railroads below and claimed 6-0-5 locomotives and numerous rail cars.

For the next several days the pilots of Eighth Air Force found few targets and the scores fell off. However, on February 20 this all changed and its pilots found a wealth of targets, both in the air and on the ground. The 20th FG led the way. They escorted bombers attacking Nurnberg, and then went down to strafe targets in the area. The Group arrived over the target at 1150 and then the squadrons split up to attack rail and aircraft targets in their respective areas. The 55th FS led by Colonel Montgomery headed east and savagely attacked a large number of rail and radio targets. In these assaults they destroyed locomotives, tank cars, some freight cars and two radio stations. Three planes were lost.

One of the pilots, Lt. Sidney Stitzer, was a victim of his own target. He strafed a tank car which was apparently loaded with a volatile cargo. When hit by Stitzer's machine gun fire the car exploded violently and threw debris and flames several hundred feet in the air. His Mustang went through the blast area and came out the other side flying straight, but one landing gear was dangling down. Shortly afterward the P-51 rolled over and went straight in.

The 77th FS led by Maj. Merle Gilbertson strafed thirty-four miles of railroads and left dozens of freight and oil cars burning on the tracks. Shortly after the strafing attack Lieutenants Fay, Kern, Reynolds and Piatkiewicz bounced a flight of six German training planes and downed four of them. Moments later three more German aircraft were destroyed by 77th pilots in a strafing run over Straubling aerodrome.

The 79th FS led by Maj. Bob Meyer came home with the scoring laurels. After arriving over Nurnberg the 79th headed northeast on the deck. Along the tracks between Nurnberg and Bayreuth they intercepted six trains and some isolated locomotives and destroyed at least seven locomotives and sixteen freight cars. When they finished with the trains Lt. Dale Jones spotted an airfield near the town of Weiden, Germany, filled with aircraft. The 79th attacked the field for the next fifteen minutes and left sixteen enemy planes destroyed and another nineteen damaged. Lt. Frank Strock led in scoring with 3-0-2 victories.

During the same mission the 479th FG teamed up with the 356th FG and strafed the Windishenlaibach airfield, destroying another sixteen E/A. Each Group claimed eight destroyed.

Mustangs of the 77th FS logging some formation time over England. J. Ilfrey

Chapter 17

The Fall of the Jets

Toward the end of February 1945 the Eighth Air Force opened a new offensive called Operation Clarion, which was an assault on German communications. It began on Feb. 22, 1945, and for the next eight days the Eighth dispatched huge 1,000–plus bomber strikes against German transportation. The fighters joined in the effort, destroying four enemy fighters in air-to-air combat and another twenty-four in strafing attacks on German airfields.

Three of the aerial victories were against Me 262 jets. Lt. Charles Price of the 486th FS, 352nd FG and Maj. Wayne Blickenstaff and Capt. Gordon Compton of the 353rd Fighter Group each got one. Blickenstaff and his squadron had sighted four of the jet-powered craft in the vicinity of Brandenburg, and the entire group gave chase. However, the jets broke formation and seemed to lose the Mustangs in and out of haze. Blickenstaff finally decided that his charges were getting too close to Russian lines, so he ordered them to break off and head for home.

Flying at 8,000 feet northwest of Berlin, Blickenstaff sighted another Me 262 flying east in haze. He put his Mustang in a dive and managed to close on the jet

and opened fire. The left jet engine began to smoke and the German pilot went into wild evasive action. When the jet went into a dive, Blickenstaff put another burst into it and more smoke poured from the left engine. The pilot went over the side and bailed out.

Capt. Gordon Compton had split off and chased after one of the original four jets the group had sighted. The four 262s had gone into diving turns and as Compton patiently waited, the number four craft in the string formation pulled up right in front of him. Compton didn't have time to set his K–14 sight so he fired a long burst through his line of flight and the right jet engine began to stream smoke. Compton quickly closed and eased his Mustang in on the German's six o'clock. Another long burst sent pieces flying, and the right engine burst into flames. The pilot bailed out.

Eight of the ground strafing victories were scored by the 4th FG when they tore up the airfield at Halberstadt. The 78th FG worked over the rail systems near Kitzingen and claimed 10–0–1 locomotives and several freight cars. The 479th also accounted for a number of planes and rail cars on the ground but the Group's real excitement came when it encountered fifteen Me 262s

Mustangs of the 350th FS, 353rd FG, laden with drop tanks headed out from England. USAAF

and dueled the jets to a scoreless draw. The 262 attack was directed against the 435th FS and took place just southwest of Berlin. The attack by an apparently very experienced group of Germans was described as follows by the squadron leader: "Squadron heading east just southwest of Berlin when bounced by 15 Me-262s at 1150 hours. Flight of four E/A attacked from south on level. Broke into E/A who crossed in front and climbed. Second flight of four bounced us from rear high. Climbing tactics by one E/A and simultaneous bounce from a rear flight kept up until we had made about four breaks into the E/A. Neither P-51s or Me-262s were able to get in a shot. E/A easily climbed ahead of P-51s, drawing away rapidly. During the engagement by friendly and enemy flights, the number four man from Jerry flight, while turning from attack by us, would fall behind and slightly above for an attack from the rear. Both friendly and enemy took advantage of the sun. Jerries were very aggressive and apparently experienced pilots. Whenever our flights broke into E/A head on, Jerries would climb rather than dive. In one particular mixup, two 262s bounced flight from above and from each side. Again the jets climbed after our flight turned into them. Fight broke up at 1210."

The report went on to say that even though the Me 262s didn't shoot any Mustangs down, they had still done their job: "Their job seemed to be to force us to drop tanks so that we would have to leave. After we had used up all but a minimum of gas for the return trip the jets did not press an attack as we left. It was apparent that they were vectored to us. Our flights found that expenditure of gas while attempting to close was very heavy, as it is necessary to use full power all the time.

Capt. Gordon Compton, veteran ace of the 353rd FG, scored victories over two Me 262s on separate occasions. G. Compton

Mustang from the 55th FG taxies out in the snow. The winter of 1944–45 was one of the worst ever recorded in northern Europe. L. Moon

The jets flew excellent formation and never allowed themselves to be caught in a bad position."

The 435th FS was apparently the first Eighth Air Force fighter squadron to mix it up with a gaggle from the newly formed JG 7. The new German unit was an all-jet Geschwader composed of three Gruppen of Me 262s flown by well-trained, experienced pilots. It was immediately obvious to the command of the Eighth Air Force that the bombers faced a new and very dangerous threat from this jet fighter force. Nevertheless, missions would have to continue, and the fighters would have to deal with the jets as best they could. The best method to contain the Me 262s was to catch them on the ground or in vulnerable takeoff or landing situations. Eighth AF fighters made a habit of hovering near jet fields hoping to catch the 262s in a vulnerable position. On February 25 the 55th FG caught a swarm of 262s taking off from their airfield at Giebelstadt, and blasted seven of them out of the sky.

Capt. Donald Penn was leading the 38th Fighter Squadron on a sweep in the Nurnberg area when he sighted two Me 262s get airborne and two more taking off from Giebelstadt aerodrome. The Mustangs were at 13,000 feet and Penn ordered them to drop tanks and engage. Penn dove on one 262, pulling fifty inches of mercury at 3000 rpm. The jet was making a slight turn to port at 1,000 feet heading back for the airfield, so Penn leveled off behind him and gave chase. The P-51 was at full power, flying at 500 mph and Penn fully expected the 262 to dive to pull away, but the jet dropped its landing gear to land. Penn cut power and started firing from 300 yards. Closing and firing, Penn broke sharply over the jet and watched as it rolled over and went straight into the ground.

Capt. Don Cummings took his flight down right across the airfield and caught one of the 262s just as it was coming in. Cummings commenced firing and followed the jet down while catching light flak from the field's AA batteries. As he pulled up over the 262 it touched the ground, cartwheeled and burned.

Cummings had lost his number three and four men in the pass so he and his wingman climbed up to 5,000 feet in search of other targets. An unidentified aircraft was sighted near Leipheim aerodrome as it crossed the drome at about 4,000 feet. As the Mustangs increased their speed, they identified it as an Me 262. The jet continued to let down for a landing as Cummings opened fire. The first burst missed, but then the 262 pilot made the mistake of going into a turn to the right. The P-51 pilot then was able to get him at ten degrees deflection and score hits all over the aircraft. The 262 continued to roll to the right and crash.

Other pilots who downed Me 262s on that memorable day for the 55th Group were Lts. Don Menegay, Millard Anderson, John O'Neil and Billy Clemmons.

In a more conventional air battle the pilots of the 20th FG destroyed another seven enemy aircraft. These engagements took place after thirty-five minutes of strafing in which the 20th destroyed seventeen locomotives and numerous rail cars, horse-drawn carts, trucks

and staff and recon cars. It was after the completion of the strafing runs that Capt. Charles Cole and his flight from the 55th FS caught a group of five FW 190s taking off from a grass airfield and bounced them. In the pass Cole destroyed two and probably destroyed two more, and Lt. Seifert damaged one. As they were pulling up, a lone Focke Wulf dove on Cole and shot him down. The FW 190 was shot from the sky by Maj. Maurice Cristadore. Cole bellied in his Mustang near Magdeburg. In the meantime, Lt. Charles Nicholson found another FW 190 stooging around and fired on it, setting the German fighter afire. As the 190 started burning, Nicholson pulled alongside it and the German waved at him. As Nicholson returned the wave, the German pilot jettisoned his canopy and climbed out on the wing. As he slid off the wing he struck the tail plane and was killed instantly.

On the way home Captain Fruechtenicht, leading Red Flight of the 55th, and a couple of strays from Blue Flight ran into a gaggle of thirty Me 109s flying at 5,000 feet near Dummer Lake. The six Mustangs charged into the German formation and sent three of them down in flames. Two of the kills were scored by Lt. Edward Kier, the single victory went to Fruechtenicht. Lieutenant Pettit damaged another.

The 4th Fighter Group also played a big part in the scoring on February 25. The 4th, led by Maj. Pierce

Capt. Charles H. Cole of the 20th FG downed two FW 190s taking off on Feb. 25, 1945, but was then shot down to become a POW. Cole was one of the 20th FG top scorers with five in the air and six on the ground. USAAF

201

McKennon, was on a free-lance sweep to the Dessau, Germany, area. Upon arriving in the area they strafed the airfields at Rohrensee and Kothen. During the attack on Kothen, Capt. Kendall Carlson of the 336th FS was hit and crash-landed on the airfield. Instead of making a quick getaway, Carlson stuck with his plane and directed the attack from his ringside seat. He added insult to injury to the German forces at Kothen when he vectored Lieutenants Brooker and Morgan on to the tail of a Focke Wulf being flown by the base commander. The 190 was in its landing pattern when the two lieutenants downed it with their combined fire. The 336th left Kothen after destroying four enemy fighters and the 334th FS added seven more to the list during their strafing at Rohrensee.

The other victory of the day for the 4th was an aerial victory over an Me 262 by Lt. Carl Payne. Payne described his victory as follows: "We were 10 minutes southwest of Leipzig at 8,000 feet when I spotted the Me–262 at about 4,000 feet at our one o'clock. I peeled off on him, calling in at the same time. I closed to about 400 yards and opened fire, holding it until about 100 yards. I hit him and knocked out his left jet. I overshot him and pulled up to the right and made another pass. I was not hitting him as I should, so I moved up to 10 to 30 feet behind him and started firing; he exploded and covered me completely with flames. After I hit him the first time, he went to the deck and stayed there until he exploded."

The strafing actions by the 4th FG on February 25 were just a warmup action for their mission of February 27. On this mission the 4th was split into A Group led by Maj. Fred Glover and B Group led by Col. Everett Stewart. A Group was sent on a free-lance sweep to Leipzig while B was to escort B–24s to Halle. After finishing its escort duties, Stewart led B Group to strafe the Weimar airfield. During the attack, A Group joined the fray and when it was all finished they destroyed forty-three enemy planes. It cost them two of their own, Lts. Harold Crawford and Bob Voyles, who became POWs. Lt. Donald Malmsten led in scoring with six destroyed, and several pilots tied for second place with three apiece.

The strafing of airfields constituted most of the fighter action for the next two days, but on Mar. 2, 1945, the tempo changed. On that date three air divisions totaling 1,167 heavy bombers escorted by 713 fighters struck at the German petroleum industry, and the strike force was met by an unusually large defensive force. The majority of the enemy fighters attacked the 3rd Air Division, which bombed Ruhland and Dresden. In that air battle fifty-four of the 66½ enemy fighters claimed by the Eighth Air Force that day were destroyed. The 78th Fighter Group's 83rd Fighter Squadron claimed fourteen of those victories. The enemy fighters were spotted near Magdeburg, flying at about 15,000 feet and the 83rd dove to the attack. The formation of twenty-four Me 109s were flying in flights of four in string. When attacked, the six enemy flight leaders dropped their tanks and turned into the attackers.

The remaining 109s retained their tanks and held formation for a while longer, then split up. The six leaders seemed experienced and aggressive but the other pilots were quite timid, and as such were no match for the 83rd's checker-nosed Mustangs. Lt. Duncan McDuffie downed four of the 109s in short order: "I pursued the one which broke to the left. We made a half turn when I gave him a radii lead while he was in a gentle climb. After a good 'squirt,' I saw generous hits on the canopy and engine. He flipped on his back and went down. I figured he'd been had, so continued on in the turn and found myself on the tail of another 109. This was a repeat of the first situation except the E/A was on fire when it went in. I was then at cloud level, so I went beneath them and saw a 109 on the deck that apparently never saw me. I bounced him, gave him a long burst and the Jerry burst into a huge mass of flame and plowed in. I sighted a fourth E/A at about 7,000 feet. He saw me and evaded into one of the semi-thick clouds. I followed, gained on him, and fired a short burst. Hits showed and he dodged back for a cloud. I followed and got in another short burst when he headed for another cloud. This dodging went on from cloud to cloud for about four or five passes with hits showing each time. On my next to last pass, I saw that his left elevator was completely gone and part of his right wing. On my last pass I saw hits on the engine and canopy. The E/A jerked and glycol began streaming. My ammo was nearly gone and the aerodrome over which we had been fighting commenced firing at me. The E/A slid off on one wing in a steep dive and I, feeling that the E/A was done for, and to avoid the flak, climbed through the clouds to rejoin Cargo Leader [Colonel John Landers]."

Col. John Landers shot down two of the 109s from the JG 301 formation. No doubt the veteran Mustang pilot would have scored more had it not been for gun stoppages. Landers pulled in on the tail-end of a formation of 109s which still had belly tanks attached. He hit the gun tit but nothing happened. Landers pulled out to the left and let his wingman, Lt. Jack Hodge, have a crack at the target. Hodge fired and scored no hits, but the pilot rolled the 109 over and bailed out.

Landers, meanwhile, was charging his guns and came back into the fight. Four of his guns fired and as he turned with an E/A, two of them stopped firing. The Luftwaffe pilot had had enough, though. He bailed out. Landers quickly lined up on another 109, fired a short burst and all guns quit once more. Again this was a sufficient scare for the inexperienced German pilot who went over the side. Landers summed up the kills: "All were freaks. The Jerry pilots were very inexperienced and still played follow the leader."

The 357th Fighter Group encountered primarily Me 109s on their way to Ruhland, and the quality of the pilots was about the same as was being encountered by the 78th Group. Capt. Alva Murphy took his flight from the 364th Squadron down after some Me 109s and soon got on the tail of one and downed it. Five minutes later he dove on another and after two turns it was earthward

Lt. Col. John D. Landers was one of the outstanding fighter leaders and aces in the Eighth AF. He came from the Pacific where he had been an ace and flew with the 55th FG, 357th FG and then went to the 78th FG as CO. J. Landers

Lt. Col. John Landers' last combat aircraft Big Beautiful Doll shown on hardstand with all its victory markings at the end of the war. J. Landers

The German pilot went in with his aircraft which exploded.

Capt. Bob Schimanski of the 364th Squadron found what appeared to be a new airfield and took his charges down to strafe. The E/A were parked in the woods which made them hard to hit, but fortunately, the flak was very light, consisting of only two machine

Capt. John L. Sublett of the 357th FG explains to Lt. Pete Pelon in fighter "hand language" how he finally got the long nosed FW 190. M. Olmsted

bound in flames. Shortly thereafter Murphy took his charges in to strafe an airfield. On a strafing pass his plane was hit by flak and he was forced to bail out, only to be killed later on the ground.

Capt. John Sublett of the 362nd Squadron dropped down on an enemy formation, sighted an Me 109 fleeing the scene and took off after him. The enemy craft ducked into a cloud, so Sublett nonchalantly circled, burning off fuel in his fuselage tank. He then dropped his wing tanks and he and his wingman dropped into the cloud to seek the enemy. Sublett reefed up after the 109, fired and got good hits causing the right gear of the E/A to drop. The 109 sought refuge in the cloud once more, but Sublett dropped below the cloud and was able to sight his victim, who came out of the cloud spinning. Another burst was sufficient to send him down to his destruction.

Sublett then found trouble with an FW 190D. This long-nosed 190 was braver and headed for the Mustang from ten o'clock. The Mustang pilot looped onto his tail and as soon as the pipper on the gunsight settled down, Sublett let him have it. The P–51 chased the 190 through the clouds, still closing, and then really clobbered it.

gun positions on either side of the field. A number of German Mistel or pick-a-backs as the Americans called them were present along with conventional He 111s, Ju 88s and Ju 188s. The Mustangs worked the field over, with some of them making as many as ten passes. Fifteen of the E/A were claimed destroyed on the ground, four of these being FW 190s which were mounted on top of He 111s.

The 353rd Fighter Group under the leadership of Lt. Col. Bill Bailey sighted a gaggle of Me 109s assembling in the vicinity of Wittenberg, Germany, and attacked. Lt. Arthur Cundy and Lt. Horace Q. Waggoner tied for high score by destroying three E/A each. Cundy described his combat as follows: "Lt. Grove was right with me and Lt. Snyder was rather far back when someone called in many Me 109s above us. In the immediately following confusion and disorder a lone Me 109 came screaming down past our flight and attacked a four ship Jockey Flight low and 10 o'clock to me. Instantly I rolled over and split-essed after him, saw that I could catch the bum and released my external tanks. This particular Me 109 pilot must have been Adolph Hitler Junior in a brand new Superman suit because, not satisfied with his unsuccessful pass on four of our fighters, he pulled right up very steeply and began giving a bomber box the works from their six o'clock low. That's when I tacked on behind and cut loose. I began to get a few scattered and unsatisfactory strikes about his wings and tail but not concentrated because I was at the moment having great difficulty with the great trim displacement from the extremes of vertical dive to stalling vertical climb. For this reason I had not accomplished a darn thing when I was right on him, overtaking and about to ram into him. Just as I booted hard right rudder to avoid collision and passed barely under his right wing the 109 stalled out and began to tumble and spin. At the very same time, I found myself in a similar situation, spinning. As we spun down side by side out of control I was extremely gratified to note that a 109 has a more rapid rate of descent in a spin than a P–51, and the 109 was below me in about one turn. This fact allowed me to see the guy in my gunsight on every turn, so every time my nose swung around to bear for a split second on my adversary I gave him a short squirt. It was good for my morale. In this manner I got a few more strikes on him before he made a flattering recovery from the spin. I was able to recover easily and did so, coming out of it right behind the 109. I followed him down to the clouds, which were at this point rather thin. Having lost the guy temporarily I went straight on through the cloud and found him down there again. As soon as he saw me this time he bailed out with no further delay and I got set to strafe him in his chute, but before I squeezed the trigger I changed my mind and took a picture of him instead.

"By then I was quite alone on the deck, my wingman having found it impossible to follow down throughout the erratic maneuvers already mentioned. Off to my right was a lone fighter plane, to which I immediately gave chase and found to be a FW 190. This 190 hadn't seen me at all, so I had no trouble driving up his tail and clobbered him good with one burst. He burst into flames and nosed down, went straight into the deck almost vertically and blew up very pleasingly.

"Low of gas I believed it time to get the hell out of there. This I was doing when I spotted a little speck far behind me. Knowing that any other plane down there was surely enemy, I turned sharply to give chase. Just as this fighter plane went into a small cloud puff and out of sight another came out, head-on to me. This suited me fine so I flew on waiting for him to make a nice target in my gunsight. I recognized it for another FW 190 and gave him a very short burst right on the kisser just when he was plenty close. His engine exploded immediately and he whizzed past me in flames, pulled up steeply and bailed out like an old hand at the game."

The 486th FS of the 352nd FG closed out the scoring on March 2 with six aerial victories. Five of the victories were claimed in a dogfight with fifteen FW 190s over the target at Rositz. After breaking off from this engagement, they sighted another small gaggle of 190s and pursued them to the vicinity of Prague. Once over Prague, Czechoslovakia, they spotted an airfield below them filled with tempting targets. In this attack the squadron scored its last aerial victory of the day when Lt. Col. Willie O. Jackson caught an FW 189 reconnaissance plane taking off and blasted it from the sky. In addition to Jackson's kill over the aerodrome, the squadron claimed two FW 190s strafing, and damaged two Mistel aircraft.

After its devastating setback on March 2 the Luftwaffe was conspicuous by its absence on March 3. A huge strike force of Eighth Air Force bombers escorted by 700 plus fighters again attacked oil facilities and marshaling yards throughout Germany, but this time they were virtually unopposed. Lt. William Sanford of the 352nd FG scored the only aerial victory of the day when he downed an Me 109 near Dresden. Since the enemy did not come up to fight, the fighters dove to the deck in search of targets. In the strafing attacks, they destroyed another nineteen enemy planes and damaged twenty-five. The 505th FS of the 339th FG laid claim to 8–0–2 of those victories when Lt. Colonel Joe Thury led an attack against the airfield at Mockburn.

Thury, one of the most accomplished ground strafers the Eighth Air Force produced, described the attack as follows: "On March 3 I was leading the upper squadron (505th) on a Ramrod to Dollberger. After chasing blow jobs to the deck in the target area I led Red, White, and Blue Flights onto a dispersal area in the vicinity of Mockburn. About 50 Ju-88s, Do–217s and pick-a-backs (Ju-88 and FW-190s) were dispersed in three clumps of trees. All of the E/A were well camouflaged and packed in the wooded areas which necessitated passes from numerous angles and directions.

"Planted in the area were five or six light flak positions which we were unable to knock out. The flak was extremely accurate and hit Lts. Jones and Ziegler on their first pass. I sustained three flak hits and Lt. Marts was hit once. On the first pass, out of the sun,

Captain Starnes destroyed one pick-a-back, Lt. Ziegler a Ju–88, Lt. Jones a pick-a-back, and I got a Ju–88.

"Lt. Ziegler bellied in, making a beautiful landing, and was seen to walk away. Lt. Jones bailed out from below 300 feet and hit the ground before his chute opened.

"Lt. Marts and I were the only ones left in the dispersal area after the first pass. So I continued my attacks from out of the sun. On one pass I dropped my tanks near two Ju–88s and on the succeeding pass one Ju–88 started to burn. I made seven distinct passes, in a left hand pattern, and destroyed three Ju–88s and one DO–217, and damaged one other Ju–88. One of my Ju–88s exploded and burned. My other three claims burned very slowly at first, then developed into large fires which exuded black smoke apparently from the gas and oil in the planes.

"When I left the area Lt. Marts and I counted eight fires. He didn't make any passes since he was covering Lt. Jones when he bailed out and continued to circle the area until I had finished my attacks.

"I attribute the destruction of three of the E/A to two of my guns firing incendiary ammo, which, at first, caused only slow burning fires. However, as I left they had begun to blaze violently."

The remaining credit for a Ju 88 destroyed and a Mistel pick-a-back damaged went to Lt. Richard Thieme.

From March 4 through March 13 the enemy hid from the fighter pilots of the Eighth Air Force. During this period only six enemy planes were destroyed, all in aerial combat. Finally on March 14 the drought ended and the flyers took advantage of it. On that day seventeen enemy planes were destroyed in aerial combat, with the 353rd FG taking the lion's share of eleven.

Capt. Bill Maguire led the 351st Fighter Squadron on a fighter sweep east of Magdeburg where they sighted a force of Me 109s. The Mustangs took off after them and Maguire sighted two 109s below him. As he pulled around to bounce the E/A, four Me 109s pulled up behind him and his wingman. Maguire pulled into a hard turn and called, "There are Me 109s up here and they are on my ass shooting at me." Lt. George Montgomery climbed up into the Lufbery and shot down one 109 on Maguire's tail. At the same time Maguire nailed a 109 in front of him.

Maguire then spotted another four Me 109s and went up after them. Montgomery went after the first two and Maguire and Capt. Gene Markham tacked onto the two remaining. Both used their K–14 sights at maximum range to clobber the two 109s, sending both straight in. Maguire's burst sawed two feet or better off the wing of his victim. Both Maguire and Montgomery were credited with two of the Me 109s. Capt. Gene Markham was high scorer for the day with three.

Four of the day's victories were against German jets. One of them went to Capt. Donald S. Bryan of the 352nd FG. The Group, still operating from its forward base in Belgium, was participating in a Ninth Air Force mission when Bryan spotted the Ar 234 bomber heading for the Remagen bridgehead in Germany. He dropped tanks and went after the bomber but could not catch it because the bomber was at least fifty miles an hour faster than Bryan's Mustang. The 234 passed over the bridge but for some reason did not drop his bomb. Just about that time a group of Ninth Air Force P–47s dove down to block the jet's escape route.

Hoping to get away from the formation of Thunderbolts, the German pilot made a fatal decision and turned toward Captain Bryan. The Arado passed under Bryan who then dove to the attack and fired from about 250 yards. On his first burst Bryan knocked out the right engine, and then after trailing the 234 through a series of maneuvers shot out the left engine. At this time the German jet rolled over on its back and dived straight into the ground carrying its pilot with it. The other jet victories were scored by the 56th FG which claimed two Me 262s and the 356th FG which downed another Ar 234. The 56th's victories were both scored by Lt. John Keeler, and the Arado fell to Lt. Robert Barnhart.

The enemy went back into hiding on March 15 and encounters were few and far between. Only one aerial victory was scored during the day but it was a significant one. The engagement took place over Berlin between a rocket-powered Me 163 and a 359th FG Mustang flown by Capt. Ray Wetmore.

Wetmore was leading his section of the 370th Fighter Squadron when they sighted two Me 163s circling at about 20,000 feet in the vicinity of Wittenberge. Wetmore positioned his P–51 above the craft and made ready to bounce. However, the 163 pilot spotted him and went up into a steep climb. At about 26,000 feet his engine cut out and he went over in a split-ess. Wetmore followed him in a high-speed dive at between 500 and 600 miles per hour. The 163 leveled out at 2,000 feet and as he did so Wetmore closed and opened fire from 200 yards. Pieces began to fly off the craft, and its pilot threw it into a sharp turn to the right. Another burst cut half its left wing off. Flames broke out and the pilot bailed out. This was the final Eighth Air Force claim for an Me 163 and it marked the twenty-first and last aerial victory for Wetmore, who was the highest scoring active ace in the ETO at the time.

Finally, on March 18 the Luftwaffe chose to attack again in large numbers, but in doing so, lost fourteen of its valuable planes and pilots to the Eighth Air Force fighters. The 55th and 339th Groups with four victories apiece led in scoring, and the 352nd FG was a close second with three victories. For the 4th FG, victory took a different shape. The Group was split into A Group and B Group, and they were both escorting bombers to Berlin. Upon arriving in the target area, B Group led by Captain Howe stayed with the bombers, while A Group led by Maj. Pierce McKennon went down to strafe the airfield at Neubrandenburg. As McKennon led his Group over the field, his P–51D *Ridgerunner III* was hit by flak and he was forced to pull up and bail out. Seeing his CO on the ground, Lt. George Green made an instant decision and announced to his squadron mates that he was going down after the major. Green then set his Mustang down gently in the plowed field where McKennon had landed, and motioned for "Mac" to get aboard. Lt. Mel Franklin of the 336th FS was one of the pilots flying cover for the rescue attempt. He described the scene as follows: "As Major McKennon was racing for concealment and Green was making his landing approach, German soldiers with dogs came charging into the area. In an instant I was streaking over the field to begin strafing. There were targets everywhere and all you had to do was fire your guns and 'fishtail' your aircraft in order to hose the area. While firing though, I couldn't help from worrying that some of those figures on the ground might be 'underground' people trying to help.

"While Lt. Franklin and the others continued to lay down their covering fire, Green climbed from his cockpit and threw his parachute away. Almost simultaneously Major McKennon leaped onto the wing and climbed into the cockpit. Once Mac was in the cockpit Lt. Green climbed back in and sat on his lap, and in this manner the two took off and headed back to base."

The Eighth Air Force returned to Germany on March 19 to strike at transportation centers, and for the second day in a row the Luftwaffe made an appearance. This time it planned to strike as the American formations crossed their border, and the 78th FG was the first force to encounter the German fighters.

Sweeping ahead of the 1st Air Division, the 78th FG led by Lt. Col. John D. Landers ran into its first opposition just as they entered Germany. They were attacked by three Me 262s. The jets made shallow dives at the Mustangs, apparently hoping to get them to drop their wing tanks and to draw them away from the area where other German fighters were forming up to attack the American bomber formations. The Mustang pilots

didn't fall for the ruse, and after turning into the jets to drive them off, continued on their mission.

Twenty minutes later as the 78th approached Osnabruck, the 82nd FS engaged four Me 109s. This was the beginning of a long battle in which the Group would claim a total of 32-1-13 enemy fighters at a cost of five of their own. According to the Group historian it was considered the toughest and most successful air battle the 78th ever engaged in. As soon as the 82nd FS went after the four 109s, the main body of the German force was spotted. There were approximately forty-five Me 109s in four gaggles at altitudes from 14,000 feet down to 7,000 feet. In addition to the 109s there were about twenty-five Focke Wulf 190s above a thin cloud layer at about 14,000 feet, and these also joined into the battle about fifteen minutes after it began.

The German pilots not only had a clear numerical advantage over the 82nd, but they were also aggressive and willing to fight. The forty-six Mustangs of the 78th FG were now battling at least 125 enemy planes. Landers reported on the battle: "It is impossible to give a general picture of the action, which rapidly developed into individual dogfights. It was an 'elevator affair' sweeping from 14,000 feet down to the deck and back up again. Some of our pilots who had shot down enemy planes found themselves tangled with up to eight to ten of the Nazi fighters."

Typical of the day's action was the swirling dogfight in which Lt. J. E. Parker of the 82nd FS engaged: "I was flying as Yellow 2 on a fighter sweep to Berlin when we encountered 15 plus Me-109s at 5,000 feet at approximately 1230 hours. We bounced them from 8,000 feet, and on the bounce, I got on the tail of an Ar-234, which came stooging along in front of our flight. I started firing dead astern at maximum range and observed many strikes on tail, jets, and fuselage. The same time as this, another P-51 was firing from high and to the right of me, also getting good hits. As I was firing, the pilot crawled out of the cockpit, attempting to bail out, but my bullets knocked him over the forward wing and I observed no chute. I claim one Ar-234 and pilot shared with Lt. A. A. Rosenblum.

"We reformed our flight and headed west. A few minutes later, Yellow Leader and I bounced two FW-190s from 4,000 feet and tailed them to the deck. Yellow Leader destroyed one. We pulled up to 3,000 feet and were immediately bounced by 12 plus FW-190s from 9 o'clock high. We turned into them and made a head-on pass. I observed strikes and claim one FW-190 damaged. I then split-s'd and got a 90 degree long burst at a FW-190 on the deck. He began to smoke and crashed into the ground, disintegrating upon impact. I claim this FW-190 and pilot destroyed.

"I looked up and saw three FW-190s coming in on my tail and firing. I pulled 9 g's in a level 360 degree turn and got a 45 degree long burst at a FW-190, observing many strikes. It was smoking heavily when I broke off with two on my tail. I claim that FW probably destroyed. I then made another tight turn and got several short bursts at 45 degrees deflection on another FW-190,

Maj. Pierce McKennon, 4th FG ace, was picked up by Lt. George Green in the final rescue act in the Eighth AF. AF Museum

observing several strikes on his tail. I ran out of ammo and broke off and headed for home. I claim this FW–190 damaged."

Of the thirty-two victories scored by the 78th FG on March 19, the 82nd FS claimed 13–2–6 of them, two of which were Ar 234s. The second Arado was shared by Capt. W. H. Brown and Lt. H. H. Lamb. The 84th FS took the brunt of the casualties, losing three of its planes against eight victories. Two of the 84th FS kills were scored by Maj. Harry Downing before he was shot down. The 83rd FS chipped in with ten victories against two losses, and the remaining kill was claimed by Lt. Col. John Landers. It was the fourteenth aerial victory for Landers.

In addition to the thirty-two victories scored by the 78th, pilots from six other Eighth Air Force fighter groups claimed eight victories. Two of those were eleventh and twelfth aerial victories scored by Maj. Robin Olds of the 434th FS, 479th FG.

Olds' last victim was an FW 190 that attempted to join up in formation with him. Olds would have none of this and broke into him. The 190 then went into a barrel roll heading down and Olds went down and clobbered him. As the pilot bailed out he released what seemed to be a stack of papers which Olds racked around to avoid. The plane continued down in flames.

The 78th FG followed up their amazing victory of March 19 with two successful missions against Me 262s. The first of these missions took place on March 21, when the Group shot six 262s out of the air and destroyed three more on the ground. The first was downed by Capt. Edwin H. Miller at 0945 hours over Wittenberge. The speeding jet was sighted just as it blew up two B–17s. Before Miller could get to the scene of the action, the 262 had come around for another pass and struck at a crippled B–17. As the jet fired at the Fort, Miller cut loose at long range and scored a few hits—enough to drive the jet away from the B–17. After being hit, the 262 broke to the left and went into a dive. Not to be denied his victory, Miller put his Mustang into a 500 mph dive and closed on the Messerschmitt as it came out of a cloud. Miller began firing at 500 yards and continued shooting until he had closed to 100 yards. His gunfire was devastating and huge chunks of metal tore away from the 262 just before it went into its final, fatal dive. Forty-five minutes later Lt. John Kirk caught another 262 attempting to attack the B–17s and downed it with two well-placed long-ranged bursts. Moments later Lt. Kuehl downed the third Me 262 of the day's air battle.

The last three Me 262s destroyed by the 78th FG in aerial combat on March 21 were disposed of at 1215 hours over Giebelstadt airfield. Lts. Walter Bourque and Robert Anderson each claimed one, and the last one was shared by Capt. Winfield Brown and Lt. Allen Rosenblum. Major Conner rounded out the day's scoring when he destroyed three more of the jets during a strafing run across Alt Lonnerwitz airfield.

Lt. Col. John Landers led the 78th FG back to Germany on Mar. 22, 1945, and they continued their

Maj. Niven Cranfill of the 359th FG, who scored three victories in the big "green nose" victory of Nov. 27, 1944, downed one of the Me 262s that attempted interception on Mar. 19, 1945. N. Cranfill

victories over the 262s. This time the 78th claimed three of the speedy jets in aerial combat. One of the claims went to Capt. Harold Barnaby who caught one of them just after takeoff and was astounded that the jet had already reached an air speed of nearly 400 miles an hour in less than three miles flying distance. Barnaby was

Maj. Robin Olds became an ace in the P–38 shortly after his entry into combat with the 479th FG, but really went to town in the Mustang. At the end of the war his score was thirteen aerial and eleven ground victories. Tabatt

indicating 425 mph in his Mustang when he overtook and downed the 262.

March 22 was also quite a day for Lt. Col. Sidney Woods' A Group of the 4th FG. Shortly after an unsuccessful bounce against some Me 262s near Berlin, A Group sighted a large gaggle of bomb-laden FW 190s forming up over Furstenwald and attacked. After a battle which lasted forty minutes, eleven of the 190s lay as burning wreckage on the fields surrounding their aerodrome. Woods personally flamed five of them and became an "ace in a day." His total aerial victories then stood at seven.

Woods was leading the 4th A Group on a sweep east of Berlin when he sighted a B–17 which was apparently damaged heading for the Russian lines. Woods let down to follow the Fortress and sighted a formation of four FW 190s carrying bombs. They seemed to be forming up to fly a mission against Russian positions. Woods dropped down on the six o'clock of the number four man and sent the craft diving into the deck.

As Woods pulled up to clear his tail he sighted another E/A firing on his Mustang from nine o'clock above. Dumping the stick, Woods got down below the 190's line of fire. The German pilot went over the top, so Woods pulled straight up and rolled off on the top bringing himself down on the tail of the enemy aircraft. The 190 went into an aileron roll, but Woods followed, hit him and sent him crashing onto an aerodrome.

By this time Woods and his flight were taking heavy and light flak from the aerodrome, so away they went. Another four FW 190s were sighted down low. Once more Woods latched onto the number four man who dropped his bomb as he took strikes. The pilot went over the side.

Woods then sighted two FW 190s on the tail of a Mustang and went to the rescue. The German pilot seemed oblivious to the presence of the P-51 on his tail and quickly absorbed enough hits to send him crashing to earth.

Having disposed of victim number four, Woods pulled up to 3,000 feet where he sighted another flight of four FW 190s. For the third time he lined up on number four and as he opened fire all the E/A broke into a tight left turn. One enemy pilot made the mistake of pulling up in a steep climbing turn. Woods lined him up and walked his fire right up to the cockpit. The 190 caught fire, crashed and burned.

On the ground, the Allied forces had crossed the Rhine and were trying to establish a bridgehead from which to launch the final drive across Germany. To help augment the Allied forces on the enemy side of the river, an airborne assault was planned for March 24. To help prepare the way for the Allied paratroopers, Eighth Air Force dispatched a huge force of bombers and fighters to hit at nearby airfields and troop concentrations. While the B–17s bombed targets in the area, and B–24s made supply drops to the ground troops, the fighters combed the area to search for the expected Luftwaffe attack. The German air force did not react as strongly as anticipated, but our pilots still managed to claim 53-0-2 aerial victories. Nearly half of those victories were claimed by the 353rd FG. It scored twenty-

Lt. Col. Andrew Evans led the 357th into its big air battle on Mar. 24, 1945, and got his sixth aerial victory. M. Olmsted

Lt. Col. Sidney Woods of the 4th FG exuberantly tells the world that "I got five! Five!" during the combat of Mar. 22, 1945. Lt. Richard Moore looks on in awe. S. Woods

three kills, and the 357th and 359th FGs combined for another twenty-seven.

The Mustangs of the 357th Group sighted fifteen to twenty Me 109s headed west and attacked. The majority of the Messerschmitts involved were from JG 27. The veteran pilots of the 357th sent the Messerschmitts one after the other crashing to their destruction. The Mustang pilots almost lost two of their squadron leaders, however. Lt. Col. Andrew Evans' guns ran away on him while making his attack on an Me 109 spraying the countryside. His target absorbed enough hits to do considerable damage and from the aircraft's performance, he probably hit the pilot, too. The plane crashed into the trees. Evans cut his gun switches, but then his engine began to act up. Even though he was trailing black smoke and his engine was making a terrific racket he took off after another 109. Evans called his wingman to take over the target but he wasn't there. Upon checking his guns he found that all of his ammunition was gone. Evans then set out for the long ride home with a bad engine and no ammo.

Maj. Bob Foy, leading the 363rd Squadron, quickly dispatched a 109 down on the deck. As he made a strafing run he almost collided with the ground. His Mustang snapped to the left and the left wing hit a fair-sized tree. The impact swung the P–51 around and the right wing tip hit a smaller tree. Foy finally regained control and set course for home. The Mustang had a badly trimmed left wing, reducing stall-out speed to just below 160 mph.

The 353rd Fighter Group, led by Lt. Col. Wayne Blickenstaff, had its finest aerial combat of the war. Its force of twenty-one Mustangs under MEW control were northwest of Dummer Lake when they were told to head south. As they were flying at 7,000 feet they encountered fifteen-plus 109s at their altitude which were flying top cover for fifteen FW 190s laden with belly tanks. These were the aircraft of JG 300. Both formations were flying line abreast in a northwest direction toward the front lines.

Blickenstaff took his formation down in a right diving turn and lined up on one of the FW 190s. As the 190 began to turn, Blickenstaff blasted it and it went straight in.

Blickenstaff entered a climbing turn, picked up an Me 109 and closed to zero range. The E/A took his licks and went into the ground. Blickenstaff thought the excitement for the day was over but then he sighted a 109 at four o'clock high bearing down on him. Blickenstaff broke hard right and after a 360 degree turn ended up on the 109's tail in a fifty-degree dive. Blickenstaff gave it a burst and it crashed into the trees.

A few minutes later Blickenstaff sighted Maj. Elder's aircraft in a left orbit with two FW 190s on the deck. Elder had already downed an Me 109 and three FW 190s when he got into the turning match just above the ground. Blickenstaff heard his call for help and told him to "keep shooting and I'll take care of the other 190 on your tail."

Elder was taking some strikes from the 190 as Blickenstaff lined up on the attacker to discover that he had only one gun working. The first burst apparently hit, as the enemy aircraft began to trail smoke. The 190 pilot rolled over to split-ess but was too low and went right into the ground.

Elder shot down his opponent also, giving him five kills for the day. Blickenstaff started a left climbing turn, but sighted a 190 that was 1,000 feet below in a left orbit. Blickenstaff didn't hesitate, but went down with his one gun and began circling while calling someone to come shoot the 190 down. No one came, so Blickenstaff decided to give it a try. He slid in behind and raked the craft across the cockpit. The E/A began to smoke, slid off and crashed to the ground, apparently with a dead pilot at the controls.

This was the only combat in which two pilots from the same unit scored five victories each in one day. Other high scorers for the day were Lt. John L. Guthrie with three, Capt. Raymond Hartley with three and Lt. Louis Lee with three. Five Mustangs failed to return to base.

The number of aerial victories dropped drastically on March 25 to a total of four. However, those four were all against Me 262s, and the kills were shared equally between P–47s and P–51s. Two of the victories went to the 56th FG, which found a number of the jets at Parchim airfield in Germany. Capt. George Bostwick claimed one 262 destroyed and damaged a second when he caught them shortly after takeoff. The other 56th FG claim went to Lieutenant Crosthwaite who caught a 262 in the landing pattern and downed it. The remaining victories were scored by Lt. Eugene Wendt of the 479th FG, who outdueled the jet over Limburg, and by Lt. Ray Littge of the 352nd FG.

Maj. Robert A. Elder of the 353rd FG destroyed five E/A and damaged another in one of "Slybird" Group's finest operations Mar. 24, 1945. R. A. Elder

Beautiful shot of Mustang Donna-mite *of the 352nd FS, 353rd FG coming in to land.* USAAF

During the next several days aerial action was virtually nonexistent, but on March 30 the German jets again came up to fight. The 78th FG added two more jets to their score on March 30 and closed out the month with another 262 kill on March 31. Several other Me 262s went down under the guns of Eighth Air Force fighter pilots during this two-day period. However, the 78th FG had really proven itself as the "jet-killer" of the Eighth Air Force. During March 1945 the Group accounted for thirteen of the forty-three jets destroyed by Eighth Air Force, and in doing so raised the 78th's morale to a new high.

The dynamic leadership of Lt. Col. John D. Landers instilled the Group's high morale and aggressiveness. He infused a new sense of pride in the 78th FG, one that put the "jinxed group" thoughts out of the minds of the Group's personnel, and their scoring during the month was the result.

The primary opposition left in the air consisted of the Messerschmitt Me 262s which finally were committed to battle the bomber stream in sizeable numbers. The primary mission of the Eighth Air Force fighters was to strafe and destroy the remaining Luftwaffe aircraft on the ground. The third primary concern during the month was the weather which proved to be atro-

cious on more than one occasion and cost the American fighters a number of aircraft.

To oppose the German jets, a number of the Eighth Air Force fighter groups made studies and set out to get the enemy craft where they lived—on their airfields. One such group was the 339th. As Col. William Clark stated: "We researched all we could into everything concerning the Me 262. Where, how it was built, where they were based, where and how the pilots were trained, where the fuel came from and how it was stored.

"Then we selected three known air bases where 262s were operational. We got photos and studied the terrain and defenses. We planned the best low altitude approaches. Our idea was to first just flush the 262s off the field and then shoot them down right after takeoff. However, we found that they didn't flush out so we shot them up on the ground and set as much of the air base on fire as we could. Always we left a whole squadron, 16 to 24 aircraft, up high to give the ground attacking squadron cover and also to get anything that became airborne. There was another flight of at least 8 aircraft which was ready to spread out and run down (force him to run out of fuel at low altitude) any 262 that got away from the high squadron. After about 20 minutes of 'beating up' the air base, we withdrew the attacking squadron (they were out of ammo anyway) and sent them home. Another flight of eight was left loitering in the area out of sight and its job was to knock down any 262 that had been missed somehow and was trying to land at home base. Almost always they got at least one.

"Tactics in the strafing flights were simple. They attacked in flights of four at low altitude and full speed, using the natural screening as much as possible. When crossing the field boundary they popped up enough so the element leaders could see and depress the guns to hit the target. Very short bursts were used, element leaders went for a target, wingmen took care of flak that was shooting at them. We tried to time at least three flights of four each across the air base at the same time from different directions but in such a way that they didn't interfere with each other. The air base was crossed at a very low altitude. Most flak was over our heads.

"Of the three air bases we picked, we were only able to attack two. On the first (just northwest of Berlin) we claimed and were awarded five destroyed in the air. We found out later that we had chased six more north to the Baltic where they flamed out and were lost. We of course never got credit for these. One more tried to land at the base after our last flight had left but flamed out off the end of the runway and crashed.

"The air base was so badly damaged that it never became operational again. I inspected it myself after the war and found that no repair work had been done after we left it. A Luftwaffe officer told me that we set their fuel supply on fire and they could get no more. Two 262s which survived the attack were put in storage. We didn't lose a single aircraft on this operation. I am more proud of this fact than anything else."

The mission described took place on April 4, and was directed at the airfield at Parchim. Just as Colonel Clark positioned his 504th Fighter Squadron to attack, eight Me 262s took off at 180 degrees to the Mustangs and flew right through them. Clark got a burst into one and it flew into the clouds smoking.

Capt. Nile Greer was leading Blue Flight of the 504th which was instructed to stay above the clouds when the attackers went after the field. Just as Clark called in the 262s taking off, Greer sighted three Me 262s coming up through a small hole in the undercast. He was 4,000 feet above the E/A and had no trouble in closing in a dive. One 262 broke away but the other two went into a gentle turn to the right. Greer lined up one on the K-14 pipper and got strikes with a short burst. The enemy craft immediately went into a reversal to the left and Greer really clobbered him. The 262 pulled up into a big cloud, but the Mustang pilot pulled up over it and sighted him. A long burst got hits all over the engines and wing roots, and black smoke began to pour out. The pilot jettisoned his canopy but did not get out in time.

The same day, Lt. Col. George Ceuleers was leading A Group of the 364th when eight Me 262s attacked the B-24s they were escorting during withdrawal from

Col. William Clark of the 339th FG helped plan and carry out his unit's operations against the German jet airfields. W. Clark

targets in central Germany. Even though the Mustangs sped to protect the bombers, two of the Liberators went down to the attacking jets before they were driven off. Ceuleers took off after one of the 262s full bore, pulling sixty inches of manifold pressure at 3000 rpm. The chase went from 22,000 feet to around 400 feet and covered over 180 miles. After twenty minutes the Mustang had finally closed the gap to 500 yards and Ceuleers opened fire. Slowly he closed the distance to 100 yards and after 1,650 rounds of ammunition, enough damage was inflicted that the pilot bailed out. Ceuleers' shooting difficulty came from the turbulence wrought by the exhaust from the jet engines. Following his success, Ceuleers stated that he felt that with a 2,000 foot advantage he could overtake and down any Me 262 by flying at full throttle.

Lt. Col. George Ceuleers of the 364th FG chased an Me 262 at high speeds for 20 minutes before he finally brought it down. He is shown with his P-51 Constance. USAAF

Chapter 18

Alles Kaput

During April 1945 the Allied bombers were roaming and bombing the Third Reich almost at will. The ability of the Luftwaffe to effectively counter these attacks had ceased long before, and the citizens of Germany were suffering horrifying attacks on their cities. As a last-ditch effort to stem the tide, the Luftwaffe formed a group of suicide commandos. This new group called Sonderkommando vowed to ram the bombers in their heavily armored Me 109s and FW 190s if that was what was needed to bring them down. This new force entered combat on April 7, 1945.

With patriotic music and statements being radioed into their headsets, the pilots of Sonderkommando Elbe headed toward the approaching bombers. In the battle that ensued, eighteen of the Big Friends went down, of which eight were lost from ramming. But once the American escort fighters entered the battle, the Germans suffered terrible casualties. At least sixty-four of their fighters went down under the guns of the Mustangs and Thunderbolts.

The 479th FG led all groups in scoring with eleven victories, five of which were scored by Lt. Richard Candelaria. The action took place southwest of Luneburg, Germany. His first target was an Me 262 which he saw headed after a flight of B-24s. Candelaria reported: "I then saw two Me-262s coming up along the bombers stream at 7 o'clock, slightly low. I came at the leader

Capt. William Cullerton of the 355th FG and his P-51 Miss Steve *ran up a score of five in the air and 15 on the ground before he went down on Apr. 8, 1945.* 355th FG Assn.

head-on, trying to make him break but he avoided my head-on pass by diving, but not altering his course, making it very difficult for me to hit him. I tried to drop my tanks on him but missed completely. I did a half roll and lined up on his tail as he opened fire on the bombers. I opened fire on the jet and observed hits on both sides of the cockpit and large puffs of smoke emitting from the fuselage and wings. In the meantime the second jet had positioned himself on my tail and opened fire on me. I saw white and red shells, like golf balls, going past me. Looking up in the rear view mirror I saw him firing away. A moment later he hit me in the right wing. At this time the first jet broke away to the left in a lazy half-roll and went straight down, trailing smoke. I broke hard into the jet behind me but he went off into a shallow dive toward his buddy, going too fast for me to ever catch up."

After his successful fight against the jets, Candelaria headed back toward the bomber formation. As he climbed he saw a force of fifteen 109s hurl themselves at the bombers, and the leader blew a B-24 out of the sky before he could attack the 109s. Seeing the bomber go down incensed Candelaria and he attacked the German formation with a vengeance. He quickly gunned two of the German element leaders out of the sky and forced the third to jump from his undamaged 109 by simply firing a burst in the direction of the 109. His fourth victim of this encounter also went down without being hit by gunfire. This one tried to follow Candelaria through his violent maneuvers and spun out and crashed. Even after downing a total of five enemy planes in rapid order, Candelaria was still not out of trouble. Just as another force of 109s was trying to box him in, six other P-51s arrived on the scene and drove them away.

Capt. Verne Hooker of the 435th FS, 479th FG also claimed a jet kill when he destroyed an Me 262 during the same air battle that Candelaria got his. In addition to the 262, Hooker also downed an Me 109 that was attacking a bomber.

The intent of the FW 190 chased by Maj. Louis Norley of the 4th Fighter Group is questionable. Norley had chased the Focke Wulf up to 23,000 feet where the pilot broke his climb and went down in a thirty-degree dive. As Norley closed to 600 yards he opened fire and at the same time sighted a formation of B-17s directly in front of the E/A. As Norley pulled off to the right the Focke Wulf dove through the box of bombers, hitting the tail of one B-17, cutting it off completely. The 190 lost its starboard wing and rear half of the fuselage. It was Norley's personal opinion that the enemy pilot

William Cullerton's Mustang Miss Steve.

didn't intentionally ram the Fortress in view of the fact that he didn't fire a shot at the bombers during his closure. Whether or not he rammed intentionally or hit it in his attempt to escape the guns of the Mustang will never be known.

Despite a Field Order restricting strafing, the 55th Fighter Group could not resist the sight of some 120 E/A parked along the autobahn south of Munich on April 9. Lt. Col. Elwyn Righetti was leading the Group which was escorting the bombers. As the second group of Big Friends let go of their loads, an Me 262 was sighted by Maj. Edward Giller who was leading Tudor Squadron. Giller dropped his tanks and chased the German jet, downing the craft when it attempted to land on Munich/Riem airfield. While they were in the area, other members of the squadron decided to strafe aircraft on the field, destroying an Me 410 before they were driven off by heavy flak.

Tudor Squadron formed up once more and Giller sighted a Heinkel He 111 being towed south of the main autobahn. He dropped down to investigate and sighted many beautifully hidden aircraft of all types, including jets, parked on the shoulders of the autobahn or backed into the woods. All the aircraft were covered with brush nets, providing excellent camouflage.

Giller got permission to fly a strafing run against the aircraft, and Righetti assigned Acorn Squadron to cover the bombers homeward while he brought Hellcat Squadron on the scene for strafing. The Mustangs made eight to ten passes because the area was defended by only three or four light, inaccurate guns. By the time

they finished, fifty-five enemy aircraft were burning or destroyed and another twenty-three were damaged.

On April 10 the Luftwaffe threw more than fifty of its jets into action against the bombers in an attempt to stop these incessant attacks. Although their massed formation was broken up by the 1st Air Division's escort fighters, the 262s were able to penetrate the formations and destroyed five bombers near Oranienburg, Germany. Five more were soon ripped out of the 3rd Air Division's formation by the speedy jets while the escort fighters could do little more than watch. Even though the German jets won the opening round of the day's air battle, the fight was not over by a long shot. As the 262s ran low on fuel they started to peel off and head toward their bases. But when they arrived they found a welcoming committee of American fighters waiting for them. In a number of battles above these aerodromes, US fighters sent at least twenty of the jets crashing to earth. The 20th FG led in the defeat of the jets with five victories.

The success of the 55th Fighter Group's strafing on April 9 had really set a fire under the seats of the leaders of the 339th Fighter Group. Not only had the 55th ignored the Field Order restricting strafing, but they had done it in what had been the exclusive territory of the 339th Group. Lt. Col. Joe Thury and Maj. Archie Tower were determined that they would fly a strafing mission the following day that would surpass any ever flown by an Eighth Air Force Squadron, and they proceeded to do so. They escorted the bombers to Neuruppin airfield then dropped their Mustangs down to

Lt. Col. Joe Thury in the cockpit of his Mustang Pauline. *Thury was an outstanding strafer in the 339th FG.* J. Starnes

types of aircraft, the majority of which were twin-engined."

From 1520 to 1545 hours Thury's Mustangs beat up the area, making ten to fifteen passes and abandoning targets only when all their ammunition had been expended. Thury returned to claim twenty-six destroyed and fourteen damaged for his eleven P–51 section.

Meanwhile, Major Tower took his eight P–51s on the deck and flew north from Neuruppin to Wittstock airfield where a gunnery pattern was set up to attack about thirty enemy aircraft dispersed in a woods to the east. Tower recalled: "After several passes from north to south we changed directions to east to west in order that we might cover a large group of planes east of the hangar and the hangar area. Smoke on the southeast corner of the field was so dense that it reached an altitude of 5,000 feet. It was difficult to count all the fires but there were over 50 when we left. I feel that we destroyed 37 E/A and believe that estimate may be low. All the planes burned beautifully . . ."

In spite of the great strafing victory of Apr. 10, 1945, Allied Headquarters decided to ban all strafing beginning on Apr. 11, 1945, because Allied ground troops were operating in close proximity to many of the German airfields. On that date over 900 fighters escorted 1,300 bombers to targets throughout Germany on a near "milk run." Only one B–17 was lost and that

the deck. Thury described the action: "I split the squadron into two task forces, taking 11 aircraft with me and sending eight with Major Tower. Just north of Neuruppin Airfield we discovered a huge dispersal which covered almost two miles. The area started from the north-south runway of the field itself, and contained all

Joe Thury's Pauline. J. Starnes

was to flak. All of the fighter groups honored the strafing ban except one—the 339th. Apparently the temptation was too great for them, and the Mustangs from Fowlmere headed to the deck. They found more packed airfields and left 118 enemy planes in wreckage before heading for home. Despite the excellent showing, Eighth Air Force Headquarters was less than pleased at the 339th's disregard of the safety orders.

Inspired by the 339th's actions on April 11, the 56th FG ignored the ban on Apr. 13, 1945, when they found Eggebeck aerodrome near Kiel jammed full of aircraft. With ninety-five destroyed on this mission, the 56th FG passed the 1,000 claims mark (this figure was later reduced), the first Eighth Air Force Group to do so. Other groups decided to ignore the ban too, and a total of 266 claims were turned in on April 13. The 479th FG escorted a combat wing to Hagenow and then dove to the deck in search of airfields. They found five of them crammed with planes and claimed a total of 47-0-33 at a cost of three pilots.

The ground strafing success of the 56th Group on April 13 marked a high point for the unit that had seen much frustration since the first of the year. The 56th chose to retain the P-47 and was the only group left in the Eighth Air Force flying Thunderbolts at the end of the war in Europe.

In January 1945 the 56th received new P-47M's which had a more powerful engine which increased its performance dramatically. The P-47M could fly 465 mph at 32,000 feet—faster than the Mustang. However, an increase in weight cut down on the Thunderbolt's range, but drop tanks combined with proper cruise

Three stars in the 339th FG strafing line-up were, left to right, Lt. Oscar K. Biggs, Capt. James R. Starnes and Capt. George T. Rich. J. Starnes

control made it possible to perform their assigned missions.

Disaster struck the 56th, however; the R-2800-57 engines developed all sorts of troubles. In flight, engine failures became rampant. Initially it was ignition troubles and when this was rectified cooling problems grounded the craft. Before it was all over, practically all the new aircraft in the group had to have new and

The 56th FG was held up at the end of the war with teething troubles on the P-47M. Shoot!! You're Faded is shown here getting guns harmonized. Note the unusual camouflage paint

job which was prominent in the 56th FG late in the war. USAAF

modified engines. By the time the P–47M really became combat proficient it was April and the end of hostilities was in sight.

While there were celebrations at Boxted, Wattisham and many other fighter bases in England after the mission of April 13, the 4th FG at Debden was in a somber mood. By honoring the strafing ban placed on them April 11, the Eagles had lost their lead in scoring and also allowed the 56th FG to cross the magic number of 1,000 destroyed ahead of them.

The 4th FG, like all the others, knew the end of the war was now in sight and for the Eagles it was a time of real pressure. They wanted the scoring honors and intended to achieve that goal by war's end. The mission of April 16 was an answer to their prayers, and their 105 victories put them into the lead to stay. The 4th was divided into two groups for the mission. A Group, led by Lt. Col. Sidney Woods, headed for Czechoslovakia on a free-lance strafing mission, and B Group, led by Maj. Louis Norley, was on an escort/strafing mission to Rosenheim/Gablingen aerodrome in Germany.

Lt. Mel Franklin of the 336th FS recalled the day's briefing and mission: "When Colonel Woods presented the briefing he was a little angry and upset that we were now in second place in scoring. He had not ignored the no-strafing order as the other Groups had, and planned to make up for lost time on this mission.

"As we flew over Prague we could see three airfields just crammed with German aircraft, and then we got the word to go down after them. The first three passes were like a shooting gallery as we got no return fire. We thought maybe we caught them at lunch or that they had abandoned the airfields. As the 336th FS lined up for their fourth pass things changed. I was flying in a frontal assault of 12 Mustangs going in together when all hell broke loose from the ground below and filled the

sky with flak. Several of the planes were hit and went down, and the rest of us received some minor damage before completing our firing pass. As I started to pull up I saw the plane in front of me run into an umbrella of solid flak and I knew that there was no way that I would try to go through that. Instead I headed my 51 straight out over the end of the field and flew into downtown Prague and made my turn while flying between the buildings. As I came back across the field on my fifth pass I spotted a Ju–52 and a Ju–88 and hoped to add them to the Ju–88 I got on the previous pass. As these aircraft were parked near each other I opened fire and 'fishtailed' my aircraft in order to hit both of them. Both aircraft exploded into flame just as I was pulling up to come around for my next pass. By now most of the aircraft were already burning or under attack so I turned my guns toward hangars, motor vehicles, and other installations and shot them up pretty well. One other pilot in the Group must have wanted to let the Germans know that their time had run out when he could find no other targets, and decided to shoot the clock out of the terminal tower. In all we made nine passes over the field, and pretty much destroyed everything in sight. We destroyed over 100 planes but not without many losses of our own, including Colonel Woods." Woods became a POW.

Woods' A Group claimed sixty-one of the enemy planes destroyed by the 4th FG on April 16. The remaining forty-four were clobbered by B Group after they completed their escort. B Group's victories were scored at Gablingen aerodrome and without loss to themselves.

The magnificent victory by the 4th FG on April 16 represented only the tip of the iceburg. On this date, fighters of Eighth Air Force destroyed an unbelievable 752 aircraft. The highest scoring group of the day was the 78th FG which scored 125 victories. Total American losses were thirty-four planes.

The nine enemy aircraft destroyed on the ground by Lt. Col. John D. Landers, CO of the 78th Fighter Group, coupled with eight that had been scored on April 10 gave him a total of seventeen E/A destroyed in a week's time. Landers reported: "When we arrived at least 80 planes were scattered around the field. When we left there were 80 funeral pyres. A dozen anti-aircraft gunners put up some light flak, at first, but it didn't bother us much and we simply set up a traffic pattern. German aircraft were blowing up and burning all over the place. We made eight to nine passes. I scored doubles on each of my first three passes, two of the six planes blowing up."

Lt. Danford Josey, Jr., of the 78th Group scored five destroyed on his first mission while Lt. Dale Sweat, who also destroyed five, was on his second. Capt. Dorian Ledington destroyed four and was banking around to finish off another when he was hit with an explosive shell that smashed through his canopy, grazed

Capt. Robert Ammon of the 339th FG claimed 13 destroyed on the ground on Apr. 16, 1945, but was credited with nine of them. USAAF

his neck and exploded in the cockpit. Shell fragments and plexiglass were embedded in his neck.

"I reached up and felt the blood streaming out and I figured I was a goner," said Ledington. "I decided that I might as well take another German plane with me. I pulled the Mustang around and made one more pass on the field destroying the plane I had already damaged. Nobody was more surprised than me when I made it back to the Channel alive."

Another veteran pilot who took a shot from the ground that day was Maj. Edward Giller of the 55th Group. He had already destroyed three E/A when he positioned himself to destroy what would have been his fourth victim. He came in on it in his set pattern from south to north and although he noted many strikes on the craft, it refused to burn. As he pulled up from his last pass a 20 mm shell came in the left side of the canopy and exploded, wounding Giller in the shoulder. Dazed and bleeding he gathered his flight together and headed for home.

The ground strafing continued on April 17 and another 286 enemy craft were destroyed. Lt. Col. Elwyn Righetti led his 55th Fighter Group on another

successful, but tragic, mission. The formation let down through a hole in the clouds over Riesa/Canitz airfield which was loaded with aircraft. As the Mustangs started their first pass Righetti instructed his wingman, Capt. Carroll D. Henry, to take care of an FW 190 that was coming in for a landing.

Henry attacked the 190 so was not on the first strafing passes. After downing the Focke Wulf, he began to search for Righetti, and as he did so made one pass and left an E/A in flames.

Finally, he sighted Righetti who now had seven fires burning, but whose aircraft was streaming coolant. Righetti called over the R/T, "I'm hit bad, oil pressure dropping fast, can't make it out of enemy territory, but I've got ammunition for one more pass." Henry then watched him make his final pass and flame two more E/A, making a total of nine for the mission.

Righetti then pulled up slightly and leveled off and flew for about five miles before he belly-landed his Mustang in a field. He then called out over the R/T, "I'm OK, broke my nose landing. Tell my family I'm all right. I got nine today. It's been swell working with you, gang. Be seeing you shortly."

Maj. Edward Giller of the 55th FG, shown here in his P-51 Millie G got another three victories strafing on Apr. 16, 1945, before he was seriously wounded by ground fire. E. Giller

This was the last word ever heard from this outstanding leader and strafing specialist. As best as could ever be determined, Righetti fell into the hands of irate German civilians who killed him. At the time of his death he had shot down 7½ E/A and destroyed another twenty-seven on the ground.

With over 1,000 enemy planes destroyed by strafing during the last two days, General Spaatz declared that the strategic battle of the Eighth Air Force was now ended. For the remainder of the war the Eighth would only concern itself with tactical targets. With opposition in the northern part of Germany virtually eliminated, the Eighth concentrated its efforts in the south. It was during this period that they fought the last aerial battle against the Me 262s.

This encounter took place on Apr. 19, 1945, when the 3rd Division which was ordered to bomb the marshaling yards in southeastern Germany, ran into a gaggle of 262s. In a running battle the jets downed six of the majestic Forts, the last Eighth Air Force bombers to fall to German fighters.

It was not a totally one-sided show, though, as the 357th FG caught sixteen of the jets taking off from their aerodrome and destroyed six of them.

Lt. Col. Jack W. Hayes, Jr., was leading the 357th on one of the final escort missions, and as the bombers neared the IP he took his squadron of Mustangs on a heading for the jet airfield at Prague, Czechoslovakia. On arrival there was no activity so the Mustangs took up a post orbiting up sun over the field. Hayes instructed his pilots to maintain their position until some of the Me 262s could get airborne. Patience paid off and soon fourteen jets were airborne. Then off came the tanks and down went the P-51s to attack.

Hayes pulled in behind two jets that had just taken off and they proceeded to break in different directions. Hayes went after the leader who turned to the left. The enemy aircraft then hit the deck and turned on power and Hayes was forced to go to full throttle to keep up. The 262 stayed right on the deck and led the Mustang pilot down the river near Prague while flak aimed at the P-51 became heavier and heavier. The 262 then went out of sight behind a tall building on the east side of the river. All this time Hayes had been firing sporadically at the jet, which had taken a number of hits. Finally Hayes' fire took effect. As he pulled up over the building to regain his target he saw the Me 262 hit the ground and blow up.

Five other Me 262s were caught on the rise by members of the 357th and sent crashing. The victors were Capt. Robert S. Fifield and Lts. Paul Bowles, Carroll W. Ofsthun and James McMullen. The sixth 262 was shared by Capt. Ivan McGuire and Lt. Gilman Weber.

The last air battle between the Eighth Air Force fighters and the Focke Wulf 190 also took place on the nineteenth when the 383rd Squadron of the 364th Fighter Group was bounced by four FW 190s after downing a Dornier 217. Lt. Ralph Queal climbed after two of the 190s and scored hits on one of them. The 190 slid away and Queal turned him over to his wingman, Lt. Donald Fisher, who followed him down and finished him off. Queal got on the tail of the second FW 190 and fired until the pilot slumped over and the aircraft went into the ground. One other FW 190 managed to get on Capt. Charles Hammett's tail and was promptly shot off by F/O Dana Healy. Then it was Hammett's turn as he proceeded to dispense with the fourth FW that had tacked onto Healy's six o'clock.

The 364th was involved in another combat that day that did not result in such a fortunate outcome. Lt. Sim Lett was leading his flight southeast of Berlin when a flight of Russian Lagg 3s passed overhead. Then a second flight of Yak 9s passed to the left at 180 degrees. Signals were given and the Russians went on, but suddenly turned and attacked Lett's wingman, Lieutenant Horner. Lett immediately started a tight turn into them to keep them from getting on Horner's tail. They started firing at Horner and after about half a turn they began getting strikes all over him.

At this time the first four were coming head-on into Lett and he turned into the second four who were firing at Horner. These four broke and started to make a pass at Lett. Then the four Russian aircraft behind them began to fire at Lett. He half rolled and went balls out on the deck, rolling and skidding all the time. Lett finally lost them in the smoke on the deck.

Horner bailed out and landed near the American lines where he was picked up by ambulance.

Another final battle was met when the 355th Fighter Group mixed it up with Me 109s in the vicinity of Prague on April 20. Lt. Col. Claiborne Kinnard was leading the group in a nonstrafing free-lance patrol when they noticed that dust was rising from the airfield at Prague-Letnany aerodrome. As the Mustangs approached, the dust stopped so they proceeded on for about fifteen minutes and then returned. This time six or seven aircraft were airborne. The P-51s dropped tanks and went down after them. Kinnard latched onto one and fired, getting strikes all over the E/A. It mushed through a turn and dove into a field where it exploded.

Kinnard lined up on another 109 but scored very few hits. When another 109 got on his tail he broke off. Kinnard lined up on another E/A, got good hits and this one rolled over on fire from 1,000 feet. The pilot bailed out and the plane crashed into a woods and exploded. When the fight was over, eight Me 109s had fallen to the guns of the 355th Mustangs.

On Apr. 25, 1945, eleven fighter groups of the Eighth Air Force departed on their last operational mission of World War II. These fighters were to escort bombers striking at targets in the Pilsen, Czechoslovakia, and Salzburg, Austria, areas. The distinction of the last aerial victory fell to the 479th FG which had escorted B-24s to Traunstein, near Salzburg. The Group was a bit southeast of the target when Lt. Hilton Thompson of the 434th FS spotted an Arado 234 jet flying along eastward at a moderate speed. Thompson dove after the Arado and came in from behind and below the jet. He clobbered the unsuspecting German in short order and sent the 234 headed to earth trailing flames and smoke. The only other encounter by the 479th nearly ended in tragedy for both sides. Colonel Riddle got into a scrape with an unidentified twin-engined bomber and had one engine smoking before he realized the plane carried Russian markings. The bomber was last seen heading eastward and seemingly under control. Riddle also limped back to base with a coolant leak.

So ended the mighty crusade of the Eighth Air Force's fighter force against the German Luftwaffe. With Germany split in half after the linkup at the Elbe River on April 26, the Eighth Air Force had no more targets. The remaining air actions in Europe fell to the Tactical Air Forces based at forward fields. Two weeks later Germany surrendered and it was all over in Europe.

From a nucleus of green and eager pilots fresh from the training fields of the United States, interspersed with a smattering of combat-wise Eagle Squadron pilots, the original VIII Fighter Command had grown to the finest, most formidable fighter force the world had ever seen. Fifteen groups strong, it wrenched air supremacy from the Luftwaffe and escorted the daylight bombers to targets that the original planners had never dreamed of striking. When the Luftwaffe wouldn't come up to do battle with them, they went to the deck and destroyed the enemy where he lived. When the curtain fell the Thunderbolts, Lightnings and Mustangs roamed the skies of Europe at will, and their engines roared in a crescendo of victory.

Appendices

Eighth Air Force Air and Ground Aces

In view of the fact that the Eighth Air Force credited its pilots with ground victories, we have compiled what we feel is an accurate and complete listing of aces as it would have appeared at the end of World War II in Europe. Some years later the US Air Force in response to public queries saw fit to draw up a new list of aces, eliminating ground credits. The primary reason for this was the fact that the associated Ninth Air Force in northwestern Europe did not grant its pilots ground victories nor did the Twelfth and Fifteenth Air Forces in the Mediterranean Theater of Operations (MTO). In the Pacific Theater (PTO) and in the China-Burma-India (CBI) Theater only the tenth and fourteenth air forces of the CBI awarded ground credits. With this ruling many former pilots of the Eighth Air Force found that they were no longer aces as far as USAF Public Information sources were concerned.

Regardless of any comparisons or arguments pro or con between the merits of air versus ground victories, we have chosen to list the aces who were so recognized by the Eighth Air Force at the end of World War II. They are ranked in order of the total number of enemy aircraft they destroyed.

Air and Ground Aces

Rank	Name	Air Victories	Ground Victories	Total	Group(s)	Remarks
Lt. Col.	John C. Meyer	24	13	37	352	
Lt. Col.	John D. Landers	14.5	20	34.5	55, 78, 357	6 Air 49 FG, PTO 4 Air 55 FG 1 Air 357 FG
Lt. Col.	Elwyn G. Righetti	7.5	27	34.5	55	KIA 4–17–45
Col.	David C. Schilling	22.5	10.5	33	56	
Maj.	George E. Preddy, Jr.	26.83	5	31.83	352	KIA 12–25–44
Lt. Col.	Francis S. Gabreski	28	3	31	56	POW 7–20–44
Maj.	James A. Goodson	15	15	30	4	1 Air RAF, POW 6–20–44
Lt.	Ralph K. Hofer	15	14	29	4	KIA 7–2–44
Capt.	Henry W. Brown	14.2	14.5	28.7	355	POW 10–3–44
Lt. Col.	Joseph L. Thury	2.5	25.5	28	339	
Capt.	Don S. Gentile	21.83	6	27.83	4	
Maj.	Robert S. Johnson	27	0	27	56	
Maj.	John T. Godfrey	14	12.66	26.66	4	POW 8–24–44
Col.	Glenn E. Duncan	19.5	6.83	26.33	353	MIA Evade 7–7–44
Col.	Hubert A. Zemke	17.75	8.5	26.25	56, 479	POW 10–30–44
Col.	Claiborne H. Kinnard, Jr.	8	17	25	4, 355, 356	
Maj.	Robin Olds	13	11	24	479	
Maj.	Ray S. Wetmore	21.25	2.33	23.58	359	
Capt.	Raymond H. Littge	10.5	13	23.5	352	
Maj.	Fred W. Glover	10.33	12.5	22.83	4	MIA Evade 4–30–44
Maj.	Duane W. Beeson	17.33	4.75	22.08	4	POW 4–5–44
Maj.	Leonard K. Carson	18.5	3.5	22	357	
Capt.	Edwin L. Heller	5.5	16.5	22	352	
Capt.	Fred J. Christensen, Jr.	21.5	0	21.5	56	
Lt. Col.	John L. Elder, Jr.	8	13	21	355	
Maj.	Walker M. Mahurin	20.75	0	20.75	56	MIA Evade 3–27–44, 1 Air 3 ACG, PTO
Maj.	Pierce W. McKennon	11	9.68	20.68	4	MIA Evade 8–28–44

Rank	Name	Air Victories	Ground Victories	Total	Group(s)	Remarks
Capt.	Gordon B. Compton	5.5	15	20.5	353	
Lt.	William J. Cullerton	5	15	20	355	POW 4-8-45
Maj.	Archie A. Tower	1.5	18	19.5	339	
Capt.	John F. Thornell, Jr.	17.25	2	19.25		
Maj.	Richard A. Peterson	15.5	3.5	19	357	
Maj.	John B. England	17.5	1	18.5	357	
Capt.	William T. Whisner	15.5	3	18.5	352	
Maj.	Walter C. Beckham	18	0	18	353	POW 2-22-44
Maj.	Robert W. Foy	15	3	18		
Capt.	B. Michael Gladych	10	8	18	56	Polish Air Force
Capt.	Robert E. Welch	6	12	18	55	
Maj.	Ernest E. Bankey, Jr.	9.5	8	17.5	364	
Maj.	Gerald E. Montgomery	3	14.5	17.5	4	
Capt.	Clarence E. Anderson, Jr.	16.25	1	17.25	357	
Lt. Col.	Gordon M. Graham	7	9.5	16.5	355	
Maj.	Gerald W. Johnson	16.5	0	16.5	56	POW 3-27-44
Lt. Col.	John H. Lowell	7.5	9	16.5	364	
Col.	Donald J. M. Blakeslee	14.5	1.5	16	4	2 Air RAF
Lt.	Glennon T. Moran	13	3	16	352	
Capt.	Michael J. Quirk	11	5	16	56	POW 9-11-44
Maj.	George W. Carpenter	13.83	2	15.83	4	POW 4-18-44
Capt.	Nicholas Megura	11.83	3.75	15.58	4	POW 5-22-44
Capt.	Charles F. Anderson, Jr.	10	5.5	15.5	4	KIA 4-19-44
Maj.	Stephen W. Andrew	9	6.5	15.5	352	POW 7-2-44 1 Air 49FG, PTO
Lt.	Carl J. Luksic	8.5	7	15.5	352	POW 5-24-44
Maj.	Louis H. Norley	10.33	5	15.33	4	
Lt. Col.	James A. Clark, Jr.	10.5	4.5	15	4	
Capt.	Alwin M. Juchiem	9	6	15	78	POW 5-28-44
Maj.	Willard W. Millikan	13	2	15	4	POW 5-30-44
Maj.	George W. Gleason	12	2.5	14.5	479	
Capt.	Kirke B. Everson, Jr.	1.5	13	14.5	339	
Capt.	Melville W. Hightshoe	0	14.5	14.5	353	
Maj.	Howard D. Hively	12	2.5	14.5	4	
Capt.	Herbert G. Kolb	0	14.5	14.5	353	
Capt.	Joseph H. Powers	14.5	0	14.5	56	
Maj.	Quince L. Brown	12.33	2	14.33	78	KIA 9-6-44
Capt.	James E. Duffy, Jr.	5.2	9	14.2	355	
Maj.	Walker L. Boone	2.0	12.13	14.13	353	
Capt.	Robert H. Ammon	5	9	14	339	
Maj.	George E. Bostwick	8	6	14	56	
Lt. Col.	Arthur F. Jeffrey	14	0	14	479	
Maj.	Leroy A. Schreiber	12	2	14	56	KIA 4-15-44
Maj.	Donald H. Bochkay	13.83	0	13.83	357	
Capt.	Woodrow W. Anderson	4.5	9	13.5	352	KIA 5-28-44
Maj.	Michael J. Jackson	8	5.5	13.5	56	
Capt.	Henry J. Miklajcyk	7.5	6	13.5	352	
Lt.	Ray S. Morris	3.5	10	13.5	355	
Capt.	Albert L. Schlegel	8.5	5	13.5	4	KIA 8-28-44
Maj.	Donald J. Strait	13.5	0	13.5	356	
Capt.	Donald S. Bryan	13.33	0	13.33	352	
Capt.	Clarence O. Johnson	7	6	13	479, 352	4 Air 82 FG, MTO 1 Air 479 FG KIA 9-23-44
Capt.	Felix D. Williamson	13	0	13	56	
F/O	Richard N. Gustke	0	12.5	12.5	353	
Lt. Col.	William T. Halton	10.5	2	12.5	352	
Maj.	William J. Hovde	10.5	2	12.5	355	

Rank	Name	Air Victories	Ground Victories	Total	Group(s)	Remarks
Col.	Ben Rimerman	4.5	8	12.5	353	
Lt. Col.	James C. Stewart	11.5	1	12.5	56	
Capt.	Horace Q. Waggoner	5	7.5	12.5	353	
Lt.	Oscar K. Biggs	0.5	11.5	12	339	
Capt.	Harry R. Corey	1	11	12	339	
Maj.	George A. Doersch	10.5	1.5	12	359	
Capt.	Frank N. Emory	2	10	12	353	
Lt.	Francis E. Harrington	4	8	12	78	
Capt.	Fred R. Haviland, Jr.	6	6	12	355	
Capt.	John A. Kirla	11.5	0.5	12	357	
Lt.	Roland J. Lanoue	1	11	12	353	
Lt.	Randel L. Murphy	2	10	12	56	
Capt.	James R. Starnes	6	6	12	339	
Lt. Col.	John A. Storch	10.5	1.5	12	357	
Capt.	Joseph L. Lang	7.83	4	11.83	4	KIA 10-14-44
Maj.	Paul A. Conger	11.5	0	11.5	56	
Maj.	Claire A. P. Duffie	3	8.5	11.5	479	
Lt. Col.	Olin E. Gilbert	2	9.5	11.5	78	MIA Evade 8-28-44
Lt.	Dale E. Karger	7.5	4	11.5	357	
Lt. Col.	Leslie C. Smith	7	4.5	11.5	56	
Capt.	Charles E. Yeager	11.5	0	11.5	357	MIA Evade 3-5-44
Capt.	Hipolitus T. Biel	5.33	6	11.33	4	KIA 4-24-44
Maj.	Norman J. Fortier	5.83	5.5	11.33	355	
Capt.	Charles H. Cole, Jr.	5	6	11	20	POW 2-25-45
Lt.	Harold W. Burch	0	11	11	339	
Capt.	Ernest C. Fiebelkorn	9	2	11	20	
Lt. Col.	Kenneth W. Gallup	9	2	11	353	
Lt. Col.	Willie O. Jackson, Jr.	7	4	11	352	
Lt.	Cyril W. Jones	6	5	11	359	KIA 9-12-44
Capt.	James N. McElroy	5	6	11	355	
Maj.	George L. Merritt	5	6	11	361	KIA 6-7-44
Lt.	Gerald J. Miller	0	11	11	353	
Maj.	James N. Poindexter	7	4	11	353	KIFA 3-3-45
Capt.	Charles E. Weaver	8	3	11	357	
Lt. Col.	George F. Ceuleers	10.5	0	10.5	364	
Capt.	Frank A. Cutler	7.5	3	10.5	352	KIA 5-13-44
Col.	Irwin H. Dregne	5	5.5	10.5	357	
Lt.	Gail E. Jacobson	4.5	6	10.5	479	
Lt.	Otto D. Jenkins	8.5	2	10.5	357	KIFA 3-24-45
Capt.	Frank C. Jones	5	5.5	10.5	4	KIA 8-8-44
Lt.	Thomas C. Olson	1	9.5	10.5	479	
Capt.	James M. Morris	7.33	2.83	10.16	20	POW 7-7-44
Maj.	Henry S. Bille	6	4	10	355	
Lt. Col.	Wayne K. Blickenstaff	10	0	10	353	
Capt.	Kendall E. Carlson	6	4	10	4	POW 2-25-45
Capt.	Claude J. Crenshaw	7	3	10	359	
Lt.	John F. Duncan	4	6	10	357	
Lt.	Billy G. Edens	7	3	10	56	POW 9-10-44
Capt.	Martin H. Johnson	1	9	10	361	
Capt.	Robert J. Keen	6	4	10	56	
Lt.	John A. Kirk III	4	6	10	78	
Lt.	Russell S. Kyler	3	7	10	56	
Capt.	Ted E. Lines	10	0	10	4	
Capt.	Joseph L. Mansker	3	7	10	20	
Maj.	Bert W. Marshall, Jr.	7	3	10	355	
Capt.	Arthur B. McCormick, Jr.	1	9	10	364	
Lt.	Joseph D. McMullen	0	10	10	353	
Capt.	Joseph E. Mellen	2	8	10	355	

Rank	Name	Air Victories	Ground Victories	Total	Group(s)	Remarks
Capt.	Charles M. Peal	2	8	10	78	
Capt.	Robert J. Rankin	10	0	10	56	
Lt. Col.	Dale E. Shafer, Jr.	8	2	10	339	4 Air 31 FG, MTO
Lt.	Dale F. Spencer	9.5	0.5	10	361	
Capt.	William J. Sykes	5	5	10	361	POW 1-25-45
Lt.	Karl M. Waldron, Jr.	3	7	10	352	
Lt. Col.	Sidney S. Woods	7	3	10	4, 479	2 Air 49 FG, PTO POW 4-16-45
Maj.	William E. Bryan, Jr.	7.5	2	9.5	339	
Lt.	Paul S. Riley	6.5	3	9.5	4	POW 4-24-44
Col.	Everett W. Stewart	7.83	1.5	9.33	355, 352, 4	
Capt.	Fletcher E. Adams	9	0	9	357	KIA 5-30-44
Lt. Col.	Donald A. Baccus	5	4	9	356, 359	
Capt.	William R. Beyer	9	0	9	361	
Capt.	James W. Browning	7	2	9	357	KIA 2-9-45
Lt.	Van E. Chandler	5	4	9	4	
Lt. Col.	William C. Clark	1	8	9	357, 339	
Maj.	Darrell S. Cramer	7	2	9	55	
Lt.	John W. Cunnick III	2	7	9	55	
Lt. Col.	Lucian A. Dade, Jr.	3	6	9	56	
Capt.	Clayton E. Davis	5	4	9	352	
Capt.	Samuel D. Gevorkian	2	7	9	55	MIA Evade 8-26-44
Maj.	Edward B. Giller	3	6	9	55	
Lt.	Rayl P. Greenwood	0	9	9	353	POW 8-12-44
Capt.	Robert B. Hatter	3	6	9	359	
Capt.	John C. Hunter	3	6	9	364	
Capt.	Edward L. Kier	2	7	9	20	
Maj.	Donald A. Larson	6	3	9	339	KIA 8-4-44
Lt.	Thomas W. Marvel	0	9	9	339	
Lt.	Duncan M. McDuffie	4	5	9	78	
Maj.	Virgil K. Meroney	9	0	9	352	POW 4-8-44
Capt.	Stanley B. Morrill	9	0	9	56	
Lt.	Leon M. Orcutt, Jr.	0	9	9	339	
Lt. Col.	Eugene P. Roberts	9	0	9	78, 364	
Maj.	Wilbur R. Scheible	6	3	9	356	
Capt.	John L. Sublett	8	1	9	357	
Lt.	Clyde E. Taylor	0	9	9	78	
Capt.	Romildo Visconte	4	5	9	364	KIA 12-5-44
Lt. Col.	Roy A. Webb, Jr.	4	5	9	361	
Capt.	Robert E. Woody	7	2	9	355	
Maj.	Shelton W. Monroe	4.33	4.5	8.83	4	
Maj.	James R. Happel	4	4.68	8.68	4	
Capt.	Victor J. France	4.33	4.33	8.66	4	KIA 4-18-44
Maj.	Edward W. Szaniawski	4	4.66	8.66	355	POW 5-19-44
Capt.	Joseph H. Bennett	8.5	0	8.5	4, 356	POW 5-25-44
Capt.	Charles J. Cesky	8.5	0	8.5	352	
Lt. Col.	Thomas L. Hayes, Jr.	8.5	0	8.5	357	
Capt.	David W. Howe	6	2.5	8.5	4	
Capt.	Donald M. Malmsten	1.5	7	8.5	4	MIA Evade 8-7-44
Capt.	Bernard L. McGrattan	8.5	0	8.5	4	KIA 6-6-44
Capt.	Sanford K. Moats	8.5	0	8.5	352	
Maj.	Joseph Myers, Jr.	4.5	4	8.5	55, 78	
Lt. Col.	Raymond B. Myers	4.5	4	8.5	355	
Capt.	Donald J. Pierce	0	8.5	8.5	4, 479	
Lt.	Henry R. Slack IV	1.5	7	8.5	78	
Capt.	Theodore J. Sowerby	2	6.5	8.5	479	
Lt.	George R. Vanden Heuval	5.5	3	8.5	361	

Rank	Name	Air Victories	Ground Victories	Total	Group(s)	Remarks
Capt.	Richard A. Hewitt	4	4.33	8.33	78	
Capt.	John J. Hockery	7	1.12	8.12	78	
Lt.	Fred H. Alexander	2	6	8	20	
Lt.	James W. Ayers	1	7	8	4	
Lt.	Robert J. Booth	8	0	8	359	POW 6–8–44
Maj.	Joseph E. Broadhead	8	0	8	357	
Maj.	Richard E. Conner	4.5	3.5	8	78	
Maj.	William S. Crombie	4	4	8	364	
Lt. Col.	Andrew J. Evans	6	2	8	357	
Capt.	Walter L. Flagg	2	6	8	56	
Capt.	James M. Fowle	8	0	8	364	
Capt.	Francis R. Gerard	8	0	8	339	
Lt. Col.	Wallace E. Hopkins	4	4	8	361	
Lt.	Bernard H. Howes	6	2	8	55	POW 3–3–45
Maj.	Jack E. M. Ilfrey	8	0	8	20	6 Air 1 FG, MTO, MIA Evade 6–13–44
Lt.	Danford E. Josey	0	8	8	78	
Lt. Col.	William H. Julian	5	3	8	78	
Lt.	Fred H. Jurgens	0	8	8	20	
Maj.	Charles W. Lenfest	5.5	2.5	8	355	POW 10–3–44
Lt.	William R. MacClarence	0	8	8	339	
Capt.	William J. Maguire	7	1	8	353	
Maj.	Donald C. McGee	6	2	8	357	5 Air 8 FG, PTO
Lt. Col.	John L. McGinn	5	3	8	55	3 Air 347 FG, PTO
Lt.	Keith R. McGinnis	2	6	8	55	
Capt.	Joseph T. McKeon	6	2	8	20	5 Air 475 FG, PTO, POW 10–7–44
Lt.	Richard A. Messinger	0	8	8	78	
Lt.	William F. Mudge, Jr.	2	6	8	339	
Capt.	Alva C. Murphy	6	2	8	357	KIA 3–2–45
Capt.	Norman E. Olson	6	2	8	355	KIA 4–8–44
Capt.	Roy W. Orndorf	4	4	8	364	
Lt.	Richard C. J. Palson	0	8	8	479	
Lt.	Malcolm C. Pickering	4	4	8	352	
Capt.	Joseph F. Pierce	7	1	8	357	KIA 5–20–44
Capt.	Glen D. Schlitz, Jr.	8	0	8	56	
Capt.	Robert G. Schimanski	6	2	8	357	
Capt.	Robert M. Shaw	8	0	8	357	
Capt.	John H. Truluck	7	1	8	56	
Maj.	John W. Vogt, Jr.	8	0	8	56, 356	
Lt.	William E. Whalen	6	2	8	4, 2SF	
Capt.	James W. Wilkinson	6	2	8	4, 78	KIFA 6–4–44
Lt.	Vincent V. Zettler	1	7	8	357	
Lt.	Grover C. Siems, Jr.	4.33	3.5	7.83	4	
Capt.	William B. Smith	3	4.75	7.75	4	KIA 9–13–44
Lt. Col.	Jack J. Oberhansly	6	1.66	7.66	4, 78	
Lt.	Vermont Garrison	7.33	0.25	7.58	4	POW 3–3–44
Lt.	Swift T. Benjamin	1	6.5	7.5	56, 353	
Capt.	Glendon V. Davis	7.5	0	7.5	357	MIA Evade 4–28–44
Capt.	Donald R. Emerson	4.5	3	7.5	4	KIA 12–25–44
Lt.	Donald Henley, Jr.	3	4.5	7.5	56	
Capt.	Joseph H. Joiner	3.5	4	7.5	4	
Maj.	Norman D. Munson	0	7.5	7.5	78	
Maj.	Donovan F. Smith	5.5	2	7.5	56	
Capt.	Robert C. Wright	3.5	4	7.5	361	
Lt.	Dudley M. Amoss	5.5	1.5	7	55	POW 3–21–45
Lt.	William O. Antonides	0	7	7	4	
Capt.	Robert H. Becker	7	0	7	357	

Rank	Name	Air Victories	Ground Victories	Total	Group(s)	Remarks
Lt.	Lloyd D. Boring	0.5	6.5	7	55	
Capt.	James W. Browning	7	0	7	357	
Capt.	John B. Carder	7	0	7	357	POW 5-12-44
Lt.	Herbert L. Caywood	0	7	7	339	
Lt.	Steve J. Chetneky	1	6	7	339	
Lt.	Claude A. Chinn	0	7	7	56	
Capt.	William F. Collins	4	3	7	359	
Maj.	Harold E. Comstock	5	2	7	56	
Capt.	Brack Diamond, Jr.	1	6	7	4	
Lt.	Urban L. Drew	6	1	7	361	
Lt.	Robert T. Eckfeldt	3	4	7	361	
Lt. Col.	Robert A. Elder	5	2	7	353	
Lt.	Charles B. Elmgren	0	7	7	479	
Capt.	Owen P. Farmer	2	5	7	339	
Capt.	Steven N. Gerick	5	2	7	56	
Maj.	Walter V. Gresham, Jr.	4	3	7	355	
Lt.	Christopher J. Hanseman	5	2	7	339	KIA 7-29-44
Capt.	Raymond E. Hartley, Jr.	3	4	7	353	2 Air 325 FG, MTO
Lt.	Neal Hepner	0	7	7	78	
Capt.	James M. Hollingsworth	0	7	7	479	KIA 12-25-44
Lt.	Ernest J. Hopcroft	0	7	7	479	
Lt.	James Jabara	1.5	5.5	7	355	1½ Air 363 FG, 9 AF
Capt.	Gilbert L. Jamison	7	0	7	364	
Lt.	Ben D. Johnston, Jr.	4	3	7	355	
Lt.	Reps D. Jones	2	5	7	20	
Maj.	Ben H. King	7	0	7	359	3 Air 347 FG, PTO
Lt.	Frank W. Klibbe	7	0	7	56	
Capt.	Edward R. Kulik	0	7	7	78	
Maj.	Robert A. Lamb	7	0	7	56	
Capt.	William H. Lewis	7	0	7	55	
Lt.	Howard Mahany, Jr.	0	7	7	55	
Lt.	William D. Martin	4	3	7	355	
F/O	Evan D. McMinn	5	2	7	56	KIA 6-6-44
Lt.	Jerome T. Murphy	0	7	7	339	
Capt.	Gilbert M. O'Brien	7	0	7	357	
Lt. Col.	Chesley G. Peterson	7	0	7	4	6 Air RAF
Capt.	Peter E. Pompetti	5	2	7	78	POW 3-17-44
Maj.	William J. Price	3	4	7	353	
Lt.	Arval J. Roberson	6	1	7	357	
Lt.	Joseph E. Shupe	2	5	7	359	KIA 5-21-44
Capt.	Stanley E. Silva	1	6	7	355	
Capt.	Robert E. Smith	1	6	7	78	
Maj.	Walter E. Starck	7	0	7	352	POW 11-27-44
Capt.	David F. Thwaites	6	1	7	356	
Capt.	Harrison B. Tordoff	5	2	7	353	
Capt.	Gerald E. Tyler	7	0	7	357	
Lt.	Carl W. Weber	0	7	7	352	
Maj.	Samuel J. Wicker	7	0	7	364	
Maj.	John H. Wilson	3.5	3.5	7	355	
Lt.	George H. Witzell	0	7	7	479	
Capt.	Vasseure H. Wynn	5	2	7	4	2½ Air RAF POW 4-13-44
Capt.	John D. Coleman	4.33	2.5	6.83	352	
Maj.	Merle J. Gilbertson	2.83	4	6.83	20	
Lt. Col.	John B. Murphy	6.75	0	6.75	359	½ Air 54 FS, Alaska
Lt.	Clinton D. Burdick	5.5	1	6.5	356	
Capt.	Raymond C. Care	6	0.5	6.5	4	POW 4-15-44
Capt.	Leslie P. Cles	0	6.5	6.5	353	

Rank	Name	Air Victories	Ground Victories	Total	Group(s)	Remarks
Capt.	Donald M. Cummings	6.5	0	6.5	55	1 Air 27 FG, MTO
F/O	Harold W. Falvey	0	6.5	6.5	355	
Lt.	William W. Furr	3.5	3	6.5	352	
Lt.	Frank L. Gailer, Jr.	5.5	1	6.5	357	POW 11-27-44
Lt.	Robert L. Garlich	0	6.5	6.5	355	
Capt.	Raymond H. Gansberg	2.5	4	6.5	356	KIA 12-5-44
Lt.	John T. Golden	1	5.5	6.5	479	POW 4-16-45
Lt.	Charles E. Goodman	4.5	2	6.5	352	
Lt.	Hans J. Grasshoff	2.5	4	6.5	479	
Capt.	Robert T. Green	4.5	2	6.5	78	
Capt.	Carroll D. Henry	1.5	5	6.5	55	
Capt.	Francis W. Horne	5.5	1	6.5	352	
Col.	Mark E. Hubbard	6.5	0	6.5	20	4 Air 33 FG, MTO POW 3-18-44
Lt.	Thomas W. Jones	0.5	6	6.5	353	
Lt. Col.	Joseph J. Kruzel	6.5	0	6.5	361	3 Air 17 PS, PTO
Col.	Einar A. Malmstrom	1	5.5	6.5	356	POW 4-23-44
Maj.	Ben I. Mayo, Jr.	4	2.5	6.5	78	
Capt.	Mark L. Moseley	6.5	0	6.5	56	
Capt.	Richard B. Olander	1.5	5	6.5	339	
Capt.	George T. Rich	1.5	5	6.5	339	
Capt.	Morris A. Stanley	5	1.5	6.5	357	
Maj.	William F. Tanner	5.5	1	6.5	353	
Capt.	Jesse L. Truett	0	6.5	6.5	364	
Capt.	Benjamin M. Watkins	2	4.5	6.5	78	
Lt.	Clarence R. Barger	0.33	6	6.33	355	
Col.	Robert P. Montgomery	3.33	3	6.33	20	MIA Evade 2-11-44
Lt.	Louis W. Adams, Jr.	4	2	6	20	
Capt.	Carl R. Alfred	0	6	6	4	KIA 4-16-45
Lt.	George A. Apple	0	6	6	55	
Lt. Col.	William B. Bailey	3	3	6	353	
Lt.	Robert V. E. Blizzard	0	6	6	339	
Lt.	Robert R. Bosworth	1	5	6	78	
Lt.	William P. Boulet	3	3	6	355	
Lt.	Arthur R. Bowers	0	6	6	4	
Lt.	J. E. Brasher	1	5	6	78	
Capt.	Harley L. Brown	6	0	6	20	
Maj.	Gillespie Bryan	0	6	6	78	
Lt.	George H. Butler	3	3	6	56	
Lt.	Richard G. Candelaria	6	0	6	479	POW 4-13-45
Maj.	James R. Carter	6	0	6	56	
Capt.	Harold W. Chase	2	4	6	353	
Lt.	Frank A. Clifton	0	6	6	339	
Lt.	Anthony T. Colletti	1	5	6	78	
Capt.	Walter V. Cook	6	0	6	56	
Lt.	Arthur C. Cundy	6	0	6	353	KIA 3-11-45
Lt.	Louis DeAnda	0	6	6	78	
Capt.	Donald J. DeVilliers	0	6	6	78	
Capt.	Lawrence J. Dissette	1	5	6	355	
Lt. Col.	Roy W. Evans	6	0	6	4, 359	1 Air 359 FG, POW 2-14-45
Capt.	Lowell E. Einhaus	0	6	6	20	
Capt.	Robert J. Frisch	0	6	6	339	
Lt.	Ray C. Gordon	0	6	6	353	
Lt.	Clifford C. Gould	1	5	6	55	
Capt.	George F. Hall	6	0	6	56	
Capt.	Cameron M. Hart	6	0	6	56	
Lt. Col.	James M. Herren, Jr.	4	2	6	479	KIA 10-30-44

Rank	Name	Air Victories	Ground Victories	Total	Group(s)	Remarks
Capt.	Verne E. Hooker	2	4	6	479	
Lt.	Kenneth R. Horner	0	6	6	364	
Lt.	Robert E. Irion	1	5	6	339	
Lt.	Loton D. Jennings	0	6	6	4	
Lt.	William A. Jones	2	4	6	339	
Lt.	William T. Kemp	6	0	6	361	
Maj.	Henry H. Kirby, Jr.	1	5	6	355	
Maj.	Henry B. Kucheman, Jr.	4	2	6	355	
Capt.	Witold A. Lanowski	6	0	6	56	2 Air RAF, Polish Air Force
Lt.	Louis W. Lee	4	2	6	353	
Lt.	Thurman C. Long	2	4	6	355	
Col.	James D. Mayden	2	4	6	352	
Lt.	Keith R. McGinnis	2	4	6	55	
Lt.	Bruce D. McMahan	0.5	5.5	6	353	
Maj.	Henry L. Mills	6	0	6	4	POW 3-3-44
Capt.	Leslie D. Minchew	5.5	0.5	6	355	
Lt.	Tom D. Neely	2	4	6	479	POW 12-23-44
Lt.	Robert F. Nelson	1	5	6	4	POW 4-22-44
Lt.	Robert A. Newman	4	2	6	353	KIA 3-16-44
Lt.	Cuthbert A. Pattillo	0	6	6	352	
Lt.	Robert H. Paul	0	6	6	339	
F/O	Douglas P. Pederson	0	6	6	4	
F/O	Charles E. Poage, Jr.	0	6	6	4	POW 12-25-44
Lt.	Edward F. Rogue	0	6	6	20	
Lt.	Lawrence J. Powell, Jr.	2.5	3.5	6	339	POW 1-14-45
Lt.	Walter A. S. Prescott	2	4	6	353	
Capt.	John F. Pugh	6	0	6	357	
Capt.	Garth L. Reynolds	2	4	6	20	
Capt.	Alexander F. Sears	5	1	6	352	
Capt.	Herbert K. Shope	0	6	6	78	
Lt.	Frank E. Speer	1	5	6	4	POW 5-29-44
Lt.	David Stewart	0	6	6	20	POW 4-10-45
Capt.	Richard M. Tracy	0	6	6	20	POW 4-10-45
Lt.	Grant M. Turley	6	0	6	78	KIA 3-6-44
Capt.	Alton J. Wallace	3	3	6	352	
Capt.	Warren M. Wesson	4	2	6	78	
Lt.	Donald Y. Whinnem	1	5	6	352	
Lt.	Howard E. Wiggins	4.5	1.5	6	356	
Lt.	James C. Woolery	0	6	6	339	
Maj.	Michael P. Yannell	2	4	6	356	2 Air 86 FG, MTO
Maj.	Earl L. Abbott	4.75	1	5.75	352	
Capt.	Brady C. Williamson	1.7	4	5.7	355	
Capt.	Walter J. Koraleski	5.53	0	5.53	355	POW 4-15-44
Lt.	Thomas E. Adams	4.5	1	5.5	357	
Lt.	Sherman Armsby	4.5	1	5.5	361	KIA 8-13-44
Lt.	Clifford T. Ashby	3.5	2	5.5	356	
Lt.	Bayard C. Auchincloss	3	2.5	5.5	353	
Capt.	Thomas R. Bell	0	5.5	5.5	4	
Lt.	Charles J. Bennette	2	3.5	5.5	352	
Lt.	Robert H. Berkshire	4.5	1	5.5	352	MIA Evade 6-27-44
Capt.	Marvin V. Bledsoe	0	5.5	5.5	353	
Capt.	Robert V. Buttke	5.5	0	5.5	55	
Lt.	Merle R. Capp	2	3.5	5.5	78	
Lt.	Joseph D. Carter	0.5	5	5.5	352	
Capt.	Archie W. Chatterly	4.5	1	5.5	2	POW 3-27-44
Lt.	Jack W. Clark	2.5	3	5.5	353	
Lt.	Randolph W. Cooper	0	5.5	5.5	355	

Rank	Name	Air Victories	Ground Victories	Total	Group(s)	Remarks
Col.	Gerald J. Dix	4	1.5	5.5	355	POW 6-8-44
Capt.	John B. Eaves	3.5	2	5.5	56	
Capt.	Lindol F. Graham	5.5	0	5.5	20	KIA 3-18-44
Capt.	Paul R. Hatala	5.5	0	5.5	357	
Maj.	Donald H. Higgins	2.5	3	5.5	352	
Capt.	Edward F. Izor	4.5	1	5.5	364	
Lt.	William J. Jordan	1	4.5	5.5	353	
Lt.	Gilbert L. Kesler	0.5	5	5.5	4	
Capt.	Robert G. Kurtz	0.5	5	5.5	355	
Lt.	Huie H. Lamb, Jr.	2.5	3	5.5	78	
Capt.	Philip M. Loveless, Jr.	0.5	5	5.5	339	
Capt.	Frank E. McCauley	5.5	0	5.5	56	
Lt.	Darrell E. McMahan	1.5	4	5.5	56	
Lt.	Harold O. Miller	2	3.5	5.5	353	
Capt.	Frank A. Morgan	0.5	5	5.5	356	
Capt.	William R. O'Brien	5.5	0	5.5	357	
Lt.	James J. Pascoe	5.5	0	5.5	364	
Capt.	Carl G. Payne	2	3.5	5.5	4	
Lt.	Eugene L. Peel	0.5	5	5.5	78	
Lt.	Vernon G. Rafferty	2.5	3	5.5	353	
Capt.	Albert J. Ramm	0.5	5	5.5	55	
Lt.	Vernon R. Richards	2	3.5	5.5	361	
Capt.	Leroy A. Ruder	5.5	0	5.5	357	KIA 6-6-44
Lt.	Robert C. Smith	2.5	3	5.5	357	
Capt.	Mark H. Stepleton	3.5	2	5.5	357	
Lt.	Robert P. Winks	5.5	0	5.5	357	
Lt.	Clemmons A. Fiedler	4.33	1	5.33	4	KIA 4-10-44
Lt.	Richard C. Brookins	4.25	1	5.25	352	
Lt.	Edmond Zellner	3.25	2	5.25	352	MIA Evade 7-13-44
Capt.	Robert W. Abernathy	5	0	5	353	
Lt.	William J. Allen	5	0	5	55	
Lt.	Clifford F. Armstrong	3	2	5	353	
Lt.	Sanborn N. Ball, Jr.	1.5	3.5	5	56	
Lt.	Raymond W. Bank	5	0	5	357	POW 3-2-45
Capt.	Harold T. Barnaby	4	1	5	78	
F/O	Donald P. Baugh	0	5	5	4	
Lt.	Richard M. Baughn	1	4	5	364	
Lt.	Eugene M. Beason	1	4	5	56	
Capt.	Edward H. Beavers, Jr.	5	0	5	339	KIA 11-27-44
Lt.	Myron A. Becraft	1	4	5	357	
Lt.	Donald Best	0	5	5	55	
Capt.	Frank E. Birtciel	0	5	5	55	
Capt.	Brooks Bline	1	4	5	339	
Lt.	Burton O. Blodgett	0	5	5	56	
Lt.	Victor E. Bocquin	4	1	5	361	
Lt.	Hugh Bodiford	2	3	5	55	
Maj.	Robert R. Bonebrake	3	2	5	78	
Capt.	Ernest O. Bostrom	5	0	5	352	
Lt.	Byron K. Bralay	3	2	5	357	
Maj.	Gerald Brown	5	0	5	55, 4	
Lt.	Carl H. Bundgoard	2	3	5	339	
Lt.	John R. Byers	0	5	5	339	
Lt.	Merle F. Caldwell	2	3	5	339	
Lt.	George W. Ceglarski	1	4	5	4, 2SF	
Capt.	Merle M. Coons	5	0	5	55	
Maj.	Ralph L. Cox	5	0	5	359	
Maj.	Niven K. Cranfill	5	0	5	359	
Lt.	J. S. Daniell	5	0	5	339	

Rank	Name	Air Victories	Ground Victories	Total	Group(s)	Remarks
Lt.	Gordon S. Denson	0	5	5	4	
Capt.	Charles DeWitt	0	5	5	78	
Capt.	Melvin N. Dickey	0	5	5	4	
Capt.	Gene C. Doss	0	5	5	78	
Capt.	Joseph L. Egan, Jr.	5	0	5	56	KIA 7-19-44
Capt.	John C. Fahringer	4	1	5	56	
Lt.	Jack M. Fletcher	0	5	5	355	
Capt.	Earl R. Fryer	4	1	5	55	
Lt.	Donald Galer	0	5	5	355	
Lt.	Richard G. Gibbs	4	1	5	55	
Lt.	Lindsay W. Grove	1	4	5	353	
Lt.	William R. Guyton	0	5	5	339	
Capt.	Harry N. Hagan	2	3	5	4	
Lt.	Robert F. Hahn	1	4	5	353	
Lt.	Thomas H. Hall, Jr.	3	2	5	364	
Capt.	Ralph W. Hamilton	4	1	5	352	
Lt.	Kenneth J. Hansen	0	5	5	479	
Capt.	Thomas L. Harris	5	0	5	357	POW 5-27-44
Capt.	Charles D. Hauver	5	0	5	355	
Lt.	Russell C. Haworth	5	0	5	55	
Lt.	Kenneth G. Helfrecht	0	5	5	4	
Lt.	Cephas Hermansen	0	5	5	339	
Capt.	Sidney H. Hewett	2.5	2.5	5	356	POW 5-4-44
Maj.	Edwin W. Hiro	5	0	5	357	KIA 9-19-44
Capt.	Robert D. Hobert	2	3	5	4	KIA 4-5-44
Capt.	William R. Hodges	5	0	5	359	MIA Evade 5-11-44
Lt.	Harlan F. Hunt	0	5	5	339	
Lt.	Joseph W. Icard	5	0	5	56	KIA 3-8-44
Lt.	James M. Jure	3.5	1.5	5	56	
Lt.	Boyd O. Jackson	0	5	5	339	
Lt.	Leedom K. John	0	5	5	55	
Capt.	Evan M. Johnson	5	0	5	339	
Lt. Col.	Herbert E. Johnson	3.5	1.5	5	20	
Maj.	Wilton W. Johnson	3	2	5	353	
Capt.	Warren E. Kerr	0	5	5	56	
Lt.	Herman E. King	1	4	5	56	
Capt.	William F. Kissell	0	5	5	364	
Lt.	William H. Krauss	0.5	4.5	5	339	
Lt.	Philip G. Kuhn	1	4	5	56	
Capt.	Earl R. Lazear, Jr.	5	0	5	352	
Capt.	Dorian Ledington	2	3	5	78	
Capt.	Charles P. London	5	0	5	78	
Lt.	William J. Lynch	0	5	5	355	POW 4-16-45
Capt.	Jack D. MacFadden	0	5	5	4	
Capt.	Robert G. MacKean	0	5	5	352	KIA 4-24-44
Lt.	John T. Maloney	0	5	5	55	
Capt.	Gene E. Markham	5	0	5	353	
Lt.	Halbert G. Marsh	0	5	5	355	
Lt.	Lester C. Marsh	5	0	5	339	
Lt.	Jay F. Marts	2	3	5	339	
Col.	Joseph L. Mason	5	0	5	352	
Maj.	Chester K. Maxwell	5	0	5	357	
Lt.	Darwin D. McCasland	2	3	5	355	POW 4-15-44
Lt.	James H. McClure	0	5	5	353	
Lt.	James L. McCubbin	4	1	5	364	POW 2-19-45
Lt.	Francis N. McCullom	0	5	5	355	POW 4-16-45
Capt.	Charles L. McGraw	3	2	5	353	
Lt.	Philip M. N. McHugh	2	3	5	355	

Rank	Name	Air Victories	Ground Victories	Total	Group(s)	Remarks
Lt. Col.	Daniel D. McKee	1	4	5	359	
Lt.	Joseph D. McMullen	0	5	5	353	
Lt.	Edward J. Moroney	3	2	5	355	
Lt.	John N. Murr	2	3	5	479	
Lt.	Jerome K. Magel	1	4	5	479	
Capt.	Thomas F. Neal, Jr.	4.5	0.5	5	355	
Lt.	Charles E. Parmalee	3	2	5	78	
Lt.	Roy L. Patterson	1	4	5	56	
Lt.	Emil F. Perry	2	3	5	355	
Lt.	Joseph A. Peterburs	0	5	5	20	POW 4-10-45
Lt.	Robert O. Peters	3	2	5	355	KIA 9-18-44
Lt.	Richard E. Phaneuf	0	5	5	78	
Lt.	Raymond G. Phillips	2	3	5	352	
Capt.	Donald J. Pierini	1	4	5	4	
Capt.	Spiros N. Pisanos	5	0	5	4	MIA Evade 3-5-44
Maj.	Jack C. Price	5	0	5	78	
Lt.	Royce W. Priest	5	0	5	355	
Lt.	Thomas P. Pryor, Jr.	0	5	5	353	
Lt.	Thomas W. Queen, Jr.	0	5	5	56	
Col.	John P. Randolph	1	4	5	20, 359	
Col.	Harold J. Rau	1	4	5	20, 356	
Lt.	William C. Reese	5	0	5	357	KIA 5-20-44
Lt.	Edwin D. Reinhardt	0	5	5	353	
F/O	John J. Rice	0	5	5	339	
Lt.	Alden P. Rigby	4	1	5	352	
Lt.	Robert T. Rose	0	5	5	353	
Lt.	Thomas D. Schank	5	0	5	55	
Capt.	Duerr H. Schuh	5	0	5	352	
Capt.	Presson S. Shane	0	5	5	479	
Lt.	Walter J. Sharbo	3	2	5	56	
Lt.	Kenneth C. Smeltz	1	4	5	20	
Lt.	Alfred J. Smigel	0	5	5	479	
Lt.	Kenneth G. Smith	5	0	5	4	POW 3-21-44
Lt.	Vernon A. Smith	0	5	5	56	
Capt.	William J. Stangel	5	0	5	352	
Capt.	Henry M. Stewart	4	1	5	352	
Lt.	Dale S. Sweat	0	5	5	78	
Lt.	Henry S. Sykes	0	5	5	352	
Capt.	Willis B. Taylor	3	2	5	20	POW 10-19-44
Lt.	Eugene J. Timony	1	4	5	56	
Capt.	Jack R. Warren	5	0	5	357	KIA 3-19-44
Capt.	William P. Wilkerson	1	4	5	56	
Capt.	William F. Wilson	5	0	5	364	
Lt.	Victor Wolski	3	2	5	479	
Lt.	Jack J. Yelton	3	2	5	20	POW 4-5-44
Capt.	Robert M. York	5	0	5	359	

Top Air-To-Air Aces

Rank	Name	Air-to-air score
Lt. Col.	Francis S. Gabreski	28
Maj.	Robert S. Johnson	27
Maj.	George E. Preddy, Jr.	26.83
Lt. Col.	John C. Meyer	24
Lt. Col.	David C. Schilling	22.5
Capt.	Don S. Gentile	21.83
Capt.	Fred J. Christensen, Jr.	21.5
Maj.	Ray S. Wetmore	21.25
Maj.	Walker M. Mahurin	20.75
Col.	Glenn E. Duncan	19.5
Maj.	Leonard K. Carson	18.5
Maj.	Walter C. Beckham	18
Col.	Hubert A. Zemke	17.75
Maj.	John B. England	17.5
Maj.	Duane W. Beeson	17.33
Capt.	John F. Thornell, Jr.	17.25
Maj.	Gerald W. Johnson	16.5
Capt.	Clarence E. Anderson, Jr.	16.25
Capt.	William T. Whisner	15.5
Maj.	Robert W. Foy	15
Maj.	James A. Goodson	15
Lt.	Ralph K. Hofer	15
Col.	Donald J. M. Blakeslee	14.5
Lt. Col.	John D. Landers	14.5
Capt.	Joseph H. Powers	14.5

Top Strafing Aces

Rank	Name	Strafing victories
Lt. Col.	Elwyn G. Righetti	27
Lt. Col.	Joseph L. Thury	25.5
Lt. Col.	John D. Landers	20
Maj.	Archie A. Tower	18
Col.	Claiborne H. Kinnard, Jr.	17
Capt.	Edwin L. Heller	16.5
Capt.	Gordon B. Compton	15
Lt.	William J. Cullerton	15
Maj.	James A. Goodson	15
Capt.	Henry W. Brown	14.5
Capt.	Melville W. Hightshoe	14.5
Capt.	Herbert G. Kolb	14.5
Maj.	Gerald E. Montgomery	14.5
Lt.	Ralph K. Hofer	14
Lt. Col.	John L. Elder, Jr.	13
Capt.	Kirke B. Everson, Jr.	13
Capt.	Raymond H. Littge	13
Lt. Col.	John C. Meyer	13
Maj.	John T. Godfrey	12.66
Maj.	Fred W. Glover	12.5
F/O	Richard N. Gustke	12.5
Maj.	Walker L. Boone	12.13
Capt.	Robert E. Welch	12
Lt.	Oscar K. Biggs	11.5

Aerial Aces in a Day

Name	Credits	Date	Group
Capt. Fred J. Christensen, Jr.	6	7-7-44	56
Maj. George E. Preddy	6	8-6-44	352
Maj. Ernest E. Bankey, Jr.	5½	12-27-44	364
Maj. William J. Hovde	5½	12-5-44	355
Lt. William H. Allen	5	9-5-44	55
Capt. William R. Beyer	5	9-27-44	361
Lt. Col. Wayne K. Blickenstaff	5	3-24-45	353
Capt. Donald S. Bryan	5	11-2-44	352
Maj. Leonard K. Carson	5	11-27-44	357
Lt. Jack S. Daniell	5	11-26-44	339
Lt. Col. Robert A. Elder	5	3-24-45	353
Lt. William H. Lewis	5	9-5-44	55

Aerial Aces in a Day

Name	Credits	Date	Group
Lt. Carl J. Luksic	5	5-8-44	352
Capt. Robert J. Rankin	5	5-12-44	56
Col. David C. Schilling	5	12-23-44	56
Capt. William T. Whisner	5	11-21-44	352
Capt. Felix D. Williamson	5	1-14-45	56
Lt. Col. Sidney S. Woods	5	3-22-45	4
Capt. Charles E. Yeager	5	10-12-44	357

Combined Air-Ground Aces in a Day

Name	Air	Ground	Date	Group
Maj. Ernest E. Bankey, Jr.	2	4	4-16-45	364
Lt. Cyril W. Jones	4	2	9-12-44	359
Lt. Robert O. Peters	3	2	7-20-44	355

Ground Aces in a Day

Name	Credits	Date	Group	Name	Credits	Date	Group
Lt. Randel L. Murphy	10	4–13–45	56	Lt. Anthony T. Colletti	5	4–16–45	78
Capt. Herbert G. Kolb	9½	4–16–45	353	Lt. Donald J. DeVilliers	5	4–16–45	78
Capt. Robert H. Ammon	9	4–16–45	339	Lt. Gene C. Doss	5	4–16–45	78
Maj. Fred Glover	9	2–27–45	4	Maj. John L. Elder, Jr.	5	11–2–44	355
Lt. Col. John D. Landers	9	4–16–45	78	Capt. Don S. Gentile	5	4–5–44	4
Lt. Gerald J. Miller	9	4–16–45	353	F/O Richard N. Gustke	5	3–21–45	353
Lt. Leon M. Orcutt	9	4–17–45	339	F/O Richard N. Gustke	5	4–16–45	353
Lt. Col. Elwyn G. Righetti	9	4–17–45	55	Lt. Kenneth G. Helfrecht	5	4–16–45	4
Maj. Walker L. Boone	8	2–27–45	353	Lt. Neal Hepner	5	4–16–45	78
F/O Frederick H. Jurgens	8	4–10–45	20	Capt. Melville W. Hightshoe	5	4–16–45	353
Lt. Clyde E. Taylor	8	4–16–45	78				
Maj. Archie A. Tower	8	4–10–45	339	Capt. Clarence O. Johnson	5	9–10–44	352
Lt. William J. Cullerton	7	9–12–44	355	Lt. Reps D. Jones	5	2–9–45	20
Capt. Kirke B. Everson	7	4–17–45	339	Lt. Danford E. Josey, Jr.	5	4–16–45	78
Capt. Edwin L. Heller	7	4–16–45	352	Lt. Neal Kepner	5	4–16–45	78
Capt. Edward R. Kulik	7	4–16–45	78	Lt. Richard L. Kier	5	4–10–45	20
Lt. David Stewart	7	4–10–45	20	Capt. Herbert G. Kolb	5	2–27–45	353
Lt. Col. Olin E. Gilbert	6½	4–16–45	78	Lt. Russell S. Kyler	5	4–13–45	56
Capt. Charles H. Cole	6	2–9–45	20	Lt. Roland J. Lanoue	5	2–27–45	353
Lt. Steve J. Chetneky	6	4–16–45	339	Lt. Howard Mahany, Jr.	5	4–17–45	55
Lt. Col. William C. Clark	6	4–16–45	339	Lt. Halbert G. Marsh	5	4–16–45	355
Lt. William J. Cullerton	6	11–2–44	355	Lt. James H. McClure	5	4–16–45	353
Capt. Lowell E. Einhaus	6	2–8–45	20	Capt. James N. McElroy	5	4–15–44	355
Capt. Robert B. Hatter	6	5–21–44	359	Lt. Duncan McDuffie	5	4–16–45	78
Capt. John C. Hunter	6	4–13–45	364	Lt. Joseph D. McMullen	5	4–16–45	353
Capt. Raymond H. Littge	6	4–17–45	352	Lt. Joseph E. Mellen	5	4–13–45	355
Capt. Donald M. Malmsten	6	2–27–45	4	Capt. Frank A. Morgan	5	2–20–45	356
Lt. Cuthbert A. Pattillo	6	4–16–45	352	Lt. Jerome T. Murphy	5	4–10–45	339
Lt. Col. Elwyn G. Righetti	6	4–9–45	55	Maj. Robin Olds	5	4–16–45	479
Lt. Col. Elwyn G. Righetti	6	4–16–45	55	Lt. Robert H. Paul	5	4–10–45	339
Col. Ben Rimerman	6	4–16–45	353	Lt. Douglas P. Pederson	5	4–16–45	4
Maj. James A. Goodson	5½	4–10–44	4	Lt. Joseph A. Peterburs	5	4–10–45	20
Lt. Bruce D. McMahan	5½	4–16–45	353	Capt. Donald J. Pierce	5	4–16–45	479
Lt. Fred H. Alexander	5	10–6–44	20	Lt. Dale S. Swett	5	4–16–45	78
Lt. William O. Antonides	5	4–16–45	4	Lt. Henry S. Sykes	5	4–16–45	352
F/O Donald P. Baugh	5	4–16–45	4	Lt. Col. Joseph L. Thury	5	4–17–45	339
Lt. Swift T. Benjamin	5	8–29–44	353	Capt. Jesse L. Truett	5	4–13–45	364
Capt. Frank E. Birtciel	5	4–9–45	55	Lt. Karl R. Waldron	5	4–17–45	352
Lt. John R. Byers	5	4–16–45	339	Lt. Col. Roy A. Webb, Jr.	5	6–29–44	361
Lt. Joseph D. Carter	5	4–17–45	352				

Alphabetical Listing of Aces

In order to facilitate ready reference to the aces the following pages list their names alphabetically with their total air and ground score. Further information on the individual ace can be obtained from the listings ranked by total score.

Name	Total victories
Earl L. Abbott	5.75
Robert W. Abernathy	5
Fletcher E. Adams	9
Louis W. Adams, Jr.	6
Thomas E. Adams	5.5
William J. Allen	5
Fred H. Alexander	8
Robert H. Ammon	14
Dudley M. Amoss	7
Clarence E. Anderson, Jr.	17.25
Charles F. Anderson, Jr.	15.5
Woodrow W. Anderson	13.5
Stephen W. Andrew	15.5
William B. Antonides	7
George A. Apple	6
Sherman Armsby	5.5
Clifford F. Armstrong	5
Clifford T. Ashby	5.5
Bayard C. Auchincloss	5.5
Joseph W. Ayers	8
Donald A. Baccus	9
William B. Bailey	6
Sanborn N. Ball, Jr.	5
Raymond W. Bank	5
Ernest E. Bankey	17.5
Clarence R. Barger	6.33
Donald P. Baugh	5
Richard M. Baughn	5
Harold T. Barnaby	5
Eugene M. Beason	5
Edward H. Beavers, Jr.	5
Myron A. Becraft	5
Walter C. Beckham	18
Duane W. Beeson	22.08
Thomas R. Bell	5.5
Swift T. Benjamin	7.5
Charles J. Bennett	5.5
Joseph H. Bennett	8.5
Robert H. Berkshire	5.5
Donald Best	5
William R. Beyer	9
Hipolitus T. Biel	11.33
Oscar K. Biggs	12
Henry S. Bille	10
Frank E. Birtciel	5
Donald J. M. Blakeslee	16
Marvin V. Bledsoe	5.5
Wayne K. Blickenstaff	10
Brooks Bline	5
Robert V. E. Blizzard	6
Donald H. Bochkay	13.83
Burton O. Blodgett	5

Name	Total victories
Victor E. Bocquin	5
Hugh Bodiford	5
Robert R. Bonebreak	5
Walker L. Boone	14.13
Robert J. Booth	8
Lloyd D. Boring	7
Ernest O. Bostrom	5
George E. Bostwick	14
Robert R. Bosworth	6
William P. Boulet	6
Arthur R. Bowers	6
Byron Bralay	5
J. E. Brasher	6
Joseph E. Broadhead	8
Richard C. Brookins	5.25
Gerald Brown	5
Henry W. Brown	28.7
Quince L. Brown	14.33
James W. Browning	9
Joseph W. Browning	7
Donald S. Bryan	13.33
Gillespie Bryan	6
William E. Bryan, Jr.	9.5
Carl H. Bundgoard	5
Harold W. Burch	11
Clinton D. Burdick	6.5
George H. Butler	6
Robert V. Buttke	5.5
John R. Byers	5
Merle F. Caldwell	5
Richard G. Candelaria	6
Merle R. Capp	5.5
John B. Carder	7
Raymond C. Care	6.5
Kendall E. Carlson	10
George W. Carpenter	15.83
Leonard K. Carson	22
James R. Carter	6
Joseph D. Carter	5.5
Herbert L. Caywood	7
George W. Ceglarski	5
Charles J. Cesky	8.5
George F. Ceuleers	10.5
Van E. Chandler	9
Harold W. Chase	6
Archie W. Chatterly	5.5
Steve J. Chetneky	7
Claude A. Chinn	7
Fred J. Christensen, Jr.	21.5
Jack W. Clark	5.5
James A. Clark, Jr.	15
William C. Clark	9
Leslie P. Cles	6.5
Frank A. Clifton	6
Charles H. Cole, Jr.	11
John D. Coleman	6.83
Anthony T. Colletti	6
William F. Collins	7
Gordon B. Compton	20.5

Name	Total victories	Name	Total victories
Harold E. Comstock	7	James M. Fowle	8
Paul A. Conger	11.5	Robert W. Foy	18
Richard E. Conner	8	Victor J. France	8.66
Walter V. Cook	6	Robert J. Frisch	6
Merle M. Coons	5	Earl R. Fryer	5
Randolph W. Cooper	5.5	William W. Furr	6.5
Harry R. Corey	12	Francis S. Gabreski	31
Ralph L. Cox	5	Frank L. Gailer, Jr.	6.5
Darrell S. Cramer	9	Donald Galer	5
Niven K. Cranfill	5	Kenneth W. Gallup	11
William S. Crombie	8	Raymond H. Gansberg	6.5
Claude J. Crenshaw	10	Robert L. Garlich	6.5
William J. Cullerton	20	Vermont Garrison	7.58
John W. Cunnick III	9	Don S. Gentile	27.83
Donald M. Cummings	6.5	Francis R. Gerard	8
Arthur C. Cundy	6	Steven N. Gerrick	7
Frank A. Cutler	10.5	Samuel D. Gevorkian	9
Lucian A. Dade, Jr.	9	Richard G. Gibbs	5
J. S. Daniell	5	Olin E. Gilbert	11.5
Clayton E. Davis	9	Merle J. Gilbertson	6.83
Glendon V. Davis	7.5	Edward B. Giller	9
Louis DeAnda	6	B. Michael Gladych	18
Gordon S. Denson	5	George W. Gleason	14.5
Donald J. DeVilliers	6	Fred W. Glover	22.83
Charles DeWitt	5	John T. Godfrey	26.66
Brack Diamond, Jr.	7	John T. Golden	6.5
Melvin N. Dickey	5	Charles E. Goodman	6.5
Lawrence J. Dissette	6	James A. Goodson	30
Gerald J. Dix	5.5	Ray C. Gordon	6
George A. Doersch	12	Clifford C. Gould	6
Gene C. Doss	5	Gordon M. Graham	16.5
Irwin H. Dregne	10.5	Lindol F. Graham	5.5
Urban L. Drew	7	Hans J. Grasshoff	6.5
Claire A. P. Duffie	11.5	Robert T. Green	6.5
James E. Duffy, Jr.	14.2	Rayl P. Greenwood	9
Glenn E. Duncan	26.33	Walter V. Gresham, Jr.	7
John F. Duncan	10	Lindsay W. Grove	5
John B. Eaves	5.5	Richard N. Gustke	12.5
Robert T. Eckfeldt	7	William R. Guyton	5
Billy G. Edens	10	Harry N. Hagan	5
Joseph L. Egan, Jr.	5	Robert F. Hahn	5
Lowell E. Einhaus	6	George F. Hall	6
John L. Elder, Jr.	21	Thomas H. Hall, Jr.	5
Robert A. Elder	7	William T. Halton	12.5
Charles B. Elmgren	7	Ralph W. Hamilton	5
Donald R. Emerson	7.5	Christopher J. Hanseman	7
Frank N. Emory	12	Kenneth J. Hansen	5
John B. England	18.5	James R. Happel	8.68
Andrew J. Evans	8	Francis E. Harrington	12
Roy W. Evans	6	Thomas L. Harris	5
Kirke B. Everson, Jr.	13	Cameron M. Hart	6
John C. Fahringer	5	Raymond E. Hartley, Jr.	7
Harold W. Falvey	6.5	Paul R. Hatala	5.5
Owen P. Farmer	7	Robert B. Hatter	9
Clemmons A. Fiedler	5.33	Fred R. Haviland, Jr.	12
Ernest C. Fiebelkorn	11	Charles D. Hauver	5
Walter L. Flagg	8	Thomas L. Hayes, Jr.	8.5
Jack M. Fletcher	5	Russell C. Haworth	5
Norman J. Fortier	11.33	Kenneth G. Helfrecht	5

Name	Total victories	Name	Total victories
Edwin L. Heller	22	William H. Julian	8
Donald Henley, Jr.	7.5	James M. Jure	5
Carroll D. Henry	6.5	Fred H. Jurgens	8
Neal Hepner	7	Dale E. Karger	11.5
Cephas Hermansen	5	Robert J. Keen	10
James M. Herren, Jr.	6	William T. Kemp	6
Sidney H. Hewett	5	Warren E. Kerr	5
Richard A. Hewitt	8.33	Gilbert L. Kesler	5.5
Donald H. Higgins	5.5	Edward L. Kier	9
Melville W. Hightshoe	14.5	Ben H. King	7
Edwin W. Hiro	5	Herman E. King	5
Howard D. Hively	14.5	Claiborne H. Kinnard, Jr.	25
Robert D. Hobert	5	Henry H. Kirby, Jr.	6
John J. Hockery	8.12	John A. Kirla	12
William R. Hodges	5	John A. Kirk III	10
Ralph K. Hofer	29	William F. Kissell	5
Wallace E. Hopkins	8	Frank W. Klibbe	7
James M. Hollingsworth	7	Herbert G. Kolb	14.5
Verne E. Hooker	6	Witold J. Koraleski	6
Ernest J. Hopcroft	7	William H. Krauss	5
Francis W. Horne	6.5	Joseph J. Kruzel	6.5
Kenneth R. Horner	6	Henry B. Kuchmen, Jr.	6
William J. Hovde	12.5	Philip G. Kuhn	5
David W. Howe	8.5	Edward R. Kulik	7
Bernard H. Howes	8	Robert G. Kurtz	5.5
Mark E. Hubbard	6.5	Russell S. Kyler	10
Harlan F. Hunt	5	Huie H. Lamb, Jr.	5.5
John C. Hunter	9	Robert A. Lamb	7
James W. Icard	5	John D. Landers	34.5
Jack M. Ilfrey	8	Joseph L. Lang	11.83
Robert F. Irion	6	Roland J. Lanoue	12
Edward F. Izor	5.5	Witold A. Lanowski	6
James Jabara	7	Donald A. Larson	9
Boyd O. Jackson	5	Earl R. Lazear, Jr.	5
Michael J. Jackson	13.5	Dorian Ledington	5
Willie O. Jackson, Jr.	11	Louis W. Lee	6
Gail E. Jacobson	10.5	Charles W. Lenfest	8
Gilbert L. Jamison	7	William H. Lewis	7
Arthur F. Jeffrey	14	Ted E. Lines	10
Otto D. Jenkins	10.5	Raymond H. Littge	23.5
Loton D. Jennings	6	Charles P. London	5
Leedom K. John	5	Thurman C. Long	6
Clarence O. Johnson	13	Philip M. Loveless, Jr.	5.5
Evan M. Johnson	5	John H. Lowell	16.5
Gerald W. Johnson	16.5	Carl J. Luksic	15.5
Herbert E. Johnson	5	William J. Lynch	5
Martin H. Johnson	10	William R. MacClarence	8
Robert S. Johnson	27	Jack D. MacFadden	5
Wilton W. Johnson	5	Robert G. MacKean	5
Ben D. Johnston, Jr.	7	Jerome K. Magel	5
Joseph H. Joiner	7.5	William J. Maguire	8
Cyril W. Jones	11	Howard Mahany, Jr.	7
Frank C. Jones	10.5	Walker M. Mahurin	20.75
Reps D. Jones	7	Donald M. Malmsten	8.5
Thomas W. Jones	6.5	Einar A. Malmstrom	6.5
William A. Jones	6	Joseph L. Mansker	10
William J. Jordan	5.5	John T. Maloney	5
Danford E. Josey	8	Gene E. Markham	5
Alwin M. Juchiem	15	Bert W. Marshall, Jr.	10

Name	Total victories	Name	Total victories
Halbert G. Marsh	5	Randel L. Murphy	12
Lester C. Marsh	5	John N. Murr	5
William D. Martin	7	James Myers, Jr.	8.5
Jay F. Marts	5	Raymond B. Myers	8.5
Joseph L. Mason	5	Thomas F. Neal, Jr.	5
Thomas W. Marvel	9	Tom D. Nealy	6
James D. Mayden	6	Robert F. Nelson	6
Chester K. Maxwell	5	Robert A. Newman	6
Ben I. Mayo, Jr.	6.5	Louis H. Norley	15.33
Darwin D. McCasland	5	Jack J. Oberhansly	7.66
Frank A. McCauley	5.5	Gilbert M. O'Brien	7
James H. McClure	5	William R. O'Brien	5.5
Arthur B. McCormick, Jr.	10	Richard B. Olander	6.5
James L. McCubbin	5	Robin Olds	24
Francis N. McCullom	5	Norman E. Olson	8
Duncan M. McDuffie	9	Thomas C. Olson	10.5
James N. McElroy	11	Leon M. Orcutt, Jr.	9
Donald C. McGee	8	Roy W. Orndorf	8
John L. McGinn	8	Richard C. J. Palson	8
Keith R. McGinnis	8	Charles E. Parmalee	5
Bernard L. McGrattan	8.5	James J. Pascoe	5.5
Charles L. McGraw	5	Ray L. Patterson	5
Philip M. N. McHugh	5	Cuthbert Pattillo	6
Daniel D. McKee	5	Robert H. Paul	6
James T. McKeon	8	Carl G. Payne	5.5
Pierce W. McKennon	20.68	Charles M. Peal	10
Bruce D. McMahan	6	Eugene L. Peel	5.5
Darrell E. McMahan	5.5	Douglas D. Pederson	6
Evan D. McMinn	7	Emil F. Perry	5
James D. McMullen	5	Joseph A. Peterburs	5
Joseph D. McMullen	10	Robert O. Peters	5
Nicholas Megura	15.58	Chesley G. Peterson	7
Joseph E. Mellen	10	Richard A. Peterson	19
Virgil K. Meroney	9	Richard E. Phaneuf	5
George L. Merritt	11	Raymond G. Phillips	5
Richard A. Messinger	8	Malcolm C. Pickering	8
John C. Meyer	37	Donald J. Pierce	8.5
Henry J. Miklajcyk	13.5	Joseph F. Pierce	8
Gerald J. Miller	11	Donald J. Pierini	5
Harold G. Miller	5.5	Spiros N. Pisanos	5
Willard W. Millikan	15	Charles E. Poage, Jr.	6
Henry L. Mills	6	Edward F. Pogue	6
Leslie D. Minchew	6	James N. Poindexter	11
Sanford K. Moats	8.5	Peter E. Pompetti	7
Shelton W. Monroe	8.83	Lawrence J. Powell, Jr.	6
Mark L. Moseley	6.5	Joseph H. Powers	14.5
Gerald E. Montgomery	17.5	George E. Preddy, Jr.	31.83
Robert P. Montgomery	6.33	Walter A. S. Prescott	6
Glennon T. Moran	16	Jack C. Price	5
Frank A. Morgan	5.5	William J. Price	7
Edward J. Moroney	5	Royce W. Priest	5
Stanley B. Morrill	9	Thomas P. Pryor, Jr.	5
James M. Morris	10.16	John F. Pugh	6
Ray S. Morris	13.5	Thomas W. Queen	5
William F. Mudge, Jr.	8	Michael L. Quirk	16
Norman D. Munson	7.5	Vernon G. Rafferty	5.5
Alva C. Murphy	8	Albert J. Ramm	5.5
John B. Murphy	6.75	John P. Randolph	5
Jerome T. Murphy	7	Robert J. Rankin	10

Name	Total victories	Name	Total victories
Harold J. Rau	5	Dale S. Sweat	5
William C. Reese	5	Henry S. Sykes	5
Edwin D. Reinhardt	5	William J. Sykes	10
Garth L. Reynolds	6	Edward W. Szaniawski	8.66
John J. Rice	5	William F. Tanner	6.5
George T. Rich	6.5	Clyde E. Taylor	9
Vernon R. Richards	5.5	Willis B. Taylor	5
Alden P. Rigby	5	John F. Thornell, Jr.	19.25
Elwyn G. Righetti	34.5	Joseph L. Thury	28
Paul S. Riley	9.5	David F. Thwaites	7
Ben Rimerman	12.5	Eugene J. Timony	5
Arval J. Roberson	7	Harrison B. Tordoff	7
Eugene P. Roberts	9	Archie A. Tower	19.5
Robert T. Rose	5	Richard M. Tracy	6
Leroy A. Ruder	5.5	Jesse L. Truett	6.5
Thomas D. Schank	5	John H. Truluck	8
Wilbur R. Scheible	9	Grant M. Turley	6
David C. Schilling	33	Gerald E. Tyler	7
Robert G. Schimanski	8	George R. Vanden Heuval	8.5
Albert L. Schlegel	13.5	Romildo Visconte	9
Glen D. Schlitz, Jr.	8	John W. Vogt, Jr.	8
Leroy A. Schreiber	14	Horace Q. Waggoner	12.5
Duerr H. Schuh	5	Karl M. Waldron	10
Alexander F. Sears	6	Alton J. Wallace	6
Dale E. Shafer, Jr.	10	Jack W. Warren	5
Presson S. Shane	5	Charles E. Weaver	11
Walter J. Sharbo	5	Roy A. Webb, Jr.	9
Robert M. Shaw	8	Carl W. Weber	7
Herbert F. Shope	6	Robert E. Welch	18
Joseph E. Shupe	7	Warren M. Wesson	6
Grover C. Siems, Jr.	7.83	Ray S. Wetmore	23.58
Stanley E. Silva	7	William E. Whalen	8
Henry R. Slack, IV	8.5	Donald Y. Whinnem	6
Kenneth C. Smeltz	5	William T. Whisner	18.5
Alfred J. Smigel	5	Samuel J. Wicker	7
Donovan F. Smith	7.5	Howard E. Wiggins	6
Kenneth G. Smith	5	William P. Wilkerson	5
Leslie C. Smith	11.5	James W. Wilkinson	8
Robert C. Smith	5.5	Brady C. Williamson	5.7
Robert E. Smith	7	Felix D. Williamson	13
Vernon A. Smith	5	John H. Wilson	7
William B. Smith	7.75	William F. Wilson	5
Theodore J. Sowerby	8.5	Robert P. Winks	5.5
Frank E. Spear	6	George H. Witzell	7
Dale F. Spencer	10	Sidney S. Woods	10
William J. Stangel	5	Robert E. Woody	9
Morris A. Stanley	6.5	James C. Woolery	6
Walter E. Starck	7	Victor Wolski	5
James R. Starnes	12	Robert C. Wright	7.5
Mark H. Stepelton	5.5	Vasseure H. Wynn	7
David Stewart	6	Michael P. Yannell	6
Everett W. Stewart	9.33	Charles E. Yeager	11.5
Henry M. Stewart	5	Jack J. Yelton	5
James C. Stewart	12.5	Robert M. York	5
John A. Storch	12	Edmond Zellner	5.25
Donald J. Strait	13.5	Hubert A. Zemke	26.25
John L. Sublett	9	Vincent A. Zettler	8

Confirmed Jet Victories

Date	Rank and name	Group	Type	Location
7-29-44	Capt. Arthur F. Jeffrey	479	Me 163	Wessermunde
8-16-44	Lt. Col. John B. Murphy	359	Me 163	SE of Leipzig
8-16-44	Lt. Cyril W. Jones, Jr.	359	Me 163	SE of Leipzig
8-28-44	Maj. Joseph Myers	78	½ Me 262	Termonda area
	Lt. Manford O. Croy, Jr.	78	½ Me 262	Termonda area
10-7-44	Lt. Urban L. Drew	361	2 Me 262	Achmer aerodrome
10-7-44	Lt. Elmer A. Taylor	364	½ Me 262	Vicinity Brux
	Lt. Willard G. Erfkamp	364	½ Me 262	Vicinity Brux
10-7-44	Maj. Richard E. Conner	78	Me 262	Osnabruck area
10-15-44	Lt. Huie H. Lamb	78	Me 262	Diepenau area
11-1-44	Lt. Walter R. Groce	56	½ Me 262	E of Arnhem
	Lt. William T. Gerbe, Jr.	352	½ Me 262	E of Arnhem
11-2-44	Capt. Fred W. Glover	4	Me 163	E of Leipzig
11-2-44	Capt. Louis H. Norley	4	Me 163	SE of Leipzig
11-6-44	Lt. William J. Quinn	361	Me 262	Bassum area
11-6-44	Capt. Charles E. Yeager	357	Me 262	E of Assen
11-8-44	Lt. Richard W. Stevens	364	Me 262	Dummer Lake
11-8-44	Lt. Anthony Maurice	361	Me 262	W of Meppel
11-8-44	Lt. Edward R. Haydon	357	½ Me 262	Dummer Lake
	Capt. Ernest C. Fiebelkorn	20	½ Me 262	Dummer Lake
11-8-44	Lt. James W. Kenney	357	Me 262	Vicinity Quackenbruck
11-18-44	Lt. John M. Creamer	4	½ Me 262	S of Liepheim aerodrome
	Capt. John C. Fitch	4	½ Me 262	S of Liepheim aerodrome
12-9-44	Lt. Harry L. Edwards	352	Me 262	Kirchheim
12-31-44	Lt. Col. John C. Meyer	352	Ar 234	Vicinity Euskirchen
1-1-45	Lt. Franklin W. Young	4	Me 262	Vicinity of Ulzen
1-13-45	Lt. Walter J. Konantz	55	Me 262	Giebelstadt aerodrome
1-14-45	Lt. Billy J. Murray	353	Me 262	Wittenberge
1-14-45	Lt. John W. Rohrs	353	½ Me 262	Wittenberge
	Lt. George J. Rosen	353	½ Me 262	Wittenberge
1-15-45	Lt. Robert P. Winks	357	Me 262	Shongau aerodrome
1-20-45	Lt. Roland R. Wright	357	Me 262	Lechfield aerodrome
1-20-45	Lt. Dale E. Karger	357	Me 262	N of Munich
2-9-45	Capt. Donald H. Bochkay	357	Me 262	Fulda
2-9-45	Lt. Johnnie L. Carter	357	Me 262	E of Giessen
2-9-45	Lt. Stephen C. Ananian	339	Me 262	Vicinity of Fulda
2-15-45	Lt. Dudley M. Amoss	55	Me 262	Vicinity of Amberg
2-21-45	Lt. Harold E. Whitmore	356	Me 262	Stettin area
2-22-45	Maj. Wayne K. Blickenstaff	353	Me 262	Berlin area
2-22-45	Capt. Gordon B. Comstock	353	Me 262	Brandenburg area
2-22-45	Lt. Charles D. Price	352	Me 262	Wahrenholz
2-25-45	Lt. Carl G. Payne	4	Me 262	SE of Naumburg
2-25-45	Capt. Donald M. Cummings	55	Me 262	Giebelstadt aerodrome
2-25-45	Capt. Donald M. Cummings	55	Me 262	Liepheim aerodrome
2-25-45	Capt. Donald E. Penn	55	Me 262	Giebelstadt aerodrome
2-25-45	Lt. Donald T. Menegay	55	Me 262	W of Giebelstadt aerodrome
2-25-45	Lt. Millard O. Anderson	55	Me 262	Giebelstadt aerodrome
2-25-45	Lt. John F. O'Neil	55	Me 262	SE of Giebelstadt aerodrome
2-25-45	Lt. Billy Clemmons	55	Me 262	SE of Mannheim
2-25-45	Lt. Eugene Murphy	364	½ Ar 234	Steinhuder Lake
	Lt. Richard E. White	364	½ Ar 234	Steinhuder Lake
3-1-45	Lt. Wendell W. Beaty	355	Me 262	Ingolstadt
3-1-45	Lt. John K. Wilkins, Jr.	2 AD Scout	Me 262	Ingolstadt
3-14-45	Lt. Robert E. Barnhart	356	Ar 234	Bislefeld
3-14-45	Lt. Sanborn N. Ball, Jr.	56	½ Ar 234	Vicinity Koblenz
	Lt. Warren S. Lear	56	½ Ar 234	Vicinity Koblenz
3-14-45	Lt. Norman D. Gould	56	Ar 234	Vicinity Koblenz

Date	Rank and name	Group	Type	Location
3-14-45	Capt. Donald S. Bryan	352	Ar 234	Vicinity Efstaffthal
3-15-45	Capt. Ray S. Wetmore	359	Me 163	Wiffenberg
3-19-45	Maj. Niven K. Cranfill	359	Me 262	Leipzig area
3-19-45	Maj. Robert W. Foy	357	Me 262	W of Giessen
3-19-45	Capt. Robert S. Fifield	357	Me 262	E of Leipzig
3-19-45	Lt. Huie H. Lamb	78	½ Ar 234	Osnabruck area
3-19-45	Capt. Winfield H. Brown	78	½ Ar 234	Osnabruck area
3-19-45	Lt. James E. Parker	78	Ar 234	Osnabruck area
3-19-45	Capt. Charles H. Spencer	355	Me 262	Kitzingen area
3-20-45	Lt. Robert E. Irion	339	Me 262	Scherwin
3-20-45	Lt. Vernon N. Barto	339	Me 262	Vicinity Hamburg
3-21-45	Lt. Harry M. Chapman	361	Me 262	Vicinity Dresden
3-21-45	Lt. Niles C. Greer	339	½ Me 262	Vicinity Wurzburg
3-21-45	Lt. Billy E. Langohr	339	½ Me 262	Vicinity Wurzburg
3-21-45	Lt. Walter E. Bourque	78	Me 262	Giebelstadt
3-21-45	Lt. John A. Kirk	78	Me 262	Vicinity Meiningen
3-21-45	Capt. Edwin H. Miller	78	Me 262	Vicinity Wittenberge
3-21-45	Lt. Robert H. Anderson	78	Me 262	Giebelstadt aerodrome
3-21-45	Capt. Winfield H. Brown	78	½ Me 262	Giebelstadt aerodrome
	Lt. Allen A. Rosenblum	78	½ Me 262	Giebelstadt aerodrome
3-22-45	Lt. John W. Cunnick	55	Me 262	Lechfeld
3-22-45	Capt. Harold T. Barnaby	78	Me 262	Giebelstadt aerodrome
3-22-45	Lt. Milton B. Stutzman	78	½ Me 262	Ulm area
	Lt. Eugene L. Peel	78	½ Me 262	Ulm area
3-25-45	Lt. Eugene H. Wendt	479	Me 262	SW of Hamburg
3-25-45	Lt. Raymond H. Littge	352	Me 262	Rechlin aerodrome
3-25-45	Lt. Edwin H. Crosthwait, Jr.	56	Me 262	Parchim aerodrome
3-25-45	Capt. George E. Bostwick	56	Me 262	Parchim aerodrome
3-30-45	Lt. John B. Guy	364	½ Me 262	Brandenburg area
3-30-45	Unknown P-51 pilot		½ Me 262	Brandenburg area
3-30-45	Lt. Thomas V. Thain, Jr.	78	½ Me 262	N of Hamburg
3-30-45	Lt. Col. John D. Landers	78	½ Me 262	N of Hamburg
3-30-45	Lt. Carroll W. Bennett	339	Me 262	Vicinity of Hamburg
3-30-45	Lt. James C. Hurley	352	Me 262	N of Magdeburg
3-30-45	Lt. Kenneth J. Scott, Jr.	361	Me 262	N of Rendsburg
3-30-45	Lt. Patrick L. Moore	55	Me 262	Lubeck airfield
3-30-45	Capt. Robert F. Sargent	339	Me 262	Vicinity Kaltenkirchen airfield
3-31-45	Lt. Marvin L. Castleberry	2 AD Scout	Me 262	SW of Brunswick
3-31-45	Lt. Wayne L. Coleman	78	Me 262	Stendal area
3-31-45	Lt. Harrison B. Tordoff	353	Me 262	Vicinity Dessau
4-4-45	Lt. Col. George F. Ceuleers	364	Me 262	Munich
4-4-45	Capt. Harry R. Corey	339	Me 262	Rostock
4-4-45	Capt. Kirke B. Everson	339	½ Me 262	Vicinity Parchim
4-4-45	Lt. Robert C. Croker	339	½ Me 262	Vicinity Parchim
4-4-45	Capt. Nile C. Greer	339	Me 262	Vicinity Parchim
4-4-45	Lt. Robert C. Havighurst	339	Me 262	Vicinity Parchim
4-4-45	Lt. Elmer H. Ruffle	355	Ar 234	Magdeburg area
4-4-45	Lt. Raymond A. Dyer	4	Me 262	SE of Parchim
4-4-45	Lt. Harold H. Frederick	4	½ Me 262	S of Ludwigslust
4-4-45	Lt. Michael J. Kennedy	4	½ Me 262	S of Ludwigslust
4-5-45	Capt. John C. Fahringer	56	Me 262	N of Regensburg
4-7-45	Lt. Hilton O. Thompson	479	Me 262	Luneburg area
4-7-45	Capt. Verne E. Hooker	479	Me 262	SE of Bremen
4-9-45	Maj. Edward B. Giller	55	Me 262	Vicinity of Munich
4-9-45	Lt. James T. Sloan	361	Me 262	W of Berlin
4-10-45	Lt. Wayne C. Gatlin	356	Me 262	Oranienburg
4-10-45	Capt. John K. Brown	20	Me 262	Neuruppin area
4-10-45	Capt. Douglas J. Pick	364	Me 262	Staaken airfield
4-10-45	Capt. John K. Hollins	20	Me 262	Vicinity of Neustadt

Date	Rank and name	Group	Type	Location
4-10-45	Lt. Albert B. North	20	Me 262	Vicinity of Oranienburg
4-10-45	Lt. Walter T. Drozd	20	Me 262	Vicinity of Oranienburg
4-10-45	F/O Jerome Rosenblum	20	½ Me 262	Berlin
4-10-45	Lt. John W. Cudd, Jr.	20	½ Me 262	Berlin
4-10-45	Lt. Jack W. Clark	353	½ Me 262	Dessau
4-10-45	Lt. Bruce D. Mcmahan	353	½ Me 262	Dessau
4-10-45	Capt. Gordon B. Compton	353	Me 262	Dessau
4-10-45	Capt. Robert J. Abernathy	353	Me 262	Dessau
4-10-45	Lt. Wilmer W. Collins	4	Me 262	Lubeck
4-10-45	Lt. Walter J. Sharbo	56	Me 262	SW of Murita Lake
4-10-45	Lt. Harold Tenebaum	359	Me 262	Gardelegen aerodrome
4-10-45	Lt. Robert J. Guggenos	359	Me 262	Gardelegen aerodrome
4-10-45	Lt. Col. Earl D. Duncan	352	½ Me 262	Vicinity of Berlin
4-10-45	Maj. Richard G. McAuliffe	352	½ Me 262	Vicinity of Berlin
4-10-45	Lt. Charles C. Pattillo	352	Me 262	E of Ulzen
4-10-45	Lt. Carlo A. Ricci	352	½ Me 262	Neuruppin
4-10-45	Lt. Joseph W. Prichard	352	½ Me 262	Neuruppin
4-10-45	Lt. Keith R. McGinnis	55	Me 262	Galworde
4-10-45	Lt. Kenneth A. Lashbrook	55	Me 262	Burg
4-16-45	Maj. Eugene E. Ryan	55	Me 262	Horsching airfield
4-17-45	Lt. John C. Campbell, Jr.	339	Me 262	Vicinity of Rokycany, Czech.
4-17-45	Capt. Roy W. Orndorff	364	Me 262	Prague, Czech.
4-17-45	Lt. William F. Kissel	364	Me 262	Falkenst
4-17-45	Capt. Walter L. Goff	364	Me 262	Pilsen, Czech.
4-17-45	F/O James A. Steiger	357	Me 262	NE of Prague, Czech.
4-18-45	Lt. Col. Dale E. Shafer, Jr.	339	Ar 234	Vicinity of Regensburg
4-18-45	Lt. Leon Oliver	356	Ar 234	Wertingen
4-18-45	Capt. Charles E. Weaver	357	Me 262	Prague, Czech.
4-18-45	Maj. Donald H. Bochkay	357	Me 262	SW of Prague, Czech.
4-19-45	Lt. Robert Deloach	55	Me 262	W of Prague, Czech.
4-19-45	Lt. Paul N. Bowles	357	Me 262	Prague, Czech.
4-19-45	Capt. Robert S. Fifield	357	Me 262	Prague, Czech.
4-19-45	Lt. Carroll W. Ofsthun	357	Me 262	Prague, Czech.
4-19-45	Lt. Gilman L. Weber	357	½ Me 262	S of Dresden
4-19-45	Capt. Ivan L. McGuire	357	½ Me 262	S of Dresden
4-19-45	Lt. James P. McMullen	357	Me 262	Prague, Czech.
4-19-45	Lt. Col. Jack W. Hayes, Jr.	357	Me 262	Prague, Czech.
4-25-45	Lt. Hilton O. Thompson	479	Ar 234	Traunstein

Eighth Air Force Fighter Groups
Enemy Aircraft Destroyed

Group	Air[1]	Ground[2]	Total	Group	Air[1]	Ground[2]	Total
4th	550.0	469.0	1,019.0	361st	222.0	105.0	327.0
20th	211.5	237.0	448.5	364th	262.5	193.0	455.5
55th	303.5	268.5	572.0	479th	155.0	279.0	434.0
56th	664.5	328.0	992.5				
78th	326.0	358.8	684.8				
339th	235.0	440.5	675.5				
352nd	504.5	287.0	791.5				
353rd	328.0	413.8	741.8				
355th	339.0	502.3	841.3				
356th	200.0	75.5	275.5				
357th	595.5	106.5	702.0				
359th	255.5	98.0	353.5				

[1]These figures were taken from Dr. Frank J. Olynyk's "USAAF Credits (European Theater) For The Destruction of Enemy Aircraft In Air-To-Air Combat World War 2."

[2]These figures were taken from Eighth Air Force Final Assessment.

Nose Art and Markings

Sweet Arlene, *pilot: Lt. Arthur R. Bowers, 4th FG*. D. Allen, via T. Ivie

Blondie, *pilot: Lt. Marvin W. Arthur, 4th FG*. D. Allen, via T. Ivie

Red Dog, *pilot: Capt. Louis Norley, 4th FG*. AF Museum

The Count, *4th FG*. D. Allen, via T. Ivie

Hot Stuff, *pilot: Maj. Willie O. Jackson, 352nd FG*. 352nd FG Assn., via T. Ivie

Ex-Lax, Shht'n Git!, *pilot: Lt. C. B. Doleac, 352nd FG*. 352nd FG Assn., via T. Ivie

Little Bitch, *357th FG.* W. O'Brien

Winged Ace, *pilot: Capt. Don Bochkay, 357th FG.* D. Bochkay

Death Angel, *pilot: Maj. Glenn Duncan, 353rd FG.* USAAF

Rocky Mt. Canary, *pilot: Lt. Thomas Schank, 55th FG.* T. Schank

Axe The Axis, *pilot: Lt. Peter Pompetti, 78th FG.* P. Pompetti

Lt. Wolf, *Lt. P. C. Dawson shown with Lt. C. McBath's aircraft, 56th FG.* F. Christensen

The Syracusan, *pilot: Lt. Henry Miklajcyk, 352nd FG*. T. Ivie

Dallas Darling, *pilot: Lt. Henry White, 352nd FG*. T. Ivie

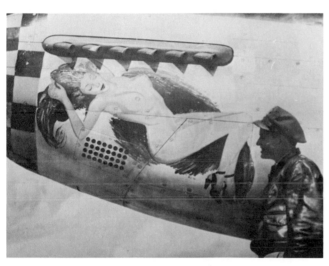

Nude, *pilot: Capt. C. E. Weaver, 357th FG*. C. E. Weaver

It's Supermouse, *pilot: F/O R. W. Dodd, 352nd FG*. R. W. Dodd, via T. Ivie

Desert Rat, *pilot: Capt. J. J. Pascoe, 364th FG*. T. Ivie

Flying Dutchman, *pilot: Capt. Neil Van Wyk, 4th FG*. AFM, via T. Ivie

Red Raider, *pilot: Lt. F. W. Miller, 78th FG.* 352nd FG Assn., via T. Ivie

Pop, *368th FS, 359th FG.* K. Miller

P-51, *504th FS, 339th FG.* J. Starnes

U've Had It!, *pilot: Capt. John England, 362nd FS, 357th FG.* M. Olmsted

Angel, *pilot: Maj. James Thorne, 356th FG.* K. Miller

Moonbeam McSwine, *pilot: Capt. William T. Whisner, 487th FS, 352nd FG.* USAAF

244

P-51, 77th FS, 20th FG. 20th FG Assn.

P-47, pilot: Capt. Ray Wetmore, 370th FS, 359th FG. USAAF

Rumboogie Jr., *pilot: Lt. William Hehn, 434th FS, 479th FG.*
D. Tabatt

Man O'War, *pilot: Col. Claiborne Kinnard, 354th FS, 355th*
FG. R. Kuhnert

P-51s, 77th FS, 20th FG. 20th FG Assn.

P-51, pilot: Lt. Col. Wayner Rhynard, 359th FS, 356th FG. K. Miller

P-47, 84th FS, 78th FG. M. Havelaar

Speed, *pilot: Lt. Col. Mark Hubbard, 354th FS, 355th FG.*
USAAF

Kraut Knocker, *343rd FS, 479th FG.* D. Tabatt

Nooky Booky IV, *pilot: Maj. Kit Carson, 362nd FS, 357th FG.*
M. Olmsted

Connie, *pilot: Capt. Fred Glover, 336th FS, 4th FG.* M.
Havelaar

Morphine Sue, *pilot: Lt. Donald McNally, 358th FS, 355th
FG.* 355th FG Assn.

Tar Heel, *pilot: Lt. O. Biggs, 505th FS, 339th FG. USAAF*

Ferocious Frankie, *pilot: Maj. Wallace Hopkins, 374th FS, 361st FG. USAAF*

Babs In Arms, *383rd FS, 364th FG. USAAF*

P–51, 503rd FS, 339th FG. USAAF

P–47, 63rd FS, 56th FG. USAAF

Anamosa II, *pilot: Lt. Russell Westfall, 63rd FS, 56th FG.* USAAF

Mick #5, *pilot: Maj. Darrell S. Cramer, 338th FS, 55th FG.* D. Cramer

It's The Kid!, *pilot: Lt. F. H. Alexander, 77th FS, 20th FG.* H. Holmes

Passion's Playground, *pilot: Lt. Herbert G. Marsh, 358th FS, 355th FG.* USAAF

P-51, 376th FS, 361st FG. USAAF

Passion Wagon, *pilot: Lt. Arval Roberson, 362nd FS, 357th FG. A. Roberson*

Bobby Jeanne, *pilot: Col. Irwin Dregne, 364th FS, 357th FG.* Kramer

Double Trouble, *pilot: Lt. Col. Bill Bailey, 352nd FS, 353rd FG. USAAF*

P-47, 335th FS, 4th FG. USAAF

Zombie, *pilot: Capt. Thomas F. Bailey, 361st FS, 356th FG.*
USAAF

Hawkeye, *62nd FS, 56th FG.* USAAF

Sweetie Face, *pilot: Lt. Sheldon Heyer, 487th FS, 352nd FG.*
S. Heyer

Blue Bonnet Belle II, *383rd FS, 364th FG.* USAAF

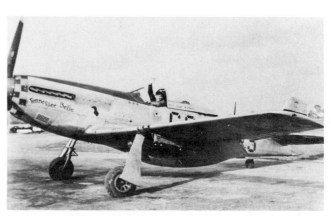

Tennessee Belle, *pilot: Capt. M. Clark, 38th FS, 55th FG.* M.
Coons

P-51, *pilot: Lt. G. Rayborn, 328th FS, 352nd FG.* S. Sox

Stasia II, *pilot: Lt. A. R. Rosatone, 352nd FS, 353rd FG.* T. Ivie

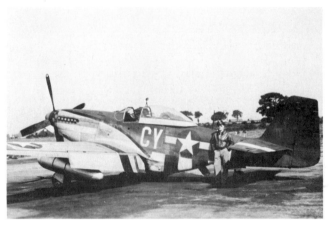

P-51, *343rd FS, 55th FG.* Giller

P-51, *pilot: Lt. Col. Don Baccus, 368th FS, 359th FG.* D. Baccus

Little Nan, *335th FS, 4th FG.* AF Museum

P-47, *83rd FS, 78th FG.* USAAF

Cile VI, *pilot: Lt. C. V. Marker, 486th FS, 352nd FG.* T. Ivie

Lucky Lady VII, *pilot: Capt. E. Bankey, 385th FS, 364th FG.*
E. Bankey

Shoo Shoo Baby, *pilot: Lt. Richard W. Gilette, 361st FS, 356th*
FG. K. Miller

Nuey V, *P–38, 479th FG.* D. Tabatt

Chief Wahoo, *pilot: Capt. Fred LeFebre, 351st FS, 353rd FG.*
USAAF

Formations

P-47s of the 62nd FS, 56th FG. Note yellow circles around the
national insignia and the white noses plus horizontal white
stripes on tail for ID purposes. USAAF

Thunderbolt formation from 84th FS, 78th FG. You can see
the 75 gallon drop tanks carried by two aircraft. USAAF

Lt. Col. William Bailey in Butch II, and Maj. Wilbert Junttila
of the 353rd FG. USAAF

P-38s from the 383rd FS, 364th FG above the clouds over England. USAAF

Mustangs of the 335th FS, 4th FG forming up for a mission. USAAF

P-51s of the 362nd FS, 357th FG tucked in tight. USAAF

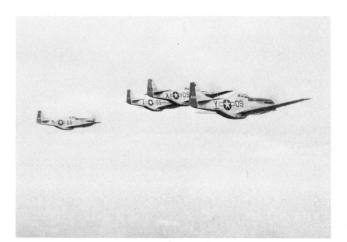

This flight from the 357th FS, 355th FG shows its heels. USAAF

The 343rd FS, 55th FG nicely formed and tucked in. USAAF

A real mixed formation from the 63rd FS, 56th FG. Some olive-drab, some silver, some razorback, some bubble canopy. USAAF

Maj. Edward Giller leading the 343rd FS of the 55th FG. USAAF

Olive-drab-painted flight from the 364th FS, 357th FG. USAAF

Very precise formation flying by this flight from the 504th FS, 339th FG. J. Starnes

Mustangs of the 376th FS, 361st FG over English countryside. Note that the P-51 with malcolm hood is marked "WW" for war weary on the vertical stabilizer. USAAF

Beautiful formation by the 369th FS, 359th FG. USAAF

Two Mustangs from the 360th FS, 356th FG looking pretty for the camera ship. K. Miller

P–51s from the 504th FS, 339th FG with big cloud build-up to their rear. USAAF

The 383rd FS, 364th FG Mustangs in tight formation. USAAF

Mustangs from the 435th FS, 479th FG outbound laden with 108 gallon drop tanks. USAAF

Black and yellow checker-nosed Mustangs from the 350th FS, 353rd FG climbing skyward. USAAF

Shoot You're Faded *from the 79th FS of the 20th FG pulls abreast of the camera. USAAF*

This Mustang flight from the 374th FS of the 361st FG laden with 75 gallon drop tanks form up in an impressive front. USAAF

Impressive formation from the 351st FS, 353rd FG climbing over England. USAAF

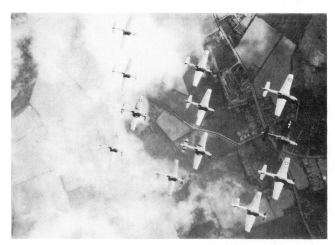

Beautiful overhead shot of P–51s from the 353rd FG. Note the olive-drab-painted craft in lead flight. Many pilots wanted to return to olive-drab upper surfaces late in the war to camouflage themselves, when so much strafing was being done. USAAF

Crashes

Floogie II, *a P-51 of the 362nd FS, 357th FG. USAAF*

Capt. John Godfrey's P-51, Reggies Reply, *336th FS, 4th FG.*
USAAF

A P-51 of the 55th FS, 20th FG. USAAF

A P-51 of the 361st FS, 356th FG. USAAF

A P-47 of the 63rd FS, 56th FG. USAAF

A P-51 of the 343rd FS, 55th FG. USAAF

A P-47 of the 352nd FS, 353rd FG. USAAF

A P-47 of the 63rd FS, 56th FG. USAAF

A P-47 of the 63rd FS, 56th FG. USAAF

Helen II, *a P-51 of the 358th FS, 355th FG. USAAF*

Index